DRUG ADDICTION
TREATMENT RESEARCH
German and American Perspectives

Edited by

GERHARD BÜHRINGER

and

JEROME J. PLATT

KRIEGER PUBLISHING COMPANY
MALABAR, FLORIDA
1992

Publisher's Note: The contributions noted in this volume are the result of an international meeting. We have attempted to conform the material as far as possible. In the interest of making the material available without delay, certain editorial inconsistancies have been allowed, for which we ask the reader's indulgence.

Original Edition 1992

Printed and Published by
KRIEGER PUBLISHING COMPANY
KRIEGER DRIVE
MALABAR, FLORIDA 32950

Copyright © 1992 by Krieger Publishing Company

Library of Congress Cataloging-In-Publication Data

Drug Addiction Treatment Research : German and American perspectives /
 edited by Gerhard Bühringer and Jerome J. Platt.
  p. cm.
 Based on the German-American Conference on Drug Addiction held in
Camden, N.J. in 1989.
 Includes bibliographical references.
 ISBN 0-89464-628-1 (alk. paper)
 1. Drug abuse — Congresses. 2. AIDS (Disease)—United States–
–Congresses. 3. AIDS (Disease)—Germany—Congresses.
I. Bühringer , Gerhard. II. Platt, Jerome J. III. German-American
Conferences on Drug Addiction (1989 : Camden, N.J.)
 [DNLM: 1. Acquired Immunodeficiency Syndrome—congresses.
2. Cross Cultural Comparison—congresses. 3. Health Policy–
–congresses. 6. Substance Dependence—therapy—congresses. WM 270
D793455 1989]
RC563.6.D78 1992
362.29'18—dc20
DNLM/DLC

 for Library of Congress   91-35392
                                                                   CIP

10 9 8 7 6 5 4 3 2

Table of Contents

PART FOUR
ADDICTION CAREERS AND PROCESS OF TREATMENT

x   Contents

Foreword

The drug problem is a worldwide problem, and consequently the Federal Republic of Germany attaches great significance to international collaboration in this area. Such collaboration may not, however, be restricted only to joint efforts to fight against drug-related crime but must also extend to all sectors capable of curtailing the demand for drugs. Research can make an important contribution in this area. The fact that the field of addiction research in Germany is characterized by considerable deficits led to the singling out of this area of research as a focus for future measures in the context of the National Drug Control Programme adopted in June 1990 by the Federal Government, the Länder, local authorities and all the essential groups in German society at a National Drug Conference chaired by the Federal Chancellor.

This report on the German-American Conference on Drug Addiction provides, above all, an overview of research on specific aspects of the problem in the United States and the Federal Republic of Germany. While problems such as treatment dropout, relapse, and HIV infection among drug addicts constitute common concerns, the American and German views of these problems and ways in which to approach them often differ significantly. Accordingly, different approaches to solving these problems have been developed. A conference which provides a forum for thorough and intensive discussions of these issues can contribute to a better understanding of the respective viewpoints and the resulting attempts to find solutions. It also can identify areas for joint action.

This volume clearly will fulfill its purpose if it stimulates questions which might lead to better answers through new and joint research projects on both sides of the Atlantic.

Bundesminister für Gesundheit
(Federal Minister of Health)

Preface

In drug abuse and drug abuse treatment, differences between Germany and the United States are obvious in many areas. These include epidemiology, socioeconomic background of drug abusers, treatment approaches, characteristics of treatment staff, treatment financing, evaluation procedures, and foci of current research. German-American differences in the understanding and treatment of drug abuse initially raised for us the issue of the practical application of this first German-American Conference on drug abuse research, the proceedings of which are contained in this volume. We concluded that there were at least two important reasons for such a meeting. First, both countries and their researchers are concerned with the same addictive behaviors and their treatment, and many facets of addiction are independent of socioeconomic and cultural influences. Second, in both scientific communities a rational, hypothesis-testing, empirically oriented scientific approach is favored in efforts to analyze and to improve both knowledge and technology about drug abuse and its treatment.

The history of German-American cooperation in the drug abuse field is about 20 years old. First contacts began in the 1970s, when the German editor of this book, Dr. Bühringer, became director of the Addiction Research Group within the Department of Psychology at the Max-Planck-Institute for Psychiatry in Munich. The former Head of this Department,

Professor Brengelmann, had invited many American researchers for study visits to the Institute, and their ideas influenced one of the first treatment research projects. In 1977 came a three-month stay by Dr. Bühringer in the United States with a "Tour d'Horizont" through the National Institute on Drug Abuse, governmental offices, and many drug abuse research locations all over the United States. The development, at the governmental level, of German-American Guidelines for Cooperation in Drug Abuse Control marked the third step. Three scientific meetings have now been held: "Evaluation of Drug Abuse Indicators" (Bonn 1980), "Treatment of Drug Dependence" (Nürnberg 1983), and "The Role of Force (Coercion) in Treatment" (Annapolis 1985). At the Annapolis meeting, the editors of this book first met and discussed further cooperation. Agreeing on the need for such cooperation, they began what has become a fruitful and exciting collaboration. As a result, three articles have been published together with other American colleagues and more are in preparation; Dr. Platt participated in addiction research conferences in Germany in 1987, 1988, and 1991; the German-American conference in Camden, New Jersey was held in 1989 when Dr. Platt was at the University of Medicine & Dentistry of New Jersey; Dr. Platt served as a visiting scientist at the IFT in Munich in the fall of 1990; and Dr. Bühringer visited New Jersey to work on this volume in early 1991.

We hope that the conference papers, the resulting discussions, and this volume will further develop mutual German-American understanding of national differences in the drug abuse situation and in strategies to cope with these problems. The conference clearly demonstrated the usefulness of future cooperation in many common areas of research such as epidemiology, trend analysis of treatment statistics, multicenter treatment evaluation studies, and basic preconditions for research such as standardization of criteria for documentation and evaluation and the improvement of diagnostic instruments. Cooperative activities between participants at the meeting already have begun, and we hope that these collaborative efforts will continue to grow in the future.

The German contributions to these proceedings also provide a relatively comprehensive introduction to West German drug addiction research prior to the integration of East Germany, as this is the first monograph in the English language which gives an overview of current research activities in the Federal Republic of Germany. We hope that this overview will enhance the understanding of the German treatment system and its various research activities as well as provide an impetus for additional cooperation within Europe.

Organizing this conference and publishing the proceedings was not just a matter of good will expressed by two colleagues, it required an extensive amount of external support and ongoing assistance. On the

German side, we wish to thank the Federal Ministry of Health for substantial financial support and the German Association for Addiction Research and Therapy for its cooperation and assistance. Many thanks also go to Charlotte Korintenberg and Jutta Künzel-Böhmer, who were extremely helpful in preparing and planning the conference, keeping in touch with the German colleagues over three years, and preparing the manuscripts for the proceedings. On the American side, special thanks are due to Kay Platt, Lee Sinclair, Cindy Rudow, and Patricia McKim, who planned and coordinated the considerable logistics of the meeting. Thanks also are due to Stephen D. Husband, who assisted in the editing and preparation of the manuscripts for the publisher. Finally, we wish to thank all of our American and German colleagues who participated in the conference and prepared manuscripts for this volume.

Gerhard Bühringer
Jerome J. Platt

List of Contributors

Thomas Arnold, Ph.D., Diplom-Soziologe, Member, Addiction Research Group, Institut für Sozialarbeit und Sozialpädagogik ISS (Institute for Social Work and Social Paedagogic), Frankfurt, Federal Republic of Germany.

John C. Ball, Ph.D., Visiting Scientist, Addiction Research Center, National Institute on Drug Abuse, Baltimore, Maryland.

Michael Böhmer, Diplom-Psychologe, Member, research group on treatment evaluation, IFT Institut für Therapieforschung (Institute for Therapy Research), Munich, Federal Republic of Germany.

Iris Bowman, Diplom-Psychologin, Clinical psychologist and family therapist, Heilpädagogische Tagesstätte (outpatient treatment program for emotionally disturbed and learning disabled children), Munich, Federal Republic of Germany.

Barry S. Brown, Ph.D., Chief, Community Research Branch, National Institute on Drug Abuse, Baltimore, Maryland.

Gerhard Bühringer, Ph.D., Diplom-Psychologe, Director, IFT Institut für Therapieforschung (Institute for Therapy Research), Munich, Federal Republic of Germany.

Donald A. Bux, M.S. Ed., Research Instructor, Division of Addiction Research and Treatment, Department of Mental Health Sciences, Hahnemann University School of Medicine, Philadelphia, Pennsylvania.

Eric Corty, Ph.D., Assistant Professor, Department of Psychology, Bradley University, Peoria, Illinois

George De Leon, Ph.D., Director of Research and Training, Therapeutic Communities of America; Deputy Director of Clinical Research, Narcotic and Drug Research, Inc.; Research Associate Professor of Psychiatry, New York University School of Medicine, New York, New York.

André Denis, Diplom-Psychologe, Dipl.-Engineer, Member, research group on treatment evaluation, IFT Institut für Therapieforschung (Institute for Therapy Research), Munich, Federal Republic of Germany.

Sherry Deren, Ph.D., Principal Investigator, Harlem AIDS Project, Narcotic and Drug Research, Inc., New York, New York.

Rudolf Egg, Professor, Ph.D., Diplom-Psychologe, Deputy Director, Kriminologische Zentralstelle (Criminological Center), Wiesbaden, Federal Republic of Germany.

Heiner Ellgring, Professor, Ph.D., Diplom-Psychologe, Head, Institut für Psychologie der Freien Universität (Department of Clinical Psychology, Institute of Psychology, Free University of Berlin), Berlin, Federal Republic of Germany.

Eva-Maria Fahrner, Ph.D., Diplom-Psychologin, Head, Research Group on AIDS and Drug Addiction, IFT Institut für Therapieforschung (Institute for Therapy Research), Munich, Federal Republic of Germany.

Roman Ferstl, Professor, Ph.D., Institut für Psychologie (Department of Clinical Psychology), University of Kiel, Federal Republic of Germany.

Barbara Haderstorfer, Diplom-Psychologin, Head, Psychosoziale Beratungsstelle "Prop-Shop" (Psychosocial Counseling Center), Freising, Federal Republic of Germany.

Elke Hanel, Diplom-Psychologin, Member, research group on treatment evaluation, IFT Institut für Therapieforschung (Institute for Therapy Research), Munich, Federal Republic of Germany.

Peter I. Hartsock, Dr.P.H., Deputy Chief, Clinical Medicine Branch, National Institute on Drug Abuse, Rockville, Maryland.

Ursula Havemann-Reinecke, M.D., Psychiatrische Klinik, Universität Göttingen (Psychiatric Hospital, University of Göttingen), Göttingen, Federal Republic of Germany.

Klaus Herbst, Ph.D., Diplom-Psychologe, Head, Research Group on Treatment Evaluation; IFT Institut für Therapieforschung (Institute for Therapy Research), Munich, Federal Republic of Germany.

Martin Y. Iguchi, Ph.D., Assistant Professor, Division of Addiction Research and Treatment, Department of Mental Health Sciences, Hahnemann University School of Medicine, Philadelphia, Pennsylvania.

Nancy Jainchill, Ph.D., Senior Research Scientist, Therapeutic Communities of America, New York, New York.

Helmut Kampe, Professor, Ph.D., Diplom-Psychologe, Fachhochschule Darmstadt, Fachbereich Sozialpädagogik (College of Social Work), Darmstadt, Federal Republic of Germany.

Walter Kindermann, Ph.D., Diplom-Psychologe, Director for Drug Problems, Hessisches Ministerium für Jugend, Familie und Gesundheit, (Hessian Ministry for Youth, Family and Health), Wiesbaden, Federal Republic of Germany.

Dieter Kleiber, Professor, Ph.D., Diplom-Psychologe, Professor for psychology and community psychology, Freie Universität Berlin, (Free University of Berlin); Guest Professor for Health Psychology, Universität Innsbruck (University of Innsbruck), Austria; Deputy Director, AIDS Research Department of the Sozialpädagogisches Institut (Social Work Institute), Berlin, Federal Republic of Germany.

Mary Jeanne Kreek, M.D., Associate Professor and Physician, Rockefeller University, New York, New York.

Arthur Kreuzer, Professor, LLD, Chair of Criminology, Juvenile Law and Penology, Institut für Kriminologie der Justus-Liebig-Universität Gießen (Institute for Criminology, Justus-Liebig-University, Gießen), Gießen, Federal Republic of Germany.

Heinrich Küfner, Ph.D., Diplom-Psychologe, Head, Research Group on Treatment Evaluation, IFT Institut für Therapieforschung (Institute for Therapy Research), Munich, Federal Republic of Germany.

Jutta Künzel-Böhmer, Diplom-Psychologin, Member, research group on prevention of drug abuse, IFT Institut für Therapieforschung (Institute for Therapy Research), Munich, Federal Republic of Germany.

Dieter Kunz, Ph.D., Diplom-Psychologe, Director, residential treatment center for drug addicts "Therapiedorf Villa Lilly", Bad Schwalbach, Federal Republic of Germany.

Klaus Kuschinsky, Professor, M.D., Institut für Pharmakologie und Toxikologie, Universität Marburg (Institute of Pharmacology and Toxicology of the School of Pharmacy, University of Marburg), Marburg, Federal Republic of Germany.

Victor Lidz, Ph.D., Assistant Professor, Division of Addiction Research and Treatment, Department of Mental Health Sciences, Hahnemann University School of Medicine, Philadelphia, Pennsylvania.

Heiner Melchinger, Ph.D., Head, research group, Institut für Entwicklungsplanung und Strukturforschung, Universität Hannover (Institute for Development Planning and Research, University of Hannover), Hannover, Federal Republic of Germany.

Robert G. Newman, M.D., President, Beth Israel Medical Center, New York City, New York.

David N. Nurco, D.S.W., Research Professor, Department of Psychiatry, University of Maryland School of Medicine, Baltimore, Maryland.

Jerome J. Platt, Ph.D., Professor of Mental Health Sciences; Director, Division of Addiction Research and Treatment, Hahnemann University School of Medicine, Philadelphia, Pennsylvania.

Klaus Püschel, Professor, M.D., Assistant Medical Director, Institut für Rechtsmedizin, Universität Hamburg (Institute of Forensic Medicine, University of Hamburg), Hamburg, Federal Republic of Germany.

Karl-Heinz Reuband, Ph.D., Sociologist, Zentralarchiv für empirische Sozialforschung, Universität Köln (Central Archive for Empirical Social Research), Cologne, Federal Republic of Germany.

Irene Roch, Diplom-Psychologin, Member, research group on treatment evaluation, IFT Institut für Therapieforschung (Institute for Therapy Research), Munich, Federal Republic of Germany.

Ruth Römer-Klees, Research Assistant, Institut für Kriminologie, Justus-Liebig-Universität Gießen (Institute for Criminology, Justus-Liebig-University, Gießen), Gießen, Federal Republic of Germany.

Hans Schneider, Ph.D., Sociologist M.A., Research Assistant, Institut für Kriminologie, Justus-Liebig-Universität Gießen (Institute for Criminology, Justus Liebig University, Gießen), Gießen, Federal Republic of Germany.

Michaela Schreiber, Diplom-Psychologin, Head of Division of General Strategies of Drug Policy, Bundesministerium für Gesundheit (Federal Ministry of Health), Bonn, Federal Republic of Germany.

Richard Sickinger, Diplom-Pädagoge, Head, research group, Jugendberatung und Jugendhilfe e.V. (Counseling center for young adults), Frankfurt, Federal Republic of Germany.

Roland Simon, Diplom-Psychologe, Head, Research Group on Epidemiology and Treatment Statistics, IFT Institut für Therapieforschung (Institute for Therapy Research), Munich, Federal Republic of Germany.

Gabriele Spies, Diplom-Psychologin, Member, research group on treatment evaluation, IFT Institut für Therapieforschung (Institute for Therapy Research), Munich, Federal Republic of Germany.

Michael Strobl, Diplom-Psychologe, Member, research group on epidemiology and treatment statistics, IFT Institut für Therapieforschung (Institute for Therapy Research), Munich, Federal Republic of Germany.

Ingolf von Törne, Diplom-Psychologe, Member, research group on AIDS and drug addiction, IFT Institut für Therapieforschung (Institute for Therapy Research), Munich, Federal Republic of Germany.

Heinz C. Vollmer, Diplom-Psychologe, Head, Prop Alternative Aiglsdorf (Treatment Center Aiglsdorf) Aiglsdorf, Federal Republic of Germany.

Herbert Ziegler, Managing Director, Sierra Tuscon Klinik (Clinic for psychosomatic medicine and addictions), Garmisch-Partenkirchen, Federal Republic of Germany.

PART ONE

Epidemiology of Drug Abuse

CHAPTER 1

The Epidemiology of Drug Use in Germany: Basic Data and Trends

Karl-Heinz Reuband

INTRODUCTION

The Federal Republic of Germany (FRG) takes a marginal position in the international literature on the epidemiology of drug use. Generally, the FRG is excluded from the discussion and no data have been presented. If any findings are cited, they are mostly fairly rudimentary; they do not allow for an exact assessment of the drug situation. The reader is thus left with the impression that the empirical basis for detailed analysis is extremely unfavorable. The reality, however, is different: though certain topics have been badly neglected in German research, the research situation concerning at least basic descriptive epidemiological figures on drug prevalence does compare relatively well with the situation in other countries. There are only a few European countries in which national surveys among adolescents or adults were conducted as frequently as in the FRG. Even in comparison to the United States, the FRG does not emerge badly in this respect: the first national surveys among adolescents that assessed attitudes toward drug use and prevalence of consumption were conducted several years ahead of comparable American surveys.

The problem of insufficient knowledge of the German epidemiological situation in the foreign literature exists at least partially because (1) The studies on the German drug situation have been published almost exclusively in German and are thus not accessible to non-German speaking researchers; (2) The majority of German epidemiological studies of the past 10 to 20 years are based on contracted research assigned to commercial institutes. Their reports are not published in most cases, and when they are, they are of little analytical value given their descriptive character. The chance of a general visibility within the "scientific community" is small; (3) The number of researchers at the universities who are concerned with the subject is small and their representation in scientific conferences respectively low.

Given the low visibility of German studies on drug use, this article attempts to provide a global view of epidemiological studies—published and unpublished—and presents some of their basic findings. This will form a foundation for the other chapters in this volume as well as suggest the prerequisites for comparisons of the drug situation in other countries. We shall hereby restrict ourselves to selected questions, including ones about the epidemiology of cannabis and heroin use and the changes in use over the course of time. Questions about the etiological determination of drug use will be excluded from this presentation.

SURVEYS ON DRUG USE: AN OVERVIEW

Whenever statements on the distribution of drug and alcohol use among adolescents have been made in West Germany, surveys have been the preferred means of data collection. At first, the issue of illegal drug use stood in the forefront of the research; issues of alcohol use were picked up with only one or two questions in passing. During the seventies, the focus changed and the subject of alcohol use—influenced by its perceived rapid growth—was increasingly studied. More recently, the repertoire was expanded again to include health-related questions (e.g., on the use of medically prescribed drugs). Research has increasingly turned into health research, and questions on possible prevention are nowadays almost exclusively seen in the context of health-related issues. Sociological questions referring to lifestyles and social networks, though often of greater substantive implications, have been badly neglected.

Until the mid-seventies, surveys of youth were primarily done among students in school, through questionnaires administered in classrooms. The surveys were limited to the communal or state levels (Table 1.1). National surveys among adolescents, including nonstudents and based on face-to-face interviews, have been conducted by the Institut für Jugendforschung (assigned by the Federal Center for Health Education) since 1973 and continued thereafter (Table 1.2). As early as 1971, surveys on attitudes (not use) had been conducted throughout the FRG for the same agency. National mail surveys by the Infratest Institute (for the Federal

TABLE 1.1

Overview of representative youth studies on drug and alcohol
use in different Federal States of Germany

No.	Year	State	Total sample	Method of assessment	Size of sample	Researcher
1	1970	Schleswig-Holstein	high school/college	Q	4,647	Schwarz et al.
2	1971	Hamburg	different schools from the 7th grade	Q	4,797	Jasinsky
3	1971	Baden-Württemberg	14–21 year-olds	I	1,871	Wickert-Institute
4	1971/1972	Schleswig-Holstein	high school/apprentices	Q	4,995	Schwarz et al.
5	1972	Hesse	different schools from the 8th grade	Q	11,521	Minister of Education and Internal Affairs
6	1972	North-Rhine Westphalia	different schools 7th–12th grade	Q	4,653	Wetz and Peterson
7	1972/1973	Saarland	different schools from 12 years	Q	2,088	Schmitt, Stein, Wolf
8	1973	Bavaria	12–24 year-olds	I	2,676	Infratest
9	1973	Hamburg	different schools from 8th grade	Q	5,168	Jasinsky
10	1973	Baden-Württemberg	14–21 year-olds	I	1,623	Wickert-Institute
11	1975	Hamburg	different schools from 8th grade	Q	5,426	Reuband
12	1976	Bavaria	14–24 year-olds	I	2,450	Infratest
13	1976	Saarland	different schools	Q	2,139	Schmitt, Stein
14	1978	Baden-Württemberg	12–25 year-olds	I	1,467	Infratest
15	1980	Bavaria	12–24 year-olds	Q	2,033	Infratest
16*	1981	Schleswig-Holstein	12–24 year-olds	M	1,408	Infratest
17*	1981	North-Rhine Westphalia	12–24 year-olds	M	1,843	Infratest
18*	1981	Saarland	12–24 year-olds	M	870	Infratest
19*	1981/1982	Hamburg	12–24 years-olds	M	720	Infratest
20*	1981/1982	Lower Saxony	12–24 year-olds	M	1,891	Infratest

No.	Year	State	Total sample	Method of as-sessment	Size of sample	Researcher
21*	1981 /1982	Rhineland-Palatinate	12–24 year-olds	M	1,475	Infratest
22*	1986 /1987	Schleswig-Holstein	12–24 years olds	M	577	Infratest
23*	1986 /1987	North-Rhine Westphalia	12–14 year-olds	M	1,828	Infratest
24*	1986 /1987	Hamburg	12–14 year-olds	M	623	Infratest
25*	1986 /1987	Lower Saxony	12–14 year-olds	M	1,969	Infratest
26*	1986 /1987	Rhineland-Palatinate	12–14 year-olds	M	1,544	Infratest
27*	1986 /1987	Bavaria	12–14 year-olds	M	2,262	Infratest
28*	1986 /1987	Berlin	12–14 year-olds	M	551	Infratest

Abbreviations for method of assessment:
Q = Questionnaires administered in group situations
I = Face-to-face interview
M = Mail survey
* = Part of a partially extended nationwide study

Ministry of Health) were added in the beginning of the 1980s. Questionnaires in classroom situations, which were formerly the preferred means for conducting representative surveys, have been seldom seen in the last few years. Whether this change in the method of data collection affects results of the survey is rather unlikely, based on the present studies, although this possibility cannot be excluded and further methodological research seems necessary.

In addition to surveys among adolescents, several representative surveys have also been conducted among the general population, including adults. These are national surveys, based on face-to-face interviews, and in contrast to the U.S. household study by NIDA (National Institute on Drug Abuse), they are exclusively multiple-topic surveys. The issue of drug use is only covered by a small number of questions in the survey and an exhaustive inventory of the use patterns—analogous to the surveys among adolescents—is lacking. Beginning in 1990, however, a large sur-

TABLE 1.2

Overview of National Surveys among Adolescents
in the Federal Republic of Germany

No.	Year	Researcher	Method of assessment	Size of sample	Age of sample	Prevalence (years) drug use
1	1973	IJF	I	1,763	14–25	18%
2	1976/77	IJF	I	1,503	14–25	14%
3	1978	Kehrmann marketing research	I	1,909	15–24	12%
4	1979	IJF	I	1,526	12–25	14%
5	1981/82	Infratest	I/M*	9,634	12–24	10%
6	1982	IJF	I	1,799	12–25	15%
7	1986	IJF	I	1,809	12–25	16%**
8	1986/87	Infratest	M	5,501	12–29	12%
9	1989	IFEP	I	1,602	12–21	15%
10	1989	Psydata	I	574	14–25	31%
11	1989/90	IJF	I	ca. 3,000	12–25	—

Survey No. 5: Without Berlin, Hesse, Schleswig-Holstein; Method of assessment:
M = Face-to-face interview
P = Mail questionnaire
– = No information available at present
* = Partially oral, partially postal inquiry (Baden-Wüttemberg and Bavaria orally)
** = In the original publication, as well as with the other presented figures, here
the weighed value has been included in the overview. The unweighed value in the
other IJF surveys differs from that only insignificantly. But in the survey from 1986,
the difference amounts to a 4% difference (unweighed prevalence = 12%)

vey among youth and younger and middle-aged adults has been begun by
the Institut für Therapieforschung (IFT) and Infratest, and it may overcome some of these limitations and cover a somewhat broader scope.

The representative surveys that are available lend themselves to a description of drug use experience and—if the size of the sample is sufficiently large—to an analysis of drug use with its full range of
manifestations. The data base is not sufficient, however, to assess heroin
addiction, which is often regarded by the public as the "real" drug problem. Even a further extension of the survey sample would not make this
possible: Heroin addicts are difficult to reach and often refuse to participate; heroin users in representative surveys among adolescents generally
reflect only "experimental users," that is, persons who used the substance
only a few times and then stopped. In order to assess permanent heroin
users, different research strategies have to be and have been selected in
the FRG: Strategies that access these persons themselves and recruit them

either through treatment facilities, correctional facilities or the drug scene (see, e.g., Middendorf et al. 1977; Berger et al. 1980; Projektgruppe TUdrop 1984), or through the recourse of analyzing existing files of institutions that were in contact with the addicts (Reuband 1979; Skarabis and Patzak 1981).

PREVALENCE OF DRUG USE AND ATTITUDES TOWARD DRUG USE

The most important findings of nationwide representative surveys among adolescents concerning the prevalence of drug use are listed in Table 1.2. If one excludes the method-dependent variations in the values, the findings appear relatively uniform: only a minority of adolescents in the FRG have ever used illicit drugs. The values range between 14% and 18% for the group of 14–25 year-olds. The higher value of 31% that was found in one recent study by the Psydata Institute is probably the result of a different, methodologically problematic, sampling strategy, and is therefore too high (street pedestrians were questioned). Further data among the adult population reinforce the impression that the proportion of people who ever used cannabis is small. Generally, the values lay between 3% and 8% (Table 1.3). If the values lay somewhat below that, it might be because of an underestimation, based on the methods.

The majority of findings both among youth and adults is fairly consistent and creates a picture that differs fundamentally from that of the United States. But it does not differ from the distribution patterns in other European countries; The FRG has cannabis-use prevalence rates similar to many other northern West European countries, even those with essentially different drug policies (such as the Netherlands). The latter is the more important when U.S. drug policy has been compared to that in European countries, it has usually been to the Netherlands only. This has often led to flawed impressions about the effect of different drug policies on prevalence rates. The findings from the Netherlands presumably reflect a fairly general European pattern of drug use rather than the consequence of its own specific drug policies (Reuband 1990d).

The available surveys grounded on identical indicators over time show, since the beginning of the 1970s, a fundamental change in the evaluation of the dangers of drugs. On the one hand, there is the indicator on which drugs one perhaps "should try." On the other hand, there is the indicator whether one should try hashish or heroin if it was "offered" at a party. Both can be seen as indicators of the willingness to use drugs. The first question measures it more in a way that assesses the globally ascribed

TABLE 1.3

Overview of National Surveys in the General Population of the FRG

No.	Year	Researcher (survey institute)	Size of sample	Age of sample	Prevalence of drug use
1	1971	IfD	ca. 2,000	16+	5%
2	1972	IfD	ca. 2,000	16+	4%
3	1977	BgA (Infratest)	2,007	14+	3%
4	1979	BgA (Infratest)	2,018	14+	4%
5	1982	Reuband (Zumabus/Infratest)	1,993	18+	6%
6	1986	IfD	1,037	16+	5%
7	1987	Reuband (GfM/Getas)	987	18+	8%

Formulation of question:
(1, 2, 6): "A question on hashish and LSD: Would you ever feel like trying hashish or LSD"? Response categories: Have tried it already; would feel like it; would not feel like it; undecided. (3, 4): "Have you yourself tried any drugs at any time or used it over a period of time?. (5): "Now, a totally different question: There are many things which almost everybody has done ever in his life. I give you a list with these common behaviors. Please—note how often have you ever done this in your life. A lot might have occured 10, 20 years ago. This includes also childhood and adolescence. Take your time. Think about it carefully and mark which applies to you. Afterwards, fold the paper [a list with frequencies is included]." (7): "Now, a totally different question. There are many things that almost everybody has done ever in his life. How is it with you—which of the following have you ever done in your life? This also includes childhood and adolescence. . . . Have you ever tried hashish? [If no:] I also mean situations in which you have only tried something and *thought* it would be hashish. The substance itself might not have had any effects. Has this ever happened?"

Basis:
Representative survey of the population, each oral face-to-face interviews. The surveys of the Institute of Demoskopie (IFD) are based on quota samples, the other on random samples.

Source:
(1, 2) Institute of Demoskopie (1982); (3, 4) Infratest (1977, 1979); (5) Reuband (1986); (6) Institute of Demoskopie (1989); (7) Survey of the author.

legitimacy of use. The second measure refers to the situation-specific willingness of the individual to try new things. The results (Table 1.4) disagree with a widely accepted assumption that adolescents have become more tolerant toward hashish or even heroin use over time. In contrast, since the beginning of the seventies, the indicators show a fairly continuous decrease. In 1976, 36% of the 14–25 year-olds thought it acceptable to try hashish; in 1986 the figure was only 19%. In 1971, 5% expressed the opinion that one may "try" heroin; in 1986 the figure was 1%. In

TABLE 1.4

Willingness to Use Different Illegal Drugs among Adolescents
(Ages between 14 and 25 Years) in the FRG

	1971	1973	1976	1979	1982	1986
One could try (1)						
hashish	. .	. .	36%	31%	23%	19%
marijuana	27%	23%	15%	15%	15%	13%
LSD	21%	14%	7%	7%	6%	3%
cocaine	. .	. .	15%	6%	7%	5%
opium	8%	6%	5%	4%	4%	3%
heroin	5%	3%	3%	2%	1%	1%
I would try myself (2)						
hashish	39%	31%	22%	24%	18%	. .
heroin	9%*	11%*	6%	5%	2%	. .

. . not assessed
* opium (instead of heroin) as drug was presented

Formulation of questions:
(1): "Which substances on this list could one try; which should not be taken at all in your opinion?" (2): "If somebody offered you heroin [1971 and 1973: opium] at a party for free or at all, would you accept it or refuse it? And how is it with hashish? Could you imagine that you would have accepted hashish?" For the first question, the percentage of "maybe try," for the second of "would accept it" is presented. The remaining percentage, which makes up the difference to 100%, consists on no-responses and missing data.

Basis:
Representative surveys among adolescents in the FRG. Random samples.

Source:
Secondary analyses of surveys of the Institute of Youth Research (for the Federal Center for Health Education), conducted by the author. Central Record Office-Studies No. 683, 1070, 1071, 1072, 1257, 1603; each unweighted samples.

the case of hashish, the percentage of persons willing to use was cut in half; the decrease is even larger for heroin. Moreover, the findings of the survey show that there is a decrease in the use of other drugs (such as LSD or cocaine).

The increasingly negative attitude toward illicit drugs is not specific to adolescents. It is embedded in a wider social context and can also be found—in the form of an increase perception of risks—among adults (Table 1.5). Thus the number of persons who attribute health and psychological risks to the use of hashish (even if it is only a single try)

Table 1.5

Attitudes toward Hashish and Heroin Use in the Population,
by Age and Course of Time

Age	18–29		30–49		50+		total	
	1982	1987	1982	1987	1982	1987	1982	1987
Large/medium risk of use								
–hashish, 1–2 times	27%	50%	42%	56%	55%	70%	44%	61%
–hashish, several times a week	80%	81%	90%	89%	90%	93%	88%	90%
–heroin, 1–2 times	88%	91%	88%	94%	87%	93%	88%	93%
–heroin, several times a week	97%	98%	96%	98%	93%	96%	94%	97%
Support of legalisation of hashish	13%	15%	7%	10%	3%	2%	7%	7%
(N) = P	445	181	726	357	792	449	1,993	987

Formulation of questions to assess dangers:
"How large are the physical and psychic risks in the use of the following drugs? Please, use the list to rate. How large is the risk if one tries hashish one or two times? Uses hashish several times a week?" The response categories range from "no risk," "little risk" to "medium risk" and "large risk." (Here listed: "large/medium risk").

Formulation of questions to assess the support of legalisation:
"What should the laws look like in your opinion? Should the use of hashish be legally permitted or not?" (Here listed: support).

Basis:
Representative surveys of the population in the FRG, subjects older than 18 years old. Assessment: May/June 1982, December 1987. Research Institute 1982: Infratest (ZUMABUS); 1987: GETAS.

Source:
Reuband (1988a)

has strongly increased in the last few years. Especially large is the change among the younger persons, of whom 27% assigned great risks to trying hashish, even if it is only once or twice. In 1987, the percentage was already 50%.

Concerning the legalization of drug use, which was discussed in the past predominantly in the United States but occasionally also in the FRG, a percentage of 7% of supporters shows that there is little support for it—less than in the United States or Australia. Even among those who have already tried hashish once, only 35% feel that the use of hashish should be legally permitted (for more details, see Reuband 1988a).

In view of the mostly negative attitude toward hashish use and the intensification of opposition over the course of time, it is not surprising that the proportion of drug users has decreased. The peak distribution of illicit drugs among the younger age groups (from 14 to 17 years) oc-curred at the beginning of the 1970s. Since then, consumption declined, and since the middle of the 1970s it has remained stable. This develop-ment can be best documented for the city of Hamburg, where many extensive surveys exist. Since the mid-1960s, similiar developments can be found in other federal states, such as Schleswig-Holstein and North-Rhine Westphalia (Reuband 1988a, 1988b). Since 1973 (the time of the first assessment in the series), there are analogous trends for Bavaria (Bayerisches Staatsministerium des Inneren und Bayerisches Staatsminis-terium für Arbeit und Sozialordnung 1985).

As far as can be seen from the few present findings, the decline in drug use is essentially a European phenomenon.[1] In sharp contrast is the case of the United States, where, in the 1970s, drug prevalence increased steadily, with the result that a majority of adolescents have experienced drug use. Only since the end of the 1970s has a certain change and slight decrease been visible. Similiar to the FRG in the beginning of the 1970s, the decline in the United States has been accompanied by an increase in negative attitudes toward drug use. In both cases, the decline is obviously a major consequence of a changed orientation toward drugs as, for ex-ample, health dangers are increasingly associated with it (see Reuband 1977, Johnston et al. 1989).

Based on the present survey data among adolescents in the FRG, the expansion phase of drug use is over for the time being. This does not exclude the possibility that—beyond the observed age groups—the use and even more, the intensive forms of use, continue to spread: Because the users grow older and continue the practice, the number of older users must increase. Furthermore, there might be a recruitment of adults into drug use, given the increasing number of "aging" users who might act as role models and propagate use among their peers. Evidence for such

1. Comparable developments over similar time periods can be also identified in other European countries such as Holland (Hulsmann 1982) or Sweden (Isaksson 1985). There though, the decline is often interpreted prematurely as a result of the practice of drug politics. Parallel development of two phenomena do not guarantee a causal relationship. Whether they are attributable to decriminalization or repression support or decreased drug use can only be evaluated by comparing different interventions. Regarding this, not one, but several contexts can build a basis for the survey.

a trend might be the increasing number of older drug users apprehended by the police.

PREVALENCE OF ADDICTION AND TRENDS

To measure the extent of drug use experience among adolescents is one thing; to assess the extent of drug addiction is another. Only a small fraction of all people who try drugs—mostly cannabis—will ever use or become addicted. Therefore, the numbers on drug use experience among adolescents only illustrate the potential recruitment basis for drug addiction but not the extent of drug addiction per se. Trends that can be generally seen in the area of cannabis use do not necessarily recur among addicts. Additional data are needed in order to comment on the spread and the form of manifestation of the use of hard drugs.

It is difficult to estimate the total extent of the present hard-drug scene in the FRG (not including the former East Germany). An empirically proven base line is lacking. The estimations, accordingly, vary considerably: The long-standing figures of the Federal Ministry of Health, which are based on estimations from government drug experts from the different states, came up with approximately 50,000 persons who are addicted to heroin, amphetamines, or cocaine. In contrast, the estimations of the Federal Criminal Office and the Federal Ministry for Internal Affairs are higher, with approximately 100,000 persons around 1989/90. How plausible are these estimations? Considering the number of hard drug users who have ever been registered by the police, one can count a number of about 91,000 users in 1988. A part of them—there were 6,283 drug deaths between 1970 and 1988—has to be regarded as dead by now (data from the Federal Criminal Office, own calculations). A further part that is difficult to estimate has to be regarded as finally recovered or in therapy, or as in a correctional facility. Another, probably larger part (Reuband 1990b), continues to belong to the population of active users.

Based on the set limitations, the number of actual users among the registered users of hard drugs has to be viewed as less than 91,000. This number will also be augmented by a different part out of the yet not identified gray area. It therefore seems realistic to assume the number of users of hard drugs as between at least 50,000 and 100,000. This number will be considerably larger if nonaddicted occasional users and those who only tried opiates and IV drug use are included in the calculation. One might then possibly reach a number of up to 200,000 persons.

Since 1984, drug use problems have intensified considerably in the FRG as assessed by the number of hard drug users who have been noticed by the police for the first time and put on file by the Federal Criminal

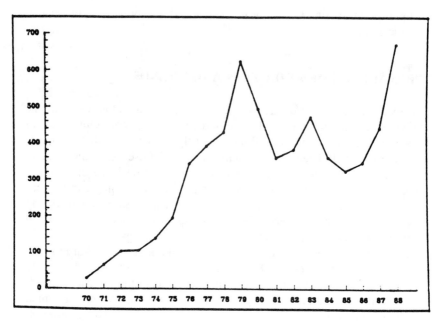

FIGURE 1.1.
Drug fatalities in Germany (1979–1988)

Office. Whereas in 1985 only 3,246 persons were registered as such, 3,921 were registered in 1986, 5,084 in 1987, and 7,456 in 1988. The number has more than doubled within three years. Not only the number of new users but also the number of complications caused by drug use— as assessed by the number of drug deaths—has increased considerably in recent years (Figure 1.1). As is the case for the first time consumers are noticed by police, the trend is not linear but has peaks and valleys. Already in 1988, the number of drug deaths exceeded the highest peak of 1979, when 623 deaths were claimed. The reason for the fluctuations and the dramatic increase in the number of drug deaths is an open question. The number is without doubt related to the number of total users, but it is also influenced by the purity of the offered substances and the physical condition of IV drug users.

FINAL COMMENTS

There are more data on the German drug situation than is usually perceived abroad. Some findings have been summarized here. However, the large quantity of data in some areas does not preclude that the analytical study of the data has been unsatisfactory. Most of the studies are descriptive in nature; relevant questions have not been asked, and—if asked at all—they have been dealt with inadequately. Questions of etiology that are closely linked to epidemiology have been unduly neglected and have almost totally given way to a clinical perspective that all too simply views drug use as some form of coping with personal and social problems. Genuinely sociological explanations are—with a few exceptions (Reuband 1990c)—lacking.

Several basic questions thus remain open: We do not know, for instance, how changes in the market or the prices affect patterns of use. We do not know how changes in behavior patterns affect overdoses. We do not know how changes in the social conditions of the drug scene and reactions of society lead to changing patterns of use and seeking help. Myths instead of facts are dominating the discussion and have given rise to often faulty social consensus among experts in many cases. In this respect, without doubt, the German situation does not differ very much from the situation in other Western European countries (Reuband 1990a). Yet it cannot be overlooked that in a number of Western European countries—such as the Netherlands or Great Britain—special, quite successful efforts have been undertaken, recently supported by government agencies, in order to get qualitatively better research. Similar research initiatives are still lacking in Germany, though there are some slight indications that conditions might change in the future.

REFERENCES

Bayerisches Staatsministerium des Inneren und Bayerisches Staatsministerium für Arbeit und Soziales (eds.). (ca. 1985). Alkohol Drogen Medikamente Tabak. Jugend fragt Jugend. Repräsentativerhebungen bei Jugendlichen in Bayern 1973, 1976, 1980, 1984. München.

Berger, H., Reuband, K. H., and Widlitzek, U. (1980). Wege in die Heroinabhängigkeit. Zur Entwicklung abweichender Karrieren. München.

Hulsmann, L. C. (1982). Die Entwicklung der Cannabisdiskussion in Holland 1964–1980. In *Haschisch: Prohibition oder Legalisierung* W. Burian, and E. Eisenbach-Stangl (eds.), pp. 157–68. Weinheim, Basel: Beltz.

Isaksson, H. O. (ed.). (1985) Report 84. On the alcohol and drug situation in Sweden. Stockholm: Swedish Council of Information on Alcohol and other Drugs.

Johnston, L. D., O'Malley, P., and Bachmann, J. (1989). Drug use, drinking and smoking: National survey results from high school, college, and young adults population 1975–1988. Rockville, Maryland: National Institute on Drug Abuse.

Middendorf, F. W., Stockert, A., Roghmann, R., Spring, R., and Algeier, R. (1977). Drogenkarriere und Entzugsversuche von Opiatabhängigen—eine katamnestische Studie. *Der Nervenarzt* 48: 170–76.

Projektgruppe TUdrop (1984). *Heroinabhängigkeit unbetreuter Jugendlicher.* Weinheim, Basel: Beltz.

Reuband, K. H. (1977). Drogen—nicht mehr "in", aber noch lange nicht "out." *Psychologie heute* 4: 58–65.

———. (1979). Drogengebrauch und soziale Merkmale von Fixern in der Bundesrepublik. *Neue Praxis. Kritische Zeitschrift für Sozialarbeit und Sozialpädogogik* 9: 85–108.

———. (1986). Die Verbreitung illegaler Drogenerfahrung in der Bevölkerung der Bundesrepublik. Versuch ihrer Messung im Rahmen der Umfrageforschung. *Suchtgefahren* 32: 87–102.

———. (1988a). Haschisch im Urteil der Bundesbürger. Moralische Bewertung, Gefahrenwahrnehmung und Sanktionsverlangen 1970–1987. *Neue Praxis. Kritische Zeitschrift für Sozialarbeit und Sozialpädagogik* 18: 480–95.

———. (1988b). Verbreitung und Erscheinungsformen des Drogengebrauchs: Umfragen unter Jugendlichen in Schleswig-Holstein 1968–1987. *Jugendforum. Fachzeitschrift für Praxis, Wissenschaft und Politik in der Jugendhilfe in Schleswig-Holstein* 9/10: 240–44.

———. (1988c). Drogenkonsum im Wandel. Eine retrospektive Messung der Drogenerfahrung Jugendlicher, 1967–1987. *Zeitschrift für Sozialisationsforschung und Erziehungssoziologie (ZSE)* 8: 149–52.

———. (1990a). Research on drug use: A review of problems, needs and future perspectives. *Drug and Alcohol Dependence* 25: 149–52.

———. (1990b). Empirische Befunde zur sozialen Zusammensetzung Drogenabhängiger. Ergebnisse einer Informantenbefragung. *Neue Praxis. Zeitschrift für Sozialarbeit, Sozialpädagogik und Sozialpolitik* 30: 526–34.

———. (1990c). Soziale Determinanten des Drogengebrauchs. Eine empirische Untersuchung des Drogengebrauchs in der Bundesrepublik Deutschland unter besonderer Berücksichtigung soziologischer Theorien abweichenden Verhaltens. Frankfurt: Campus, in press.

———. (1990d). Drogenkonsum und Drogenpolitik. Ein Vergleich der Bundesrepublik Deutschland und der Niederlande. Unpublished manuscript.

Skarabis, H., and Patzak, M. (1981). *Die Berliner Heroinszene.* Weinheim: Beltz.

CHAPTER 2

Drug-Related Death

Klaus Püschel

INTRODUCTION

Deaths resulting from drug addiction are of enormous medical, legal, and social significance. Drug addiction is of great concern to the individuals involved and to society as a whole. Crime connected with deaths caused by drug addiction poses special tasks and questions for forensic scientists. Leading experts representing the judiciary and the police estimate that the negative effects of drug-connected crime are more severe than the effects of terrorism for our society. The increased number of drug deaths reflects the extent and the changing nature of drug addiction.

The following review summarizes our forensic-medical experiences from the investigation of more than 500 drug-related fatalities in Hamburg and the surroundings within the last decade. Some remarks are made concerning the situation in the FRG. Literature with findings from other European countries and the United States can be discussed only briefly and cited incompletely.

DEFINITIONS, STATISTICS, AND EPIDEMIOLOGY

Definitions

For epidemiological analyses a standardized definition of the term *drug death* is absolutely necessary. In practice, however, different criteria are used in different countries. Deaths directly caused by overdose of illicit drugs are registered everywhere. The differences relate especially to the interpretation of the causal connection between drug addiction and death. A worldwide accepted definition of drug death is imperative for nation-wide investigations and comparisons because the problem of drug addiction does not stop at national borders.

In the FRG the following definition has been worked out by a special group of the crime police (*Bundeskriminalamt*) and is designed to record all deaths where a causal connection to drug addiction (illicit drugs or substitutes) is evident:

1. Death due to intentional or accidental overdose ("golden shot").
2. Death due to long-term abuse of drugs (e.g., myocarditis, hepatitis, liver cirrhosis, AIDS).
3. Suicides connected with drug addiction (e.g., hanging, shooting, jumping from a high structure).
4. Fatal accidents influenced by drugs (e.g., traffic accidents, falls from heights, fire, and carbon monoxide intoxication).

Group 1, the so-called golden shot, represents the majority of all drug deaths in Hamburg (about 66% some years ago, about 90% nowadays). However, the official statistics concerning drug deaths suffer from a serious disadvantage; in only some areas are the statistics based on the results of regular autopsies and toxicological investigations.

The classification of drugs by the World Health Organization (WHO) distinguishes seven types of psychic and physical dependence on the one hand and habituation to drugs on the other. The most severe consequences are attributed to heroin. In the FRG a drug is defined by the Narcotics Act (*Betäubungsmittelgesetz*). The term "narcotic" is purely a nomen juris. It is not identical with pharmacological or medical terminology and can be changed by decrees to bring it up to date. In this act not only are drugs registered (i.e., heroin, morphine, codeine, methadone, amphetamine, cocaine, mescaline, LSD, hashish) but also many substances that are taken as alternatives to or substitutes for drugs (i.e., benzodiazepines, barbiturates, apart from medical prescription, methaqualon). The so-called designer drugs, however, are not registered. These are new synthetic substitute drugs derived from amphetamine, fentanyl or meperidin. They can produce many problems in toxicological analysis. To some extent they have qualities that have remained unknown until now.

TABLE 2.1

Illegal Drugs Confiscated by the Police in Hamburg 1985–1988

	1985 kg	1986 kg	1987 kg	1988 kg
Hashish	43.3	199.9	49.6	21.6
Marihuana	5.5	193.1	20.5	8,516.4
Heroin	9.6	2.2	12.1	19.3
Cocaine	0.6	1.3	2.3	41.6
Opium	1.1	1.5	0.7	1.6
Amphetamine	2.1	—	1.9	5.5
LSD	922 trips	40 trips	125 trips	12 trips

Statistics

The prevalence of drugs can easily be demonstrated by looking at the amounts confiscated by the police. The figures published in Hamburg (Table 2.1) show that

- the confiscated amounts of heroin were especially large,
- seizure of products of cannabis was high,
- the use of cocaine is increasing,
- the amount of confiscated amphetamine is changing,
- LSD trips show a decreasing trend.

It is estimated that about 100,000 people in West Germany inject narcotics intravenously; 300,000 to 500,000 people are dependent on prescribed psychoactive drugs. Since 1970 drug deaths have been centrally registered in the *Bundeskriminalamt*. The number shows a steady increase until 1979, when over 600 drug victims were counted. After 1979 the number of drug deaths decreased to 300 to 500 annually (Figure 2.1). In 1988 there was a dramatic increase in drug deaths (674 cases in 1988; more than 700 cases up to September 1989). A similar development can be registered for Hamburg (Figure 2.2). Fifty-one drug deaths were registered in 1987. This unfortunate trend continued in 1988 (75 drug deaths) and in 1989 (more than 60 victims up to September).

Together with Frankfurt and West Berlin, Hamburg has the most problems with drugs and drug-related fatalities in the GFR. Compared with other European countries, the FRG had the highest absolute number of

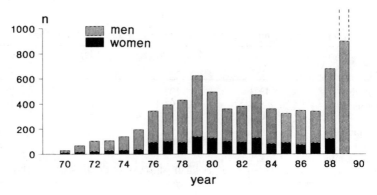

FIGURE 2.1.
Drug-related fatalities and sex distribution in FRG since 1970

drug deaths in the years 1980 to 1985 (about 400 yearly), followed by Italy (about 300) and France (about 200). However, in Denmark and Switzerland the drug mortality rate was higher. In 1986 Italy took first place in Europe in the number of drug deaths. Drug deaths in 1988 were as follows: Italy, 781; FRG, 674; Great Britain, 330; France, 236; Switzerland, 199; Denmark, 150; Norway, 115; The Netherlands, 70.

During the entire period of investigation, male drug addicts predominated in Germany. But it must be mentioned that in comparison with earlier times more women are counted among the drug deaths. The sex distribution has changed from 5 : 1 to 5 : 2 between 1975 and 1985. The average age of the drug victims has risen during the last two decades from 25 years of age to approximately 30 years of age.

Drug Career

In Hamburg it takes 1 to 2 years on average for a drug addict to be registered by the police for the first time. On average, 6 to 8 years pass from the start of the drug career until death. Sometimes the survival period is only several months—on the other hand, drug victims have survived for more than 20 years. One percent to 2% of the drug addicts die every year or, in other words, after 10 years 10% to 15% of the addicts registered by the police have died. Not all drug addicts die. About 40% to 50% of the consumers of hard drugs (especially the older ones) break free of the drug habit; we don't know exactly why. Therapeutic success is comparably poor.

One-quarter to one-third of the drug deaths in Hamburg investigated

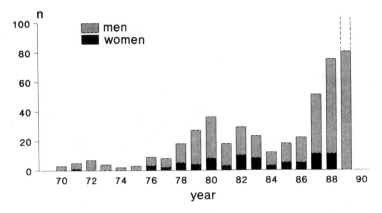

FIGURE 2.2.
Drug-related fatalities and their sex distribution in Hamburg since 1970.

by autopsy and by toxicological examinations were not registered as drug addicts with the police before death. It has to be presumed that the number of unreported drug-related fatalities is even higher. We don't know exactly the rate of intended suicides among the drug addicts. Ten years ago it made up about 20% of all drug deaths. Nowadays it seems to us that this rate has declined. Others suppose an increase of suicidal tendencies among drug addicts because of HIV infections.

FORENSIC-MEDICAL INVESTIGATIONS

It has to be emphasized that conditions for our investigations are good in Hamburg. There is close cooperation between the drug squad of the police and the University's Institute of Forensic Medicine. The frequency of autopsies of those registered as drug addicts is about 90% to 100%, however, we are not quite sure about the number of unreported cases. Our own experiences are based on more than 500 examined cases from Hamburg and the surrounding areas.

External Findings

The drug deaths mostly occurred in the inner-city areas of Hamburg. However, decentralization of drug traffic and consumption has taken place with drugs moving to the suburbs. Most drug deaths occur in private homes. Other places are hospitals, rest rooms, public places, and hotel rooms. The circumstances surrounding the death sometimes are clear, e.g., the syringe·in the vein and the utensils near the corpse. Otherwise, friends or relatives of the junkie systematically remove all traces. Needle marks are the most important signs of an intravenous drug addiction and must be recognized during the external examination of the corpse. Sometimes the drug addicts inject themselves in areas that are difficult to spot (e.g., the mouth, the feet, the lower legs, and the neck). In a few cases we didn't find any injection mark at all, although intravenous drug abuse could be proved by toxicological investigations. Sometimes we find drug-specific tatoos as hints of the addiction (Figure 2.3).

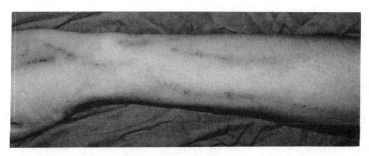

a)

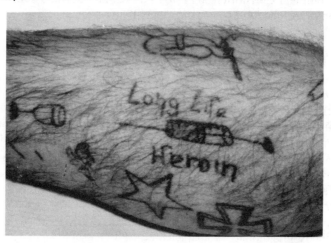

b)

FIGURE 2.3.
External findings: a) Needle marks on the forearm; b) Drug-specific tatoos.

Cause of Death

The following causes of death of drug victims could be diagnosed during the last 10 years: intoxication 70%, "natural" death 10%, external violence 20%. Fatal intoxication with heroin alone is dominant. The most common infections in drug addicts are hepatitis, myocarditis, pneumonia and HIV infection. External violence includes suicide, e.g., by hanging or drowning, or accident involving a fall from a height, fire in the home, or traffic accidents. Within the last two years, the "supply" of heroin has apparently become so copious that almost all death cases in Hamburg (more than 90%) were caused by heroin intoxication.

The so-called body packers or drug-couriers die because of the rupture of cocaine or heroin-filled condoms (Figure 2.4) in the stomach or the intestine (Introna and Smialek, 1989; Schmoldt, Koops, Püschel and Stobbe, 1988). They are generally not dependent on drugs themselves and don't take drugs intravenously.

Histology

The most important organs involved in the histological investigations in drug deaths are the liver (Beckmann and Püschel, 1982; Kringsholm and Christoffersen, 1982; Trübner, Püschel and Laufs, 1989) the lungs (Kringsholm and Christoffersen, 1987; Püschel and Schoof, 1987; Rajs, Hörm and Ormstad, 1984) and the heart (Dressler and Roberts, 1989; Kringsholm and Christoffersen, 1987; Rajs and Falconer, 1979). The histomorphological findings of these organs correspond either to direct effects of the drug addiction or to concomitant infections, hypoxias or bleedings. The proof of foreign body-granulomas is of special diagnostic importance (Figure 2.5). These are traces of intravenous drug abuse. These granulomas were found in the lungs of 60% of the drug deaths. Other places where granulomas can be detected are the skin around the needle marks, the liver and other organs. Mostly talc or starch or even other unidentified substances were found in the granulomas (Kringsholm and Christoffersen, 1987, 1989; Püschel and Schoof, 1987). These are auxiliary substances for the production or tablets and they are sometimes used for "stretching" the drugs.

The histological pattern and time dependent structure of pulmonary foreign body granulomas is characteristic (Püschel and Schoof, 1987): Early findings are pulmonary microthrombi consisting of platelets, fibrin and aggregation of leucocytes adjacent to the talc particles. The consecutive granuloma formation is mainly influenced by activated macro-

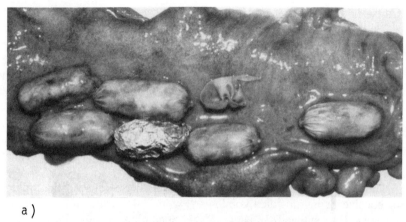

a)

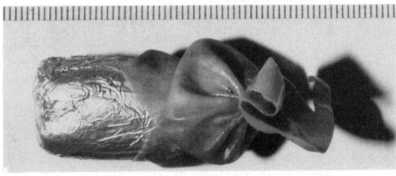

b)

FIGURE 2.4.
Body-packing: a) Cocaine-filled condoms in the intestine, partly ruptured; b) The different layers of a body-pack.

phages. Multinucleated giant cells can be found after about one week. Within a time period of some weeks talc is incorporated in the vascular wall and deposited in perivascular foreign body granulomas. The final stadium is focal perivascular fibrosis. Talc partly is eliminated by phagocytes migrating into the alveoli.

Common findings in the lung are edema, bleeding and many macrophages in the alveolar spaces (Gerlach, 1980; Rajs, Hörm and Ormstad, 1984). In our material intraalveolar siderophages were distinguished in 20% of the cases. The pattern of distribution shows typical small foci. Presumably these are the residues of intraalveolar hemorrhages during episodes of intoxication, lung edema and coma. The myocardium sometimes shows degenerative and inflammatory changes (about 5% to 10%

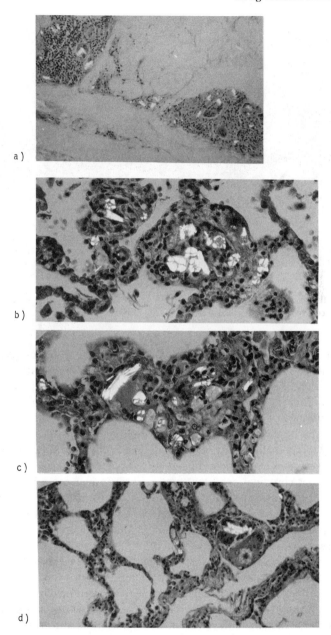

FIGURE 2.5.
Microscopy of foreign-body granulomas. The birefringent material can be visualized by polarized light. a) Subcutaneous tissue; b–d) Lung: starch particles (cross-like appearance) and talc in the vessels and in the interstitium of the alveolar wall, partly incorporated in macrophages and multinuclear foreign-body giant cells.

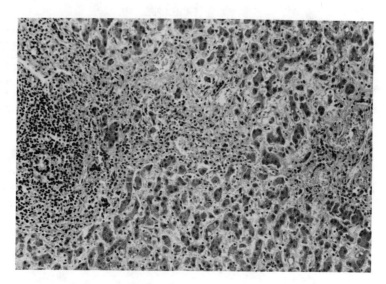

FIGURE 2.6.
Microscopy of chronic aggressive hepatitis

of the cases in our material), mostly with unspecific scattered mononuclear infiltrates and local myocardial fibrosis (so-called borderline myocarditis according to the Dallas classification). Active infective endocarditis (i.e., right-sided valve vegetations) was scarcely found.

Alterations of liver cells (i.e., lipofuscinosis and cytoplasmatic granules), can be caused by a long-term abuse of medical drugs.

The inflammatory liver diseases found in 70% to 80% of our cases are mostly due to unsterile injections. These were mostly of unspecific reactive or chronical persistent types. Chronic aggressive hepatitis (Figure 2.6), liver cirrhosis, and acute viral hepatitis make up for about 10% of all cases. Morphologically the HBs-Ag can be visualized with the aldehyde-fuchsine or orcein stain, by in situ hybridization and immunocytologically.

In a special series, undecalcified sections of jaw bones with teeth and attached soft tissues of drug-related fatalities were examined histologically. In comparison with controls, the striking findings in the users consisted of focal subgingival calcifications with granulomas, pigmentation of the deeper epithelial layer at the transition of the attached gingiva and the alveolar mucosa as well as of the periodontium and fat cells of the bone marrow. There was no inflammation of the salivary glands; the sialoporia of users is thought to be caused by drug action versus the

TABLE 2.2

Serological Hepatitis B markers in Drug-related Deaths (N = 206)

anti-HBc	95	(46.1%)
anti-HBs	67	(32.5%)
anti-HBe	8	(3.9%)
HBsAg	9	(4.4%)
HBeAg	3	(1.5%)

central nervous system or the peripheral vegetative innervation. Concerning the massive dental caries and high frequency of periodontal diseases the histologic findings correspond with clinical studies of drug-users (Donath and Püschel, 1983; Gerlach and Wolters, 1977).

Postmortem Serology

For the detection of the etiology of the inflammatory liver changes immunocytological and postmortem serological investigations have proved to be of great help. In nearly 50% of 206 serologically investigated drug deaths antibodies against the hepatitis-core-antigen could be proved. Nearly every second drug victim had had contact with hepatitis B-viruses during his life. The antibodies against HBs-antigen that are responsible for immunity protection were present in 33 of the cases (Table 2.2). The Hbs-Ag was provable in 9 cases (Trübner, Bartsch, Polywka, Püschel and Laufs, in press; Trübner, Püschel and Laufs, 1989).

The drug addicts are a risk group for the HIV infection and AIDS. Therefore, drug death, too, is connected increasingly with the problem of AIDS (Kringsholm, Theilade and Geertinger, 1989; Püschel, Lieske, Hashimoto, Karch, Laufs, Racz and Janssen, 1987; Wetli, 1972). Since 1985 we have examined all drug deaths serologically in Hamburg. The findings of ELISA, IFT, and Western Blot are postmortem very reliable and reproducible.

Up to now only very few of the drug related fatalities in Hamburg and in the FRG were caused by full blown AIDS. Of course, this number is increasing. With the advent of HIV infections the morphological findings in the drug deaths have enormously widened (Figure 2.7). The final stage of AIDS can be characterized by a lymphadenopathy syndrome, Kaposi's sarcoma, other neoplasms and opportunistic infections (i.e., cytomegaly, toxoplasmosis, pneumocystis carinii pneumonia, etc.).

The development of the HIV-1 prevalence among drug deaths (n =

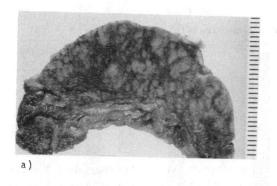

a)

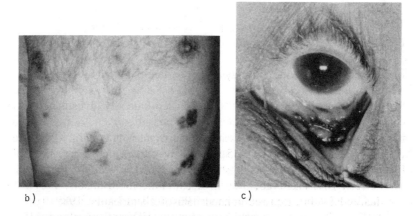

b)   c)

d)

FIGURE 2.7.
**HIV infection, lymphadenopathy-syndrome and AIDS: a) Transverse section of an axil-
lary lymph node with follicular hyperplasia; b) Cutaneous Kaposi's sarcoma on the
chest; c) Infiltration of the conjunctive; d) Sarcoma-infiltrated abdominal lymph-node
(paraaortic).**

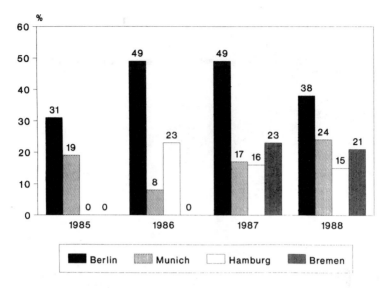

FIGURE 2.8.
Development of HIV-1-prevalence in drug deaths in various big cities of Germany since 1985.

565) in several German cities (West Berlin, Bremen, Hamburg, Cologne, Munich and Stuttgart) from 1985 to 1988 was evaluated. In 1988 36% of the 674 deceased drug addicts were examined. The prevalence rate was between 10% and 30%; only in Berlin were more than 40% of the drug deaths HIV infected (cumulated data of all cities over the 4-year-period: 27%). There was no uniform or steady regional development of HIV-1 prevalence in the different cities (Figure 2.8). The ratio of men to women among drug deaths was 3 to 1. The HIV-1 prevalence among males was 21%; among females, 41%. HIV-infected individuals were 2 to 3 years older than seronegatives. Predictions concerning the trend of prevalence rates are not possible at this point. Continuous monitoring of the HIV status of drug deaths seems to be a worthwhile means for evaluating the spread of this disease among the risk group of intravenous drug addicts.

Toxicology

The evaluation of every drug death should be established in close cooperation between the forensic pathologist and the toxicologist. Toxicolog-

Drug deaths in Hamburg 1988
Cause of death

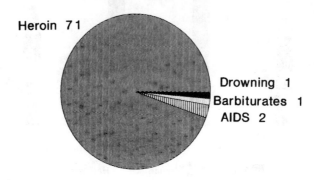

FIGURE 2.9.
Drug deaths in Hamburg 1988 (n = 75)

ical investigations are indispensable and most decisive for the evaluation of the cause of death. The range of lethal morphine concentrations in the blood of the corpse is quite wide. The lethal concentration depends on the individual disposition of the drug addict. It is not rare that relatively low doses are found in the blood and in the urine of the drug dead. The term "overdose" is very relative and depends on actual susceptibility. Death sometimes occurs when low doses are found in the blood and in the urine after periods of longer abstinence (e.g., while the user is in prison, or when the drug interacts with other substances, such as alcohol or medications, or after survival periods in a comatose state). If the drug victims were "clean" before their deaths, a small amount can be lethal even if they had tolerated the same dose previously.

The percentage of acute intoxications by heroin in Hamburg has been steadily increasing. In 1988 nearly 95% of the drug deaths were caused by heroin intoxication (Figure 2.9 and Table 2.3). Mixed intoxication, especially with alcohol, barbiturates, and benzodiazepines form the next biggest group (within the last decade). The situation in Hamburg reflects the situation for the Federal Republic of Germany as a whole. Deaths from cocaine—mostly after IV injections—are relatively infrequent.

Special investigations are required to prove the presence of opiates in the mucous membrane of the nose in the case of snorting, and in hair

TABLE 2.3

Drug Deaths in Hamburg 1988 (n = 75)
Toxicological Findings

Heroin	73
Cocaine	8
Barbiturates	6
Benzodiazepines	13
Hashish	4
Amphetamines	1
Others	6
Alcohol > 1%	21

to prove long-time abuse. The mucous membrane of the nose should be examined for a chronic granulomatous rhinitis and for traces of heroin (Hirsch and Adelson, 1972; Püschel, Schulz, Naeve and Arnold, 1980). The hair can be subjected to toxicological investigations for heroin and other narcotics from the root to the tip of the hair. Thereby certain conclusions can be drawn concerning the drug career and the drugs consumed (Baumgartner, Jones, Baumgartner and Black, 1979; Klug, 1980; Püschel, Thomasch and Arnold, W., 1983).

CONCLUSIONS

1. Every questionable drug death should be subjected to an autopsy and detailed micromorphological, toxicological, and serological investigations. The epicritical analysis should be performed in close cooperation between pathologists and toxicologists.
2. The corpse is the most important evidence in establishing the cause of death. The examination of the corpse gives the first indications of a trace to the dealer.
3. Detection of the cause of death and the source of the drug are important steps toward the prevention of drug-related death.
4. Pathological and toxicological investigations of drug-related fatalities may contribute to the evaluation of first aid, therapeutic approaches, and clinical interventions in case of intoxication.
5. Even when the quality of the statistics of the drug deaths is questionable, one may find indications about the extent of drug abuse and signals of changes in the scene.
6. Drug deaths are—to a certain extent—a parameter of the effective-

ness of the control programs for drugs, for measures of therapy and the preventive prescribing of drugs.

7. Serological screening is very useful for the epidemiology of hepatitis and HIV infections. Continuous monitoring of the HIV status of drug deaths shows the spread of this disease among the risk group of intravenous drug addicts.
8. Toxicological investigations very quickly reflect the change of illicit substances in the drug scene.
9. The "Supply" of heroin has apparently become so copious that almost all overdose deaths in Hamburg as well as in the rest of the FRG within the last two years have been caused by heroin intoxication. Other narcotics have been of minor importance up to now.
10. Obviously, it is difficult to distinguish between drug-induced deaths and deaths among drug addicts. An international agreement about a definition of what constitutes a drug death is absolutely necessary for nationwide analyses.

REFERENCES

Baumgartner, A. M., Jones, P. F., Baumgartner, W. A., and Black, C. T. (1979). Radioimmunoassay of hair for determining opiate-abuse histories. *J. Nucl. Med. 20*, 748–52.

Beckmann, E. R., and Püschel, K. (1982). Histologische Leberveränderungen bei Rauschgifttodesfällen. Proceedings XII. Kongress der Internationalen Akademie für gerichtliche und soziale Medizin, Wien: Verlag H. Egermann, pp. 885–88 Wien

Donath, K., and Püschel, K. (1989). Histologische Befunde an Zahnsystem, Weichgewebe und kleinen Speicheldrüsen bei Rauschgifttoten. *Beitr. gerichtl. Med. 41*, 349–57.

Dressler, F. A. and Roberts, W. C. (1989). Infective endocarditis in opiate addicts: Analysis of 80 cases studied at necropsy. *Am. J. Cardiol. 63*, 1240–57.

Gerlach, P. (1980). Post mortem investigations of fatal cases of narcotic addiction. *Forensic Sci. Int. 15*, 31–39.

Gerlach, P., and Wolters, H. D. (1977). Zahn- und Mundschleimhautbefgunde bei Rauschmittelkonsumenten. *Dtsch. zahnärztl. Z. 32*, 400–404.

Hirsch, C., and Adelson L. (1972). Acute fatal intranasal narcotism. Report of two fatalities following narcotic "snorting". *Hum. Pathol. 2*, 71.

Introna, F. Jr., and Smialek, J. E. (1989). The "mini-packer" syndrome. Fatal ingestion of drug containers in Baltimore, Maryland. *Am. J. Forensic Med. Pathol. 10*, 21–24.

Klug, E. (1980). Zur Morphinbestimmung in Kopfhaaren. Z. *Rechtsmed. 84*, 189–193.

Kringsholm, B., and Christoffersen P. (1982). Liver pathology in fatal drug addiction. *Forensic Sci. Int. 20*, 141–151.

Kringsholm, B., and Christoffersen P. (1987). Lung and heart pathology in fatal drug addiction. A consecutive autopsy study. *Forsensic Sci. Int. 34*, 30–51.

Kringsholm, B., and Christoffersen, P. (1987). The nature and the occurence of birefringent material in different organs in fatal drug addiction. *Forsensic Sci. Int. 34*, 53–62.

Kringsholm, B., and Christoffersen, P. (1989). Morphological findings in fatal drug addiction. An investigation of injection marks, endocrine organs and kidneys. *Forensic Sci. Int. 40*, 15–24.

Kringsholm, B., Theilade P., and Geertinger P. (1989). The occurrence of HIV antibodies in drug addicts autopsied at the University Institute of Forensic Medicine in Copenhagen in 1987. *Forsensic Sci. Int. 41*, 281–284.

Oehmichen, M., and Staak, M. (1988). Der Tod des Drogenkonsumenten: Geschehensablauf, Häufigkeit sowie Nachweisbarkeit und Prognose. In: Staak M. (ed): *Betäubungsmittelmißbrauch*. Berlin-Heidelberg: Springer, pp 8–23.

Püschel, K., and Penning, R. (in press). HIV-1-Prävalenz bei rechtsmedizinisch untersuchten Todesfällen (Hamburg und München 1989). *Beitr. gerichtl. Med.*

Püschel, K., and Schoof, W. (1987). Zur Morphogenese hämatogen entstandener Fremdköpergranulome im Lungenparenchym. *Beitr. gerichl. Med. 45*, 121–28.

Püschel, K., Schulz, F., Naeve W., and Arnold, W. (1980). Todesfälle nach nasaler Applikalion von Heroin. Z. *Rechtsmed. 84*, 270–300.

Püschel, K., Thomasch, P., and Arnold, W. (1983). Opiate levels in hair. *Forensic Sci. Int. 21*, 181–86.

Rajs, J., and Falconer, B. (1979). Cardiac lesions in intravenuous drug addicts. *Forensic Sci. Int. 13*, 193–209.

Rajs J., and Hörm, T., and Ormstad, K. (1984). Postmortem findings of pulmonary lesions of older datum in intravenous drug addicts. A forensic pathological study. *Virchows Arch. (Pathol. Anat.) 402*, 405–14.

Richards, R. G., Reed, D., and Cravey, R. H. (1976). Death from intravenously administered narcotics. A study of 114 cases. *J. Forensic Sci. 21*, 467–88.

Trübner, K., Bartsch, N., Polywka, S., Püschel, K., and Laufs R. (in press). Zur Hepatitis B-Prävalenz bei Todesfällen in der Rechtsmedizin. *Beitr. gerichtl. Med.*

Trübner, K., Püschel, K., and Laufs, R. (1989). Hepatitis bei Rauschgifttoten. Z. *Rechtsmed. 102*, 199–205.

Wotli, C. V. (1972). Narcotic addiction in Dade County Florida: An analysis of 100 consecutive autopsies. *Arch. Pathol. 93*, 330–43.

CHAPTER 3

Drug Abuse and AIDS
in New Jersey:
Issues and Interventions

Jerome J. Platt, Martin Y. Iguchi, Victor Lidz,
and Donald A. Bux

CURRENT TRENDS

United States

The impact of AIDS as a result of intravenous (IV) drug use in the
United States has been tremendous. Although male homosexual activity
continues to be the largest risk category for infection with AIDS, con-
stituting 59% of the cumulative number of AIDS cases to date, this risk
category represents a decreasing proportion of new cases diagnosed: the
12-month period ending May 31, 1990 saw 57% of AIDS cases attributed
to this risk factor, whereas the next 12-month period showed only 55%
of cases in this risk category (CDC 1991a). Conversely, intravenous
drug users (IVDUs) represent an increasing proportion of cases in the
nation. Nationwide, intravenous (IV) drug use was implicated as a sole
or coexisting risk factor in 29% of all AIDS cases reported to date, a
proportion which is expected to continue to climb (CDC 1991a).
    Minorities in the United States, particularly blacks and Hispanics, rep-
resent a disproportionate number of cases of AIDS. The incidence rates
of AIDS among heterosexual Hispanics and non-Hispanic blacks are approximately 9 and 12 times, respectively, that of heterosexual, non-Hispa-

nic whites (Ellerbrock, Bush, Chamberland et al. 1991). In several states in the northeastern United States where IV drug use is the primary risk factor for AIDS, minorities actually constitute a majority of AIDS cases (CDC 1991b). This fact can largely be accounted for by the much greater role played by IV drug use in the transmission of AIDS among minorities. Among blacks, for example, IV drug use constitutes the primary risk factor for AIDS, accounting for 39% of cases nationwide, versus 36% of cases occurring among homosexual/bisexual, non-Hispanic, black males (CDC 1991a). Among Hispanics, each of these risk categories accounts for 40% of AIDS cases (CDC 1991a). These figures are in sharp contrast to the risk profile of whites: IV drug use was identified as the means of transmission in only 8% of AIDS cases among non-Hispanic whites, versus 77% of cases attributed to male homosexual activity (CDC 1991a).

Largely as a result of spread through IV drug use, AIDS is increasingly becoming a disease spread through heterosexual contact as well. Indeed, as of 1990 heterosexual transmission (along with the closely related perinatal transmission) was the only risk category which appeared to show no signs of a leveling off of new cases reported (CDC 1991b). For the period from 1989 to 1990, heterosexual transmission was the fastest growing risk category in the United States (CDC 1991b). Among heterosexually transmitted cases of AIDS, 53% were a result of sexual contact with IV drug users. An additional 14% of heterosexually transmitted cases were a result of sexual contact with HIV-infected individuals whose risk was not specified; presumably a substantial proportion of these also were IV drug users. Not surprisingly, heterosexually transmitted AIDS also shows a higher incidence among minorities, accounting for 6% and 11% of AIDS cases among Hispanics and non-Hispanic blacks, respectively, versus only 2% of cases among non-Hispanic whites.

IV drug use-related and heterosexually transmitted AIDS has also had a dramatic effect on women. IV drug use has been implicated as the source of infection in 51% of cases reported to date in women in the United States; an additional 21% were attributed to sexual contact with an IV drug user, for a total of almost three-quarters of all AIDS cases among women related to IV drug use (CDC 1991a). The overall number of AIDS cases among women is growing at an alarming rate: from June, 1990 to May 1991 AIDS cases diagnosed in women increased by over 40%, as compared to a 31% increase among men in the same time period (CDC 1991a). Moreover, it has been argued that the current AIDS case definition overlooks many of the disease's manifestations in women; thus, if a revised case definition for AIDS currently under consideration by the CDC (Centers for Disease Control) is implemented, women are likely to show the greatest increase in reported cases (Anastos and Marte 1989;

Gladwell and Booth 1991). Overwhelmingly, women with AIDS are black or Hispanic: these minorities comprise 72% of AIDS cases among women in the United States, and the incidence rates of AIDS among black and Hispanic women are 8 and 13 times, respectively, the incidence for white women (Ellerbrock et al. 1991).

Of children born to HIV-infected mothers, 30% can be expected to develop AIDS (Palmer 1990). Thus, due to perinatal transmission of AIDS from at-risk mothers, statistics on AIDS among women have ominous implications for children as well. Of a total of 3,089 pediatric AIDS cases reported as of June, 1991, 41% were attributed to IV drug use by the mother, and an additional 18% to the mother's having had sexual contact with an IV drug user (CDC 1991a). Among Hispanics and non-Hispanic blacks, a total of 85% of pediatric AIDS cases can be attributed to one of these risk factors in the mother, again demonstrating the disproportionate impact of IV drug use-related AIDS among minorities.

Current CDC figures attribute 22% of AIDS cases in the United States directly to IV drug use. However, if one considers cases where male homosexual behavior also was present and cases resulting indirectly from IV drug use (through sexual contact with an IV drug user or perinatal transmission by a mother who is an IV drug user or the sexual partner of an IV drug user), fully one-third of AIDS cases in the United States can be linked to IV drug use (CDC 1989). Because most cases of AIDS thus related to IV drug use occur among minority and inner-city populations, the prognosis for these individuals is particularly bleak: poor health histories, health habits, and/or lack of regular medical care among IV drug users, their sexual partners, and their children, lead to shorter survival periods after diagnosis (Selwyn, Hartel, Wasserman et al. 1989; Shulman, Mantell, Eaton et al. 1990). Furthermore, the lack of knowledge about and access to early medical treatment for HIV infection often leads to delays in diagnosis and the early medical intervention which might extend life.

New Jersey

In the northeastern United States* IV drug use is the principal risk factor for AIDS, accounting for just over 50% of all AIDS cases reported in 1988 (CDC 1989). Nowhere is this more evident than in New Jersey: at 21.4 reported cases per 100,000 population, the state has the highest per capita incidence of IVDU-associated AIDS of any state in the country

---

*Includes Connecticut, Maine, Massachusetts, New Hampshire, New Jersey, New York, Pennsylvania, Rhode Island, & Vermont.

and is second only to the Commonwealth of Puerto Rico (CDC 1989). As of December 31, 1990 approximately 55% of the reported cases of AIDS in New Jersey were associated with heterosexuals who reported IV drug use, whereas 27% of the reported cases were associated with males reporting homosexual behavior, with an additional 4% of cases associated with males in both risk categories (NJSDH 1991). The New Jersey experience thus reflects nearly the reverse of the national picture. If heterosexual and perinatal transmission of AIDS by IVDUs is taken into account, IV drug use can be related to as many as 69% of all AIDS cases in New Jersey (NJSDH 1990).

The impact of AIDS on minorities in New Jersey has been even greater than in the nation as a whole. Hispanics and non-Hispanic blacks together accounted for two-thirds of AIDS cases in the state, while making up only 22% of the state's population (NJSDH 1991; Cendata database 1991b). Among women, 93% of AIDS cases in New Jersey may be attributable to IV drug use or to heterosexual transmission by IV drug-using sexual partners* (NJSDH 1991). The rate of pediatric AIDS cases in New Jersey, at 20.3 per 100,000, is the second highest in the nation, and in the vast majority of cases (approximately 90%) are the result of IV drug use by the mother or the mother's having had sexual contact with an IV drug user (NJSDH 1990).

In many ways the cities of Newark and Jersey City represent the worst of the AIDS epidemic in New Jersey. These cities currently report the highest concentration of AIDS cases in the state and, with a combined total of 6,669 cumulative cases reported through May 31, 1991, these two metropolitan areas alone have reported nearly 60% of the total number of AIDS cases in New Jersey (CDC 1991a). The Jersey City metropolitan area ranked first in the state and third in the nation in per capita AIDS cases for the 12-month period ending May 31, 1991, with Newark ranking second in the state and seventh in the United States. These rates can largely be attributed to the high incidence of IV drug use in these cities. For example, in Newark IV drug use can be linked directly or indirectly (i.e., through heterosexual contact with an IVDU or perinatal transmission from mothers infected through IV use or sex with an IVDU) to over 80% of all cases in that city. AIDS among women in Newark can be related to IV drug use in a staggering 94% of all cases (NJSDH, unpublished data, 1990).

---

*Although the risk category of the women's sexual partners in heterosexually transmitted cases was not reported by the NJSDH, given the prevalence of AIDS and IV drug use in the state it is likely that most heterosexually transmitted cases were the result of transmission from an IV drug using partner.

The impact of AIDS on these communities cannot be overstated. Current estimates place the IVDU population in New Jersey between 40,000 and 50,000 addicts, and in some areas the infection rates are as high as 45% (NJSDH, personal communication, 1991; Iguchi, unpublished data, 1991). It is clear from current data that New Jersey's AIDS epidemic is far from having peaked and will continue to increase for at least several more years as larger numbers of HIV-infected individuals progress to AIDS. Improved efforts to reduce AIDS-risk behavior among IVDUs and their sex partners in New Jersey and to provide access to early interventions for people already infected with HIV are crucial for managing a crisis that will continue to grow in the early to mid-1990s.

Interventions

Given the major role of IV drug use in the spread of AIDS, risk reduction efforts targeted at IVDUs must continue to be emphasized. Current prevention strategies among IVDUs in the United States have focused largely on eliminating or reducing injected drug use and treating drug addiction. Treatment programs have shown promise as interventions by reducing injected drug use among patients who remain in treatment and by providing much-needed AIDS education (Iguchi and Stitzer 1991; Des Jarlais, Friedman, and Casriel 1990; Ball, Lange, Myers, et al. 1988). At any given time, however, only about 20% of all addicts are in treatment (National Institute of State Alcohol and Drug Abuse Directors, unpublished data). This is due in part to difficulties in obtaining access to treatment, and in particular to prohibitive initial payment requirements in the programs (Shulman et al. 1990; Des Jarlais and Friedman 1988) as well as to the reluctance of most drug users to enter treatment. Encouraging IVDUs to initiate and remain in drug treatment and removing barriers to treatment entry should be key components of AIDS-risk reduction among IVDUs. Other interventions, designed to reach IVDUs who are not and do not wish to be enrolled in treatment, have included distribution of bleach and other equipment for cleaning needles and street-based outreach and health education. While this has shown great promise in areas where it has been initiated (e.g., Watters, Case, Huang, et al. 1988), the distribution of bleach for the disinfection of illicit drug injection equipment has remained a topic of extreme controversy in many parts of the country. Needle exchange programs, although promising in some European and U.S. cities (e.g., Coutinho 1990; Navarro 1991) and endorsed by federal investigators (National Commission on AIDS 1991), nevertheless have been implemented only on a very limited, experimental basis in the United States, again due to public reluctance to give the appearance of condoning illicit drug use by making available the paraphernalia for drug use.

Intervention efforts among the sexual partners of IVDUs are confounded by the wide variety of socioeconomic factors which affect their lives. In primary relationships, many of the women have great difficulty in introducing condom use; in fact, only 25% to 30% of IVDUs report ever using condoms during sexual intercourse (Harris, Langrod, Herbert, et al. 1990; Lewis, Watters, and Case 1990). Women's reluctance to insist on condom use may be explained in part by a fear of verbal or physical abuse by the partner as a result of the apparent challenge to the partner's power, fidelity, and/or to his denial of drug use and the serious possibility of his infection with HIV. In a relationship where the woman may depend on the partner for financial support and where there is no other reliable source of income or assistance (an especially acute problem for those poor, minority women at greatest risk for AIDS), the immediate risks of insisting on a condom may outweigh a more remote probability of eventual infection with HIV (Mays and Cochran 1988; Anastos and Marte 1989). Current research provides further evidence that these women's concerns focus on urgent needs for food, housing, and financial and medical assistance for themselves and their children rather than longer term issues such as preventive health measures (Iguchi 1991). Helping these women to meet the immediate "survival" needs of their families may be a critical first step in enabling them to give more attention to HIV prevention for themselves and their children.

The lack of access to drug treatment programs, failure to enter treatment when available, generally poor health, lack of access to financial and medical services, inadequate housing, unemployment, and prevalence of unsafe sexual practices all are socioeconomic factors which contribute to the spread of HIV. Because these difficulties occur simultaneously among IVDUs and their sex partners in poor, inner-city neighborhoods, they constitute powerful social forces impeding most intervention strategies. This is particularly true when interventions address only one problem area and fail to address other gaps in service which contribute to the cycles of difficulty experienced by both IVDUs and their sexual partners (Rugg, O'Reilly, and Galavotti 1990). An effective intervention strategy requires comprehensive, coordinated services which are able to address the major concerns facing IVDUs and their sexual partners simultaneously. Moreover, it must be able to reach the target populations when they are not easily accessible through treatment programs, jails, health clinics, and the like.

THE CENTER FOR ADDICTION RESEARCH

In response to these concerns, the Center for Addiction Research has implemented an intervention program targeting intravenous drug users (IVDUs) not in treatment and the sexual partners (SPs) of IVDUs. The Center has plans to launch another project which will attempt to address, among other things, the institutional and socioeconomic barriers which prevent drug users from entering treatment.

The Health Behavior Projects

The Health Behavior Projects of Newark and Jersey City, New Jersey were begun in 1989 by Dr. Platt and his associates under funding from the National Institute on Drug Abuse as part of its National AIDS Community Outreach Demonstration Projects. The Demonstration Projects were established to gather information about AIDS risk behaviors among IVDUs and SPs and to provide risk reduction interventions for them. In Newark and Jersey City, subjects are initially recruited at a centrally located, storefront office. At the storefront, respondents provide informed consent and are interviewed by trained project staff using a structured questionnaire (AIDS Initial Assessment; AIA, v. 8.0). Information is collected regarding demographics, general health status, current and past drug use, routes of administration and frequency of use, needle sharing and needle cleaning, sexual practices, AIDS knowledge, and locator information for follow-up. Subjects also are asked to provide a blood sample for HIV testing. A follow-up interview (AIDS Follow-Up Assessment; AFA) is conducted at approximately six months post-intake. The AFA investigates factors similar to the AIA and attempts to identify any behavioral changes.

In addition to the basic research noted above, the Health Behavior Projects (HBPs) have attempted to address some of the issues surrounding AIDS prevention discussed earlier by intervening in several areas. These include: (1) Outreach recruitment and street health education on the risks of IV drug use and unprotected sexual relations; (2) HIV testing with pre- and posttest counseling on HIV infection, means of preventing HIV infection, and medical treatment for HIV infection; (3) Provision of coupons for either 21 or 90 days of free methadone detoxification; (4) Case Management and Case Referral Services, provided under three different protocols in a research comparison; and (5) Training in Interpersonal Problem Solving, a cognitive-behavioral group training program designed to enable IVDUs and SPs to implement AIDS-risk knowledge and reduce high-risk activities. Each of these interventions is described in detail below.

Outreach and Street Health Education

Street-based outreach has been widely endorsed as the best means for reaching IVDUs and SPs who are not involved in treatment programs or other agencies which would otherwise allow easy access to these populations. Iguchi and his colleagues have reported on the value of street outreach as a cost-effective means of reaching IVDUs who are not or who do not wish to be in drug treatment; continuing to disseminate information about HIV; promoting behavioral change; encouraging entry into drug treatment; and reducing the spread of HIV (CDC 1990b). This opinion has been similarly voiced by numerous other authors (Watters et al. 1988; Danila, Shultz, Osterholm et al. 1990; Jackson, Rotkiewicz, and Baxter 1990; Newmeyer 1989).

At the start of the Project indigenous outreach workers were hired, many of whom were recovering addicts. Along with a staff ethnographer, the workers identified neighborhoods in which intravenous drug use was concentrated. The outreach workers were trained to provide AIDS prevention education and to distribute literature on the transmission of HIV, including preventive information about condom use and needle disinfection. Although current NJSDH policy still prohibits the distribution of sterile needles or of bleach for disinfecting needles, literature is distributed on methods of disinfection. Moreover, plans are in progress between the HBPs and NJSDH to begin a pilot program to distribute bleach to IVDUs for disinfecting needles. Meanwhile, the researchers continue to advocate experimentation with a needle exchange program. In addition to providing health education, outreach workers explain the HBP programs to individuals they contact in the community and encourage participation in interviews, blood tests, counseling, case management or case referral, and TIPS (Training in Interpersonal Problem Solving) services.[1]

As the project progressed, the outreach staff learned of additional neighborhoods and locations to target in recruitment, and these places were added to the outreach effort. In addition, the spread of information by word-of-mouth among IVDUs and SPs in the two cities has played an increasingly important role in recruiting new subjects to the HBP. As of July 1, 1991, 4,283 IVDUs and 449 SPs had been recruited into the HBPs.

---

[1]This paragraph describes conditions at the time field operations were being conducted. New Jersey's policies have since changed.

HIV Testing and Pre-/Posttest Counseling

All subjects having blood drawn for HIV antibody testing are counseled prior to the blood draw and encouraged to return to the HBP for the results when they become available. The general guidelines for pre- and posttest counseling have been adapted from standard HIV counseling materials provided by federal agencies, the NJSDH, and academic sources. Along with risk reduction techniques, the counseling addressed the importance for seropositive clients not to transmit their infection and not to become reinfected, and for seronegatives not to become infected. The importance of early medical intervention for HIV infection is also stressed in both pre- and posttest counseling as a significant benefit of knowing one's antibody status.

Distribution of Methadone Treatment Coupons

In response to concerns over lack of accessibility of drug treatment to a substantial number of IVDUs in northern New Jersey and to provide added incentive for participation in the research, the HBP, in cooperation with the NJDOH and area drug treatment centers, has been offering coupons for free methadone detoxification for subjects who report heroin use in the AIA. Coupons cover either 21 or 90 days of treatment and are randomly distributed to the subjects. The goals of this intervention are to facilitate access to treatment for IVDUs by circumventing the high costs of medical and other testing required when patients enter methadone detoxification and to evaluate the relative cost and efficacy of 21- and 90-day detoxification protocols as means of attracting out-of-treatment subjects into methadone treatment. Data are being collected on: (1) Length of time the individual remains in treatment; (2) Proportion of patients who extend treatment past the free period covered by the coupon (i.e., transfer to methadone maintenance); (3) Reduction in HIV-risk behavior, as reported at AFA; and (4) Reduction or cessation of drug use, as reported at the follow-up interview. As an added incentive for clients to return for follow-up, and to increase further the accessibility of treatment, treatment coupons are also offered at AFA.

Referral and Case Management Services

Early in the project, it became clear to the researchers and project staff that a large number of the HBP's clients lacked access to such basic services as food, shelter, and medical care and that previous informal efforts at providing referrals were little more than marginally effective.

As discussed above, it has been suggested by a number of research teams that lack of basic services may be a major factor contributing to the extremely high rates of HIV infection among poor and uneducated IVDUs and SPs as well as their comparatively rapid progression to AIDS and death. Therefore, the research team initiated a program designed to provide potentially crucial AIDS services on a more direct and practical level of personal helping. This program includes a comparison of three levels of intervention involving progressively greater levels of individualized attention and support for clients: Standard Care, Enhanced Case Referral, and Focused Case Management.

The Standard Care (SC) intervention is a formalization of the referral procedures in place from the start of the project. In SC, the interviewer gives AIA and AFA respondents basic information on various services in the area immediately after completion of the interview. Subjects are told briefly about services provided by various agencies and, if they express an interest in receiving specific services, they are given appropriate telephone numbers and names of contact persons and are encouraged to call the agencies to make appointments from the interviewer's office. Enhanced Case Referral (ECR) amplifies the referral procedures of SC by having an HBP staff member who has specialized knowledge of agencies and services in the community review and supervise the referral activities of the interviewers. Focused Case Management (FCM) is a time- and resource-limited, intensive modality of social case work. In FCM, clients are assigned to a case manager who ordinarily will spend up to four sessions providing services, including a comprehensive needs assessment, assistance with appropriate service placements, and supportive counseling to enable the client to take effective steps toward helping him- or herself. Priority is given to placing HIV-infected clients in continuing medical care and in assisting seronegative individuals to make personal life changes to reduce the risks of HIV infection. In some cases, FCM may be extended in order to ensure that the client has access to the case manager when the results of his or her HIV antibody test become available or if termination at the prescribed point would defeat crucial progress that has already been made.

The goals of these interventions are to provide improved access to basic social, medical, and financial services which might be required by the clients and to evaluate the relative efficacy of all three interventions according to five general criteria. These were: (1) Use of social, medical, and financial services offered; (2) Continuing placement with, and use of, appropriate medical services by HIV infected clients; (3) Reduction or elimination of drug use, particularly IV drug use; (4) Reduction of unprotected sex in which one or both partners are at risk for HIV infection or actually infected with HIV; (5) Cost effectiveness of the three types of intervention. Data for evaluation of the interventions will be collected by process analysis and through the AFA.

Training in Interpersonal Problem Solving

Another intervention modified especially for the HBP is a problem-solving training curriculum known as Training in Interpersonal Problem Solving: Enhanced Health Promotion and AIDS Prevention Program (TIPS-AIDS). For this project, TIPS-AIDS is an eight-session psycho-educational intervention designed to provide education to IVDUs and SPs on AIDS transmission and prevention and training in how to translate this information into behavior in everyday interpersonal situations. The underlying assumption is that the target behavior, i.e., HIV-risk behavior, is mediated by cognitions and by external contingencies. It is hoped that, by teaching participants better skills for problem solving in social situations, they will do better in negotiating the often sensitive interpersonal aspects of safer sex and needle use.

Earlier studies of TIPS with heroin addicts, using a modification of the TIPS program originally developed by Platt and Duome (1979), have demonstrated that the acquisition of problem-solving skills is related to various outcome variables, such as employment (Platt, Metzger, Hermalin, Husband, and Cater, submitted), and lower arrest and recommitment rates (Platt, Perry, and Metzger 1980).

Preliminary Findings

HIV Testing and Risk Factors Associated with HIV Seropositivity

As of mid-June, 1991, results were available on the HIV antibody tests on over 4,400 IVDUs and over 300 SPs. Among SPs in the sample, the seroprevalence is approximately 17%, whereas among IVDUs the rate is slightly over 42%. These data appear consistent with other seroprevalence studies conducted in the greater New York City area (e.g., Nemoto, Brown, Foster, et al. 1990; Des Jarlais, Friedman, Novick, et al. 1989).

One of the most important findings of the Project to date has been the identification of variables which predict a given individual's likelihood of being infected with HIV. Over 500 variables from the AIA related to demographics and risk behavior were initially examined. From these variables, a linear discriminant function was constructed consisting of thirteen variables identified as independently and most significantly related to HIV serostatus. Initially the analyses were conducted separately for each site; however, because the results were similar the samples were combined. The 13 variables and their unadjusted and adjusted odds ratios are shown in Table 3.1. The variables which were identified corroborated earlier findings by a number of other authors (e.g., Chaisson, Bacchetti, Osmond, et al. 1989; D'Aquila, Peterson, Williams, et al. 1989; Marmor, Des Jarlais and Cohen 1987; Schoenbaum, Hartel, Selwyn, et al. 1989; Raymond 1988).

Employing a discriminant classification function with the 13 variables, 68% of the seronegative cases (416 of 611) were correctly classified as seronegative, 74% of the seropositive cases (490 of 667) were correctly classified as seropositive, and 34 cases were not classified. Overall, 71% of the cases (906 of 1278) were correctly identified with respect to HIV serostatus (Iguchi, French, Baxter, et al. 1990; Iguchi, Baxter, Platt, et al. in press).

Using the discriminant function coefficients from the discriminant analysis described above, a clinical risk index was calculated for each of the first 1278 IVDUs interviewed and HIV antibody-tested by the Newark and Jersey City HBPs (Iguchi, Rosen, Musikoff, et al. 1990). Overall, the risk index values ranged from -9.3 to 29.0. Figure 3.1 depicts the relative distribution of subjects testing HIV antibody positive and negative by risk score. Noteworthy is the clear separation of the two distributions and the relatively normal distribution of the two groups. The relative odds ratio for the 94 cases with a risk score ≥ 20 (80 HIV+, 14 HIV−) and the 100 cases assigned a risk score of <1.0 (15 HIV+, 85 HIV−) was 41. The risk index is currently being used as part of the FCM program to identify respondents at highest risk for infection so that we may intervene with these individuals as rapidly as possible and to ensure that they remain in FCM long enough to receive appropriate assistance after they learn the results of their HIV antibody tests. Further studies on the risk index are still in progress.

Methadone Treatment Coupon Program

As of March 1, 1991, 3,729 IVDUs interviewed for AIA have been offered coupons for either 21 or 90 days (randomly assigned) of free methadone detoxification. Of these, 3,396 (91%) accepted the coupons. Over half of the coupons distributed by the HBPs have actually been redeemed at the designated clinics within the week's time permitted. There has been no apparent difference in the rates of coupon acceptance and redemption for the 21-day versus 90-day coupons, nor between the

TABLE 3.1

Crude and Adjusted Odds Ratios for Multivariate Analysis Items

Variables	Crude Odds Ratio	Adjusted Odds Ratio	95% Confidence Interval
Male sex (vs. female)	1.2	1.4	1.0–1.8
Black race (vs non-black)	1.4	1.8	1.4–2.4
Non-completion of high school (vs. completion)	1.6	2.6	2.1–3.3
In jail more than twice in the past 5 years (vs. 2 or less times)	1.9	3.4	2.7–4.3
Years of IV drug use			
3–4 years	2.1	3.3	1.1–10.3
5–9 years	3.5	5.2	2.0–14.2
10–14 years	5.5	15.1	6.1–39.9
15–19 years	8.8	35.3	14.3–92.4
20–24 years	10.2	61.71	24.6–164.0
25+ years	11.6	312.1	87.2–1237.1
Use of IV heroin & cocaine (speedball) in past 6 months (vs. no use)	5.2	21.1	10.7–43.0
Daily use or more of IV cocaine in past 6 months (vs. less than daily use)	2.3	4.7	3.7–6.0
Absence of crack cocaine use in past 6 months (vs. use)	2.3	4.6	3.4–5.9
Absence of non-IV heroin use in past 6 months (vs. use)	2.4	5.0	3.9–6.3
Abuse of glue/paint in lifetime (vs. no history of use)	2.1	4.2	3.1–5.6
Absence of sexual partners in past 6 months (vs. presence)	1.9	2.0	1.6–2.6
Self rating of "high" or "sure" chance of developing AIDS (vs. "no" or "some" chance)	2.7	7.9	5.8–10.8
Presence of more than one HIV-related health problem in past 6 mos (vs. ≤ 1)*	2.1	4.0	2.9–5.4

* HIV-related health problems included: endocarditis, tuberculosis, pneumonia, hepatitis, syphilis, genital herpes, gonorrhea, and chlamydia)

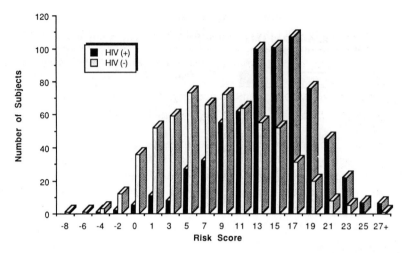

FIGURE 3.1.
Distribution of HIV (+) and HIV(−) Subjects by Risk Score.

rates of redemption for women and men. Women made up approximately 25% of the total number of people who redeemed coupons, a proportion roughly equivalent to that of women in the entire IVDU sample at the HBPs.

A closer examination of treatment retention trends has led to several interesting findings. For example, it was of interest whether clients would elect to remain in treatment on a maintenance dosage of methadone after the term of free treatment provided by the coupon was over. Of 436 coupon redeemers examined in a preliminary analysis, 41 (9.4%) elected to transfer to methadone maintenance at their own expense rather than taper off methadone at the end of the term of the coupon. When 90-day coupon holders were considered alone, this rate increased to 11.64% compared to 3.42% for 21-day coupon holders. While these findings should be interpreted with caution due to the small sample size, they may nevertheless suggest that a longer period of free treatment may serve to increase the patient's motivation for continued abstinence from drug use. A more thorough examination of these findings using the full sample of coupon redeemers is currently in progress.

Another finding of interest is that, once in treatment, women seem to remain in treatment considerably longer than men. For example, an examination of the average number of medication days (days on which patients actually received a dose of methadone) revealed that, among women holding 90-day coupons, the mean was 75.96 days, whereas the mean was only 55.09 days for men. This may indicate that, once the initial commitment is made, women are more likely to sustain a commitment to treatment for addiction than are men. Interestingly, this gender difference was not apparent among holders of 21-day coupons, where the average number of medication days was 13.55 for women and 12.20 for men. Moreover, women did not appear any more likely to convert to a program of methadone maintenance than men. It is hoped that analyses of a larger sample will yield a stronger relationship among these latter variables.

To date, no data are yet available on the relative impact of each treatment program on HIV-risk behaviors. However, the trends described above suggest that the apparently more successful 90-day treatment program would generate greater decreases in HIV-risk behaviors. Analyses of these factors are still in progress.

Case Management

As of June 1 1991, 312 subjects (209 IVDUs and 103 SPs) had been referred to the FCM staff and 231 (74%) elected to receive the service. Of those who accepted FCM, 32% returned for at least one session with a case manager. The rate of participation in FCM has been especially high for SPs, of whom 80% elected to receive this service; moreover, among SPs who accepted FCM, 43% returned for at least one session with a case manager. One reason for this is hypothesized to be partly the result of these women having a greater need and willingness to address personal problems. Another reason may be that the process of recruiting SPs at the HBPs has involved a particularly synergistic relationship among outreach, interviewing, and case management staff, which may enhance the SPs' comfort and sense of rapport with the HBP personnel.

The needs most commonly addressed by the FCM staff have included food, medical care, assistance in finding or preparing for employment, housing, mental health services, welfare, and support groups for HIV-related and/or psychiatric difficulties. The range and kinds of services most needed by this clientele dramatically highlights the depth of their social deprivations.

An interesting finding in FCM has been the tendency for clients not to keep regularly scheduled appointments, but rather to drop by the office to meet with their case managers "when they are in the neighborhood." These unscheduled visits have included both brief "check-in" visits and full-length case management sessions. Indeed, nearly one-third of all full-length FCM sessions have been in the context of such impromptu visits. The FCM staff have adjusted their style of service provision to accommodate this trend, and by so doing have enhanced clients' rapport with and commitment to FCM.

HBP staff are in the final stages of preparation for the introduction of FCM at the Newark site of the project. In view of the project staff's experiences in Jersey City, several changes are being implemented with the hope of increasing client participation. One possible obstacle to client participation identified in Jersey City was the use of the term "case management." Most clients at the HBP have had previous experience with some form of case management services, not all of which was positive. Thus, it was believed that the use of the term by the HBP might influence the clients' perceptions and expectations of the program and possibly lead to some clients deciding not to participate on the basis of negative preconceptions. Further, given that clients are initially recruited as volunteers for research activities, the introduction of the term "case management" as something they need could give clients the impression that they are being labeled as having problems, in effect drastically changing their perceived role in the project from "volunteer," to "case" or "problem" in such a way as to be potentially alienating. For these reasons the HBP staff restructured the basic message delivered in FCM to de-emphasize the idea of a client being a "case" needing to be "managed" and instead chose the term "networking" as a less formal, more neutral way of describing the services offered in the FCM protocol. The rates of acceptance of "networking" in Newark, relative to current participation levels in "case management" in Jersey City, should give some indication of whether this change is meaningful to clients. In addition to these changes, the HBP staff in both cities are attempting to develop a more streamlined process of IVDU recruitment into the HBP, in effect duplicating the synergy and rapport which currently exists in the recruitment of SPs. It is hoped that this will increase participation in FCM and networking among IVDUs.

TIPS

As of January 1, 1991 224 individuals initiated the HBP's Training in Interpersonal Problem Solving (TIPS). Of these, complete follow-up data have been collected for 47 subjects. Therefore, with respect to this intervention in particular, thorough assessment must await the collection and analysis of additional AFA interviews. Nevertheless, process data and correlations between AIA data and the assessment of subjects for Means-Ends Problem-Solving abilities (MEPS Tests) before they participate in TIPS groups have provided some preliminary data.

The modest numbers of subjects recruited from AIA interviews who subsequently enrolled in TIPS reflect the practical difficulty of (1) mobilizing the clientele of the HBP to participate in an eight-session training program and (2) doing so in settings with marginal institutional supports and fragile routines, whether the setting was local methadone clinics or community outreach offices. Once clients are recruited into TIPS, however, the rates of success have been notable. Average attendance at TIPS has been 5.15 sessions for men and 5.49 sessions for women. It is important to note that these rates of attendance are substantially higher than attendance for the control groups, for which subjects can earn the same stipend for significantly less time and effort. Participants have been predominantly black, in proportions notably higher than the percentage of black HBP clients. Although TIPS sessions provide a wide range of AIDS information, the group trainer has noted that participants are generally well informed at the start and are not often dependent on the program for basic AIDS information. Group activity has concentrated on development of the underlying cognitive abilities that are essential to AIDS-risk reduction. It is apparent from clients' feedback about the TIPS program that they appreciate and take satisfaction in the attention and feelings of support they receive from both the group leader and one another. Many clients have expressed relief that they could discuss such matters as intravenous drug use and other AIDS-risk activities without encountering abrasive accusations, ridicule, or recriminations. Several indicated that the cognitive focus of group discussions in itself facilitated their becoming more disciplined in personal behavior, that their participation in TIPS led to enhanced feelings of self-worth and increased personal responsibility.

A special TIPS program was initiated in early 1990 to focus specifically on the needs of sexual partners of IVDUs with particular attention to the prevention of sexual transmission of AIDS. Although the training program was designed to incorporate situations of concern to SPs, the program met with limited success. Through anecdotal information, it became clear that many SPs tended to be so concerned with problems of basic survival such as obtaining housing, child care, money, and food that they saw very limited utility in a training group for the prevention of HIV infection. This impression is borne out through the much higher participation rates of SPs, relative to IVDUs, in the case management services offered by the HBPs.

SUMMARY

The Center for Addiction Research is attempting to deliver a multifaceted service to a population at extraordinary risk of HIV infection. Through a thoughtful process analysis, it has been possible to institute changes in procedures which have greatly enhanced the services provided by the HBP and to guide the design of similar services in the future. The detailed examination of factors which predict risk of infection has produced results which can be used in assessing applicants for a wide variety of medical and social services as well as in more focused prevention efforts. The critical evaluation of a variety of interventions in the prevention of HIV infection will assist in designing future interventions on a multitude of levels, and it is hoped that the Center's activities will make an important contribution in stemming the tide of the AIDS epidemic.

REFERENCES

Anastos, K., and Marte, C. (1989). Women: the missing persons in the AIDS epidemic. *Health/PAC Bulletin, Winter, 1989:* 6–13.

Ball J., Lange, R., Myers, P., and Friedman, S. (1988). Reducing the risk of AIDS through methadone maintenance treatment. *Journal of Health and Social Behavior, 29(September),* 214–26.

Centers for Disease Control (CDC) (1989). Update: acquired immunodeficiency syndrome associated with intravenous drug use—United States, 1988. *Morbidity and Mortality Weekly Report, 38(10):* 165–70.

CDC (1990a). Estimates of HIV prevalence and projected AIDS cases: summary of a workshop, October 31–November 1, 1989. *Morbidity and Mortality Weekly Report, 39(7):* 110–19.

CDC (1990b). Update: Reducing HIV transmission in intravenous-drug users not in drug treatment—United States. *Morbidity and Mortality Weekly Report, 39(31):* 529, 535–38.

CDC (1991a). HIV/AIDS Surveillance, June, 1991.

CDC (1991b). Update: acquired immunodeficiency syndrome—United States, 1981–1990. *Morbidity and Mortality Weekly Report, 40(22):* 358–63, 369.

CDC (1991c). The HIV/AIDS epidemic: the first 10 years. *Morbidity and Mortality Weekly Report, 40(22):* 357.

Cendata Database (1991a). Race and Hispanic origin for the United States and Regions: 1990.

Cendata Database (1991b). 1990 Population by race and Hispanic origin and housing unit count: New Jersey.

Chaisson, R. E., Bacchetti, P., Osmond, D., Brodie, B., Sande, M. A., and Moss, A. R. (1989). Cocaine use and HIV infection in intravenous drug users in San Francisco. *Journal of the American Medical Association 261(4):* 561–65.

Coutinho R. A. (1990). Epidemiology and prevention of AIDS among intravenous drug users. *Journal of Acquired Immune Deficiency Syndromes, 3(4),* 413–16.

D'Aquila, R. T., Peterson, L. R., Williams, A. B., Williams, A. S. (1989).

Race/ethnicity as a risk factor among Connecticut intravenous drug users. *Journal of Acquired Immune Deficiency Syndromes, 3(5):* 503–13.

Danila, R. N., Shultz, J. M., Osterholm, M. T., Henry, K., Simpson, M. L., and MacDonald, K. L. (1990). HIV-1 counseling and testing sites, Minnesota: Analysis of trends in client characteristics. *American Journal of Public Health, 80(4):* 419–22.

Des Jarlais, D. C., and Friedman, S. R. (1988). HIV infection among persons who inject illicit drugs: Problems and prospects. *Journal of Acquired Immune Deficiency Syndromes, 1(3):* 267–73.

Des Jarlais, D. C., Friedman, S., and Casriel, C. (1990). Target groups for preventing AIDS among intravenous drug users: The "hard" data studies. *Journal of Consulting and Clinical Psychology, 58(1),* 50–56.

Des Jarlais, D. C., Friedman, S. R., Novick, D. M., Sotheran, J. L., Thomas, P., Yankovitz, S. R., Mildvan, D., Kreek, M. J., Maslansky, R., Bartelme, S., Spira, T., and Marmor, M. (1989). HIV-1 infection among intravenous drug users in New York City, 1977–1987. *Journal of the American Medical Association, 261:* 1008–12.

Ellerbrock, T. V., Bush, T. J., Chamberland, M. E., and Oxtoby, M. J. (1991). Epidemiology of women with AIDS in the United States, 1981–1990: A comparison with heterosexual men with AIDS. *Journal of the American Medical Association, 265(22):* 2971–2975.

Gladwell, M., and Booth, W. (1991). "US May Redefine AIDS." *Philadelphia Inquirer:* June 9, p. 1A.

Harris, R., Langrod, J., Herbert, J., Lowinson, J., Zang, E., and Wynder, E. (1990). Changes in AIDS risk behavior among intravenous drug users in New York City. *New York State Journal of Medicine, 90(3),* 123–26.

Iguchi, M. Y. (1991). "Strategies for coordination of care." *Invited Presentation: NIDA National Conference on Drug Abuse Research and Practice, Washington, D.C.*

Iguchi, M. Y., Baxter, R., Platt, J. J., French, J., Kushner, H., Lidz, V., Bux, D. A., Rosen, M., and Musikoff, H. (in press). Predictors of human immunodeficiency virus seropositivity among intravenous drug users not in treatment. *Journal of Drug Issues.*

Iguchi, M. Y., French, J., Baxter, R., Kushner, H., Lidz, V., Rosen, M., Musikoff, H., and Platt, J. (1990). Predictors of HIV seropositivity in Newark and Jersey City injection drug users: A retrospective and prospective evaluation. *Paper presented at the Second Annual NADR Conference, Rockville, MD.*

Iguchi, M. Y., Rosen, M., Musikoff, H., Platt, J. J., Baxter, B., French, J., Lidz, V., and Grant, C. (1990). An index of risk factors predicting HIV seropositivity in Newark and Jersey City intravenous drug abusers (IVDAs) not currently enrolled in drug treatment. *Poster presentation at the Sixth International Conference on AIDS, San Francisco, June, 1990.*

Iguchi, M. Y. and Stitzer, M. L. (1991). Predictors of opiate drug abuse during a 90-day methadone detoxification. *American Journal of Drug and Alcohol Abuse, 17(3),* 279–94.

Jackson, J. F., Rotkiewicz, L. G., and Baxter, R. C. (1990). The role of drug abuse treatment programs in AIDS prevention and education programs for intravenous drug users: the New Jersey experience. *In*: C. G. Leukefeld, R. J. Battjes, and Z. Amsel (eds). *AIDS and Intravenous Drug Use: Future Directions for Community-Based Prevention Research*. Rockville, MD: National Institute on Drug Abuse.

Lewis, D., Watters, J., and Case, P. (1990). The prevalence of high-risk sexual behavior in male intravenous drug users with steady female partners. *American Journal of Public Health, 80(4)*, 465–466.

Marmor, M., Des Jarlais, D. C., Cohen, H., Friedman, S. R., Beatrice, S. C., Dubin, N., El-Sadr, W., Mildvan, D., Yancovitz, S., Mathur, U., and Holtzman, R. (1987). Risk factors for infection with human immunodeficiency virus among intravenous drug abusers in New York City. *AIDS, 1:* 39–44.

Mays, V., and Cochran, S. (1988). Issues in the perception of AIDS risk and risk reduction activities by Black and Hispanic/Latina women. *American Psychologist, 43(11)*, 949–57.

National Commission on AIDS (1991). Report: The twin epidemics of substance use and HIV. Washington, DC: Author.

Navarro, M. (1991). "Yale study reports clean needle project reduces AIDS cases." *The New York Times*, August 1.

Nemoto, T., Brown, L. B., Foster, K., and Chu, A. (1990). Behavioral risk factors of Human immunodeficiency virus infection among intravenous drug users and implications for preventive interventions. *AIDS Education and Prevention, 3(2):* 116–26.

New Jersey State Department of Health (NJSDH) (1991). AIDS cases in the State of New Jersey as of 31 December, 1990.

NJSDH (1990). Pediatric AIDS and HIV infection in New Jersey: supplemental report, December, 1990.

Newmeyer, J. (1989). Outreach education among intravenous drug users: Use CHOWs. *Journal of the American Medical Association, 282(22):* 3130–31.

Palmer, R. (1990). "AIDS looms larger as threat to children." *Philadelphia Inquirer*, Sept. 26, p. 3-A.

Platt, J. J., and Duome, M. J. (1979). *Training in Interpersonal Problem-Solving Skills (TIPS): A structured group process for use in drug and alcohol treatment programs*. Philadelphia, Department of Mental Health Sciences, Hahnemann University.

Platt, J. J., and Metzger, D. S. (1987). Cognitive interpersonal problem-solving skills and the maintenance of treatment success in heroin addicts. *Psychology of Addictive Behaviors, 1*, 5–13.

Platt, J. J., Husband, S. D., Hermalin, J., Cater, J., and Metzger D. S. (in press). A cognitive problem-solving employment readiness intervention for methadone clients. *Journal of Cognitive Psychotherapy*.

Platt, J. J., Perry, G., and Metzger, D. (1980). Evaluation of a heroin addiction treatment program within a correctional environment. In R. R. Ross and P. Gendreau (eds.), *Effective correctional treatment*. Ontario: Butterworth.

Raymond, C. A. (1988). Study of IV drug users and AIDS finds differing infection rate, risk behaviors. *Journal of the American Medical Association, 260(21):* 3105.

Rugg, D., and O'Reilly, K., Galavotti, C. (1990). AIDS prevention evaluation: Conceptual and methodological issues. *Evaluation and Program Planning, 13(1),* 79–89.

Schoenbaum, E. E., Hartel, D., Selwyn, P. A., Klein, R. S., Davenny, K., Rogers, M., Feiner, C., and Friedland, G. (1989). Risk factors for human immunodeficiency virus infection in intravenous drug users. *New England Journal of Medicine, 321:* 874–79.

Selwyn, P., Hartel, D., Wasserman, W., and Drucker, E. (1989). Impact of the AIDS epidemic on morbidity and mortality among intravenous drug users in a New York City methadone maintenance program. *American Journal of Public Health, 9(10):* 1358–62.

Shulman, L., Mantell, J., Eaton, C., and Sorrell, S. (1990). HIV-related disorders, needle users, and the social services. *NIDA Research Monograph Series, 93,* 254–76.

Watters, J. K., Case, P., Huang, K., Cheng, Y., Lorvick, J., and Carlson, J. (1988). HIV sero-epidemiology and behavior change in intravenous drug users: Progress report on the effectiveness of street-based intervention. *Paper presented at the Fourth International Conference on AIDS, Stockholm.*

PART TWO

Policy Perspectives

The Drug Problem in the Federal Republic of Germany: Measures Taken by the German Government, with Special Emphasis on Pilot Projects and the AIDS Problem

Michaela Schreiber

INTRODUCTION

The German Federal Government has always looked upon the drug problem as a particular challenge to its societal and health policy. Within its constitutional framework, it has launched two programs of action for drug-abuse control. In these programs, drug abuse is understood as a psychological alarm signal, and drug addiction as a psychosocial disease. The federal government has initiated several pilot projects with different objectives for various target groups of addicts. State-funded pilot projects have stimulated a wide-ranging network of residential and outpatient treatment facilities which permanently change when the drug situation changes. The objectives of the pilot projects are to find new solutions and alternative strategies for a new problem. Federal funding has undergone a four-stage process:

1. The phase of experimentation
2. The phase of qualification

3. The refinement phase
4. The coordination phase

For each phase of funding several pilot projects are briefly described.

SUMMARY OF THE DRUG SITUATION

The abuse of illicit drugs began to spread over the Federal Republic of Germany almost 20 years ago. During these years considerable changes have taken place regarding the kinds of illicit drugs used and also in the age and socioeconomic background of the abusers. In the late sixties hashish and LSD were the preferred drugs, and they were predominantly abused by older students. Some time around 1970 the abuse of these drugs spread to school-age children. At the same time opiates, especially heroin, appeared on the illicit market. After a tremendous increase in the late seventies, heroin abuse markedly decreased between 1983 and 1986. Since then, however, cocaine and amphetamines have been abused. At present there is an overwhelming supply of all kinds of illicit drugs and their purity is increasingly high and prices are low.

Fortunately, the age of the incipient abusers has not declined further. The average age of the incipient abuser is 17 years old; the addict—on average—is in his late twenties. The addict has serious psychological problems, has often had a criminal career before becoming addicted, and abuses all drugs available. The amount of illicit drugs coming into the country has fluctuated over the last 20 years, and today we are facing a peak level similar to that in 1979.

In 1988 the number of people who died as a result of drug abuse, 673, was higher than ever before. In 1989 nearly 1,000 drug deaths were expected. For the first time in 1988 more than a ton of hard drugs was seized. This trend persisted during the first months of 1989. It is not clear whether the increase in the police data corresponds to an actual rise in the demand, for the figures in the police reports may only reflect the extent of drug supply and the efforts of the law enforcement agencies. The health indicators are not very precise, but it is assumed—and there is some supporting evidence—that the overwhelming supply of drugs combined with low prices has led to a greater demand. It seems that the total of 60,000 addicts has to be considered the minimum estimated number of addicts in the Federal Republic of Germany.

The situation is even more complex regarding cocaine. In the large cities cocaine is available on the street, but in general it seems to be abused mostly by artists and upper-class users. The abusers are in their twenties and socially well established. There is reason to doubt whether the present drug treatment system will be prepared for these addicts who "enter the scene from the top."

THE FEDERAL GOVERNMENT'S PROGRAMS OF ACTION ON DRUG-ABUSE CONTROL

Governmental measures in the field of health often face the dilemma of having to react very quickly to a problem like drug abuse or AIDS without any reliable statistics about the number of persons affected or about the roots of the problem, which would allow a direct approach to its causes. The demand of the public, however, is very precise: to prevent the spread of the problem and to confine the damage. This was the situation facing the federal cabinet when it passed the first federal government's program on drug-abuse control in 1970. The program was revised in 1980, after drug abuse reached its peak level. Both programs promote the strategies of the law enforcement agencies, as well as legislation, research and documentation, prevention, and assistance to addicts and persons at risk. The Minister of Health is responsible for the coordination of the entire program. In October 1989 the Federal Chancellor decided to develop a national plan for drug abuse control which would unite all governmental and nongovernmental agencies in a comprehensive approach to the drug problem.

The drug abuse control program of 1980 saw drug misuse as a form of deviant behavior at the root of which one is likely to find disturbed personality development and/or a special conflict situation. Drug abuse is understood as a "psychological alarm signal" that serves to draw attention to a life situation the young people in question do not feel capable of handling on their own. Under these circumstances, a number of factors, such as the widespread availability of illicit drugs and the risk and group behavior peculiar to young people and certain habits of consumption, favor the drift to drug abuse. The basic understanding of the issue makes it clear that drug-specific measures can enjoy only limited success in coping with the problem; effective drug policy must be understood more as a part of comprehensive societal policy. Three principles determine drug policy:

1. It is just as important to control demand as it is to control supply; in other words, health education and treatment measures are as equally important as repressive ones.
2. The substances involved are to a great extent interchangeable; this explains why isolated special programs to control single drugs have not been particularly fruitful.

3. National drug policy has always had impacts of international scope, especially in Western Europe. It is important that in 1992—the year when the borders between the countries of the EC are to be abolished—these countries come up with a joint view and policy on the drug problem.

FEDERAL PILOT PROGRAMS

According to the constitution of the Federal Republic of Germany, the federal länder (i.e., states) bear the main responsibility for the health care system. The federal government therefore is only allowed to give funds where it is necessary to fulfil a federal law or when federal expertise is required to cope with a new nationwide problem. Aside from research projects, the means to acquire such expertise have mainly been accomplished through pilot projects. As a rule pilot projects do not deal with a single facility; rather, they comprise a number of facilities, scattered about in the various länder whose structure, too, varies: for example, Bavaria is a more rural state, as opposed to Berlin, which is a city-state. Pilot programs are aimed at finding new solutions to a clearly defined problem and at applying those solutions on a general basis. They must reach their goals and answer the questions they are confronted with in a limited period of time (i.e., 3 years). For this reason, their equipment is of high quality and they have a large staff with the best qualifications at their disposal.

One important purpose of the funding of pilot projects is to guarantee the transfer of the expertise acquired by this means to other facilities in the same field. Thus, pilot projects usually generate recommendations that the federal länder and private organizations are supposed to put into practice as well. According to the federal structure of the country, the pilot projects of the federal government have been planned and coordinated with the federal länder. The Standing Working Party of the Drug Commissioners of the Government and the Federal Länder, which is chaired by the Federal Health Ministry, dedicates a major part of its efforts to the planning and coordination of these projects.

All pilot programs are assigned to a continuous scientific project evaluation study group. The group is also supported by federal funds, and its task is to supervise the development of the programs, to identify problems as early as possible, and to offer assistance to the facilities. The permanent scientific project-evaluation group therefore can be regarded as the link between those who work at the front line and the ministry staff who ask the questions and set the goals.

THE DIFFERENT PHASES OF FEDERAL FUNDING

Throughout the years federal funding has also undergone some changes. Four different phases of funding can be identified. The first phase (1971– 1977) was characterized by experimentation in the drug field. The objective of federal funding was to identify the best therapy for drug addicts; thus residential and outpatient facilities, self-help groups, therapeutic communities, clinics, and counseling centers were supported. The range of funding was large, and the standards required for receiving funds were low. It soon became clear that there were not one but several answers to the questions posed, all of which deserved further study. To a certain extent these early pilot programs stimulated the work of counseling and treatment opportunities for drug addicts and persons at risk throughout the whole country. Thus the phase of experimentation led to the creation of a basic care system for this problem group.

The second stage of federal funding (1978–1984) concentrated on outpatient facilities. For the first time it became necessary for the facilities and their staff to prove their qualifications before being offered state aid. For some time the debates centered on whether the government had the right to stipulate these conditions, and occasionally some facilities refused to cooperate. In general the second phase of federal funding resulted in well-equipped facilities and in qualified and highly trained staff in counseling centers for drug addicts.

In 1984 the third phase of federal funding was initiated. Its objective was the refinement of the present residential and outpatient drug treatment system so that different facilities would be provided for different groups of addicts (e.g., juvenile and adult addicted offenders, women and young mothers). Furthermore, the therapeutic measures had to be modified and enlarged to include outpatient and day treatment services in addition to residential and long-term treatment respectively.

The Law on the Reform of Narcotic Drug Legislation, which came into force in 1981, was the first to contain legal provisions that took into account the principle that drug addiction is a disease. The addicted offender whose expected penalty would not exceed two years could choose either imprisonment or treatment in a state-recognized therapeutic facility. Due to the increase in the number of drug-dependent offenders since 1980, a pilot program that targeted addicted offenders was initiated in 1984 in recognition of the principle of the new Narcotic Law. The basic idea behind the program was to confer greater validity to the philosophy embodied in the Narcotics Law and to use all legal means available to provide addicts with therapy as early as possible. This meant social workers would meet with addicts against whom preliminary or criminal proceedings had been initiated, those in pretrial confinement, and those serving sentences of imprisonment or other penalties to inform them of the possibilities open to them and to encourage them to take advantage of these opportunities.

In 1987 50% of all drug-dependent offenders decided to choose therapy instead of imprisonment under the new Narcotics Law. That percentage has steadily increased, compared with previous years, probably as a result of the work done by the 53 social workers who participated in the pilot program "Social Work Outreach with Drug-dependent Offenders," which was financed for that purpose. (See Arnold's chapter in this volume.) In this connection it is also important to mention those pilot projects which were established for juvenile offenders sent to detoxification and therapy by court order. There was much skepticism when the projects were started, but the results, especially the treatment outcomes, are more encouraging than expected.

The management of drug addicts in the Federal Republic traditionally was by long-term residential treatment. The dropout rate in these institutions was, however, very high, so efforts to reduce the rate had to be undertaken. The "Inpatient Crisis Intervention" program finances highly qualified staff at these institutions whose tasks are to identify potential dropouts at an early stage, to intervene intensively and, if necessary, to seek better alternatives for the clients at other facilities. (See the chapters by Küfner, Denis, Roch, and Böhmer as well as Denis, Küfner, Roch, and Böhmer in this volume.) This very important program deals with 45% of all the places available in long-term therapy facilities in the Federal Republic. This prevention of interruption of therapy is one more step toward a multiform residential treatment system for drug addicts.

Today many drug addicts have had several unsuccessful attempts at long-term therapy, and many of them are no longer prepared to undertake residential treatment. Often they are also much older than the average client in those facilities. Two new pilot programs have been conceived as alternatives to residential treatment. One is called "Full-Time Outpatient Care for Hard-core Drug Addicts," where in addition to outpatient therapy, assistance is offered in all the other areas of an addict's life: organizing recreational activities, fostering interests, providing education and vocational training, and family help. Each land (state) has one facility in this program which is very different according to the specific region's needs.

Outpatient and part-time residential treatment as well as day-care facilities are included in the second program entitled "Social Work Outreach for Hard-Core Addicts." The basic idea of this program is to reach hard-core addicts with long histories of dependence by offering low-threshold alternatives, mostly apartment-sharing projects and work and training projects. In other countries the group of addicts usually would be placed in methadone maintenance programs.

The last pilot program that must be mentioned is the program for HIV-infected drug addicts. A variety of programs in the field of AIDS have been started since 1984, and they are addressed to the various risk groups. In the Federal Republic drug addicts rank second among the groups at highest risk for HIV infection and AIDS. Although all of these AIDS programs also include drug addicts, there is only one pilot program that concentrates exlusively on drug addicts who are HIV infected. The "Pilot Program for the Care and Treatment of HIV-infected Drug Addicts" was launched at the end of 1987 in 18 specially qualified drug-counseling centers. It focuses on providing a low-threshold alternative and easy access to the counseling facilities, with the aims of encouraging addicts to take a test, introducing them to counseling and treatment alternatives, and persuading them to adopt a "healthy" lifestyle. In the process, the traditional tasks of the outpatient centers take on responsibilities such as health education and nutritional and sex counseling. This approach has considerable potential as an HIV prophylactic measure since addicts are more likely to be persuaded to change their behavior by personal communication and counseling rather than by general information campaigns.

In 1988 the fourth phase of federal funding was initiated with two central goals: (1) To set up low-threshold forms of care for drug addicts without demanding that they undergo any kind of treatment, and (2) To concentrate and coordinate various specialized offerings in one facility. These two objectives are the core of the so-called Booster-Program. This program is aimed at the target group of addicts who have either not been reached or could not be persuaded to continue utilizing the services offered previously. Increasing the number of addicts reached and improving the retention rate constitute the fundamental objectives of three alternatives, which make minor demands on the addicts:

1. "Intensification of outreach social work." This type of work differs from previous street work in that, in cases where it can be justified, former drug addicts working alone or in collaboration with a professional make selective attempts to talk to and pick up drug addicts on the drug scene, at home, or at other meeting points.
2. "Contact points." These offer services which may range from a warm meal to the first contact with counseling. The "contact point" is the alternative "scene" or a "substitute home" for the addict.

3. "Shelter." Most addicts make repeated attempts to kick the habit on their own. They reduce their intake steadily and enjoy short "clean" periods. The shelter serves to support this individual initiative. It gives the addicts temporary shelter where they can live for a specific period of time. The addict can leave the facility without the stigma of being a "dropout" and he or she is always free to return if necessary. This "stop-and-go" approach must be accepted as an intermittent motivation to make a break with drugs.

Concentrating and bringing together different alternatives is the second target of the Booster-Program. In response to the multifactor causes of drug addiction, a multifactor treatment of the illness has been pursued for quite some tine. The fact that the facilities necessary for the individual phases of the disease were scattered across a region and sometimes even run by different organizations has in the past often been deleterious. Moreover, the medical aspect was long relegated to a position of secondary importance in the treatment of addicts. Changes in the composition of the clientele emphasize the need for more cooperation among institutions. In the future, the aim will be to provide each region in need with a "socio-therapeutic center" that covers all the facets of drug-related assistance, such as outreach social work, "contact points," drug-counseling centers, a shelter, a drug withdrawal ward, apartment-sharing and work projects, and cooperation with general practitioners. The Booster-Program will run for an initial period of three years.

REFERENCES

Bundesministerium für Jugend, Familie, Frauen und Gesundheit. (1970). Aktionsprogramm der Bundesregierung zur Bekämpfung des Drogen- und Rauschmittelmittelmißbrauchs, Bonn.
Der Bundesminister für Jugend, Familie, Frauen und Gesundheit. (1980). Federal government programme of action on drug abuse control. Bonn.
Der Bundesminister für Jugend, Familie, Frauen und Gesundheit, Der Bundesminister des Inneren. (1990). National Programme on drug abuse control. Measures for drug abuse control and help for addicts and persons at risk. Bonn.

CHAPTER 5

The Treatment of Drug Addicts: Fluctuations of Health Policy or a Well-Organized, Adaptive Learning System?

Gerhard Bühringer

LEGALIZATION, SUBSTITUTION, PUNISHMENT, OR EXECUTION?

The range of suggestions on how to manage the drug problem, which has increased throughout the world, is striking: On the one hand, there are American politicians who want to legalize even heroin use and to add to their budget with high supplementary taxes. On the other hand, there are countries in Asia that already punish possessors of hashish with the death penalty. What causes such extremes?

The polarization of reactions to the problem and the range of suggested solutions are not only phenomena of modern times: The history of society's handling of the addiction problem is also a history of a sudden change in health policy strategies. It is remarkable that many critics of the present situation favor a change in course, either toward "liberalization" or "tightening up," but have little direct contact with drug addicts. Is this polarization of attitudes based on the blindness of drug experts in their own field or on the ignorance of the critics?

The discussions about improving treatment services for drug addicts also exemplify the more or less subtle enmeshment of science and values, as it is obvious, for instance, in the methadone question or in the outpatient versus residential treatment debate. Whatever opinion is presented, one always finds some data to support the respective view. However, nothing at all is said against values. In contrast, health policy as well as therapeutic actions would be a hodgepodge if values were not included. It is necessary to label values as such instead of buttressing them with scientific arguments, but the opposite strategy of basing a health policy for drug addicts only on values also must be criticized. A good example for Germany was the extreme emphasis on long-term residential treatment for drug addicts over the past 20 years. This strategy was supported mainly by treatment facilities in spite of all critical scientific data of recent years which showed, on the one side, that only a small proportion of drug addicts could be attracted by long-term residential treatment, and on the other side that short-term residential treatment, outpatient treatment, and combinations of both, including a broader range of treatment goals, would attract many more clients than before.

Health policy for drug addicts should always be based on two components: (1) scientific data and analysis, and (2) clear values. For the first component adequate and ongoing information-gathering and analysis are needed; for the other component, explicit value concepts based on a society's general view of how to deal with social problems, diseases, and minorities is required.

This chapter has the following purposes: first, to describe the German treatment system, its basic concepts, and current problems; and second, to support a comprehensive treatment service analysis as a framework for an ongoing effort to improve the system and for a systematic funding of research and demonstration projects.

TREATMENT SERVICE SUPPLY AS AN ADAPTIVE LEARNING SYSTEM

Goals of the German Treatment Service System

Disregarding for the moment primary prevention, the treatment service system must strive for the following goals:

1. Early treatment of "first-time users" who develop initial problems in connection with experimental use (secondary prevention to avoid a permanent "drug career").
2. A short time span between the development of pronounced addiction

problems and the first treatment (decreasing the time interval to reduce the later complications of a severe addiction).

3. A high percentage of persons with addiction problems should be in therapeutic contact at a given point in time (to improve the quota of accessed persons).
4. A high percentage of clients who complete treatment as planned (high adequacy of treatment to reduce dropout rate).
5. A low percentage of persons with a relapse after the termination of treatment (to reduce relapse rate and extend drug-free intervals).
6. A short time span between recurring problems based on abuse and renewed treatment (to shorten intervals with drug use).
7. Minimizing the harm based on abuse by actual consumers who are presently unwilling to give up their abuse (harm reduction).

The Concept of an Adaptive Learning System

Nearly 1,000 residential and outpatient specialized facilities with about 5,000 employees participate in the therapeutic treatment services of drug addicts. Not included are employees of welfare organizations, health insurance groups, the justice system, and similar social services that deal with drug addicts. Therapists in particular often overlook the fact that their facility does not represent a coincidental accumulation of therapy sessions, but is rather a service organization that must best adapt its "supply" to the "demand," and must provide these services effectively and efficiently. This view applies to a single facility, a local or regional catchment area, and to the entire Federal Republic of Germany. It addresses the fundamental idea of a research system that, based on an ongoing, documented treatment service structure, attempts to routinely analyze demand, supply, and utilization of the supply, as well as the resulting outcome, and to optimize the fine tuning of the individual elements of this system (NTIS 1974). Therefore, treatment service system research goes beyond therapy research, which is only concerned with the relationships among patients, therapeutic interventions, and results.

Areas of Necessary Information

Figure 5.1 illustrates the areas for the analysis of the treatment service system for which information is needed. First, data are needed regarding demand (e.g., the number of addicted persons in the population), and on the relevant characteristics that determine the treatment service structure

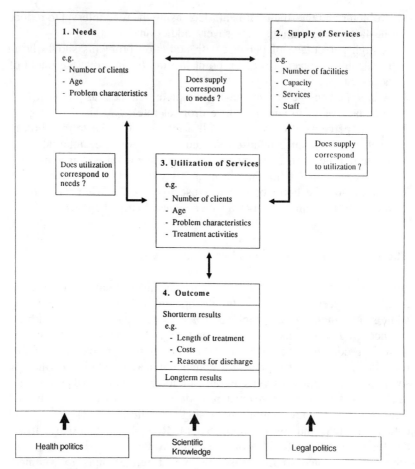

FIGURE 5.1.
Scheme for an analysis of the treatment service system in the area of addiction.

(e.g., on the types of physical illnesses or on the age structure). Second, information on the treatment service supply is needed (e.g., the number and equipping of facilities, the types of services, and the training of the staff).

The third area concerns the utilization of the treatment service supply, and the fourth involves the results that can be obtained with this treatment service. The latter is not only based on the traditional evaluation of therapy outcome, such as abstinence, but also on a more global view that includes costs and adequacy of the treatment supply.

The treatment service system does not act in a vacuum, but is influenced by numerous other circumstances. Three central influential factors are selected, including health policies (e.g., the question about the use of methadone substitution), legal policies (e.g., the configuration of the narcotic laws), and scientific knowledge (e.g., information on the therapy of drug addicts).

Utilization of Information

Basically there are three purposes for the collection of data: (1) documentation of activities, (2) analysis of trends, and (3) evaluation of activities. Depending on the level of data utilization these three purposes differ slightly. At the level of a single treatment facility, the first purpose of data collection is documentation of the staff's work. This is a necessary basis for further analysis and evaluation, because the annual report is a basic requirement for obtaining financial support from public authorities and health insurance agencies. The analysis of trends over several years gives the staff of the treatment facility detailed ideas for further activities or changes in service supply. If, for example, the average age of the clients gets older over the years, the staff must decide either to implement new activities for younger clients (if this is supported by epidemiological data) and/or to modify their treatment activities to meet the needs of older clients, which may often differ from those of the younger ones. Finally, they can evaluate the effectiveness and costs of recently implemented activities. For example, they can check if the defined goals for previous years were reached (i.e., the increase of the number of clients in preventive activities).

At the level of cities, regions, states, or the Federal Republic the three purposes of data collection are similar: Primarily, it documents service supply, service utilization, outcome, and cost. This documentation is necessary for the information of the public and for future financial support. The analysis of trends is of extreme importance at these levels because it provides ideas for future decisions at the political level, for modifying laws, for implementing demonstration projects by the government, and for stimulating research. This function has been widely used since 1970, because many demonstration projects of the federal government are based on data regarding certain trends or problematic results within the treatment service system (see Bühringer 1981). Finally the documentation of data also serves for the evaluation of the activities of the past years, e.g., to reduce the dropout rate by national demonstration programs.

CURRENT STATUS OF DATA COLLECTION
AND ANALYSIS

In the following sections some examples of available data as well as of areas that have specific needs for future research are given.

Needs

In order to comment on the condition of the population of drug addicts in the FRG, it is not sufficient to analyze data on those who attend therapeutic facilities, because an unknown percentage of drug addicts rarely if ever, seeks therapeutic help. Because of the illegality of the behavior, this population and its characteristics are difficult to assess.

Number of Drug Addicts

The number of persons who are addicted to hard drugs (the number includes not only heroin addicts, but also consumers of all opiate substances, opiate surrogates, and cocaine) is estimated to be between 50,000 and 120,000 in Germany; typically, a number of about 80,000 is currently assumed.

Reuband (1989) bases his calculations on 91,000 consumers of hard drugs who were registered by the police from 1970 until the end of 1988. At the same time, slightly more than 6,000 drug addicts died, leaving approximately 85,000 still living. It is problematic to consider those who became drug free in the meantime through treatment or other factors and who decrease the estimated prevalence, as well as the unknown number of those who have not yet had contact with the police and therefore increase this estimated prevalence. In this respect, the following estimations can be made: In the past 19 years (until 1988), about 120,000 drug addicts were treated in specialized residential facilities. (Calculations are based on published capacity of beds, the average stay, and the quota of working at full capacity; presently, these are approximately 8,000 clients per year.) Assuming a recovery rate of 25% for the use of hard drugs, a figure which can be supported by different follow-up studies of up to 8 years after the termination of the treatment, these include approximately 30,000 drug addicts. In contrast, we know from a few studies that the average preceding time span, meaning the time between the onset of addiction and first contact with the police, is approximately 3 to 5 years. In 1987/88, the number of hard-drug consumers who had contact with the police for the first time was approximately 6,000 to 7,000 per year. Consequently, a preceding time span of 4 years results in approximately 25,000 drug addicts who had no contact with the police until the end of 1988. That would lead to an estimated prevalence of approximately 80,000 until the end of 1988. This calculation formula has to be considered with great caution, because the data base of the correctional factors "therapy outcome" and "dark figure" (an estimated number of unreported/undetected cases) are based on a weak empirical foundation. However, at the same time, the formula shows that more precise estimations would certainly be possible if more research efforts to estimate these unknown numbers were undertaken.

It cannot be assumed that all drug addicts actually use drugs on any fixed day. From calculations, based on studies of the utilization of therapeutic facilities, follow-up studies about the capacity of the treatment service system, and a longitudinal analysis of untreated drug addicts by Kindermann (1989), it can be estimated that approximately 30% of drug addicts experience a drug-free interval on any given day. Unfortunately, we have little overall knowledge about drug-free intervals of drug addicts over longer periods of time. (See the chapter by Sickinger and Kindermann in this volume.)

Drug Fatalities

Figure 5.2 represents the cases of drug fatalities in the FRG between 1970 and 1988. The absolute number has increased in 1989 to 991 and in 1990 to 1,491. The longitudinal analysis shows considerable variations over the course of the past 20 years, whereby there are only speculations about the causes of these variations. Reuband (1989) claims, among other things, that extensive variations in the degree of purity of the used substances increases the risk for overdose, and, furthermore, that hopelessness spreads among long-term addicted persons, which would also be confirmed by the higher suicide rate among the older drug addicts. Altogether, the knowledge about the factors that influence drug fatalities is very small. (See the chapter by Püschel in this volume.)

Health Condition

Drug addicts suffer from poor health conditions caused by the use of contaminated syringes (e.g., abscesses), failure to recognize pain (e.g., dental diseases), and malnutrition. They are especially at risk for hepatitis and HIV infections. About 20% of drug addicts in Germany are HIV infected (with variations of 5% to 50% depending on the risk) and approximately 13% of all AIDS patients are drug addicted. (See the chapter by Kleiber in this volume.)

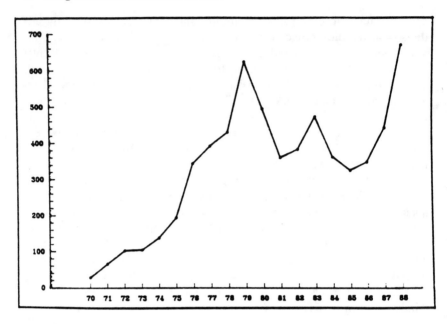

FIGURE 5.2.
Drug fatalities in Germany 1970–1988 (Reuband 1989)

Treatment-relevant Characteristics

The average age of drug addicts has not decreased; for years, all indicators pointed at a counter-rotating development (i.e., for years, the average age of drug addicts has *increased*). Figure 5.3 illustrates the percentage of adolescents and younger adults at the age of 24 and younger among the consumers of hard drugs over a period of years. This illustration is drawn from information regarding first-time users who had contact with the police, from drug addicts in outpatient treatment, and from drug facilities (Reuband 1989). The percentage of persons up to 24 years has been cut in half during this time period. This fact is of great importance for the organization of the treatment service system. It means, for example, that content and structure of treatment have to be changed to respond to the needs of older patients. Questions on education and employment, as well as on a more individual orientation for future life, play a greater role for older patients than for very young patients.

Unfortunately, we know little about further treatment-relevant characteristics. It would be necessary, for example, to study more thoroughly

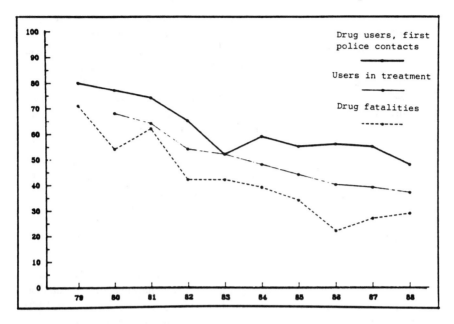

FIGURE 5.3.
Percentage of adolescents age 24 years or younger among consumers of "hard drugs"
1979–1988 (Reuband 1989).

the life situation of yet untreated drug addicts who have not had contact with the police; *e.g.*, To what extent are they still integrated in everyday processes? What kind of problems do they objectively have and which do they subjectively consider as most important? What are their attitudes and evaluations of outpatient and residential facilities, or their willingness to enter treatment at all? How do they estimate their risk for HIV infections and what is done to avoid them? Also, we generally have knowledge about psychiatric problems or psychological disorders only from the files of treated patients, and not from the population of drug addicts. The result is that the treatment service system adapts too little to drug addicts who have only recently become addicted or who refuse treatment for some reason despite their long-term career.

One possible source for more detailed data are epidemiological studies. In Germany several national studies with nearly identical questionnaires were carried out in 1982, 1986, and 1990 under grants from the Federal Ministry of Health and from 1973 to 1990 in 4-year intervals by the Federal Center for Health Education. Unfortunately, only a very few scientific analyses have been carried out with these data (e.g., Reuband

1989). (See also the chapter by Reuband in this volume). There is a lack of long-term analysis and international comparative studies. In 1990 a new research group at the IFT in Munich was implemented to increase and improve scientific analysis of epidemiological data in Germany.

Since epidemiological studies do not obtain much information about severe drug addicts, further studies to analyze this group in detail must be implemented. Unfortunately, very little information has been available in Germany up to now. The pertinent data would have to include detailed analysis of drug deaths (e.g., risk factors) and of drug addicts in early phases of their drug careers without any treatment contact; studies of drug-addict behavior over longer periods of time (Kindermann 1989); and studies of older drug addicts within the phase of "maturing out."

Treatment Service Supply

The following three information areas (treatment service supply, utilization, and short-term outcome) are based on the national documentation system, EBIS, which was developed in 1975 and implemented in 1980 in Germany, first for outpatient facilities and later for residential centers. (For detailed descriptions see the chapter by Simon, Bühringer and Strobl in this volume.)

There is a network of residential and outpatient therapeutic facilities in the FRG. The 500 to 600 larger facilities (of a total 910), which meet the usual standards with a certain minimal number of employees, essentially treat all forms of substance abuse with few exceptions. (See the chapter by Ziegler in this volume.) An average of approximately 20% of the clientele are dependent on illegal drugs.

Seventy-nine residential facilities with approximately twenty-five hundred beds are specifically for drug addicts; another 58 facilities treat drug addicts among other groups. This amounts to a capacity of about three thousand on a given day or about eight to nine thousand treatment slots per year. Additionally, while approximately two hundred residential aftercare facilities have approximately twenty-five hundred slots available, the percentage used for drug addicts is unknown. The number, capacity, and categorization of drug use in part-time residential facilities also is unknown, and a more extensive assessment of the treatment service supply would be beneficial in this area.

All of the presented numbers refer to specialized facilities for drug addicts. Not included are additional capacities in nonspecialized facilities. For example, only those psychiatric hospitals are listed that specialize in treatment of drug addiction. However, every psychiatric state hospital treats drug addicts in a more or less intensive form. Therefore, the therapeutic capacity represents a lower limit of the true value.

Treatment Service Utilization

Figure 5.4 presents the development of patient numbers in outpatient facilities during the years 1980 to 1989. The total number of patients has increased from slightly more than 500 to almost 700; the number of intensively treated patients has increased from about 160 to approximately 260 (these were patients admitted in 1989). The percentage of drug addicts among the intensively treated patients is about 19%, or an average of almost 50 patients. Therefore, because the number of staff has remained constant over the last 10 years, this increase in patient numbers has resulted in each therapist having a larger caseload than in the past.

Outcome

The quota of completed treatments is between 20% and 30% for outpatient facilities and around 30% for residential treatment. Interestingly, the range of variation for the individual facilities is between 10% and 80%, which contradicts a hypothesis that has been expressed for many years, wherein the outcome is about the same for all facilities. The quota of therapy dropouts is important in that a regularly completed therapy represents the most important prognostic factor for long-term stability. It may be shown in a demonstration project sponsored by the Federal Ministry for Health that the 90-day dropout quota can be reduced from about 44% to 28% by simple means (see the chapters by Küfner et al. and Denis et al. in this volume).

The outcome of long-term stability is relatively uncertain in the outpatient area, because there are still few studies available. Abstinence from hard drugs six months after the termination of treatment is between 25% and 40%, depending on the calculation formula (Bühringer, Dehmel and Hanel 1989; see the chapter by Spies et al. in this volume). The percentage of persons who are abstinent from hard drugs 2 to 10 years after termination of treatment can be found between 25% and 40% for residential treatment (De Jong and Henrich 1978), (See the chapters by Hadersdorfer et al. and Vollmer et al. in this volume) while the percent-

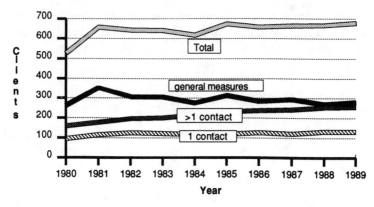

FIGURE 5.4.
Number of patients in outpatient facilities 1980–1989 (Simon et al. 1990)

age of persons with stable social adjustment ranges from 50% to 70% (Raschke and Schliehe 1985).

Altogether, the course of the clients' lives after the termination of treatment are much more complex than was assumed in the past. The simple dichotomy of abstinence versus relapse is not appropriate with respect to the course of life. Basically stable patients may have one or several intervals of drug use of differing intensity, while relapsed patients also have longer periods of abstinence from drugs. This complex picture requires more effort in the area of longitudinal studies. Moreover, in the future more attention must be given to the increase in drug-free intervals during the course of years, in that such intervals are considered as a measure of success in therapy.

Based on all outcomes it can be concluded that therapy has a positive effect. There is still a lack of research to show which factors of treatment and which factors of the life experience of addicts influence the treatment outcome positively or negatively. (See the chapters by Hanel, Herbst, Kampe, and Kunz and by Vollmer et al. in this volume.)

Analysis of the Treatment Service System

With the extracted information given above, the treatment service system of the FRG can be analyzed with respect to adequacy (Is there an adequate therapeutic supply for all persons?) and quality (outcome and costs). The state of affairs can be summarized as follows:

Positive Characteristics of the Treatment Service System

1. Germany has a network of treatment services with about 600 larger and 300 smaller outpatient facilities as well as three thousand residential treatment beds. There is a moderate waiting time, facilities are comparably well equipped and also financially secure considering that health and pension insurance finances a great part of the treatment.
2. The majority of the staff in the facilities has received a good professional education, and a very high percentage has also completed specific training for the treatment of addictive behaviors. The personnel situation is favorable in the outpatient as well as residential area. The staff of outpatient facilities treat decidedly more patients than in the past.
3. The access rate is average to high in comparison to other countries. Every year, about 25,000 drug addicts are treated in outpatient facilities and 7,000 to 8,000 receive care in residential facilities, with only partial overlap. Altogether, it can be concluded that 30% to 40% of drug addicts are assessed therapeutically every year, depending on the assumed prevalence rate.

Aspects That Require Improvements

4. The German system places too much emphasis on residential treatment. Despite all debate, residential therapy is still presented as primary to patients. Therefore, the number of drug addicts who are (yet) unwilling to enter residential treatment are accessed too late or not at all. The supply of ambulatory treatment must be increased radically.
5. The treatment service system as a whole is too undifferentiated with its dichotomy of outpatient versus residential care. Part-time residential facilities such as day and night clinics, work settings with partial therapeutic support, as well as therapeutic group homes are lacking. (See the chapter by Arnold in this volume.) The service supply is also not differentiated enough within the system. For example, there is a lack of short-term residential treatment possibilities or a combination of residential and outpatient treatment.
6. The lack of differentiation in the system is connected with a diagnostic assessment that strongly needs improvement. The often heard statement from practitioners, that all programs lead to the same outcome, is not true and this attitude makes individual assignment of therapeutic interventions, patients, and facilities difficult. In this context, initial diagnostic assessment (referral to certain residential or outpatient facilities) and the accompanying treatment assessment for individually

assigned interventions should depend on the characteristics of the patient.

7. Detoxification resources need quantitative and qualitative improvement in many areas of the FRG. The thresholds for entering detoxification are too high in the eyes of drug addicts, and the time during detoxification is not geared sufficiently toward central therapeutic activities (e.g., HIV prevention, relapse prevention) that can be provided to drug addicts who are unwilling to continue any form of long-term treatment.

8. Many facilities lack sufficient knowledge of modern therpeutic approaches including interventions to increase motivation, relapse prevention, HIV prevention, and support of cognitive processes for achieving abstinence.

9. The treatment service system is not sufficiently directed toward single regions. The supraregional orientation of most residential facilities makes close cooperation with local and regional sections as well as a coordinated treatment plan with several facilities difficult.

In past years, there were attempts to improve the critical points presented through the various demonstration programs of the Federal Ministry of Health. (See the chapter by Schreiber in this volume.) These attempts resulted, in part, in the modification of the relapse rate in residential facilities (see the chapters by Küfner et al. and Denis et al. in this volume), the improvement of the treatment of HIV-positive drug addicts (see the chapter by Fahrner et al. in this volume), and the improved cooperation between the justice and therapeutic systems. However, considerable efforts to improve the therapeutic service structure are still needed. Transitional processes are difficult and involve great professional, financial, and organizational investment. They require breaking new ground in research as well as in practice. It is therefore not surprising that many experts and many facilities see the necessity for improvements, but that progress proceeds slowly.

BASIC CONCEPTS FOR THE TREATMENT
SERVICE SYSTEM

For nearly 20 years long-term residential treatment dominated the health policy for assisting drug addicts. This system was especially promoted by the treatment staff and its representatives and not so much by the Federal Ministry of Health, which already in 1975 had begun to fund the first pilot projects for outpatient treatment of drug addicts. Because of this long domination by a single system in Germany, intense debate about ways to modify the treatment service system has recently begun.

The Traditional Concept

In order to elucidate the traditional treatment philosophy, it is presented here in a simplified form: It is based on the assumption that an addicted person has to more or less "hit bottom" before he or she can be treated at all. The addicted person should experience the negative consequences of the addiction strongly enough to be unable to live self-sufficiently and therefore must seek treatment to survive. In order to prevent so-called unmotivated addicts from entering treatment, the principle of a maximal threshold for admission has been developed. Multiple contacts with a detoxification facility before admission to treatment or unpleasant admission interviews as a precondition for beginning residential treatment are examples of such thresholds.

Based on the concept of the addicted personality, which assumes a uniform configuration of personality traits of addicts, it has been postulated that all addicts should be treated in approximately the same manner. Accordingly, the traditional treatment programs were relatively uniform and rigid. Cases of conflict were frequently worked out with confrontation, wherein patients had to submit themselves to the therapist or other patients, or else were dismissed prematurely. This was done to let them experience the negative consequences of further drug consumption and convince them that they are "finally ready" for treatment. The motivation for therapy was the patient's responsibility. He or she had to be motivated and also sustain this motivation over long periods of treatment. "Lack of motivation" was a frequent reason for premature dismissal. But waiting for a patient to become "motivated" by later-stage consequences as well as the all-or-nothing principle of the treatment (abstinence through long residential treatment or no treatment) are unethical and undignified, especially if we consider the severity of the consequences of addiction.

Alternatives in the Further Development of the Therapeutic Concept

All critics, whether conservative or liberal, agree that the traditional concept has to be reformed, because it does not access enough addicts and has too little success. Nevertheless, they disagree on possible strategies for a solution.

Legalizing Drug Use

On the surface, the strategy of legalizing drug use appears to be very simple and is supported by many scientists and practitioners in the United States and Western Europe. Through this approach, it is expected that the international drug crime rate would decrease and that governmental control of the substances also would prevent impurity and its accompanying health consequences. Moreover, it is suggested that higher taxes could partially be used for prevention and addiction research. Despite the seeming simplicity of these interventions, the strategy is more harmful than useful in the long term. It is naive to assume that the criminal element that is internationally connected with the cultivation, purchase, processing, and distribution of drugs would disappear. Although drug-related crimes would probably be reduced, international drug rings are not likely to ask for social welfare, but will only direct their activities to other areas like gambling.

Second, it is very likely that the presently low number of drug addicts (compared to the number of persons addicted to alcohol and prescribed medication) would increase. Third, legal and practical problems of control of prescribed drugs will increase considerably. It would be very difficult to rationalize to the public that psychoactive medications, including those with potential for addiction, should be increasingly controlled by specific prescription policies or taken off the market, but that similiar substances which were formerly considered illegal would now be freely available. Additionally, consumer protection laws would not permit such an eventuality.

Since there is a large consensus saying that the use of legalized drugs, like alcohol, would remain dangerous for adolescents, the efforts of international drug rings would concentrate on this age group, which would also lead to the need for extensive legal regulations and controls for obtaining drugs.

Substituting Methadone for Illegal Drugs

In recent years there have been vehement discussions, particularly in Germany, about substitutes for heroin and other opiates. This discussion is a very good example of the enmeshment of science and values. This is not the place for an extensive illustration of the arguments (see, Ministerium für Arbeit, Gesundheit und Soziales 1987). But according to the present literature, weighing advantages and disadvantages does not favor one particular treatment for all or nearly all opiate addicts. Also, at present, no clear data are available on particular treatment indications for selected subpopulations. Further research will probably find better defined groups for methadone maintenance programs. Currently, in individual cases, such programs are seen as sensible and are supported by the National Medical Association of Germany and the National AIDS Council of the Federal Government.

Punishing Illegal Drug Use

Supporters of this strategy regard past therapeutic efforts as failures, and they assume that only stricter enforcement and punishment will prevent drug addicts from further use. They believe that this approach will prove to be preventive. It should be noted here that punishment alone generally does not lead to a change in behavior: it either leads the addict to become more creative in his or her efforts to continue the behavior, despite the threat of punishment, or causes the addict to become more aggressive or depressed to the point of suicide. In addition, drug addicts do not acquire a basis for long-term drug abstinence in prison, but instead their situation deteriorates and thus supports the conditions for a relapse. Consequently, everything possible should be done to ensure that as many drug-addicted criminals as possible are diverted from imprisonment.

Linking Judicial Pressure and Treatment

This strategy is based on the assumption that sooner or later addicts will have to confront numerous pressures that occur over the course of a drug career. These include negative health consequences (e.g., suicidal thoughts and depression), social consequences (e.g., threat of job loss), as well as legal consequences (e.g., police interrogations, detention pending trial, and imprisonment). These negative consequences *in the long run* are effective pressures for the beginning of treatment, but the price the addict must pay for waiting so long is high. Therefore, the discussion should focus on to what extent *early* judicial pressure could be applied as leverage to force the addict into treatment and possibly stop drug use earlier than would be the case if the addict continued use until the consequences appear on their own.

Analyses concerning the lifestyle of addicts provide two possible areas for judicial pressure:

1. Intensification of negative consequences of addiction. Judicial pressure could contribute to a more effective balance between the strongly positive and the initially very weak negative consequences of drug use—a prerequisite for the drug addict to begin to consider entering

treatment. Hence, an attractive supply of treatment services must be available.
2. Experiences of the therapeutic reality and an abstinent lifestyle. Judicial pressure could contribute to drug addicts' knowledge about the daily situation of treatment, the staff, and an abstinent lifestyle, at least for a certain period of time. This is especially important for drug addicts who never or only briefly were in treatment, and who might construct negative biases based on third-party reports.

In general, judicial pressure could contribute to interrupting the addict's career for at least the time needed for a trial or another limited period. Judicial pressure can help to sustain health and prevent death by reducing or interrupting continuous phases of use. Moreover, these pressures have the advantage that they are sustained, especially at the beginning of therapy, when the negative physical and emotional sensations and part of the negative social consequences are already reduced through treatment. Because memories of the positive effects of drug use are still very strong then, there is generally a phase of ambivalence between relapse and future abstinent behavior at the beginning of treatment.

In addition, judicial pressure helps drug addicts experience the daily therapeutic situation and abstinent lifestyle at least for a brief period of time. Only this experience gives them the chance to weigh the consequences of continuing drug use against the advantages of stopping drug use and pursuing an abstinent lifestyle. This "enforced" collection of experiences of a life model that competes with addiction is seen as one central argument for justifying judicial pressure in the treatment of drug addicts. It opens up the chance for drug addicts to evaluate the generally undifferentiated escape to drugs, or with therapeutic help, to gain the knowledge and experience to recognize alternative life options.

The few available studies on judicial pressure (e.g., Bühringer et al. 1989) presume that it is effective with respect to therapeutic goals. They indicate that patients who are forced into therapy by judicial pressure (e.g., court-ordered treatment), cause more problems than usual for therapists at the beginning of treatment, but over the course of time a good therapeutic atmosphere similar to that of other patients can be established. Also, the outcome of therapy is at least the same or sometimes even better than that of patients who are in treatment voluntarily.

The strategy of applying judicial pressure would work toward assigning a form of treatment to drug addicts that would be more effective than fines or imprisonment. This approach should take into consideration the option of outpatient treatment. In any case, the treatment should be combined with an extended probation following therapy. It would also be necessary to provide intensive therapeutic contacts and probation officers with extensive training. Additionally, the German principle of "treatment instead of punishment" should be enlarged and handled more flexibly in order to significantly reduce the number of drug addicts in detention pending trial or imprisonment. (See the chapters by Egg, Kreuzer, and Melchinger in this volume.)

Improvement of Therapeutic Facilities

Several suggestions for improving therapeutic facilities have been made. They all point in the direction of (1) providing "more" supply, (2) lowering the thresholds for admission into therapeutic facilities, and (3) improving outcome through a more individualized treatment that considers the situation of each patient. All three points are important, but expectations for improving the treatment service system alone must be kept in perspective. Addiction is a severe illness and the addict's "inability to stop" is its central and determining characteristic. Although both improvement and expansion of treatment services are both necessary, as isolated interventions they are not sufficient prerequisites for the goal of treating more addicts and achieving better results.

The five basic strategies presented all have advantages and disadvantages at the technical-pragmatic level. It is easy to get into trouble if one justifies the selection of a single strategy or some combination for activities in health policies. It becomes obvious that in addition to the assumed advantages and disadvantages of each strategy, superior health policies and guiding principles must be formulated, based not only on scientific outcome but on values as well.

The Attempt to Formulate Health-policy Maxims for the Treatment of Drug Addicts

Since the French Revolution, the attempt to free human beings from the hierarchical and collective pressures of former centuries and to give them the opportunity for self-actualization appears as a common trend in all philosophies. This includes the personal independence of third parties and the individual's free choice of lifestyle as long as it does no harm to others. In the lives of human beings, there are phases or situations in which individual independence and self-actualization are restricted in order to protect the individual or third persons. Examples are childhood and adolescence, periods of severe illness, and the prevention of crime. In these cases as well the basic goal of all public action, no matter whether it concerns the police or law, welfare or treatment, is to keep these restrictions of freedom as minimal and as short-lived as possible.

In addition to and related to the aforementioned abstinence, independence from medication and further therapeutic treatment is always the primary goal in the treatment of addicts. Independence from severe addiction and accompanying restriction of freedom are not easy to obtain. Generally, several attempts and adequate public resources over many years are required to achieve these goals. However, care should be taken —and this is a distinction between modern therapy philosophy and the traditional abstinence-directed confrontation—that the efforts of the addict to achieve abstinence do not turn into unnecessary torture simply because it cannot be achieved immediately. Respect for human dignity entails helping an addict even if he or she is not able to be abstinent. This statement appears self-evident, but for years, it was not very relevant to many treatment concepts in Germany.

Such efforts do not mean, however, that addiction is considered an acceptable lifestyle. In Germany terms like "addiction accepting care" or "addiction accompanying work" are therefore regarded as dangerous. The addict must be clear that addiction is not an acceptable lifestyle, but that the addict is accepted as a person who is not able to change his or her behavior at the moment. The emphasis here is on the concept of "at the moment." Our own studies and numerous others show that there is very rarely a course of drug addiction that continuously deteriorates and allows for a cutoff point from which every therapeutic intervention aimed at abstinence becomes pointless. Studies have shown that the willingness to change does not decrease linearly but takes a cyclic course, and that even continued treatment attempts do not reduce the probability of a positive outcome.

To accept the momentary inability of an addict to stay abstinent, however, requires intensive treatment. All suitable possibilities to minimize the risk of further use have to be explored. "Life-sustaining" interventions like housing or overnight shelter, interventions to prevent HIV infections (e.g., helping to sterilize syringes, needle-exchange programs), and interventions to improve sexual hygiene are necessary: in short, everything that reduces the risk of further use in the life of addicts and their surroundings. In this context, the indication for substituting methadone in individual cases has significance. It should be based on a careful analysis that suggests that attempts to achieve abstinence are not always successful and that the risk of methadone substitution is lower than the risk of further illegal use.

Characteristics of a Modern Therapy Concept

The following characteristics must be considered in the organization of treatment services based on the background of the described health policy reflections.

Early Intervention

Instead of waiting until addicted persons seek help of their own accord because of late stage complications, every means should be used to reach addicts soon after the onset of the first negative consequences or after new relapse. An attractive supply of treatment facilities should be part of that attempt and all obstacles to accepting the offer of treatment should be removed (Bühringer 1990b).

Individual Treatment

The myth that all addicted persons are the same and that their resulting problems should be treated the same must be dismissed. The earlier one reaches addicts, the larger are the differences in the history of the development and the actual problem situation. Individualized treatment requires an individual diagnostic assessment and, hence, additional competencies from the therapists. Individuality must be considered with respect to the contents of the treatment, the duration of treatment (which is typically very long), and the form of organization such as outpatient, residential, or part-time residential care (Bühringer 1990a).

Promotion of Motivation

Building and maintaining motivation for continuing therapy and for changing one's life should not be perceived as the sole responsibility of the patient. The therapist should continuously include motivation-promoting interventions as an integral part of treatment. It is also necessary to acquaint therapists with more modern procedures for promotion of motivation from psychotherapy research.

Relapse Prevention

Relapse is an event that cannot be ruled out after the termination of treatment, and the possibility should not be ignored by either therapists or patients. Rather, it must be actively addressed in the therapeutic process. The latest research presents numerous interventions for relapse prevention. The combination of possible relapse triggers, the cognitive processing of situations preceding relapse, the possible approaches to solutions, and role-playing are all means of improving the addicts' mastery of critical relapse situations. Additional training in these techniques is also necessary.

Use of Judicial Pressure to Enter Treatment Early

Under all circumstances, drug addicts should be prevented from entering detention pending trial or imprisonment. Rather, an attempt should be made to respond to law violations by addicts with court-ordered outpatient or residential treatment in order to put them into contact with life concepts alternative to drug use, as often and as early as possible.

Gradual Therapeutic Goals for Risk Reduction

Drug addicts who temporarily are not able to change their dependent behavior should nevertheless be treated intensively. The goal is to try to minimize the risks of drug use. In the context of risk reduction, it can be adequate to apply a methadone substitute in individual cases. Necessary organizational structures must be developed toward that end.

FINAL COMMENTS

The health policy concept of the treatment service system for drug addicts was selected as an example of an area of possible coordination of scientific knowledge and the value systems of society. For this purpose it is necessary to accept and support scientifically based long-term data collection and analysis. It is also important to make values explicit and not to mix values with scientific arguments. Health policy should always clearly state which components are based on values and which on scientific knowledge.

This article should be understood as a plea, directed to all concerned, for a careful analysis of the treatment service structure for drug addicts in Germany and in any other country. Analysis should be optimalized through single but well-coordinated interventions in an adaptive process. In the opinion of the author, those interventions that bring more addicts into some form of social care or early treatment and that have fewer addict dropouts should be emphasized. The individualized treatment that is necessary to accomplish this is partially a matter of gaining additional financial means, changing structures, and implementing laws. However, for the most part, individualized treatment is dependent on the further development of the therapeutic philosophy of the employees, and further model testing and the extension of research are required.

The procedures suggested are not very spectacular, but they avoid making drug addicts possible victims of unnecessary risks. Finally, in this context the Helsinki Convention principles should be remembered; although they referred to medical experiments with clients, they may also be applied to the treatment of drug addicts. If all suggestions for further developments in the treatment system, and if all liberals or conservatives within the treatment system would be oriented toward these principles, much could be accomplished.

REFERENCES

Bühringer, G. (1981). *Planung, Steuerung und Bewertung von Therapieeinrichtungen für junge Drogen- und Alkoholabhängige*. München: Gerhard Röttger Verlag.

Bühringer, G. (1990a). Individualisierung der Suchttherapie-Forschung und Praxis. In *Individualisierung der Suchttherapie*. M. Heide (ed.), pp. 27–48. Saarbrücken: Dadder.

Bühringer, G. (1990b). Frühzeitige Behandlung von Abhängigen. Paper presented at the Dresdner Symposium, Ambulante und stationäre Behnadlung von Alkoholkranken in der BRD. Voraussetzungen— Schlußfolgerungen— Ergebnisse, Dresden.

Bühringer, G., Dehmel, S., and Hanel, E. (1989). Early intervention for drug dependence. In *Addictive Behaviors: Prevention and Early Intervention*. T. Loberg, W. R. Miller, P. E. Nathan, and G. A. Marlatt (eds.), pp. 185–205. Amsterdam: Swets & Zeitlinger.

Bühringer, G., Herbst, K., Kaplan, C. D., and Platt, J. J. (1989). Die Ausübung von justitiellem Zwang bei der Behandlung von Drogenabhängigen. In *Therapieverlläufe bei Drogenabhängigen. Kann es eine Lehrmeinung geben?* W. Feuerlein, G. Bühringer, R. Wille, (eds.), pp. 43–74. Heidelberg: Springer.

De Jong, R., and Henrich, G. (1978). Ergebnisse eines stationären Programms zur Behandlung jugendlicher Drogenabhängiger: Katamnesen nach einem bzw. nach zwei Jahren. In *Ein verhaltenstherapeutisches Stufenprogramm zur stationären Behandlung von Drogenabhängigen*, R. De Jong, G. Bühringer (eds.). München: Gerhard Röttger Verlag.

Kindermann, W. (1989). Komplexität von Drogenkarrieren. In *Therapieverläufe bei Drogenabhängigen. Kann es eine Lehrmeinung geben?* W. Feuerlein, G. Bühringer, R. Wille (eds.). Heidelberg: Springer.

Ministerium für Arbeit, Gesundheit und Soziales (ed.) (1987). *Medikamentengestützte Rehabilitation bei Drogenabhängigen*. Düsseldorf.

NTIS (1974). Planning and designing for juvenile justice. Springfield, WA: U.S. Department of Commerce.

Raschke, P., and Schliehe, F. (1985). Therapie und Rehabilitation bei Drogen-konsumenten. Langzeitstudie am Beispiel des "Hammer Modells." Der Minister für Arbeit, Gesundheit und Soziales des Landes Nordrhein-Westfalen.

Reuband, K.-H. (1989). Illegale Drogen. In *Jahrbuch '90 zur Frage der Suchtgefahren*, Deutsche Hauptstelle gegen die Suchtgefahren (ed.), pp. 113–55. Hamburg: Neuland.

Simon, R., Strobl, M., Schmidtobreick, B., Ziegler, H., Bühringer, G., and Helas, I. (1990). Erweiterte Jahresstatistik 1988 der ambulanten Beratungs- und Behandlungsstellen für Suchtkranke in der Bundesrepublik Deutschland (Referenzstichprobe). Berichtszeitraum: 1. Januar 1988–31. Dezember 1988. EBIS-Berichte, Bd. 13, Hamm: EBIS-AG der Deutschen Hauptstelle gegen die Suchtgefahren.

CHAPTER 6

Policy Issues Pertaining to the Treatment of Heroin Addicts in the United States, with Particular Reference to Methadone Maintenance Therapy*

John C. Ball and Eric Corty

The problem of opiate addiction has a long history in the United States (Terry and Pellens 1928; Ball and Chambers 1970). As a consequence, various prevention and treatment policies pertaining to the problem of heroin addiction have been, and continue to be, advocated. In the present context of renewed apprehension about the spread of intravenous drug abuse and AIDS, a review of basic policy issues about coping with the contemporary problem of heroin addiction in the United States is in order.

First, we will review current prevention policies, because these often are advanced in conjunction with, or as substitutes for, treatment. We will then turn our attention to treatment policy issues.

There is far-reaching public support for a policy of educating youth about the dangers of drug abuse as a principal means of eliminating the problem of compulsive drug abuse. This emphasis upon didactic or moral teaching is commendable in its intent, but such efforts at preventing or

*The material herein does not necessarily reflect the opinions, official policy, or position of the National Institute on Drug Abuse, or of the Alcohol, Drug Abuse, and Mental Health Administration of the U.S. Department of Health and Human Services.

changing peer-group behavior of adolescents has had only limited effect. In this regard, it has been found that there are three discrete domains that need to be reached for prevention: knowledge, attitudes, and behavior. Change is most readily achieved with knowledge. Attitudes about drug abuse are more difficult to change. Behavior is the least amenable to change through education (Grant 1986).

The role of formal education in affecting the later behavior of student populations should not be minimized, but it has definite limitations in preventing the start and continuation of unacceptable behavior. Thus, crime remains endemic in human societies and other "undesirable" behaviors persist: drunkenness, cigarette smoking, obesity, child abuse, teenage pregnancy, and more. It is therefore unrealistic to look to education as a comprehensive solution to the problem of drug addiction. Formal education has a limited impact.

One reason for education's limitations is that there are countervailing institutional forces at work in society. These include societal influences that denigrate family life, religious values, and community responsibility while extolling drug abuse and other forms of deviant behavior.

The family also has a crucial but limited role to play in the prevention of drug abuse among children. The difficulty is that many children do not have responsible parents and, consequently, they are deprived of suitable early socialization. There are not only orphans and unwanted children, but parents who are themselves opiate addicts, criminals, or prostitutes (Goldstein 1979).

A word about the slums of our big cities. These extensive yet forgotten neighborhoods are a principal breeding ground of heroin addiction. In a very real sense, addiction is a community problem rather than merely an individual problem (Chein, Gerard, Lee, and Rosenfeld 1964) because it maintains itself and is spread by drug-using cohorts from generation to generation in metropolitan slum areas (Mieczkowksi 1986). Furthermore, the fact that minority group members constitute a major portion of these poor slum dwellers only exacerbates the problem of awakening public interest and support for reform.

The role of law enforcement is crucial to any policy which seeks to control heroin addiction. As with crime, it is necessary to develop policies to reduce the spread and continuation of the problem. It is important that law enforcement efforts and programs be integrated with community needs and interests. It is not productive for one city to blame its heroin addiction problem on another city; nor is it efficacious for one nation to blame another for its addiction problem.

It follows that no one approach (no single institution) will be sufficient to deal with the problem of heroin addiction in the United States. Rather, a coordinated societal approach is necessary in which increased resources will consistently be organized to meet prevention, education and treatment needs of communities, occupations, and other populations.

THE ROLE OF TREATMENT IN CONTROLLING THE PROBLEM OF HEROIN ADDICTION

The role of treatment in controlling the continuation and spread of heroin addiction is also limited. Treatment alone can hardly be expected to contain and reduce the problem, for, as noted, other societal forces are at work and, furthermore, no single institution should be expected to resolve such a pervasive national problem as heroin addiction.

Still, the importance of treatment in containing and reducing heroin addiction is crucial: Treatment fulfills two basic functions in ameliorating the pervasive impact of addiction upon society. First, public support for treatment proclaims that a legitimate human need exists (Jaffe 1979). This recognition is important because it constitutes a tangible commitment on the part of society to respond and provide assistance.

Second, the availability of treatment provides a means for improvement and rehabilitation. Through treatment society offers an opportunity for improvement or cure. That some can profit from treatment while others do not is part of the human condition. But we cannot formulate social policy on the basis of pessimism and despair; democracy is predicated on a belief in the opportunity to improve, and treatment supplies this opportunity. Thus, all major modalities of treatment for heroin addiction are successful with some patients.

BASIC POLICY ISSUES PERTAINING TO THE TREATMENT OF HEROIN ADDICTS

It is worthwhile to enumerate specific policy issues regarding the role of treatment in controlling the spread of heroin addiction in the Unites States. Several specific issues are addressed:

(1) What are the causes of opiate addiction?
(2) Is prevention an adequate solution?
(3) Why is there ambivalence about the role of treatment in the overall

national policy of reducing the scope and consequences of heroin addiction?

(4) Is methadone maintenance an effective modality of treatment for opiate addiction?

(5) Does methadone maintenance institutionalize, legitimize, or otherwise encourage opiate addiction? And, is methadone maintenance similar to long-term welfare support, which often leads to intergenerational dependency?

(6) Are other treatment modalities more effective than methadone maintenance?

(7) How does methadone maintenance treatment differ from plans for free heroin distribution?

The first issue pertains to the causes of heroin addiction in the United States. A considerable body of research has been addressed to this issue, and it has been found that numerous factors promote heroin use (e.g., peer-group friends who are addicts, residence in metropolitan slums, prior delinquency) while others inhibit such use (e.g., nondrug-using friends, stable family life in better neighborhoods, absence of delinquency). Given these findings, it is evident that there is no single cause of heroin addiction and that, consequently, there is no simple solution. Furthermore, the findings from epidemiology indicate that populations at risk for opiate addiction change by historical period, nation, and locale, so that causal factors must also vary. This is not to say, however, that we cannot ascertain contemporary causal factors that are significant as mentioned above.

The second issue raises the question whether education, religion, or law enforcement can solve the problem: The answer is no. None of these institutions has been able to stem the tide of heroin addiction, much less eliminate the problem. Each of these institutions and others (mass media, sports, recreation enterprises) has a contribution to make but, as yet, there is a lack of consensus and coordination among them.

The third issue concerns the current position of treatment on the national policy agenda. As a nation we have a decidedly ambivalent attitude toward treatment of heroin addiction and, indeed, toward treatment of drug abusers in general. On one hand, we proclaim a belief in rehabilitation and reform and, therefore, do provide some treatment. On the other hand, we continue to complain and believe that the social problem of intravenous heroin addiction should not have been foisted on us. Why does it exist? Who brought it about? Why should I be responsible? Why can't we just lock them up? Or just give them drugs? And so, an intellectual dichotomy persists. The result of this ambivalence is that we grudgingly provide some treatment services (which are often inadequate) while hoping that somehow the problem will dissipate.

The effectiveness of methadone maintenance therapy, like all major modalities of treatment for heroin addicts, is successful for some patients. Methadone maintenance, therapeutic communities, psychiatric therapy, group counseling, and individual therapy are all effective. The question becomes one of ascertaining which modalities of treatment are appropriate for which patients in which neighborhoods or communities.

Deciding what constitutes successful treatment for heroin addicts is not a straightforward question, for getting addicts completely off opiates, or all illicit drugs, is only one criterion of success, because we cannot ignore their criminal behavior, psychiatric illness, or other aspects of their lives. Furthermore, patients have varying problems associated with their addiction careers (e.g., some addicts work full time, others are professional criminals). As a consequence of this diversity of lifestyles and concomitant problems, it is necessary to measure patients' improvement in a number of areas. The most widely used instrument for determining addicts' need for treatment and progress in treatment, the Addiction Severity Index, measures seven specific areas of functioning: medical status, employment, alcohol abuse, drug abuse, crime, family life, and psychiatric status. Within this context, treatment effectiveness is calculated on the basis of demonstrable improvement in each of these areas. To the extent that a given modality of treatment produces improvement in these behavioral areas, it is more or less effective. Consequently, evaluating treatment effectiveness is not a matter of success or failure, but a question of how much improvement is effected, for how many patients, over how much time.

When patients' improvement has been measured in a comprehensive manner, methadone maintenance treatment is found to be effective for many patients. The extent and type of improvement which occurs due to treatment has been described in several studies (Cooper et al. 1983; Dole and Nyswander 1965; Dole and Joseph 1978; McLellan et al. 1982).

Methadone maintenance treatment in the United States commonly provides an oral daily dose of methadone to outpatient (former) heroin addicts over an extended period of time. While in treatment, these patients receive varying amounts of counseling, medical, and other services depending upon their individual needs and the availability of clinic resources. The more effective programs provide rather comprehensive rehabilitative services on a regular basis (Ball et al. 1986).

The fifth policy issue concerns length of patient stay. The fact that many methadone maintenance patients stay in treatment for extended periods of time (a sizeable number continue for five or more years) raises the question of whether these programs seek to cure addicts as rapidly as possible by making them completely abstinent, or whether they seek to improve their functioning while they stay in the program over a long period of time.

The answer is that methadone maintenance treatment seeks to meet the varied current needs of patients. It attempts to improve patient functioning in all of the areas previously mentioned. It does this by endeavoring to have patients attend clinics to take daily oral doses of methadone, to eschew use of illicit drugs, and to stop intravenous use. Time frame and ultimate objectives of treatment are neither doctrinaire nor unrealistic. Many heroin addicts may require years of treatment before rehabilitation occurs. It is recognized that some patients have stable employment and otherwise require few treatment services other than methadone and regular monitoring. It is also known that some patients are not suited to methadone maintenance treatment. While a few patients may detoxify, leave treatment and remain abstinent, other patients, perhaps most, need methadone maintenance support for extended periods if they are to function adequately in society.

The rationale of methadone maintenance treatment accepts stabilization, improvement, and cure as objectives. Each of these objectives is an acceptable outcome for some patients. Methadone maintenance programs are able to effect significant improvement for most patients who remain in treatment but stabilization of their improved way of life generally occurs only after two years of treatment. "Cure" is uncommon, which indicates only that these three goals have differential rates of attainment. It is relevant to note that the goal of total abstinence from all opiates (both licit and illicit) and all illegal drugs is extremely unrealistic for most addict patients. Indeed, this treatment goal has never been reached by a majority of opiate addict patients anywhere in the world (Ball 1972).

The issue of whether prolonged methadone maintenance treatment tends to institutionalize patients and promote a welfarelike dependency is crucial to public policy deliberations. Three observations seem apt for answering this question. First, it should be stated that it certainly would be best if there were no problem of heroin addiction. The 500,000 addicts involved pose numerous problems for their communities and sometimes seem to threaten the very fabric of society through their self-destructive predatory acts and criminal behavior. But they do exist. Therefore, long-term treatment must be considered. Second, most of those addicts who enter methadone maintenance programs are markedly improved, especially in reducing heroin abuse and criminality (Ball et al. 1987), while they remain in treatment. Thus, the programs are effective in this sense, and this is a major benefit to society. Third, the degree of institutional dependency involved in outpatient methadone maintenance treatment is minimal; most patients make some two to five brief daily visits to the clinic per week. Furthermore, the number of clinic visits tends to decrease after the first year or two as the patients remain in treatment and progress in their rehabilitation.

The programs provide a framework for social improvement for those who want assistance. This is not to say, however, that the process of rehabilitation is quick, easy, or even desired by many addicts, for the obverse is often true. Rehabilitation is slow, difficult, and often perceived as worthwhile and attainable only after years of treatment. From this perspective, the danger of institutional dependency upon methadone maintenance seems to be an inappropriate concern.

The issue of whether other modalities of treatment are more or less effective than methadone maintenance in treating opiate addicts is a red herring: This is not the issue. Rather, the appropriate question is how do we determine the specific effectiveness of each modality of treatment and, then, provide appropriate support for them. The time for intermodality rivalry is past. There is a place and need for various treatments: methadone maintenance, therapeutic communities, psychiatric therapy, group counseling, Narcotics Anonymous, family therapy, narcotic antagonists, and others.

Lastly, proposals which advocate the free distribution of heroin or other drugs as a solution to the drug-abuse problem are quite different from methadone maintenance and other modalities of treatment. *Treatment* approaches are based upon concepts of personal improvement, provision of medical, counseling and other services, recognition of staff responsibility, the existence of individual needs among clients, and many other aspects of medical and social ethics. Proposals for distribution of free drugs to addicts do not address these considerations.

CONCLUSION

Although opiate addiction has a long history in the United States, recent influences have resulted in an awakened concern about the scope and consequences of this problem. It is held that methadone maintenance treatment is effective for most of the 72,000 former addicts currently in treatment, especially in reducing illicit drug use and crime. The question remains, however, as to which patients can (and cannot) be treated successfully.

REFERENCES

Ball, J. C., and Chambers, C. D. (1970). *The Epidemiology of Opiate Addiction in the United States*. Springfield, Ill.: Charles C. Thomas.

Ball, J. C. (1972). On the treatment of drug dependency. *American Journal of Psychiatry 128*, Editorial.

Ball, J. C., Corty, E., Petroski, S. P., Bond, H., Tommasello, A., and Graff, H. (1986). Medical services provided to 2,394 patients at methadone programs in three states. *Journal of Substance Abuse Treatment 3*: 203–9.

Ball, J. C., Corty, E., Bond, H. R., Tommasello, A., and Myers, C. P. (1987). The reduction of intravenous heroin use, non-opiate abuse and crime during methadone maintenance treatment—Further findings. Paper presented at the Annual Meeting of the Committee on Problems of Drug Dependence (June).

Chein, I., Gerard, D. L., Lee, R. S., and Rosenfeld, E. (1964). *The Road to H.* New York: Basic Books.

Cooper, J. R., Altman, F., Brown, B. S., and Czechowicz, D. (eds.) (1983). *Research on the Treatment of Narcotic Addiction—State of the Art*. National Institute on Drug Abuse, Treatment Research Monograph Series.

Dole, V. P., and Joseph, H. (1978). Long-term outcome of patients treated with methadone maintenance. *Recent Developments in Chemotherapy of Narcotic Addiction*, Annals of The New York Academy of Sciences *311*: 181–89.

Dole, V. P., and Nyswander, M. E. (1965). A medical treatment for diacetyl-morphine (heroin) addiction: A clinical trial with methadone hydrochloride. *Journal of the American Medical Association* 193: 646–50.

Goldstein, P. J. (1979). *Prostitution and Drugs*. Lexington, Mass.: Lexington Books.

Grant, M. (1986). Elusive goals and illusory targets: A comparative analysis of the impact of alcohol education in North America and Western Europe. In Babor, T. F. (ed), *Alcohol and Culture: Comparative Perspectives From Europe and America*, pp. 198–210. Annals of the New York Academy of Sciences, Vol. 472.

Jaffe, J. H. (1979). The swinging pendulum: The treatment of drug users in America. In Dupont, R. L., Goldstein, A., and O'Donnell, J., (eds), *Handbook on Drug Abuse*, p. 9. National Institute on Drug Abuse. U.S. Government Printing Office.

McLellan, A. T., Luborsky, L., O'Brien, C. P., Woody, G. E., and Druley, K. A. (1982). "Is treatment for substance abuse effective? *Journal of the American Medical Association 247*, no. 10 (March 12): 1423–27.

Mieczkowski, T. (1986). "Geeking up and throwing down: Heroin street life in Detroit. *Criminology 25*: 645–66.

Terry, C. E., and Pellens, M. (1928). *The Opium Problem*. New York: Bureau of Social Hygiene, Inc. Reprinted in 1970 by Patterson Smith.

CHAPTER 7

Methadone in the Treatment of Narcotic Addiction*

Robert G. Newman

INTRODUCTION

I do not have an answer to the problem of drug addiction, nor, I respect-fully suggest, do any of the other distinguished contributors assembled from Germany or from overseas. Indeed, I would recommend great skep-ticism should anyone claim to have the blueprint for wiping out drug abuse. At the same time, however, I would also recommend wariness of those who would condemn any given approach on philosophical grounds, unless they have something better to propose.

With regard to my own testimony, I make no secret of the fact that I am a strong proponent for the use of methadone as a critically impor-tant—though not exclusive—resource in the effort to contain the problem by affording treatment to those currently addicted. However, my purpose in the following is not to persuade others to follow this or any other course. Rather, I will try to explain the pharmacological rationale which underlies the use of methadone in addiction treatment, and describe what has been accomplished in the battle against narcotic addiction elsewhere in the world.

*This chapter is based on a presentation to the Symposium on "Therapy and Rehabil-itation of Drug Addicts—Possibilities and Limits of Medication-Supported Rehabilitation", which took place in Duesseldorf, Federal Republic of Germany, October 16–17, 1986

THE PHARMACOLOGICAL RATIONALE FOR
METHADONE TREATMENT

I can not emphasize too strongly that the pharmacology of methadone is not and never has been the subject of debate among knowledgeable professionals. There are moral issues, political issues, economic issues, and pragmatic issues that can provoke respectful disagreement and thoughtful discussion, but the way methadone affects (and does not affect) the body is unequivocal.

Methadone is a narcotic medication, which merely means that it has a series of actions similar to those of morphine. Figure 7.1 provides a partial listing of these actions. There are obviously many drugs which produce one or more of the individual effects listed, but unless they are capable of eliciting the entire spectrum they are not classified as narcotics.

One notes that among the pharmacological effects of narcotics are nausea and vomiting, and yet, it is obvious that addicts do not experience these exceedingly unpleasant consequences when, three or four times each day, they put needles in their arms and inject heroin. If this were the case, we clearly would not be faced with a problem of narcotic addiction in our society. But why does the addict *not* experience these effects, when they indeed are listed appropriately among the pharmacological actions of narcotics? The answer is a simple one: Repeated exposure to a narcotic (and indeed, to most substances) produces a tolerance to the drug's effect. Clinically, this is known to physicians and

FIGURE 7.1

Methadone as a narcotic: a drug which has a *series* of actions similar to those of morphine

Central Nervous System Depression
  Respiratory Depression (death)
  Sleepiness
Analgesia
Euphoria
Cough Suppression
Pupillary Constriction
Nausea and Vomiting
Increased Respiratory Tract Secretions
Constipation
Diaphoresis
Itching, etc.

patients alike who experience the great frustration in treating pain, only to find that a tolerance to the analgesic properties of even the most potent narcotics develops quite quickly and soon reaches a stage where no relief is obtainable.

There are several characteristics of tolerance which must be stressed. First of all, tolerance does not develop to the same degree or with the same speed to each of the various actions of the drug. Thus the addict soon develops tolerance to the adverse effects of nausea and vomiting, but is still able to achieve euphoria, and risks overdose as a result of the central nervous system depressant effect.

Second, although tolerance develops as a result of repeated exposure to a specific drug, it applies to *all* drugs in the same class. Thus a patient whose pain has been treated exclusively with morphine, and who develops tolerance as a result, is unable to get analgesic relief from codeine, demerol, or any other narcotic. Similarly, although the street addicts' exclusive drug may have been heroin, they develop a tolerance to morphine, methadone, and all other narcotics as well.

Third, although tolerance is defined as a level of drug concentration in the body which must be exceeded before the pharmacological effect will be experienced (as shown in Figure 7.2), that level may be so high that it is unreachable regardless of the amount of drug taken. A nonnarcotic example of this phenomenon is common decongestant nose drops. Initially the sufferer experiences great relief, but the tolerance quickly develops to such an extent that even an endless flow of the medicine will produce no effect whatsoever. As mentioned previously, precisely the same phenomenon precludes continued analgesia being achieved

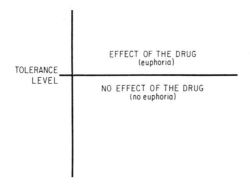

FIGURE 7.2.
The tolerance level denotes the level of drug concentration in the body which must be exceeded before pharmacological effect can be experienced.

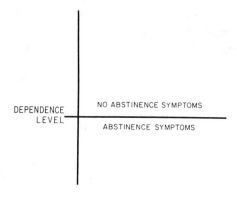

DEPENDENCE
LEVEL

NO ABSTINENCE SYMPTOMS

ABSTINENCE SYMPTOMS

FIGURE 7.3.
Withdrawal symptoms result when the concentration of narcotics in the body of a physically dependent individual falls below the dependence level.

through the administration of narcotics, even in progressively higher dosages.

Along with tolerance, there is another phenomenon which is a consequence of repeated exposure to narcotics, and that is dependence. Dependence also refers to a level of drug concentration in the body, but it has nothing to do with the pharmacological actions of the drug. Rather, it is the level which must be exceeded in order to avoid the symptoms associated with *absence* of the drug. As Figure 7.3 indicates, when the concentration of narcotics in the body of a physically dependent individual falls below the dependence level, withdrawal symptoms result; when the concentration is above this level there are no such symptoms.

As in the case of tolerance, the dependence—even when it is a consequence of exposure to only a single specific drug—is in fact a dependence on the entire class of drugs. This means that withdrawal symptoms in an addict who has never taken anything but heroin can be treated effectively by the administration of *any* narcotic drug.

What is critical to the understanding of the use of methadone in the treatment of addiction is that a range exists between the dependence level and the tolerance level. As indicated in Figure 7.4, as long as the concentration of narcotics in the body falls below the tolerance level (thus precluding the patient experiencing any of the narcotic effects), and yet is above the dependence level (thus precluding withdrawal symptoms), the patient will look and feel completely normal. The most astute clinical observer will be unable to distinguish the addict from the nonaddict under these circumstances. Of course, the heroin-dependent user, if unable to

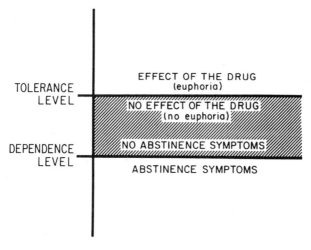

FIGURE 7.4.
The patient appears to have no drug effects or abstinence symptoms as the concentration of drugs falls below the tolerance level and above the dependence level.

obtain another fix, will experience withdrawal symptoms in a matter of hours as the drug from previous injections is metabolized and the concentration falls below the dependence level.

The objective in the administration of methadone for the treatment of addiction, whether the goal is short-term detoxification or long-term maintenance, is very simple: to maintain the patient in a state of physiological normalcy by keeping the narcotic concentration in the body in the range between the tolerance level and the dependence level. This objective is relatively easy to achieve with methadone for two reasons. First, methadone has a very predictable effectiveness even when taken by mouth; and second, the duration of effectiveness is in the neighborhood of 24 to 36 hours, while those of virtually all other narcotics are no more than 3 to 6 hours. Theoretically one could try to "stabilize" a patient with heroin or morphine, but this would require the administration of the drug at least four or five times each day, and by injection rather than by the oral route. Obviously, such a treatment regimen would be impossible.

In countries throughout the world where methadone treatment has been employed, it has been demonstrated that an initial dose of methadone of 30 to 40 mgs. will prevent withdrawal symptoms without producing any significant untoward effects. This is true regardless of the amount of heroin being consumed by the individual addict, the purity of the drug, or the route of administration. The body quickly adjusts to the starting

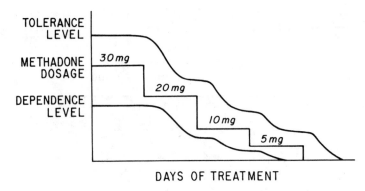

FIGURE 7.5.
Detoxification treatment of narcotic addiction

dosage so that the concentration of the narcotic in the body is maintained approximately mid-way between the dependence and tolerance levels.

METHADONE USED FOR DETOXIFICATION

Since we are dealing with a range between the two levels, and a relatively broad range at that, it is possible to increase or decrease the dosage by 5 or 10 milligrams without crossing either of the two levels. Thus, in detoxification treatment, a decrease of 5 milligrams will not be accompanied by withdrawal symptoms, and after several days at the new reduced level, the dosage can be lowered once more; and this process can be repeated until the methadone administration has been discontinued altogether (see Figure 7.5). In this way, generally in no more than about 14 days, the acute physical dependence can be eliminated successfully without the patient experiencing withdrawal symptoms.

The benefits of such short-term addiction treatment with methadone are very substantial. It is a completely safe, very effective, relatively inexpensive (particularly when provided on an outpatient basis) medical intervention in the chronic problem of heroin addiction. It lends itself to very rapid and large-scale implementation—to the extent that virtually unlimited numbers of patients can be accommodated promptly. In this way, it can ease significantly the unconscionable situation in which addicts who desperately want treatment must remain on "waiting lists" because the long-term rehabilitation programs are filled to capacity. In addition, we know from the experience in many parts of the world that no other form of treatment generates as much demand among the addict population. For example, in New York City a network of only five ambulatory detoxification clinics admitted over 22,000 individuals yearly in the early 1970s—before the program was terminated by government officials who, shortsightedly, were determined to reduce expenditures.

On the other hand, there is a major limitation of detoxification treatment: We know that once withdrawal from physical dependence has been accomplished, the former heroin user almost invariably will revert to illicit drug use. This might occur after a matter of days or, in some cases, many months, but sooner or later relapse is the rule rather than the exception. For this reason, there is another application of methadone in the treatment of heroin addiction, and that is as a maintenance medication for patients who are motivated to give up heroin use and the lifestyle that is associated with it.

METHADONE IN THE "MAINTENANCE" TREATMENT OF ADDICTION

Methadone "maintenance" is really a relative term and does not denote any specific duration of treatment. It should be clear from the pharmacological description above that, first, any patient *can* be maintained—in any amount—for an indefinite period of time. Constant doses will maintain the concentration of methadone in the range between the dependence and the tolerance levels, and thus neither withdrawal symptoms nor narcotic effects will be experienced. It also should be obvious that any patient can be detoxified from methadone through gradual reduction of dosage, in precisely the manner described previously, regardless of how long and in what dosage methadone has been prescribed.

But there are questions, of course, and the first is: "Why do it?" The answer is simple: Empirically, it has been demonstrated in countries throughout the world that individuals are able to give up illicit heroin use and to resume (and in many instances assume for the first time) a normal, productive, socially acceptable, and self-fulfilling lifestyle while maintained on constant doses of methadone.

The second question commonly raised is: "How long should this treatment continue?" The response, again, is both simple and empirical: as long as it is effective! As in any other form of medical treatment, the success of the treatment regimen is determined by how the patient responds, and a desirable therapeutic outcome is not diminished in the slightest by the fact that the patient continues to receive medication.

What underlies the response to both of the above questions is the reality that heroin addicts, following treatment, have a tendency to relapse to illicit drug use regardless of the form of care which has been provided, its duration, or its apparent effectiveness. This being the case, the conservative approach is to continue that which is effective.

Some have rejected as nihilistic the notion that a persistent risk of recidivism is inevitable. Frankly, such a position is nonsense and ignores the experience of all addiction treatment specialists, regardless of their individual techniques and regardless of the locale. In addition, it is worth considering the situation in the field of alcoholism, which in many respects is analogous. Alcoholics Anonymous, the most respected voice in the field of alcoholism treatment, has as the cornerstone of its philosophy the premise that no alcoholic is ever cured and that the illness of alcoholism persists even after a decade or more of total abstinence. The universal experience with narcotic addiction suggests most strongly that precisely the same premise applies to that form of substance abuse as well.

And finally, a word about dosages. One of the greatest absurdities in the field of addiction treatment is the perception that there is some inherent goodness in prescribing the lowest possible dose of methadone. The only consideration that matters is the effectiveness of the medication; if the patient is comfortable at a particular dosage, reports no drug craving, and is doing well clinically, it is inconsequential what dosage of medication is contributing to this outcome. Thus, the answer to the question of "optimal" dosage is once again an empirical one: whatever dosage is effective! Here, too, the conservative approach is to give more rather than less, as long as no side effects occur, and indeed there are no significant side effects which have been associated with methadone in either low or high dosage.

But there is a pharmacological rationale for relying, in general, on relatively higher amounts of medication. As demonstrated in Figure 7.6, the tolerance level does *not* rise in parallel with the administered methadone dosage. The individual who is maintained at 30 or 40 mgs. of methadone has little difficulty in reaching and exceeding the tolerance level through supplemental narcotics (methadone, heroin, or any other drug in this class) and thereby experiencing euphoria. As the maintenance dose increases, however, the proportionate increase in the tolerance level is much greater, so that it takes steadily more and more supplemental narcotics to achieve any effect. Ultimately, at a maintenance dose of approximately 80 to 90 mgs., the tolerance level is so exceedingly high that for practical purposes it is impossible for the patient to achieve euphoria or other central nervous system effects of narcotics regardless of the amount of additional narcotics that might be taken. The sole ex-

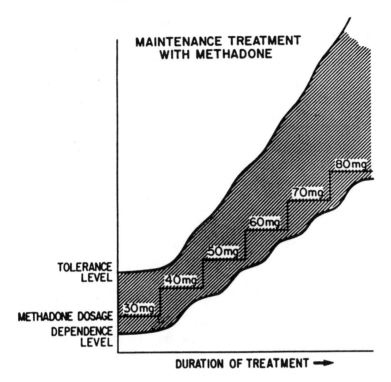

FIGURE 7.6.
Maintenance treatment with methadone

ception is with respect to the analgesic effect; patients are tolerant to the analgesic action of the methadone dosage being taken, but *this* tolerance level can be exceeded by normal pain-killing doses of any narcotic medication. But again, the patient is pharmacologically unable to achieve euphoria through misuse of narcotics and will not be tempted to do so regardless of the circumstances or opportunities that might arise.

It must be stressed again that none of the above pharmacological phenomena are speculative or theoretical or the focus of controversy among knowledgeable individuals. They reflect what is known to every doctor, nurse, and medical student who has prescribed narcotics for pain medication or for any other purpose. To summarize: methadone maintenance is associated with no euphoria whatsoever and, indeed, at appropriate dosages renders the patient pharmacologically unable to achieve euphoria even with supplemental narcotics. It is safe and effective and in tremendous demand by addicts throughout the world who are motivated to give up illicit narcotic addiction and the associated lifestyle, even as they recognize that they will also give up the euphoria they once enjoyed.

It is inappropriate to seek to compare different treatments for narcotic addiction and to try to determine which is "better" than another. The problem is complex and difficult, and any treatment which offers help and which is acceptable to addicts should be made available. There is no question, however, that only methadone treatment lends itself to implementation on a massive scale. Any country which refuses to include methadone treatment as part of the therapeutic armamentarium is guaranteeing that only a tiny percentage of those who need and who want treatment will get it. Rejecting methadone treatment, therefore, amounts to dooming the vast majority of addicts, including those desperately motivated to give up the habit, to continued illicit drug use, to their own detriment and to the incalculable harm of the general society.

A MODEL WORTHY OF CONSIDERATION

Although the physiological and pharmacological characteristics of drugs and their effects on the body are the same throughout the world, the problem of drug addiction clearly is shaped in large measure by political, economic, cultural, and other characteristics unique to each country. For this reason, the response to this complex problem must be customized for each locale, and it would be foolish to believe that an approach which seems to be effective in one country can simply be replicated in another. This qualification notwithstanding, however, there indeed is much that can be learned from the failures and successes of colleagues in other parts of the world. While, regrettably, there are a great many more failures than successes, this at least makes it easier to select a desirable model.

On what country would I suggest Germany focus its attention? Certainly not the United States. It is true that our federal government claims to be dealing with drugs through domestic and international law enforcement, as well as through treatment, prevention, and research, but this is largely lip service. While the law enforcement budget under President Reagan increased 70% in past years, the treatment and prevention budget—never very large to begin with—was reduced. And this despite strong evidence that abuse of a variety of drugs has been increasing steadily. As a consequence, while President Reagan took pride in the American helicopters participating in raids on Bolivian cocaine laboratories (every one of which was abandoned before the helicopters came near), and while he proudly urinated in a bottle, stating that he would seek to have at least 1.5 million federal workers do the same (at a cost of as much as a half billion dollars), there is today not one city in the United States where those addicts motivated to accept treatment can be admitted to a program promptly.

Waiting lists exist everywhere—except in those communities where there is no treatment for which to wait. In New York City, waiting lists for methadone maintenance as well as drug-free programs number well over two thousand, and that clearly is only the tip of the iceberg. It is common knowledge on the streets that all the programs are filled, and that the time and energy devoted to filling out application forms in one of the clinics will achieve nothing but having one's name placed on a list for a period of as long as six months. Addicts are hardly known for their tendency to plan ahead and to "delay gratification," and it is not unreasonable to speculate that for every addict who goes to the trouble of applying, another 10 or 20 would seek treatment if it were known to be readily available. The gap, therefore, between voluntary demand for treatment and availability of treatment services is enormous.

It is possible that the Netherlands represents a good model to follow, but I am not personally familiar with the programs there and since the conference has wisely included colleagues from the Netherlands to describe first-hand experience, it would be presumptuous of me to comment. But I do have extensive personal familiarity with the programs which have been developed during the past 11 years in Hong Kong, and I believe those programs are indeed outstanding and worthy of consideration by Germany and every other country which has an extensive illicit drug problem.

There is one fundamental characteristic of the Hong Kong approach which distinguishes it from virtually every other country in the world: the government there made a determination some 10 years ago that one component of its efforts to deal with the narcotic drug problem would be to ensure the immediate availability of treatment to every addict who wants it. No philosophical or practical obstacle to the achievement of this goal would be tolerated.

I had the honor of being called to Hong Kong early in 1975 to advise on the establishment of a large methadone treatment program. Included in my recommendations were guidelines regarding "adequate" staffing by physicians, nurses, social workers, and vocational rehabilitation specialists to provide a comprehensive treatment package to address all of the many needs associated with drug addiction throughout the world. My Chinese hosts listened attentively, smiled politely, and then (thank goodness) ignored every suggestion I made which would have prevented expansion on the scale that they recognized as being imperative.

The methadone treatment clinics in Hong Kong have extremely limited staffing. There are posters in each facility stating that referral can be made to various community resources such as medical clinics, welfare agencies, and so forth. But it was recognized that it would be impossible to replicate these services within the methadone treatment clinics, and thus this was not even attempted.

And what has been the outcome? First of all, Hong Kong is in a position which is probably unique in the world in that it can (and does) publicize through posters displayed throughout the colony and through nightly television announcements that every person who has a heroin addiction problem can get help immediately. The response has been dramatic, and the daily attendance is in the neighborhood of 8,000 to 10,000 people. Whenever there is a successful law enforcement seizure of incoming narcotics, the price promptly rises—and so does attendance in the treatment facilities. Without such treatment, it is certain that the drug users would be compelled to ever greater criminal activity. In addition, there has been a steadily growing core group of approximately 6,000 former heroin users who remain in treatment and abstain from illicit drug use regardless of the street market.

Just before the program was developed, the prisons were bursting at the seams and there were five drug units within the Corrections Department; additional facilities were in the planning stages. But within five years after the expansion of the methadone treatment network, the number of addicts entering prison had declined by 70%. Three of the previous five addiction facilities in the prisons had been closed, and the other two were underutilized: A dramatic result indeed!

It should be emphasized that Hong Kong did not embrace methadone as *the* answer to its drug problem. It has a proud record of close and effective cooperation with other governments to curtail the importation of narcotics; it has a quite effective internal law enforcement program which has been greatly strengthened by a major anticorruption campaign; it vigorously pursues prevention and education with respect to drugs; and even in the treatment arena, it has continued to support drug-free residential programs and new research initiatives. But it is absolutely clear and universally acknowledged in Hong Kong that the methadone treatment program there is the cornerstone of the antinarcotics campaign and that it is this program which has played the key role in determining the successes to date.

CONCLUSION

The problem of addiction is exceedingly complex and defies solution by a narrowly focused, simplistic approach. It is a problem which requires law enforcement and treatment, prisons and programs, punishment and help, firmness and patience, pressure and encouragement. Nor can one ignore prevention and education programs to keep our young people from becoming addicts tomorrow, while we treat the problem posed by those who are already addicted today.

My basic message is to consider *every* course that holds promise for having a significant favorable impact. Obviously, I believe methadone is one such course and that it is an essential component of any comprehensive program. In considering the arguments of the critics and the advocates, the conclusions reached should be based on experience and facts, and not on philosophical dogma. The problem we face, after all, is not a philosophical one, but a tragically real one which affects every member of our respective communities.

And finally, to end as I began, I urge that, before dismissing a role for methadone, those involved in addiction treatment ask what alternatives exist for the tens of thousands of potential patients who would accept and could benefit from it.

PART THREE

The Treatment Service System

CHAPTER 8

Treatment Facilities in Germany: Number and Type of Services, Organization, and Funding

Herbert Ziegler

TYPES OF SERVICES

The existing treatment service system for addicts can be divided into outpatient, residential and part-time treatment facilities (Deutsche Hauptstelle gegen die Suchtgefahren 1989):

- Outpatient facilities:
  Counseling and treatment centers
  Self-help and temperance groups
- Residential or inpatient facilities
  Special treatment centers for addicts
  Psychiatric hospitals
  Aftercare facilities
- Part-time facilities
  Day clinics
  Aftercare facilities
  Therapeutic communities
  Halfway houses

In the early 1970s, when the problem of illegal drugs increased in Germany, many new treatment facilities were opened for this specific clientele. There was a dual system that provided for alcohol addicts on the one side and drug addicts on the other side. In the last 20 years this separation has increasingly disappeared. Today the outpatient counseling and treatment centers usually deal with all types of addictions including alcohol, illegal drugs, and pharmaceuticals. But many of them still have major interests in one type of addiction, either alcohol or illegal drugs. Especially in the north of Germany the outpatient counseling and treatment centers also deal with other psychosocial problems and illnesses, for example, partnership and sexual problems, gambling, and eating disorders. The residential facilities are mostly still distinguished according to the type of the drug. But here also there is a tendency, as drug addicts get older and alcohol addicts grow younger, to separate the treatment facilities not by the type of drug but by the age group.

CURRENT TREATMENT APPROACH IN GERMANY

Treatment for addicts is usually carried out in four different steps. The first step involves the motivation phase for the addict, the selection of an appropriate treatment center, and administrative matters relating to the treatment costs. Usually these activities are handled by counselors. In outpatient treatment centers the first contact with the addict is often made outside the agency by visits to prisons or hospitals or by street work. Another important role in the motivation phase involves work with parents and relatives of the addict (Wille 1987).

The second step of the standard treatment usually is a short detoxification in a hospital, followed by the client's transfer to a residential treatment center. Traditionally the standard treatment for drug addicts in Germany is the long-term residential or inpatient treatment, but more and more outpatient centers have begun to offer comprehensive treatment programs. The addict stays in treatment from a minimum of 4 to 6 months up to 18 or sometimes even 24 months. Only a few programs have shorter stays (Wille 1987), but this number is increasing.

The final step of treatment should be the reintegration of the addict into society. This is accomplished partly through residence in halfway houses followed by outpatient treatment and crisis intervention in counseling centers. This gradual integration into "normal" social life is difficult, especially today: unemployment among young people is high and competition for good jobs is intense. It is also difficult for recovered addicts to rent apartments. Therefore apartments are often supervised by social workers of outpatient treatment centers.

NUMBER OF TREATMENT SERVICE CENTERS

It is difficult to constantly monitor the exact number of treatment facilities and treatment places because they are run by different organizations that are independent from each other and independent from official authorities. According to current figures there are 910 outpatient counselling and treatment facilities in Germany. There are about 6,550 self-help and temperance groups, and 175 parents' groups, which are mostly linked in one way or another to the outpatient treatment centers; 703 of the 910 treatment centers are run by large national welfare organizations (e.g., by Protestant and Catholic churches and by nonreligious societies), and 207 are organized within a city administration or by other independent organizations. The number of self-help and temperance groups has increased steadily in recent years. About 500 to 600 of the 910 outpatient centers meet the standards of an adequately equipped and professionally run outpatient center.

The type and number of residential treatment facilities are shown in Table 8.1. This table does not show the exact distribution of the facilities as the complete data on some of them were not available. There are at least 3,000 treatment places[1] for drug addicts, for in facilities for all three types of addictions 15% to 20% of the places are reserved for drug addicts. Pensions and health insurance companies now finance treatment in 226 out of 336 institutions; the rest are financed by public welfare. There are 209 houses with 2,516 places altogether for aftercare. There are no data available on day and night clinics. The average size of residential treatment centers is 20 to 50 slots for drug addicts and 80 to 150 slots for alcohol addicts.

STAFF[2]

Nearly all treatment centers are run by professional teams (physicians, psychologists, social workers, and therapists). The only larger self-help community for addicts without professional staff in Germany is Synanon. Former addicts are very seldom employed in treatment centers, but often

---

1. Treatment places: capacity of a residential treatment facility on any given day. For example, three clients can be treated in one year in every place, if the average treatment duration is four months.

2. Some of the following data are taken from the EBIS documentation system. For further details see the chapter by Simon and Bühringer in this volume.

TABLE 8.1
Type, Number and Capacity of German Residential Treatment Facilities

Number/Places	Alcohol		A+PrD		A+PrD+D		Illegal Drugs		Total	
	N	Slots	N	Slots	N	Slots	N	Slots	N	Slots
Charity organizations	13	443	85	4,102	22	673	63	1,957	183	7,175
Private and other organizations	3	151	49	4,785	5	237	8	244	65	5,417
Psychiatric hospitals	7	538	32	1,585	31	2,460	8	250	78	4,833
Total	23	1,132	166	10,472	58	3,370	79	2,451	326	17,425

(A: Alcohol; PrD: Prescribed drugs; D: Illegal drugs)

TABLE 8.2
Average Staff in 303 Outpatient and Counseling Treatment Centers
(Data from EBIS-System)[1]

Profession	Average number	Percentage of the total number of staff
Social worker	2.6	57.7%
Psychologist	0.4	8.8%
Physician	0.05	1.0%
Management	0.79	17.5%
Other	0.68	15.0%
Total	4.52	100.0%

("Average number" means for example that in the average there are 2.6 social workers in a treatment center.)
[1]Data from EBIS System: Simon, R., Helas, I., Schmidtobreick, B., Ziegler, H. and Bühringer, G. (1988). Jahresstatistik 1987 der ambulanten Beratungs- und Behandlungsstellen fr Suchtkranke in der Bundesrepublik. Berichtszeitraum: 1.1.1987 -31.12. 1987. EBIS-Berichte 10, Hamm: EBIS-AG.

TABLE 8.3

Staff in Residential Treatment Centers

Physician	1 : 25	Usual staff-client ratio:	
Psychologist	1 : 25		
Social worker	1 : 7	Alcohol addiction:	1 : 6
Occupational therapist	1 : 20	Drug addiction:	1 : 2.5
Sport therapist	1 : 30		

they are responsible for aftercare units of self-help groups of addicts. Tables 8.2 and 8.3 give an overview of the staff in outpatient and residential treatment centers. In residential treatment centers in particular, there has been a qualification campaign (in terms of professional status and a special two to three-year postgraduate training course for the treatment of addicts) since 1975, when insurance companies began to fund treatment. In counseling centers nearly 75% of the staff has also received this type of special training.

FUNDING

The German Insurance System

It is necessary here to present a short overview about the German insurance system. The system is divided in three parts:

1. Public social assistance/welfare (e.g., for long-term unemployed people),
2. Health insurance companies (public or private) provided by law. Responsible for treatment costs for all people who are employed, their relatives, and pensioners.
3. Annuity or pension insurance companies provided by law. Responsible for the rehabilitation of those suffering from chronic diseases in order to reintegrate people into the working process.

Employers and employees are required to pay equal shares of fees into the last two systems. The work of the insurance companies is regulated by federal laws, but the companies are run by representatives of employer organizations and trade unions (so called self-administered organizations). Private insurance companies play virtually no role in the field of addiction.

Funding of Outpatient Centers

Nearly 80% of the outpatient centers are run by nonprofit private organizations and are usually members of one of the five large German welfare organizations. Their annual budget is funded by the organizations themselves, by temporary funding of the Federal Ministry of Health (Model Projects), by the federal states, and by regional divisions and municipalities (Table 8.4). The funding of counseling centers differs slightly from one federal state to another. The average annual budget for one outpatient center is about DM 310,000 ($180,000). During the last few years there has been increasing discussion about funding outpatient treatment by insurance companies. The first regulations were implemented in 1991.

TABLE 8.4

Funding Sources for Outpatient Treatment (Data from EBIS-System)

Municipalities	34.0%
Charity organizations	28.0%
State authorities	27.0%
Annuity insurance/	3.0%
Health insurance	
Federal authorities	2.0%
Other	7.0%

TABLE 8.5

Funding Sources for Inpatient Treatment

Annuity insurance (worker)	59.0%
Annuity insurance (employee)	21.9%
Health insurance	9.7%
Other insurance companies	5.1%
Public social assistance (welfare)	2.6%
Other	1.7%

Funding of Inpatient Centers

Inpatient treatment is almost entirely financed by insurance companies (Table 8.5). In 1988 the social insurance companies spent a total of DM 538 million for the residential treatment of addictions; DM 429 million was spent for rehabilitation; and DM 109 million was paid as transitional financing. The total budget for all treatments was DM 5.005 billion, and the expenses for addictive diseases amount to 10.7%. When the medical measures are broken down into measures for men and women it becomes clear that 16% of the women come under the diagnostic group "Psychiatric Diseases," but only 1.6% fall under the group "Addiction" (Table 8.6). The same diagnosis group shows only 12% of the men, but 4.8% fall under the diagnosis "Addiction." Without over interpreting these data, one may hypothesize that the diagnosis "Addiction" is much more taboo for women than for men. Thus men might have a greater chance of receiving the right treatment.

Inpatient treatment is paid on a day by day client basis. The average costs for one day of detoxification in a general hospital are between DM 300 and DM 400, and for one day of long-term residential treatment

TABLE 8.6
Medical Diagnoses of Inpatients under Annuity Insurance in Germany (1988)

	Men	Women
Diseases of the skeleton, muscles, and connective tissue	45%	46%
Psychiatric diseases	12%	16%
addictions	4.8%	1.6%
Cancerous diseases	5%	13%
Circulatory diseases	19%	9%
Diseases of the digestive organs and metabolism	8%	6%
Diseases of the respiratory organs	6%	5%
Diseases of the nervous system and sense organs	2%	2%
Skin diseases	1%	1%
Diseases of the urinary organs and genitals	1%	1%
Other diseases	2%	3%
	100%	100%
Total	(423,728)	(303,606)

TABLE 8.7
Numbers and Source of Funding for Addicts in Inpatient Treatment

		1982	1984	1986	1988
Arv	Men	12,369	14,249	14,716	15,708
	Women	1,351	1,751	1,781	2,082
	Both	13,720	16,000	16,497	17,790
Anv	Men	1,575	3,368	3,398	3,760
	Women	1,083	2,352	2,390	2,545
	Both	2,840	5,720	5,788	6,305
Bkn	Men	248	364	336	317
	Women	5	18	7	6
	Both	253	382	343	323
	Total	16,813	22,102	22,628	24,418

Arv: Social Insurance for Workers ("blue collar")
Anv: Social Insurance for Employees ("white collar")
Bkn: Miner's Insurance

TABLE 8.8

Numbers and Age Distributions for Addicts in Inpatient Treatment

Age	Men		Women		Men + Women	
	N	%	N	%	N	%
< 20	44	0.2	14	0.3	58	0.2
20–24	1,042	5.3	261	5.6	1,303	5.3
25–29	2,498	12.6	586	12.6	3,084	12.6
30–34	3,454	17.4	715	15.4	4,169	17.1
35–39	3,358	17.1	789	17.0	4,174	17.1
40–44	2,956	14.9	776	16.7	3,732	15.3
45–49	3,215	16.2	786	17.0	4,001	16.4
50–59	2,256	11.4	479	10.3	2,735	11.2
> 60	810	4.1	191	4.1	1,001	4.1
	125	0.6	36	0.8	161	0.7
Total	19,785	100.0	4,633	100.0	24,418	100.0
Average age	39.1		39.2		39.1	

(nonmedical but professional settings) between DM 80 and DM 150 ($50–90).

UTILIZATION OF INPATIENT TREATMENT

About 250,000 addicts contacted outpatient and residential facilities in 1988. In addition, about 100,000 addicts were reached by self-help groups. The following data were collected by the annuity insurance companies. Table 8.7 shows the figures for residential treatment in recent years. The number of the applications for treatment of addicts varies between 27,000 and 30,000 each year. Due to various reasons not all the granted treatments are carried out. It is interesting that the proportion of addicted men and women is 60:40 in the Anv (Social Insurance for Employees, "white collar"), whereas it is 90:10 in the Arv (Social Insurance for Workers, "blue collar"). This proportion has not changed over the past several years. Unfortunately, we have no data from the public and private health-care insurance companies.

The distribution of the age groups (Table 8.8) remained nearly the same as compared with previous years. The average age was 39.1 years old. The distribution shows a considerably younger age structure in comparison with other medical rehabilitation measures. The average length

TABLE 8.9
Average Duration of Inpatient Treatment (1988)

	Men	Women	Men + Women
Alcohol addiction	123 days	127 days	124 days
Addiction to prescribed drugs/ illegal drugs	155 days	136 days	150 days
All types of addiction	127 days	129 days	128 days
Other rehabilitation treatment	35 days	33 days	35 days

of treatment is shown in Table 8.9. Taking into account the high number of people dropping out of treatment, one must differentiate between the average length of all the measures, including those that are broken off, and the length of the measures that are carried out to the end. Compared with 1987 the average length of treatment has gone down slightly: three days for men, two days for women.

ORGANIZATIONS

Many different organizations are working at different levels in the treatment of addictive disorders. At the federal level the DHS Deutsche Hauptstelle gegen die Suchtgefahren (German Council on Dependence Problems) represents 17 organizations with nationwide activities. These organizations keep their autonomy, but work together in this private, non-profit-oriented umbrella organization. The DHS is in close contact with the Bundesministerium für Gesundheit (Federal Minstry of Health), the Bundeszentrale für gesundheitliche Aufklärung (Federal Center for Health Education; a public agency of the Federal Minstry of Health), and the Bundesvereinigung für Gesundheitserziehung e.V. (National Association for Health Education) as well as with other authorities and institutions. The DHS is financed by funds of the Federal Minstry of Health as well as by grants of the Federal Pension Insurance Organization. The necessary international exchange of experience is ensured by its membership in the International Council on Alcohol and Addiction (ICAA) in Lausanne. Corresponding State Councils on Dependence Problems work at the state level. They cooperate closely with the DHS in the Bundesarbeitsgemeinschaft der Landesstellen (National Working Group of the State Councils).

CONCLUSIONS

Germany has a varied supply of outpatient and counseling treatment centers and residential treatment centers. Nearly 40% of all drug addicts get in touch with the different services, but many still stay in prison for a longer time than in treatment facilities. The standard of the treatment programs is high in many areas but public opinion about the treatment centers is low. Insurance companies, public administration, and courts are often not flexible enough to find suitable treatment centers for drug addicts who are motivated for therapy. Therefore our task for the future will be to improve the different parts of the system and to reduce deficits in a cooperative and coordinated manner.

REFERENCES

Deutsche Hauptstelle gegen die Suchtgefahren. (1989). *Jahrbuch '90 zur Frage der Suchtgefahren.* Hamburg: Neuland.
Wille, R. (1987). Drug addiction in the Federal Republic of Germany: Problems and responses. *British Journal of Addiction* 82: 849–56.

CHAPTER 9

Trend Analysis of Treatment Service Data from the EBIS Information System*

Roland Simon, Gerhard Bühringer, and Michael Strobl

INTRODUCTION

Documentation and analysis of clients and therapeutic activities are essential for the evaluation of the health care system for drug addicts. When the first German demonstration project for the treatment of drug addicts was begun in 1973, a standardized documentation system was developed for residential and outpatient facilities. When the project was finished, the documentation system was modified and implemented nationwide in 1980 (Hachmann and Bühringer 1980). This system, called *EBIS* (Facility [*Einrichtung*] *Based Information System*), has since been used for collecting and analyzing annual nationwide statistics in the Federal Republic of Germany. In the first section of this chapter, the topics covered by the system and the organization of data collection and data analyses are described. Some data regarding present-day conditions, trends in facilities, and clients are subsequently presented to demonstrate how the documentation system is used.

*The research reported here was supported by the German Federal Ministry of Health.

AIMS AND ISSUES OF EBIS

There are two groups of items in EBIS:

1. Facilities are described (i.e., in terms of number of staff members, funding, number of clients, and other variables).
2. Clients' characteristics are documented and basic data regarding treatment and outcome are collected in three major areas:

- Situation at the beginning of treatment (covering drug and other problems), socioeconomic data, and drug history.
- Treatment process as described by therapeutic activities, duration of treatment, and number of treatment sessions.
- Short-term outcome in drug use, social behavior, and overall psychological state at the end of treatment.

When EBIS was implemented in 1980, the system had to meet several needs. It was to document the activities and client data of the treatment facilities. Such documentation is required for the facilities to receive public funds. The comparison of similar facilities and statistics from the previous year's clientele form part of the informational background for planning further development and activities. New treatment entries can be monitored and controlled. EBIS also may be used by authorities to monitor the regional and national activities and to compare regions. The overall purpose of the documentation system is to monitor treatment facilities in the Federal Republic of Germany according to the needs of the clients on one side, and the utilization of services on the other. Since these factors vary over time, the services must change accordingly. EBIS thus forms the basis for an adaptive learning process to constantly improve the treatment service system for addicts. (For further details see the chapter by Bühringer in this volume.) Within this process EBIS should help to answer three questions: (1) Does the supply of services correspond to the needs of addicts? (2) Does the supply of services correspond to its utilization? (3) Does the utilization of services correspond to the needs? The analysis of needs (e.g., epidemiological studies) and long-term follow-up studies are not part of EBIS, which is a low-cost, annually collated information system. These data must be gathered in seperate studies.

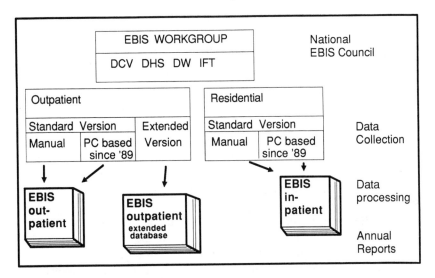

FIGURE 9.1.
Organizational structure of EBIS

ORGANIZATIONAL BACKGROUND

The organization of EBIS consist of four layers (Figure 9.1): The EBIS Workgroup defines items and further developments of the system. The IFT Institute for Therapy Research, the German Council on Dependence Problems (DHS), and two nationwide charity organizations are members of this council. Data for all clients who are treated with more than one contact are collected on special index cards. At the end of the year client data are collected by the facilities' staff according to a questionnaire and sent to the central unit for data processing. One-time contacts and data about facility and staff are added on a special questionnaire. A representative quota sample of 35 out of about 300 outpatient treatment facilities use the Extended Version of EBIS Outpatient, wherein additional data about the clients' drug use, drug history, and abuse of pharmaceuticals are asked.

In an increasing number of standard facilities, a PC-based version of EBIS is used. Data are compiled in a data base within the facility. At the end of the year they are collected and sent on a floppy disk to the central unit for data processing. The EBIS Inpatient Version also began as a manual version; a PC-based version was introduced in 1989. Altogether about 350 facilities use one of the different versions of EBIS on a volunteer basis.

In the central unit at the IFT, the data for each facility are processed and a printout is generated in order to guarantee rapid feedback. Then the data analyses for the different regions and states, and for the national level are carried out. All printouts for the facilities and the different areas are sent back within two months (usually in March for the previous year). The data of the Standard and the Extended Version of EBIS for outpatient care are integrated in the annual report "EBIS Outpatient" (see, e.g., Simon et al. 1990); for residential facilities a special report entitled "EBIS Inpatient" is published (e.g. Simon 1990a). Additional data and data on abuse of pharmaceuticals are published seperately (see, e.g., Strobl et al. 1990).

There are several training sessions conducted each year in which users of EBIS learn how to code and how to work with the information provided by EBIS. Special courses help users learn to operate PCs and EBIS software package. There are different elaborate manuals (Hanel, Herbst, and Simon 1984, Simon et al. 1986, Simon 1989, Simon 1990b) which contain exact definitions for questions, categories, and organizational instructions.

RESULTS

In the following description of treatment facilities, means are used. Data collected from individuals who began or terminated treatment in 1989 are examined to determine client characteristics. Trend analysis data from 1980 to 1989 are included. All data are from the system "EBIS-Outpatient." (For detailed information see Simon et al. 1990.)

Number of Clients and Staff

In 1989 data from 301 treatment facilities were reported to EBIS. On average, each treatment center had nearly 260 clients with at least two contacts. About one-third began treatment before 1989, and nearly 40% continued treatment in 1990. A total of more than 75,000 clients were treated in all facilities, from which about 50,000 began and 46,000 finished treatment in 1989 (Figure 9.2).

One important figure that is significant in planning social services are trends in utilization of services. The EBIS data from 1980 to 1989 show

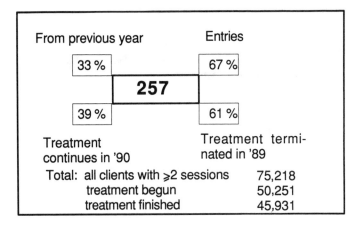

FIGURE 9.2.
Clients per facility (1989)

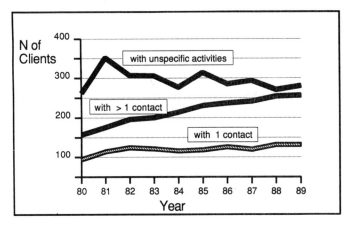

FIGURE 9.3.
Clients per facility (1980–1989)

a constant increase in client figures. The number of clients who received more than one contact was about 150 in 1980 and increased to nearly 260 in 1989 (Figure 9.3). This increase of more than 70% is handled by nearly the same number of staff members as in 1980. Facilities and social welfare organizations are thus using these data to support their claims for the need for more staff. The number of "one-time contacts"

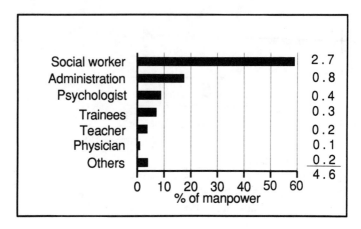

FIGURE 9.4.
Staff (1989; full-time manpower)

remained nearly the same from 1982 to 1989, but general measures such as preventive activities and street work were gradually decreasing. This may be an effect of the heavy work load.

There are several professions represented in outpatient treatment facilities (Figure 9.4). Most prominent are social workers: nearly 60% of the facilities' personnel, which amounts to four to five full-time workers, is based on them. Another 18% are administrative and technical staff, while less than 10% are psychologists. The share of physicians is nearly invisible in this graph. The personnel structure of outpatient work with drug addicts is quite different from residential facilities in Germany, where more psychologists and medical staff are found.

Clients: Status and Trends

The clients' ages range from less than 14 to more than 60 years. Most male and female clients are in the age groups between 30 and 50 years. There is no significant difference between sexes. Most of the treatment centers treat primarily alcohol dependence, thus the clients' age is rather high on the average. Most of the opiate addicts belong to the group aged from 20 to 30 years old (Figure 9.5). The womens' group is slightly older than the male group. As a matter of fact, some years ago there were very few clients over 30 years old with opiate problems.

About two-thirds of all male clients and 40% of all female admissions

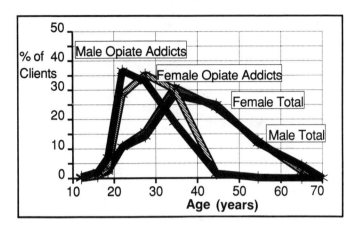

FIGURE 9.5.
Age of clients (admissions, 1989)

TABLE 9.1

**Drugs abused by Male and Female Admissions to
Outpatient Treatment Centers (1989)**

| | *Male* | | *Female* | |
	Addiction	*Abuse*	*Addiction*	*Abuse*
Alcohol	66%	15%	40%	11%
Pharmaceutics	7%	6%	11%	11%
Opiates	8%	2%	6%	2%
Other ill. drugs	6%	6%	3%	4%
Total	28,043		14,878	

in 1989 show an alcohol addiction (Table 9.1). More than 10% abuse
alcohol without symptoms of an addiction. Addiction and abuse of opiates
and of other illegal drugs are found less often.

Little data exist that can be used as reliable indicators for the extent
of the drug problems in a country. Data sources like police data or court
sentences are confounded by different variables. It seems a good idea,
then, to use several indicators to estimate the number of addicts. One
possible indicator is the number of treated addicts. Moreover, changing
numbers of clients for different substance groups are of some importance
to the development of treatment services. For comparison, all data for

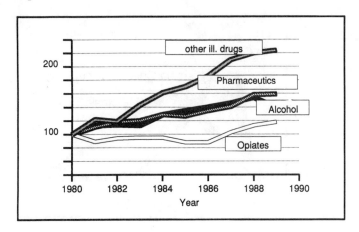

FIGURE 9.6.
Drugs used by male addicts (admissions, 1980-1989; 1980 = 100%)

male addicts from 1980 to 1989 were based on the values from 1980 (Figure 9.6). While the number of opiate addicts fluctuates somewhat, all other groups show an increase of at least 30%. Addictions of "other illegal drugs" show a sharp increase of more than 100%. Therapists from treatment facilities usually assume cocaine to be the cause for this dramatic change. First data on cocaine use from the Extended EBIS Version support this hypothesis.

There are some sex differences in the trends of drug taking (Figure 9.7). While female and male clients are similar in the alcohol and pharmaceutic trends, there is a decrease for female opiate addicts from 1980 to 1986 of nearly 40%. For the first time since 1980 an increase was observed from 1986 to 1987. There is a really astonishing sex difference for addictions to other illegal drugs. While the number of male clients in this group doubled from 1980 to 1989, female clients showed nearly no changes from 1980 to 1986, and there is just a 20% increase from 1980 to 1989.

In order to analyze the effects of age on drug behavior, two age groups were defined with a cutoff at 25 years. Figure 9.8 shows the total number of clients with illegal drug use in all facilities. The number of clients younger than 25 years old did not increase during the last 7 years. There was a sharp decline for opiate addicts until 1986. On the other side the number of people addicted to opiates and other illegal drugs increased every year for adult clients aged 25 and older. Thus the clientele became older, and opiate addiction and addiction to other illegal drugs was no longer a "youth problem."

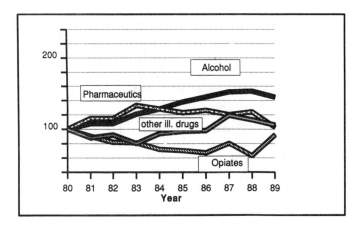

FIGURE 9.7.
Drugs used by female addicts (admissions, 1980–1989; 1980 = 100%)

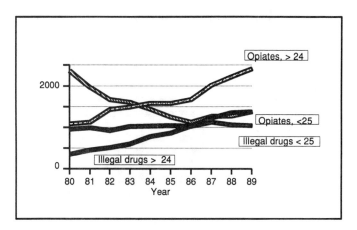

FIGURE 9.8.
Drugs used and age (admissions, 1980–1989)

Treatment and Outcome Data

A variety of therapeutic activities are available during the clients' treatment. The frequency of distribution of activities is nearly unchanged since 1980 (Figure 9.9). The pattern of treatment seems to have remained rather constant over the years. There are only slightly fewer referrals to residential treatment and some more outpatient therapies.

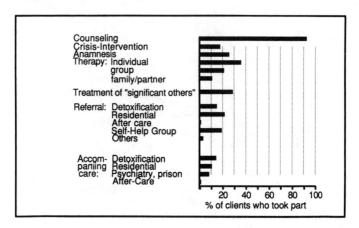

FIGURE 9.9.
Activities of treatment facilities in 1989

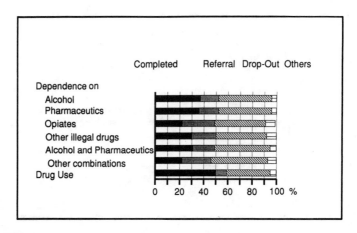

FIGURE 9.10.
Termination of treatment for different groups of clients (terminations, 1989)

Counseling is done most often; nearly every client took part in this activity. Almost 40% of all clients have been in individual therapy.

Several kinds of treatment terminations are possible. Treatment can be terminated by completion, referral, or dropout. As Figure 9.10 shows, the different groups of clients have different patterns of termination. Clients with opiate addiction alone or combined with one or more other

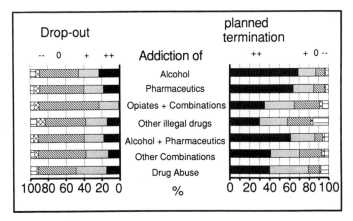

FIGURE 9.11.
Outcome (terminations, 1989)

addictions seldom complete therapy; only about 20% belong to this group. A large number of clients are referred to residential treatment. More than 40% of all clients with drug abuse without addiction symptoms complete treatment as planned. The dropout rate for clients with an addiction to alcohol and pharmaceuticals is rather high, while all other groups are similar.

At the end of treatment therapists rate drug abuse on a 4-point scale, from abstinent to worse, as compared to the clients' status at the beginning of treatment. In Figure 9.11 the scale is defined by (+ +) for abstinence to (− −) for worse. Dropouts are on the left-hand side, regular discharges are shown on the right. The comparison between terminators and dropouts shows much better results for the first group. But even for dropouts some positive effects seem to emerge. The results for addicts to opiates or other illegal drugs are worse than the results for alcohol addictions or pharmaceuticals.

FINAL COMMENTS

EBIS is in use in more than 300 facilities. About a thousand staff members are coding information according to this system. The reliability checks show good results, so trends in EBIS data can be seen as reflecting true changes in clientele and therapeutic work. The increase in the number of facilities with computer-based EBIS will open some extended possibilities for documentation and information systems as well as for epidemiological studies.

REFERENCES

Hachmann, E., and Bühringer, G. (1980). Beschreibung des einrichtungsbezogenen Informationssystems EBIS mit beispielhaften Ergebnissen aus der Erprobungsphase von 1977 bis 1979. *Suchtgefahren 26*: 97–111. Hamburg: Neuland.

Hanel, E., Herbst, K., and Simon, R. (1984). *Systembeschreibung EBIS-stationär. Ein Handbuch für Benutzer*. München: IFT Institut für Therapieforschung.

Simon, R. (1989). *Systembeschreibung zum Programm EBIS-A. Programmsystem für Einrichtungen der ambulanten Suchtkrankenhile im einrichtungsbezogenen Informationssystem. IFT-Manuale 26*. München: IFT Institut für Therapieforschung.

Simon, R. (1990a). *Jahresstatistik 1988 von stationären Einrichtungen für die Suchtkrankenhilfe (Bezugszeitraum: 1.1.1988–31.12.1988). IFT-Berichte 52*. München: IFT Institut für Therapieforschung.

Simon, R. (1990b). *Systembeschreibung zum Programm EBIS-R. Programmsystem für Referenz-Einrichtungen der ambulanten Suchtkrankenhilfe im einrichtungsbezogenen Informationssystem. IFT-Manuale 27*. München: IFT Institut für Therapieforschung.

Simon, R., Bühringer, G., Helas, I., Schmidtobreick, B., and Ziegler, H. (1986). *Systembeschreibung EBIS ambulant (Randlochversion). Ein Handbuch für Benutzer. EBIS-Berichte 7*. München: IFT Institut für Therapieforschung.

Simon, R., Helas, I., Schmidtobreick, B., Ziegler, H., and Bühringer, G. (1988). *Jahresstatistik 1987 der ambulanten Beratungs- und Behandlungsstellen für Suchtkranke in der Bundesrepublik Deutschland (Berichtszeitraum: 1.1.1987–31.12.1987). EBIS-Berichte 10*. Hamm: EBIS-AG.

Simon, R., Strobl, M., Bühringer, G., Ziegler, H., Helas, I., and Schmidtobreick, B. (1990). *Jahresstatistik 1989 der ambulanten Beratungs- und Behandlungsstellen für Suchtkranke in der Bundesrepublik Deutschland (Berichtszeitraum: 1.1.1989–31.12.1989). EBIS-Berichte 12*. Hamm: EBIS-AG.

Strobl, M., Simon, R., Helas, I., Schmidtobreick, B., Hüllinghorst, R., and Bühringer, G. (1990). *Erweiterte Jahresstatistik 1989 der ambulanten Beratungs- und Behandlungsstellen für Suchtkranke in der Bundesrepublik Deutschland (Referenzstichprobe) (Berichtszeitraum: 1.1.1989–31.12.1989). EBIS-Berichte 14*. Hamm: EBIS-AG.

CHAPTER 10

The Challenge of Counseling and Care of Long-Term Drug Addicts: The German Experience with the Demonstration Project "Social Work with Long-Term Drug Addicts" (SLD)*

Thomas Arnold

INTRODUCTION

Despite such positive developments as expansion and differentiation of the care system for drug addicts, male and female workers in counseling centers ever more frequently encounter clients of both sexes who have had long drug careers and many relapses. Because of their previous experience in residential treatment many of them reject renewed treatment. Experience to date shows that this attitude is attributable to numerous causes and to a problem complex whose contours cannot be easily defined. Specific determinants of their present way of life result partly from the clients' aging process, that is, by the increase in their average age. To this must be added their experiences associated with a life of crime, which increasingly militates against a return to so-called reality.

* The study was funded by the German Federal Ministry of Health.

The methods and possibilities of social and educational work are to be explored by means of the model project SLD (Social Work with Long-Term Drug Addicts), with the aim of finding new ways to contact and provide intensive counseling for this group of clients.

STRUCTURE OF FACILITIES

The SLD project is subdivided into the following three areas:

- outreach and counseling
- live-in projects
- job projects

Outreach and Counseling

One important feature of outreach and counseling activities is establishing direct contact with clients. Such contact is realized through social work within the typical environment of drug addicts, including public parks, barrooms, streetcorners, and psychiatric clinics. Once a certain level of mutual trust between the social worker and the client is established, the relationship can be intensified so that effective counseling can take place. This may result in support for possible referral to detoxification clinics, residential treatment, or outpatient, drug-free programs. Furthermore, advice on how to claim social security benefits and other services rendered by the federal, state, or local governments can be given. In some cases the counseling itself develops into something close to actual therapeutic work. The clients are also contacted in detention centers after being arrested or convicted with the aim of arranging for therapeutic treatment as an alternative to imprisonment.

Live-in Projects

Providing a "healthy" and drug-free environment through adequate housing is the major goal of the live-in projects and is accomplished by putting together small groups (6–10 inhabitants) of clients who are counseled by social workers. Twenty-four-hour counseling is not provided, so that clients can achieve a certain degree of independence. The previous lifestyles of those admitted vary considerably. Some have just gone through detoxification programs, others have just been released from residential treatment or psychiatric clinics. Admission is made possible without the usual bureaucratic procedures. Upkeep is the responsibility of the clients; they must come up with their fair share of the rent and other common expenditures such as heating, water, and food. The necessary financial means have to be supplied through personal income or social security benefits. Counseling is financed by the funds of SLD.

One essential feature of the live-in projects is the partial transfer of responsibilities to the groups themselves. This applies to daily recreational activities and to future plans for admission and release of individual members. As far as admission or release is concerned, each member of the group has the right to voice his or her opinion and to vote on issues. The stability and smooth functioning of the groups depend heavily on a specific number of so-called core-members who are usually familiar with therapeutic procedures and group counseling.

Job Projects

The conceptual foundations of the job projects are mainly a consequence of the huge problems drug addicts face in finding and keeping jobs. The job projects within SLD focus on various aspects, such as arranging supervision on the job during vocational training. Another aspect includes participation in self-help enterprises. A third aspect is to provide basic job training to put the clients in a position to find satisfying and lasting employment by themselves.

The job projects comprise groups under the supervision of social workers. For organizational reasons the number of members of each group must be kept relatively low (6 to 12 members). Again, regarding admission to and release from the group, each member has the right to vote on issues. It is vital that the groups are organized so that members learn to cope with the market society. This approach may lead to a form of contradiction between therapeutic and educational goals on the one had and the demands of management in the free-market system on the other. The dilemma of dealing with relapse poses a major problem in this context. The job projects have to be furnished with adequate equipment including tools, machines, or cars. This equipment is financed through extra government funding or private donations.

It is clear that lasting independence from social security services can only be achieved if a certain level of self-support can be reached. Above all, the live-in projects and job projects are based on the principle that comprehensive attempts at achieving social integration should not merely concentrate on certain forms of deviant behavior but must also develop auxiliary forms of support.

AIMS AND METHODS OF DOCUMENTING CLIENTS

Detailed information regarding male and female clients were recorded for the model project by documenting relevant biographical data, and, during the course of counseling, for all those male and female clients in 1987 and 1988 counseled within the framework of the SLD project conceived for the control group. Data on the course of counseling have been compiled for each calendar year, making possible a comparison between the situation before and after completion of treatment. The systematic nature and compilation of the biographical data of those in the project allow for its use even after treatment has been completed, and that data may then be related to other material collected up to that point of time. Among other things this procedure allows informed evaluation as to the degree to which counseling already broken off might be resumed later.

Project workers completed questionnaires together with the clients. The documentation includes three major areas:

• the way of life before counseling began
• the course of counseling
• the change in the way of life during and after treatment.

The documentation includes 429 persons for 1987. The number of first contacts for 1988 (together with those admitted again from 1986 and earlier) totaled 272. This makes a total of 701 people counseled for 1987 and 1988.

SOCIODEMOGRAPHIC DATA

Age and Sex

For both years covered by the study, the mean age of male and female clients in the model project was 28 years at the time of admission. In comparison with other studies in the German-speaking world, the results here display the highest mean age. But it must be borne in mind that corresponding studies were carried out or completed primarily during the early 1980s. On the other hand, experts often point out that there is a tendency toward a higher average age in the drug scene. Some institutions for residential treatment approach the average age shown in this study (Drogenhilfe Tübingen 1988; Hanel and Herbst 1988). The age variable here can be interpreted as an indication that a group of drug addicts was reached that shared the tendency toward an above-average value. Special individual studies are needed to ascertain to what factors to attribute the overall tendency toward a higher mean age and that of those counseled within the project and whether such tendencies stabilize over time.

The 72% of males in the sample available is notably higher than the 28% of females. There are no major differences in this factor for either year investigated. At first sight the continuing uneven proportion of males and females is conspicuous. Males predominate by some 44%. To be sure, results of other studies and documentation compiled from residential treatment show that a disproportion of sexes has often been reported. This is also true for the treatment of outpatients. In the institutions cited the female proportion is uneven at 25% and 33% respectively. Studies to date show that the proportion of female opiate users decreases with increasing age (Projektgruppe TUdrop 1984; Skarabis and Patzack 1981). An explanation could be that females give up using opiates at a younger age than do males. However, a caveat must be entered that the evaluation study and other studies have included data on clients who have contact with institutions for drug users. Consequently, an unexplored territory remains of those who have no contact with drug-care institutions or with the police.

With regard to the relevant aspects of drug delinquency in terms of sex, a study conducted at the German national level (Kreuzer et al. 1981) ascertained that a considerable proportion of the delinquency of female drug addicts resembled that of the males. This resemblance appeared closest when related to a basis of various modes of delinquent behavior. To be sure, even among the females studied there are differences according to form and gravity of delinquency. Females adopt modes of behavior less liable to indictment; among indictable crimes, females opt for less easily detectable and less aggressive and active forms. The forms of crime favored by females are those such as payoff and go-between crimes, of aiding and abetting theft, petty theft from practitioners' surgeries, theft in situations of social proximity, receiving stolen property, and prostitution (Kreuzer 1986b).

Family Situation and Partnership

Tables 10.1 and 10.2 depict the clients' family situation and partner living arrangements at the time of admission to the project. For both 1987 and

TABLE 10.1
Marital Status

	Outreach		Live-in		Work Projects		Total	
	1987 (257)	1988 (151)	1987 (68)	1988 (69)	1987 (99)	1988 (50)	1987 (424)	1988 (270)
Not married	72.8%	78.8%	79.4%	71.0%	72.7%	76.0%	73.8%	76.3%
Married	14.4%	11.9%	13.2%	15.9%	17.2%	10.0%	14.9%	12.6%
Divorced	12.5%	8.6%	7.4%	11.6%	9.1%	12.0%	10.8%	10.0%
Widowed	0.4%	0.7%	0.0%	1.5%	1.0%	2.0%	0.5%	1.1%
Total	100%	100%	100%	100%	100%	100%	100%	100%

TABLE 10.2
Partner Living Arrangements

	Outreach Projects		Live-in Projects		Work Projects		Total	
	1987 (258)	1988 (152)	1987 (68)	1988 (69)	1987 (99)	1988 (51)	1987 (425)	1988 (272)
Mainly single	57.0%	59.9%	66.2%	56.5%	60.6%	66.7%	59.3%	60.3%
Steady relationship	36.4%	33.6%	26.5%	42.0%	37.4%	29.4%	35.1%	34.9%
Unknown/No answer	6.6%	6.5%	1.4%	1.5%	2.0%	3.9%	5.6%	4.8%
Total	100%	100%	100%	100%	100%	100%	100%	100%

1988 some three-quarters of the male and female clients were single and about one-third had a permanent partner. These results correspond closely to other findings in the literature. In the various studies (Berger et al. 1980; Kreuzer et al. 1981; Projektgruppe TUdrop 1984) that describe the addicts' way of life—the overwhelming majority of those questioned are single. These data correspond to the high quota of those mainly living alone. Here the sample of heroin dependents differs from the overall picture of the so-called normal population and contrasts with relevant data on results of investigations into alcoholism (Küfner et al. 1986). In this instance the quota of those married was 55%, some 19% were divorced, and 25% were single.

Education

Sixty percent of the clients in the project had no higher than secondary school education. This figure is below the German national average and documents a trend noted in other studies of the German heroin scene (Kreuzer et al. 1981; Skarabis and Patzack 1981; Projektgruppe TUdrop 1984). This contrasts with findings reported by Platt and Labate (1976) for the educational levels of American drug users, which show a wider range of below average and above average educational levels. The underrepresentation of higher educational levels (vocational and high school) in the West German drug scene permits us to ask if the use of hard drugs leads to a new orientation of users by which higher education loses subjective relevance. Some interpretations impute that low educational attainments themselves lead to greater inclination to use illegal drugs. A third view stresses the consequences of illegality and the threat of penal sanctions. The social marginality and illegality characterizing the drug scene exposes users more intensely to penal sanctions and isolation. As a result, intended educational goals can no longer be realized.

Vocational Training

Table 10.3 depicts the results of the findings in this field. Notable here is the high proportion of male and female clients who had either not begun (about 22%) or had prematurely broken off vocational training (about 40%). This tendency corresponds to many other findings to date (Kreuzer et al. 1981). Here 80% of those questioned have begun some form of vocational training.

In the group of those questioned both with and without completed vo-

TABLE 10.3
Job Training and Apprenticeship

	Outreach		Live-in		Work Projects		Total	
	1987 (231)	1988 (146)	1987 (63)	1988 (60)	1987 (86)	1988 (51)	1987 (380)	1988 (257)
Apprenticeship or training scheme (not completed)	36.4%	40.4%	39.7%	25.0%	47.7%	52.9%	39.5%	39.3%
Apprenticeship or training scheme (completed)	36.4%	36.3%	36.5%	41.7%	26.7%	27.5%	34.2%	35.8%
University (no degree)	2.2%	2.7%	4.8%	5.0%	5.8%	2.0%	3.4%	3.1%
University graduate	0.0%	0.7%	0.0%	0.0%	0.0%	0.0%	0.0%	0.4%
No special training	25.1%	19.9%	19.0%	28.3%	19.8%	17.6%	22.9%	21.4%
Total	100%	100%	100%	100%	100%	100%	100%	100%

cational training, many attempts were made in a number of cases to complete training in various vocations. Sometimes up to five starts with vocational training were made. The investigations oriented to qualitative aspects demonstrate that a variously recurring motive for prematurely breaking off vocational training was related to an increasing incompatibility of drug consumption with the discipline of job requirements. Reference to an disproportionally high degree of unemployment among youth and the known difficulty of finding a place for vocational training is often regarded as a factor promoting the use of hard drugs or to a considerable degree as working in the direction of determining their use.

Social Origins

For a theory on the origins of addiction worthy of the name "social scientific," ascertaining connections with social factors assumes a high degree of relevance. There is, of course, nothing new in attempts to analyze individual characteristics (for example, drug use or dependence) in the context of social-structural variables. Studies of socialization in relation to social strata represent an analogy for this research strategy.

The question as to the social origin of drug dependence has been variously pursued in studies related to West Germany. Explicitly or implicitly this is often a matter of a variant of the so-called proletarian hypothesis, according to which drug use and drug dependence can either be assumed to be predominantly attributable to characteristics of the lower social strata or to those who approximate the features of the lower social strata. The much-discussed problem of the valid criteria for determining social strata is thematically relevant here (Oevermann et al. 1976; Müller 1978; Dahrendorf 1968; Geiger 1932). Even in view of the backdrop of the difficulties in determining valid criteria for differentiating social strata discussed in this literature, it would be a mistake not to pursue the question of classifying the social strata of drug dependents. Vocational status and respective main vocation of the clients' fathers is depicted in Table 10.4. In order to compare this data in the records of the German Federal Bureau of Statistics, a relatively simple model has been drawn up; it includes the categories blue-collar worker, white-collar worker, civil servant, local government official, and self-employed worker. For problems mentioned in this context it is obvious that only a crude approximation is possible here.

Table 10.4 demonstrates an unequivocal result regarding the issue of overrepresentation or underrepresentation of certain social strata. The samples in the categories white-collar worker and civil servant/local government official reveal parity with the German national average. Devia-

TABLE 10.4

**Main Occupation of Father (Guardian or Substitute Father)
up to Client's Completion of 18th Year of Age**

	Sample (1987 and 1988) (v = 406)	National Average*
Blue-collar worker	41.3%	48.7%
White-collar worker	26.8%	27.8%
Civil-servant / Local government official	12.6%	11.5%
Self-employed	17.5%	11.0%
Total	100.0%	100.0%

* Based on mean age of clients, 1978 has been taken as the year of reference.

tions can be observed in the samples, namely below the national average for blue-collar workers and above average for self-employed. The difference in each case is 6%. Based on the criterion occupation of father blue-collar worker there is no reason to confirm overrepresentation of members of the lower social strata, for in that case a higher share than the national average could be expected. (For the dichotomy blue-collar/not blue-collar worker cf. Uchtenhagen and Zimmer-Höfler 1985).

Family Origins

The background of family origins, including the milieu of origins and relevant modes of behavior or traits—in this case the use of heroin—is correlated with the dependents' educational attainment and experience during socialization. The so-called broken home is regularly stressed as a factor in the literature. The general characteristic of the associated formative milieu is that one parent is in general terms frequently or permanently absent. The family is then accordingly classified as structurally incomplete. The results of the evaluation of the samples presented here must be seen against this background, and they are summarized in Table 10.5. The table shows that barely more than 60% of those questioned grew up within a "complete family." These results confirm the relatively high quota of structural incompleteness already depicted in other studies.

The general problem emerging from the attempt to describe the conditions of socialization of heroin addicts or users turns on the need to bear in mind that the criterion "broken home" must be regarded as a

TABLE 10.5

Residence until 18th Birthday (Multiple responses possible)

	Outreach Projects		Live-in Projects		Work Projects		Total	
	1987	1988	1987	1988	1987	1988	1987	1988
One year or longer with relatives	10.7%	12.2%	13.1%	8.3%	5.8%	10.6%	9.9%	11.0%
Foster parents	7.0%	3.4%	6.6%	5.0%	5.8%	4.3%	6.6%	3.9%
Children's home	24.7%	17.0%	19.7%	18.3%	11.6%	12.8%	20.7%	16.5%
Adoptive parents	0.9%	0.0%	1.6%	1.7%	0.0%	2.1%	0.8%	0.8%
Mainly parents	61.4%	61.9%	52.5%	63.3%	73.3%	72.3%	62.7%	64.2%
Mainly one parent	19.5%	30.6%	34.4%	25.0%	15.1%	17.0%	21.0%	26.8%
Others	4.2%	6.1%	9.8%	6.7%	2.3%	4.3%	4.7%	5.9%
Total	(215)	(147)	(61)	(60)	(86)	(47)	(362)	(254)

TABLE 10.6

Heroin Use

	Outreach Projects		Live-in Projects		Work Projects		Total	
	1987	1988	1987	1988	1987	1988	1987	1988
Average period of consumption in years (mean)	8.3	7.3	9.2	7.7	6.9	7.2	8.2	7.4

somewhat superficial concept, mainly because it cannot appropriately reflect the pathogenetic potential in families. For example, the question is excluded as to, if at all (and if so how), functionally incomplete families can be properly conceived. Many investigations exclude the question whether substitute figures have played a significant role in "incomplete" families. However, a notable finding is that a relatively high quota of some 30% of female and male clients up to their eighteenth year grew up over a lengthy period in alien surroundings, that is, outside the milieu of parental socialization. This relatively high quota agrees with results obtained elsewhere (Projektgruppe TUdrop 1984; Uchtenhagen and Zimmer-Höfler 1985). For one control group a quota of formative development in so-called alien surroundings was ascertained at 1% and 2%.

DATA AND RESULTS ON CAREERS IN DRUGS

Use of Heroin

For this sample the duration of heroin use is presented in Table 10.6. The point of time taken as reference for heroin use was admittance to the care offered in one of the model projects. Only regular, dependent use of heroin was taken as a factor for ascertaining the mean length of use. Phases of abstinence, above all before, during, and after periods of therapeutic treatment, were not taken into account. Comparison with other investigations is restricted because in some studies, concepts such as "initial use of drugs" or "initial use of opiates" are used. This primarily means the initial use of heroin, which does not necessarily coincide with dependence on heroin. A period of a year or more can elapse between initial use and the onset of dependence. Similarily, in individual cases it cannot be determined how periods in penal institutions can be evaluated. They could have been spent in abstinence or with more or less regular use of heroin (Kreuzer et al. 1981).

Experience with the Treatment System

Drug-Counseling Centers

As a branch of the social services, drug-counseling centers pursue the manifold tasks of counseling young adults and their relatives on various problems and offering and obtaining help. Of the clients referred to in the documentation, approximately 90% had already had some contact with drug-counseling centers.

Residential Treatment

The share of patients admitted to residential treatment and who success-fully complete it according to plan varies between 30% and 50% (Hanel and Herbst 1988). The share of those who break off therapy prematurely contrasts greatly with institutions admitting alcoholics (Küfner et al. 1986). The figure for prematurely breaking off treatment in this case is 20%. But the 39-year mean age of alcohol addicts is well above the corresponding figure for drug addicts. Table 10.7 illustrates that for both years 60% of the clients have to date received residential treatment at least once. Notable here is that up to one-third of those questioned to date have never undergone therapy. If one compares the group with and without experience of residential treatment, a picture emerges which, con-trary to usual expectations (according to which the probability of having received residential treatment increases with age), the age of each group displays only a minor difference (26.6 versus 27.8). Consequently, the age factor alone can hardly be cogently related to the findings on therapy to date.

By contrast, there are significant differences between each group of clients with regard to the length of time of heroin consumption (8.4 years versus 6.5; $p = 0.001$) and the age at which consumption began (18.9 years of age versus 20.3; $P = 0.001$). Clients with at least one period of residential treatment have had on average a longer career with drugs and began using them at a younger age than other clients. The experience is also reflected here that, with an increasing length of a career in drugs, the probability also increases of having received residential treat-ment at least once. The difference between each group with regard to having served a period of detention is equally significant. Among those with experience in residential treatment, there is a significantly higher proportion who have been in detention at least once ($P = 0.025$).

Table 10.8 shows the amount of treatment of clients in residential therapy. There is a nearly steady slight rise in the average figures over these periods. The values obtained deviate only slightly from results ob-tained for two periods. However, the findings also show that some four or more periods of residential treatment are still by no means the rule for drug addicts.

Experience with Penal Institutions

Users of illegal drugs are equally exposed to criminalization and criminal prosecution in several ways. The actual use of illegal drugs is not an indictable offense in Germany. However, the general phrasing of the Ger-

TABLE 10.7

Previous Residential Treatment

	Outreach Projects		Live-in Projects		Work Projects		Total	
	1987 (259)	1988 (152)	1987 (71)	1988 (69)	1987 (99)	1988 (51)	1987 (429)	1988 (272)
Yes	58.0%	52.6%	55.0%	66.7%	68.7%	70.6%	59.9%	59.6%
No	30.1%	43.4%	23.9%	23.2%	21.2%	21.6%	27.0%	34.2%
Unknown / No Answer	11.9%	3.9%	21.1%	10.1%	10.1%	7.8%	13.1%	6.3%
Total	100%	100%	100%	100%	100%	100%	100%	100%

TABLE 10.8

Amount of Residential Treatment

	Outreach Projects		Live-in Projects		Work Projects		Total	
	1987	1988	1987	1988	1987	1988	1987	1988
Mean number of treatments	1.8	1.9	1.6	2.2	1.8	1.7	1.8	1.9

man law on narcotics, according to which possession of illegal drugs is a criminal offense, allows for the possibility of prosecution of those using them. Moreover, experience to date shows that some drug addicts themselves procure money needed for their own consumption of drugs by petty dealing in illegal drugs (Albrecht 1987; Kreuzer 1986a).

The negative consequences of criminalization of drug addicts in the Federal Republic of Germany have been variously assessed in the relevant studies (Kreuzer et al. 1981, Projektgruppe TUdrop 1984). Involvement with the police and trials for crimes or conviction have often served as the point of reference. This study assumed that the most relevant feature in this context for those concerned is the experience of being in detention and took this as a parameter for the degree of criminalization. Of those questioned some 51% had been in detention at least once. The average number of times in detentions was 2.4, and the average duration of detention was approximately 2.4 years.

The findings reveal clear differences in terms of sex and age. A relatively close correlation exists between the variable "age" and "frequency of detention" (Cramer's $V = 0.27$; $p = 0.004$). The results also show that females have proportionally less experience with detention or have served relatively shorter terms of detention. These data also document the relatively lower degree of criminalization of females in comparison to that of males discussed above.

The Problem of HIV

With regard to the issue of infection with HIV, drug addicts are often considered to be one of the main groups open to risk or one of the major groups already infected. Their share of actual infection with AIDS has risen steadily in West Germany over the past few years, increasing in 1988 from 7% to 11%. The findings for West Germany on the degree of infection with HIV among intravenous drug users vary greatly. According to present knowledge one can assume with a high degree of probability an overall rate of infection between 15% and 30% (Kleiber 1989; see also the chapter by Kleiber in this volume).

A year-by-year comparison of male and female clients tested for HIV shows strikingly that the quota of those testing positive has actually fallen (Table 10.9). At the least, widespread dissemination of the HIV virus among intravenous drug users cannot be proven by the results of these samples (Arnold and Frietsch 1988). To be sure, it must be borne in mind that they are based on a response rate of 55% to the question "HIV

TABLE 10.9

HIV-Test Results

	Outreach Projects		Live-in Projects		Work Projects		Total	
	1987 (143)	1988 (74)	1987 (48)	1988 (52)	1987 (31)	1988 (28)	1987 (222)	1988 (154)
Result "negative"	60.1%	75.7%	83.3%	76.9%	71.0%	57.1%	66.7%	72.7%
Result "positive"	31.5%	18.9%	10.4%	9.6%	22.6%	28.6%	25.7%	17.5%
Result not definite	0.7%	1.4%	2.1%	0.0%	0.0%	3.6%	0.9%	1.3%
Result unknown	7.7%	4.1%	4.2%	13.5%	6.5%	10.7%	6.8%	8.4%
Total	100%	100%	100%	100%	100%	100%	100%	100%

TABLE 10.10

Counseling Completed*

	Outreach Projects		Live-in Projects		Work Projects		Total	
	1987 (258)	1988 (305)	1987 (70)	1988 (101)	1987 (99)	1988 (102)	1987 (427)	1988 (508)
Yes	51.9%	59.7%	67.1%	68.3%	50.5%	35.6%	54.1%	56.5%
No	48.1%	40.3%	32.9%	31.7%	49.5%	64.4%	45.9%	43.5%
Total	100%	100%	100%	100%	100%	100%	100%	100%

* Because of the overlap of one year into the next, the figures of those counseled for the individual years are greater than the total sum of 701 for 1987 and 1988.

test, yes or no?" and on statements by the clients themselves (Friedman et al. 1988).

If one again compares the group of clients with and without experience of residential treatment, a highly significant difference emerges as to the question of tests conducted for HIV. Among those with residential treatment tested for HIV there is clearly a higher quota (63.2 versus 46.8; $p = 0.001$). This is almost certainly attributable to the fact that over the past few years HIV tests have become a rule with residential treatment before or directly after therapy starts. The quota of those with experience in residential treatment lies accordingly at 63.2% and those without residential treatment at 47%. By contrast, the differences in the reported results of the tests are not significant, which initially indicates that the rate of infection with HIV is evenly divided between the groups.

COUNSELING SITUATION

Table 10.10 depicts all clients counseled in both years. After the data on the situations of those counseled in 1987 had been completed on 31 December 1987, the same analysis was analogously carried out on 31 December 1988 for those counseled in 1988. The proportion of those who had already left the project at the end of the year has tended to rise slightly from 54% to 56%.

In Table 10.11 the group which has completed the counseling is differentiated in terms of reason for termination. Both years show that overall the highest proportion lies with those who completed the counseling "according to plan." A comparison between the years even shows an increase from 37.5% to 47.5%.

WAY OF LIFE AFTER COUNSELING

Of the total of 701 male and female clients counseled in both years, treatment was completed for 463 (66%) by 31 December 1988. At the time of sampling, 26.6% of those male and female clients were in residential treatment or in penal institutions. Eighty-five percent of this 26.6% of clients were counseled within the framework of the SLD project with a focus on outreach work. The following details refer to the remaining 73.4% of the male and female clients who when sampled were no longer being counseled. The variables selected to depict the way of life after completion of counseling are those related to being "clean," the social environment, and work.

TABLE 10.11

Reasons for Termination of Counseling (Multiple responses possible)

	Outreach		Live-in		Work Projects		Total	
	1987	*1988*	*1987*	*1988*	*1987*	*1988*	*1987*	*1988*
Scheduled termination	41.5%	51.4%	36.2%	41.2%	28.0%	40.0%	37.5%	47.5%
Violations of regulations	3.0%	1.1%	40.4%	45.6%	40.0%	51.4%	18.5%	18.1%
No contact over a longer period of time	23.0%	32.4%	2.1%	1.5%	4.0%	0.0%	14.7%	20.9%
Referral to other institutions	45.2%	38.0%	17.0%	5.9%	8.0%	5.7%	31.5%	26.2%
Other	33.3%	21.2%	27.7%	19.1%	46.0%	20.0%	34.9%	20.6%
Total *N*	(135)	(179)	(47)	(68)	(50)	(35)	(232)	(282)

Of those clients no longer counseled, 42.5% were reported to be "clean"; 22.6% used drugs occasionally, and 34.9% showed renewed or continuing drug addiction; 34.9% of the male and female clients reported that the drug scene was predominately or exclusively their social field of activity. Thirty-three percent reported living in a social environment free of drugs and 32.1% reported living in a mixed form of these social environments. For the third variable, results shows that 50.3% were either at school or in vocational training or had permanent or part-time jobs; 46.2% were unemployed.

The mean length of time since completion of counseling was 11 months. Comparison of the results of the follow-up investigations to the pilot project with the findings in the literature, especially the studies on the outcome of treatment (Raschke et al. 1985), shows some differences from the results mentioned above. In this study the quota of clients who had been "clean" is 44%, 47% were living in a social environment free of drugs, and 64% had an occupation or were in vocational training. But the average period of time of 6 years since release from residential treatment was notably higher than the average 11 months of this study.

CONCLUSIONS

In summary, one can state that the framework of the SLD project makes it possible to gain access to a specific group of drug addicts who differ from others in certain social parameters such as age, length of period of drug use, time spent in penal institutions, education, and vocational background. The typical SLD client is 28 years old and first used heroin at the age of 19. Consumption of heroin stretches over a period of about 8 years. The client has undergone residential treatment once or twice and has spent about 30 months in penal institutions. There is no conclusive evidence of affiliation to a social class. Educational and vocational accomplishments are well below the national average. The HIV-infection rate is 19%, which is surprisingly low for this social group. The client is likely to have been socialized in an "incomplete" family, and to have experienced periods of long-term unemployment.

The social workers involved in SLD manage to establish contact with a group of clients, who, for various reasons, turn away from traditional institutions. In many instances they succeed in convincing drug addicts that adequate treatment and facilities are helpful and available. The manifold negative social repercussions of the "drug problem" need to be countered by the effective support of the responsible authorities. The

158   Drug Addiction Treatment Research

dedication of social workers and the willingness of drug addicts to become "clean" must be supported by imaginative projects such as SLD.

REFERENCES

Albrecht, H. J. (1987). Drogenpolitik und Drogenstrafrecht. *Bewährungshilfe* 34(3): 267–79.

Arnold, T., and Frietsch, R. (1988). Aids-Problematik und Drogengebrauch— Zur Sichtweise der betroffenen Drogenkonsumenten. *Suchtgefahren* 34: 303–15.

Arnold, T., Frietsch, R., and Korndorfer, G. (1989). Erfahrungen mit bisherigen niederschwelligen Angeboten für langjährig Drogenabhängige. *Suchtgefahren* 35: 120–24.

Berger, H., Reuband, K. H., and Widlitzek, U. (1980). *Wege in die Heroinabhängigkeit. Zur Entwicklung abweichender Karrieren.* München: Juventa.

Dahrendorf, R. (1968). *Gesellschaft und Demokratie in Deutschland.* München: Piper.

Drogenhilfe Tübingen (1989). *Tätigkeitsbericht 1988.* Tübingen: Drogenhilfe Tübingen.

Friedmann et al. (1988). Biological validation of self-reported AIDS risk reduction among New York City intravenous drug users. *Annals of the New York Academy of Sciences* 529: 257–59.

Geiger, T. (1932). *Die soziale Schichtung des deutschen Volkes.* Stuttgard: Enke.

Gerdes, K. H., and Wolffersdorff-Ehlert, V. (1974). *Drogenszene, Suche nach Gegenwart.* Stuttgart: Enke.

Hanel, E., and Herbst, K. (1988). Beschreibung und erste Ergebnisse einer prospektiven Studie zur stationären Behandlung von Drogenabhängigen. *Suchtgefahren* 34: 1–21.

Kleiber, D. (1989). HIV-Infektion bei i.v. Drogenabhängigen in der Bundesrepublik. Unpublished manuscript.

Kreuzer, A., Gebhardt, C., Maasen, M., and Stein-Hilbers, M. (1981). *Drogenabhängigkeit und Koutrolle.* Wiesbaden: BKA-Forschungsreihe 14.

Kreuzer, A. (1986a). Kriminologische Grundpositionen einer Drogenpolitik. *Bewährungshilfe* 33(4): 395–409.

Kreuzer, A. (1986b). Cherchez la femme?. In *Gedächtnisschrift für Hilde Kaufmann*, H. J. Hirsch, G. Kaiser, H. Marquardt (eds.). Berlin, New York: DeGruyter.

Küfner, H., Feuerlein, W., and Florschütz, T. H. (1986). Die stationäre Behandlung von Alkoholabhängigen: Merkmale von Patienten und Behandlungseinrichtungen, Katamnestische Ergebnisse. *Suchtgefahren* 32: 1–86.

Ladewig, D., and Graw, P. (1985). Entwicklungschancen Drogenabhängiger. Weinheim: Beltz.

Müller, W. (1978). Der Lebenslauf von Geburtskohorten. In *Soziologie des Lebenslaufs*, Kohli, M. (ed.). Darmstadt: Luchterhand.

Oevermann, V. et al. (1976). Die sozialstrukturelle Einbettung vonj Sozialisationsprozessen: Empirische Ergebnisse zur Ausdifferenzierung des globalen Zusammenhangs von Schichtzugehörigkeit und gemessener Intelligenz sowie Schulerfolg. *Zeitschrift für Soziologie* 5(2): 167–99.

Platt, J. J., and Labate, C. (1976). *Heroin Addiction.* New York: Wiley.

Projektgruppe TUdrop (1984). *Heroinabhängigkeit unbetreuter Jugendlicher.* Weinheim: Beltz.

Raschke, P. et al. (1985). *Therapie und Rehabilitation bei Drogenkonsumenten. Langzeitstudie am Beispiel des Hammer Modells.* Düsseldorf. Ministerium für Arbeit, Gesundheitand Soziales des Landes Nordrhein-Westfalen.

Skarabis, H., and Patzack, M. (1981). *Die Berliner Heroinszene.* Weinheim: Beltz.

Uchtenhagen, A., and Zimmer-Höfler, D. (1985). *Heroinabhängige und ihre "normalen" Altersgenossen.* Bern, Stuttgart: Haupt.

PART FOUR

Addiction Careers and Process of Treatment

CHAPTER 11

Development of Dependence and Dopaminergic Mechanisms

Ursula Havemann-Reinecke and Klaus Kuschinsky*

INTRODUCTION

Dopamine is a catecholamine and functions as a neurotransmitter in the brain. In comparison with other neurotransmitter systems that are widespread in the brain (e.g., noradrenaline and serotonin), its distribution is more limited to distinct areas. Most pathways containing dopamine originate in the mesencephalon and terminate in the basal ganglia. The largest dopaminergic pathway, the nigro-striatal pathway, originates in the substantia nigra and leads to the striatum (Figure 11.1). There are other pathways, somewhat parallel to this pathway, that originate in the ventral tegmental area of the mesencephalon and end in nucleus accumbens, tuberculum olfactorium, septum, or amygdala (the mesolimbic pathway) or in several cortical areas (e.g., the frontal cortex, entorhinal cortex, cingulate cortex), the mesocortical pathway (see Ungerstedt 1971 and Lane et al. 1983). These pathways were extensively studied in the rat brain, but almost identical pathways exist in the human brain as well.

Dopamine in the nigrostriatal pathway plays an important role in the performance of voluntary movements, whereas that in the mesolimbic (and perhaps also the mesocortical) pathway seems relevant in motivation and positive reinforcement (see Havemann and Kuschinsky 1982;

*The studies of K. K. were supported by grants of the Deutsche Forschungsgemeinschaft. The studies of U. H. were performed in the Max-Planck Institute for Experimental Medicine, D-3400 Göttingen, F.R.G.

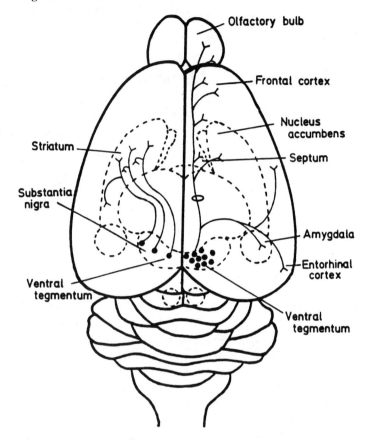

FIGURE 11.1.
Scheme of nigrostriatal dopaminergic pathways (left side) originating mainly in the substantia nigra and ending in the striatum. The mesolimbic dopaminergic pathways (right side) originate in the ventral tegmental area and end in nucleus accumbens, amygdala, septum, frontal cortex, and entorhinal cortex.

Wise 1987). There is increasing evidence that an enhancement in dopaminergic neurotransmission produced by drugs can lead to addiction and psychic dependence: opioids, cocaine, amphetaminelike drugs, nicotine and, at least in part, ethanol seem to act in this way (DiChiara and Imperato 1988). These drugs are either prototypes of central stimulants (cocaine, amphetamine) or they produce a mixture of stimulant and depressant effects (opioids, nicotine, ethanol). Whether addictive drugs with merely depressant actions (e.g., benzodiazepines) also enhance dopaminergic neurotransmission is as yet unsettled.

ANIMAL MODELS

There are various animal models that enable us to predict, with at least high probability, whether a drug has addictive properties in humans. Rats can be used in models that seem to be important in evaluating the neuronal mechanisms responsible for the formation of addicted behavior and thus of psychic dependence. Self-administration of the drug via an implanted cannula can be used as a tool in this respect: Rats show a high tendency to self-administer drugs that are addictive in humans (Weeks 1962; Yokel 1987). Another animal model is the conditioned place preference: When rats are repeatedly treated with the drug and subsequently put into a certain place, they ultimately prefer this place when given the choice (Bozarth 1987; Phillips and Fibiger 1987). Both animal models strongly suggest that dopaminergic mechanisms are of crucial importance for the addictive properties of the drugs mentioned above (Bozarth 1983). A third model involves electrical self-stimulation via an implanted electrode located in certain brain areas; some areas are coincident with dopaminergic pathways, others are not (Reid 1987). The self-stimulation can be so pronounced that the animals neglect any other requirements of the organism (e.g., fluid intake). Similarly, rats can self-administer some drugs (e.g., central stimulants) in lethal doses. These aspects closely resemble some self-destructive aspects of drug-taking behavior in humans.

We would like to present some of our own studies that deal with aspects that are probably also relevant to analysis of the addictive properties of drugs. Experiments concerning individual differences in the reaction of rats to drugs that enhance dopaminergic activity (Havemann et al. 1986) are of particular interest.

Apomorphine is a drug that directly activates dopamine receptors. In humans it has emetic effects, at least in larger doses, whereas in rats (which have no brain center for emesis) it produces locomotor activation and stereotyped sniffing, and, after increasing doses, licking and gnawing. All these effects are induced by activation of postsynaptically located dopamine receptors. The pattern of behavior produced by the drug is in part dependent on the test environment and the dosage. In general, however, the striatum seems more important for licking and gnawing responses, the regions innervated by the mesolimbic dopaminergic pathways for locomotor activation and sniffing (Ungerstedt 1979). An interesting apparent result is that a test dose of apomorphine (2 mg/kg s.c.) produces mainly sniffing and increased locomotor activity in some rats (well reproducible in another test), whereas it induces a licking, and in part gnawing reaction, with significantly less locomotor activation, in other rats under the same experimental conditions. It seems likely that sniffing animals are less sensitive to dopaminergic stimulation and might have a different balance between the nigrostriatal and the mesolimbic system after dopaminergic stimulation than do "licking and gnawing" rats.

This conclusion is supported by a later series of experiments (Havemann 1988) in which rats pretested with apomorphine as described above were then repeatedly treated with a large dose of morphine (15 mg/kg). First administration of this dose produces akinesia (stop of motility) and muscular rigidity, followed by signs of dopaminergic activation (stereotypies and locomotor activation). After repeated administration of apomorphine, the signs of dopaminergic activation (locomotor activation, sniffing, licking, gnawing) predominate more and more. Animals classified as "sniffing rats" by the apomorphine test showed little tolerance for the akinetic and rigidity-producing effects of morphine, in contrast to the gnawing rats that demonstrated a clear tolerance to the akinetic and rigidity-producing effects. Furthermore, animals classified as "sniffing rats" after apomorphine showed sniffing also after repeated morphine administration, whereas rats classified as gnawing mainly showed gnawing reactions after morphine. Obviously, the rats that were less sensitive to dopaminergic stimulation, the sniffing rats, were also less sensitive to the effects of morphine and showed less dependence on the opioid. These remarkable results might present a model for individual differences in liability to drug addiction as suggested by differences in reaction to dopaminergic stimulation.

Another kind of phenomenon, conditioning, seems to be relevant for the development of drug addiction and psychic dependence. It is well known that a former "fixer" who has been drug free for a long time feels a strong craving for the drug or even withdrawal signs when he is reexposed to stimuli previously associated with the drug effect (Wikler 1980). Similar phenomena can be observed and quantified in animals, and it was reported by several groups that behavioral effects of cocaine, amphetamine, and morphine can be conditioned: When the animals are repeatedly treated with the drug and, during the onset of the drug effect, exposed to well-defined environmental stimuli (conditioned stimuli), the appearance of these stimuli alone leads to conditioned responses similar to the pharmacological (unconditioned) responses (Barr et al. 1983; Ellinwood 1971; Schiff 1982).

It was the goal of some of our own experiments to study the relationship between conditioned and unconditioned (pharmacological) drug effects in more detail. Therefore, a number of conditioning experiments were performed using the protocol in Table 11.1. *Conditioned* rats were treated with the drug in association with the test cage and various defined stimuli (auditory, olfactory, tactile), and with inert solvent in association

TABLE 11.1

Conditioning Scheme

	Conditioning Period	Test Day
Naive Rats	Solvent + Home Cage Solvent + Test Cage	Drug or + Test Cage Solvent
Pseudoconditioned Rats	Drug + Home Cage Solvent + Test Cage	Drug or + Test Cage Solvent
Conditioned Rats	Solvent + Home Cage Drug + Test Cage	Drug or + Test Cage Solvent

with the home cage. *Pseudoconditioned* animals were treated with the drug in association with the home cage and with solvent in association with the test cage. Accordingly, both groups of rats underwent the same number of exposures to drug and environmental stimuli, but only in the conditioned rats was a positive association formed between both. *Drug-naive* rats were always treated with solvent, but exposed to the stimuli (test cage) with the same frequency as both other groups.

The conditioned stereotypies produced by apomorphine (sniffing, licking, and gnawing) were manifest and relatively long lasting when the conditioned rats were exposed to the conditioned stimuli alone (a combination of auditory, olfactory, and tactile stimuli), with the drug. The pseudoconditioned rats showed practically no response (Möller et al. 1987). Similarly, nicotine-induced behavioral effects, the locomotor activation and stereotyped sniffing, could also be conditioned (Walter and Kuschinsky 1989).

DISCUSSION

There is much evidence that the stereotypies described are induced in the terminal regions of the dopaminergic neurones in the basal ganglia (Figure 11.1). The stimuli mediating the pharmacological effects (via the dopaminergic pathways) and those mediating the conditioned stimuli (probably via corticostriatal pathways, or by thalamostriatal, possibly cholinergic, pathways) might converge in the striatum and the adjacent nucleus accumbens and eventually form neuronal associations (Figure 11.2). Beyond the site of convergence, the same neuronal pathways are likely to be activated both by pharmacological and conditioned responses. Due to this convergence, the activation of dopaminergic systems by drugs seems to be positively reinforcing and rewarding, and the manifestation of conditioned responses may be rewarding as well, although to a smaller degree. A small dose of a reinforcing drug often leads to the urgent need to consume more of the drug. This is a priming effect which seems to be dopamine dependent. A similar priming effect might be induced by the conditioned responses and might lead to another cycle of drug intake.

It seems likely that the various phenomena described above that contribute to "psychic dependence" are more relevant in the complex phenomenon of drug addiction than is physical dependence. This assumption is supported by the following facts: First, some drugs, like cocaine and amphetamine, produce little physical dependence but have a strong likelyhood for addiction; second, patients who are free of the drug for a long period of time and have no more withdrawal signs are nevertheless threatened by a great risk of relapse, suggesting that something other than

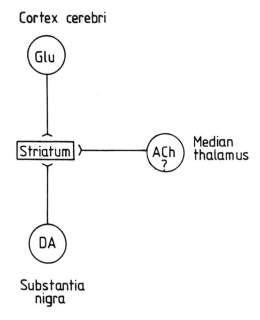

FIGURE 11.2.
Hypothesis about the pathways that may be involved in conditioning of dopaminergic drug effects. The dopaminergic nigrostriatal pathways mediating the unconditioned, pharmacological effects, and the corticostriatal pathways, with glutamate as a transmitter, mediating the conditioned responses converge in the striatum and form associations there. Additional pathways that may mediate conditioned responses are the thalamostriatal pathways, which probably have acetylcholine as neurotransmitter.

physical dependence must be the main factor in drug addiction. It seems reasonable to assume that some important phenomena contributing to drug addiction can be studied in animal experiments. Animal experiments are doubtless necessary for finding effective pharmacological and non-pharmacological therapies for drug addiction. Only close interaction and cooperation among clinicians, psychologists, epidemiologists, and experimental pharmacologists can lead to a solution to the problem of drug addiction.

REFERENCES

Barr, G. A., Sharpless, N. S., Cooper, S., Schiff, S. R., Paredes, W., and Bridger, W. H. (1983). Classical conditioning, decay and extinction of cocaine-induced hyperactivity and stereotypy. *Life Sci.* 33: 1341–51.

Bozarth, M. A. (1983). Opiate reward mechanisms mapped by intracranial self-administration. In *The Neurobiology of Opiate Reward Processes*. J. E. Smith and J. Lane (eds.), pp. 331–59. Amsterdam: Elsevier Biomedical Press.

Bozarth, M. A. (1987). Conditioned place preference: A parametric analysis using systemic heroin injections. In *Methods of Assessing the Reinforcing Properties of Abused Drugs*, M. A. Bozarth (ed.), pp. 241–73. New York: Springer-Verlag.

DiChiara, G., and Imperato, A. (1988). Drugs abused by humans preferentially increase synaptic dopamine concentrations in the mesolimbic system of freely moving rats. *Proc. Natl. Acad. Sci. USA* 85: 5274–78.

Ellinwood, E. N., Jr. (1971). Accidental conditioning with chronic methamphetamine intoxication: Implications for a theory of drug habituation. *Psychopharmacol* 21: 131–38.

Havemann, U. (1988). Does individually different sensitivity to dopaminergic stimulation determine the degree of tolerance and dependence to opioids? *Pharmacopsychiatry* 21: 314–16.

Havemann, U., and Kuschinsky, K. (1982). Neurochemical aspects of the opioid-induced "catatonia." *Neurochem. Internat.* 4: 199–215.

Havemann, U., Magnus, B., Möller, H.-G., and Kuschinsky, K. (1986). Individual and morphological differences in the behavioural response to apomorphine in rats. *Psychopharmacol.* 90: 40–48.

Lane, J. D., Smith, J. E., and Fagg, G. E. (1983). The origin and termination of neuronal pathways in mammalian brain and their putative neurohumors. In *The NeuroBiology of Opiate Reward Processes*, J. E. Smith and J. D. Lane (eds.), pp. 3–58. Amsterdam: Elsevier Biomedical Press.

Möller, H.-G., Nowak, K., and Kuschinsky, K. (1987). Conditioning of pre- and postsynaptic behavioural responses to the dopamine receptor against apomorphine in rats. *Psychopharmacol.* 91: 50–55.

Phillips, A. G., and Fibiger, H. C. (1987). Anatomical and neurochemical substrates of drug reward determined by the conditioned place preference technique. In *Methods of Assessing the Reinforcing Properties of Abused Drugs*, M. A. Bozarth (ed.), pp. 275–90. New York: Springer-Verlag.

Reid, L. D. (1987). Tests involving pressing for intracranial stimulation as an early procedure for screening likelihood of addiction of opioids and other drugs. In *Methods of Assessing the Reinforcing Properties of Abused Drugs*, M. A. Bozarth (ed.), pp. 391–420. New York: Springer-Verlag.

Schiff, S. R. (1982). Conditioned dopaminergic activity. *Biol. Psychiatry* 17: 135–54.

Ungerstedt, U. (1971). Stereotaxic mapping of the monoamine pathways in the rat brain. *Acta Physiol. Scand.* Suppl. 367; 1–48.

———. (1979). Central dopamine mechanisms and unconditioned behaviour. In *The Neurobiology of Dopamine*, A. S. Horn, J. Korf, and B. H. C. Westerink (eds.), pp. 577–96. London: Academic Press.

Walter, S., and Kuschinsky, K. (1989). Conditioning of nicotine effects on motility and behaviour in rats. Naunyn-Schmiedeberg's *Arch. Pharmacol.* 339: 208–13.

Weeks, J. R. (1962). Experimental morphine addiction: Method for automatic intravenous injections in unrestrained rats. *Science* 138: 143–44.

Wikler, A. (1980). *Opioid Dependence.* New York and London: Plenum Press.

Wise, R. (1987). The role of reward pathways in the development of drug dependence. *Pharmacol. Therap.* 35: 227–63.

Yokel, R. A. (1987). Intravenous self-administration: response rates, the effects of pharmacological challenges, and drug preference. In *Methods of assessing the reinforcing properties of abused drugs.* M. A. Bozarth (ed.), pp. 1–33. New York: Springer-Verlag.

CHAPTER 12

Recovery from Opiate Addiction: A Longitudinal Prospective Study

Richard Sickinger and Walter Kindermann

INTRODUCTION

Public opinion regarding the chances drug addicts have for terminating their drug careers is usually negative, especially in cases of heroin addiction. Statements such as "Once an addict, always an addict" or "They have no chance to quit using drugs" are frequently heard. This attitude is because the media often report only the negative view of the addicts' prospects. Additionally, the generally pessimistic attitude toward recovery from opiate addiction in Germany stems from a lack of research on this issue. Studies that emphasize the social resources and personal competences addicts have, even during the addiction period, are very rare. Even many treatment facility staff members are pessimistic regarding recovery because they most often are confronted with clients who relapse after treatment rather than those who successfully stay clean; the same experience holds true for judges, policemen, street workers, and others. In order to determine whether a more optimistic point of view of addiction recovery is justified, a longitudinal prospective study with drug addicts was initiated. Two studies that were conducted in Berlin provide part of the historical background for the AMSEL Study (Ambulante Therapie und Selbstheilung):

1. In 1979/80 the TUdrop Study interviewed over 500 addicts who had to that point not been treated through any help system. The study

tried to answer the question "What is the profile of the heroin addict today [1979/80]?" (Projektgruppe TUdrop 1984).

2. Once this study was completed, the same research group began a longitudinal prospective study in 1981 in order to answer the question "How do adolescents become addicts?" (Silbereisen and Eyferth 1983).

The recent AMSEL Study tries to answer the question: "What happens to a group of drug addicts with whom we have contact over a long period of time?" (Kindermann et al. 1989). In German-speaking areas three research strategies have been used to answer this question: (1) studies of criminal files (Lange 1986), (2) follow-up studies of clients after treatment (Raschke and Schliehe 1985; Stosberg et al. 1985; Uchtenhagen and Zimmer-Höfler 1985), and (3) single case follow-ups. The first two research strategies have the drawback that documentation of the process of cessation of drug taking is difficult; and the third strategy does not obtain results that can be generalized for a greater group of addicts.

In order to avoid such difficulties we chose the research strategy of a longitudinal prospective study. The main objective of this study is to document prospectively the process of recovery and to answer such questions as "What helps and what hinders an addict's recovery from drug dependency? How many of a known group of addicts will terminate their drug careers? What are the influences of residential and outpatient treatment settings? What is the impact of the "double-bind situation," wherein drug addicts sometimes are treated arbitrarily as sick persons, sometimes as criminals?"

THEORETICAL CONCEPT

The underlying theoretical concept of the study is based on a developmental psychology perspective of how drug abuse begins, the course of the drug career itself, and the chances of terminating the drug dependency. The key words of this theoretical approach are *developmental tasks* (Havighurst 1972; Newman and Newman 1979; Oerter 1978), *critical life events* (Filipp 1981), *coping strategies* (Lazarus 1966, 1981), and *social support*. Adolescents must cope with a series of demands resulting from the physical, social, and individual changes they experience in the process of growing up. Some classic examples of the developmental tasks adolescents face are:

• learning to accept their bodies
• learning their gender-role identity

- achieving emotional autonomy from their parents
- obtaining an accepted position in a peer group
- preparing for a job/career
- establishing a satisfying sexual relationship

During this difficult time some adolescents try to cope with problems by using drugs in order to "soften" or moderate their intensity (Labouvie 1980) without solving the developmental tasks. Therefore drug addicts are largely people with many unresolved developmental tasks, and the life as an addict does not support the process of solving these tasks. We assume that termination of the drug career is more likely or could be managed more easily if the addict has the chance to cope with these unresolved developmental tasks and finally solve them. Professional help, either on a residential or outpatient basis, provided the addict with one means of social support, in addition to others (e.g., peer integration or support resulting from establishing an intimate relationship, which is important for solving the "missed" developmental aims).

METHOD

Sample Selection

From mid-1985 to mid-1986 we interviewed 324 drug addicts in a variety of living circumstances that are typical for drug addicts: residential treatment center (58.4%), prison (13.9%), psychiatric or general hospital (2.1%), the drug scene and streets (15.1%), and outpatient treatment center (10.5%). Because the characteristics of the addict population are not fully known, we tried to obtain a sample with an optimal allocation. The sample is perhaps not representative, but very typical for attainable drug addicts in the Frankfurt area in 1985 and 1986. In order to explore the process of termination of the drug career, we looked for a sample with a longer lasting drug history. Therefore addicts we reached for initial interviews in institutions are overrepresented. But we consider the institutions as a "sluice," where the addicts were more accessible for us at a certain time. We assumed that the place of the initial interview within a certain limit could be at choice, because the addicts at other times also live at different places before and after coming through the sluice (Figure 12.1).

The study is based on personal, tape-recorded, unpaid interviews with each addict every year over a period of four years (1985/86–1989/90). We tried to conduct five personal interviews with each participant until the end of the study. These included an initial interview dealing with the

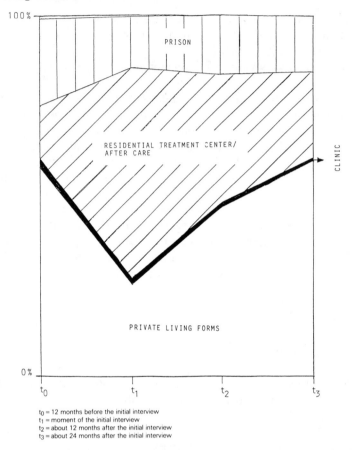

FIGURE 12.1.
Dominant life situations of the interviewed addicts at specific times

client's biography, three follow-ups, and one closing interview. The interview, a combination of standardized and open-ended questions, created an atmosphere similar to that of a conversation with "a good friend." Each interview lasted from 1 1/2 to 3 hours. This interview style allowed us to make both quantitative and qualitative assessments.

Subjects

Of the 324 interviewed drug addicts, 26.2% (85) are women; 91.4% had used heroin, 90.4% cocaine, and almost all cannabis, alcohol, and nicotine. For 84.6% heroin was the primary drug of abuse. The average age at the time of the first interview was 26.2 years. The first cannabis use was 11.6 and the first heroin use 7.9 years before the first interview. In the sample 64.8% had been in prison at least once; the average time spent in prison was 27 months; 14.2% (46) thus far had had no contact with a residential treatment center; 26% (84) had more than two admissions, and the average admission rate was 1.9. The seropositive rate among the 248 addicts tested for HIV antibodies, and whose primary drug of abuse was heroin, is 27.4% (68).

RESULTS

Because the study is still in progress, we cannot make any final assessments regarding the termination of a drug career. The data we present relate only to the 274 addicts whose primary drug of abuse is heroin, and we can describe the personal and social development of the interviewed drug addicts in the last three years. These first results revealed changes and shifts within the sample concerning: drug use, circle of friends, employment, and intimate friendships.

The data are based on the three personal interviews we conducted within the last two years. For those we could not reach for each follow-up interview, we collected additional information from friends, family members, or social workers, so that we had basic information about the life paths of about 80% of the sample two years after the initial interview.

Drug Use and Drug-Related Contacts

When we analyze the drug-use history of the interviewed addicts before the initial interview, we find that at no time was the entire sample addicted to drugs. The intensity of drug use ranged from no drug use to daily heroin use. About two-thirds of the interviewed addicts reported drug-free time periods within their drug careers outside of institutions (e.g., treatment centers, prisons) lasting twenty-six weeks (Kindermann et al. 1989). The data of the drug use of the 274 heroin addicts two years after the initial interview do not justify the assumption that drug-free participants are currently on their way to terminating their drug careers. Nevertheless, it is surprising that 50% (137) of the former heroin addicts were not addicted to any drug at the time of the third interview (Figure 12.2).

Any drug-free period could lead to a longer lasting period. All drug-free periods are, at the least, important preconditions for preparing the addict

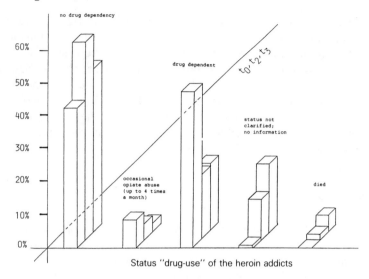

t_0 = 12 months before the initial interview
t_2 = about 12 months after the initial interview
t_3 = about 24 months after the initial interview

FIGURE 12.2.
Drug-use of heroin addicts at various times

for changes in other life areas. The data concerning reduced drug use correspond to changes in social contacts. Integration within conventional groups/friendships (drug-free social contacts) versus nonconventional groups/friendships (drug scene/street contacts) increased in the last three years: About 75% were more integrated in the drug scene one year before the initial interview in contrast to two years after the initial interview when it was just the opposite: 75% were more integrated in conventional groups/friendships (Figure 12.3). This means that they had more social contacts with persons who did not belong to the drug scene and did not use illegal drugs. These data related only to participants who lived outside of institutions (treatment centers, clinics, prisons) at the different times of the interviews.

We can see the same development when we look at the data concerning intimate friendships/sexual relationships. The relationships with drug-free intimate friends increased during the last three years from 24.8% (68) to 53% (80), while the relationships with persons who abused drugs decreased from 34.6% (95) to 7.3% (11) (Figure 12.4). It is a remarkable change, even when one considers that the case number also decreased (the data relate only to interviewed persons).

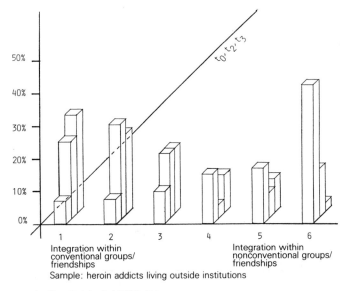

Integration within
conventional groups/
friendships

Integration within
nonconventional groups/
friendships

Sample: heroin addicts living outside institutions

t_0 = 12 months before the initial interview
t_2 = about 12 months after the initial interview
t_3 = about 24 months after the initial interview

FIGURE 12.3.
**Integration within conventional groups/friendships versus nonconventional
groups/friendships at various times (Sample: heroin addicts living outside institutions)**

Work

Changes concerning the employment status or the addicts' participation
in school/training programs are only visible for a small part of the sample. The number of unemployed persons not in school or in a training
program decreased from 39.3% (108) to 24.8%. The number of persons
who were employed full-time or who were attending school/training programs increased from 19.5% to 27.4% (Figure 12.5). When we take
into consideration that those 17.1% from whom we could not get any
information are more likely to be unemployed and still addicted
(because we could reach those who were drug free more easily for a
personal interview), the employment status of the sample is not very
encouraging.

The generally difficult situation in the job market also influences the
rehabilitation process. More participants are in school or training programs than are employed. This could imply that they first try to obtain
better job qualifications in order to improve their chances in the job
market later. We assume that changes within the sample in the different

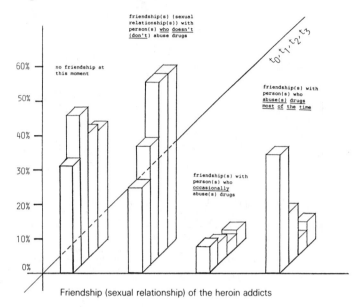

FIGURE 12.4.
Friendships (sexual relationships) of heroin addicts at various times

life areas are likely related to improvements in the process of solving some of the heretofore unsolved developmental tasks. Our hypothesis is that a basic condition for the termination of one's drug career is an improvement in this process and that this progress is linked to substantial changes in the way they cope with problems that occur in their relations with friends or employers. Thus far, we found some evidence for this hypothesis, but further, detailed analysis of the different coping strategies of different groups of addicts (drug free versus addicted) must be conducted at the end of the study.

Drug Use, Prison, and Treatment

Currently in the study the development of a nearly representative part (n=62) of the total sample gives us some ideas for the next steps in the assessments. When we divide the sample according to developments in

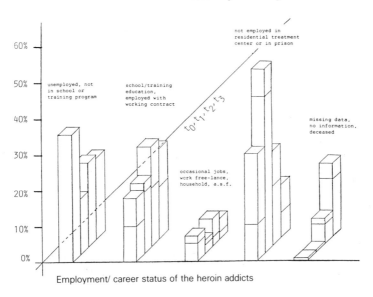

Employment/ career status of the heroin addicts

t_0 = 12 months before the initial interview
t_1 = month of the initial interview
t_2 = about 12 months after the initial interview
t_3 = about 24 months after the initial interview

FIGURE 12.5.
Employment/career status of heroin addicts at various times

the last two years into four different groups, and compare those relating to some important variables, we found several interesting results that must be considered when we discuss chances for cessation of drug dependency. In Table 12.1 Groups 1 and 2 differ from Groups 3 and 4 significantly in "duration of drug-dependency" (p = 000). The drug career of those who are still addicted lasts 12.7 years, more than 5 years longer than those who lived 2 years without drug dependency after the initial interview. Only Group 1 differs significantly in age from Group 4 (p = .05). Furthermore, Groups 1 and 2 are significantly different from Group 3 in terms of "age at the beginning of drug-dependency." Though many other factors could be responsible for the "drug status" at the third interview, it seems that those study participants with a relatively short time of drug dependency who were over twenty-one years old when they started to become addicted are more likely to live without drug dependency 2 years after the initial interview.

Furthermore, Groups 1 and 2 differ significantly from Group 4 (p = .0015) on the measure "planned residential treatment discharge."

TABLE 12.1

Drug Use, Prison, and Employment (Means)

(n = 18, 14, 22, 14)

	Age at the third interview (yrs.)	Age at the beginning of drug-dependency (yrs.)	Duration of drug dependency (yrs.)	Time in prison (mths.)	Planned discharge from at least one residential treatment program (%)	Duration of residential treatment (weeks)
Group 1	28.4	21.6	6.8	15.5	61.1	55
Group 2	29.4	22.2	7.2	17.8 (median: 4)	64.3	77
Group 3	30.1	17.4	12.7	28.9 (median: 20)	36.7	50
Group 4	32.2	19.7	12.5	29.4 (median: 24)	14.3	29

Group 1: No problematic drug use since the initial interview
Group 2: No problematic drug use at the time of the interview
Group 3: Drug-dependent or in prison or treatment
Group 4: Deceased participants (This group includes all deceased participants from the complete sample.)

More than 60% of those who are drug free had a planned discharge at least once from a residential treatment program in contrast to only 14.3% of those who had died. This indicates that the chances of surviving drug dependency increase for those who graduated from a residential treatment program. Those who died since the first interview spent less time in treatment but most of the time in prison. But Groups 1 and 2 do not differ significantly from Groups 3 and 4 on the measure of time in prison.

Drug Use and Employment

Groups 1 and 2 in Table 12.2 did much better in terms of employment or educational training than did Group 3 (p = .000) and Group 4 (p = .003). Two explanation are possible: (1) intensive drug use does not allow for regular work or participation in a school or training program; (2) the difficulties developing a work orientation as a (former) drug addict does not support the termination of the drug career.

Drug Use and HIV Infection

We found no significant group differences regarding HIV-infection rates among the four groups (Table 12.3). Having knowledge of a seropositive test result does not automatically lead to continuation of the drug career or to a "radical break" with the drug-using habit. However, we found that 50% of the deceased addicts tested positive, as opposed to the total sample of heroin addicts (274), of whom "only" 27.4% tested positive. Two participants from Group 4 died as a result of AIDS. It is very difficult to determine whether the other deaths were suicide or unintentional overdoses. Nevertheless, HIV and AIDS can weaken physical condition, so that death related to drug use is more likely.

DISCUSSION

Termination of the drug career is a dynamic process. As we daily gather new information about the life paths of our participants, we are frequently surprised. Often, our individual prognosis about further development is proven wrong: sometimes in a positive sense, other times with a more negative outcome. Even if not all of the 137 (former) heroin addicts who were clean at the final day of data collection finally succeed in terminating their drug careers, we admire the courage, spirit, and strength

Table 12.2

Drug Use and Employment
(n = 18, 14, 22, 14)

	Group 1	Group 2	Group 3	Group 4
Unemployed	1	—	17	12
Employed/job, training program, school	16	12	—	1
In residential treatment	—	—	2	—
In prison	—	—	3	—
Other	—	1	—	1
No information	1	1	—	—
Total	18	14	22	14

Group definitions: see Table 12.1

TABLE 12.3

Drug Use and HIV Status
(n = 18, 14, 22, 14)

	Group 1	Group 2	Group 3	Group 4
HIV+	4	5	6	7
HIV−	14	9	14	6
No information	—	—	2	1

Group definitions: see Table 12.1

they mobilized in order to find new life perspectives. Despite the difficult social hurdles they have to overcome, including lack of work and housing, heavy debts, health problems, and social prejudices they face, they are working their way back into society.

REFERENCES

Filipp, S. H. (1981). *Ein allgemeines Modell für die Analyse kritischer Lebensereignisse*. München: Urban & Schwarzenberg, 1–52.
Havighurst, R.-J. (1972). *Developmental Tasks and Education*. New York: Mc-Kay.

Kindermann, W. (1981). Komplexität von Drogenkarrieren. In *Therapieverläufe bei Drogenabhängigen*, Feuerlein, W., Bühringer, G., Wille, R. (eds.), 28–39 Berlin, Heidelberg: Springer.

Kindermann, W., Sickinger, R., Hedrich, D., and Kindermann, S. (1989). *Drogenabhängig. Lebenswelten zwischen Szene, Justiz, Therapie und Drogenfreiheit*. Freiburg: Lambertus-Verlag.

Labouvie, E. (1980). Jugendentwicklung und Drogen. In *Entwicklungspsychologie—Ein Handbuch in Schlüsselbegriffen*, Silbereisen, R. K., Montada, L. (eds.), München: Urban & Schwarzenberg.

Lange, K.-J. (1986). Neuere kriminalistische Beobachtungen zum Verlauf von Opiatabhängigkeit. *Suchtgefahren* 32: 112 ff.

Lazarus, R. S. (1966). *Psychological Stress and the Coping Process*. New York: McGraw-Hill.

———. (1981). Streß und Streßbewältigung—ein Paradigma. In *Kritische Lebensereignisse*, Filipp, S. H. (ed.). München: Urban & Scharzenberg.

Newman, B. M., and Newman, P. R. (1979). *An introduction to the psychology of adolescence*. Homewood, Illinois: Dorsey Press.

Oerter, R. (ed.). (1978). *Entwicklung als lebenslanger Prozess: Aspekte und Perspektiven*. Hamburg: Hoffman & Campe.

Projektgruppe TUdrop. (1984). *Heroinabhängigkeit unbetreuter Jugendlicher*. Weinheim, Basel: Beltz.

Raschke, P., and Schliehe, F. (1985). *Therapie und Rehabilitation bei Drogenkonsumenten. Langzeitstudie am Beispiel des "Hammer Modells."* Düsseldorf: Ministerium für Arbeit, Gesundheit und Soziales des Landes Nordrhein-Westfalen.

Silbereisen, R. F., and Eyferth, K. (1983). *Jugendentwicklung und Drogen. Zweiter Fortsetzungsantrag an die Deutsche Forschungsgemeinschaft. Berichte aus der Arbeitsgruppe TUdrop Jugendforschung*. Berlin: Technische Universität. 24.

Stosberg, K., Pfeiffer-Beck, M., and Lungershausen, E. (1985). *Wege aus der Heroinabhängigkeit*. Erlangen: Perimed.

Uchtenhagen, A., and Zimmer-Höfler, D. (1985). *Heroinabhängige und ihre "normalen" Altersgenossen*. Bern, Stuttgart: Haupt.

CHAPTER 13

Client Characteristics and the Therapeutic Process in Residential Treatment Centers for Drug Addicts*

Elke Hanel

INTRODUCTION

Thirteen residential treatment facilities have been analyzed in the Munich Multicenter Treatment Evaluation Study (MTE-Study) since 1985. The study's main goals are the documentation of programs, therapeutic staff, client characteristics, and results, as well as a process analysis of treatment and a prognosis of dropout and therapy outcomes. Clients and therapists are investigated several times during treatment, and clients are followed up 3, 12, and 24 months after planned discharge or dropout. This is the first multicenter study to be carried out in German-speaking countries.[1]

This paper first describes the type of clients who are treated in the 13 facilities, and next deals with the progress in treatment in relation to some psychological variables. Special emphasis is given to sex differences. The 13 facilities present different treatment concepts with various psychological programs, planned times in treatment, and so forth. The size of the facilities ranges from 12 to 30 treatment slots; most treatment facilities are characterized as therapeutic communities (TC). The entire range of residential programs for drug addicts in Germany is covered.

*The study was funded by the German Federal Ministry of Health.
[1]See also the chapters by Haderstorfer and Künzel as well as by Herbst in this volume.

TABLE 13.1

Demographic Characteristics and Education*

		female: 24
Average age at time of admission	26	male: 26.5

Sex	
Female	21%

Marital status	
Single	80%
Married	11%
Widowed	1%
Divorced	6%

Education	
Failed to complete high school	75%
High school graduate	25%

* The separate scores for females and males are only indicated when significant differences have been found.

(See also Hanel and Herbst 1988; Herbst and Hanel, 1989a, b; Herbst et al. 1989; Hanel 1989.) The data were collected between November 1985 and the beginning of 1987; 70% of all clients took part in the study. Of the 302 participants 63 were female and 239 male.

CLIENT CHARACTERISTICS

Demographic Characteristics

There is a wide range of age at admission: the youngest client was 15 and the oldest 42 years old. The average age at admission has tended to increase in the last 10 years. The women began consuming illegal drugs regularly 2 years earlier than the men, and thus their average age at admission is 2.5 years younger (Table 13.1). The percentage of female clients is only 21%. In many treatment centers there are one or two female addicts among two dozen male clients. Only in two treatment centers was the ratio of women and men roughly equal. While almost half of the male clients completed professional training, the rate for female clients is only 23%. More than half of all the clients are unemployed, so it is not surprising that about 30% of the clients report that they earned money from illegal activity.

TABLE 13.2

Drug-Use History Reported at Time of Admission (Median, percentages*)

Age at first marijuana, hashish, LSD use	15	female: male:	14 16
Age at first regular opiate/cocaine use	18	female: male:	17 19
Duration of opiate/cocaine addiction	8		
Never used opiate/cocaine	12%		

Opiate/cocaine in the last 3
   months prior to admission
   not used
   sometimes used
   frequently / daily used
	
	24%
	13%
	64%		

Frequent / daily alcohol intoxification	34%		

*The separate scores for females and males are indicated only when significant differences have been found.

Drug-Use History

For the following data analysis, clients with heroin, other opiate, or cocaine dependence were included in the opiate/cocaine group. In this group heroin addiction was most often reported (almost 80%), and clients with marijuana, hashish, and LSD use are included in a separate group (Table 13.2). Perceived addiction to hashish, marijuana, or LSD usually occurred at about age 15, while opiate/cocaine addiction was commonly reported at age 18; but there is a small group that became opiate addicted before the age of 14 and over the age of 25. The duration of opiate dependence ranges from 1 to 22 years; half of the clients were addicted for almost a decade.

In the sample 24% reported that they had not used opiates in the last 3 months prior to admission. This number includes both clients who used other drugs or were already detoxificated and clients who never used opiates or cocaine; each group amounted to 12% of the clients. They were treated because they had alcohol or other nonhard drug problems. In general most of the clients were severe drug dependents according to DSM III. Correspondingly, the drug involvement was severe: 82% of the women and 64% of the men had frequent contact with opiate users. In

TABLE 13.3
Criminal Histories*

		female	male
Convictions (median)	3	2	4
fine only	8%		
sentence	69%		
Imprisonment	62%	35%	65%
Months of imprisonment (median)	14	7.5	16
Age of first imprisonment (median)	20.5		

* The separate scores for females and males are only indicated when significant differences have been found.

addition, women had longer lasting partnerships, and the partners were more often addicted as well.

Criminal Histories

The following data are self-reports, as are all the other variables mentioned up to now. The typical addict was sentenced at least once. The conviction rate for men is double that for women (Table 13.3). A small group was sentenced to fine only, but most of the sample was sentenced to imprisonment. Almost two-thirds were imprisoned with an average sentence of 14 months. There are also significant differences between men and women. Illegal activities such as drug dealing or theft were reported by 31%.

Treatment Prior to Admission

Almost half of the sample had previous residential treatment experience, but most had not completed treatment and had stayed in the program not longer than 5 months. This result is in accordance with the results of other recent German studies (Raschke and Schliehe 1985; Stosberg et al. 1985; Kampe and Kunz in this volume). A small group dropped out in the last 12 months before starting this treatment.

TABLE 13.4

Physical and Psychosocial Histories*

		female	*male*
Suicide attempts:			
one	20%		
more than one	25%	40%	23%
Sexual abuse in childhood and adolescence	16%	41%	7%
average age (years)	14		
Diseases acquired as a consequence of			
drug use:			
liver	35%		
teeth	43%		

* The separate scores for females and males are only indicated when significant differences have been found.

Physical and Psychosocial History

In terms of physical and psychosocial history the female drug addicts experienced more disadvantages. Women tried to commit suicide more often than did men. Forty percent were the victims of sexual abuse as children or adolescents. There is no difference between the sexes regarding diseases acquired as a consequence of drug use (Table 13.4).

PSYCHOLOGICAL SITUATION DURING TREATMENT

The following presents the psychological situation of the clients during treatment. Depressiveness is assessed by the "Depressivitäts-Skala" (v. Zerssen 1976; Figure 13.1). It is interesting to note that the average sample score is within the range of psychiatric patients. Except at the time of the regular termination of treatment, the scores of the women are significantly higher than those of the men. At the beginning of the treatment they score even higher than a psychiatric patient group. With both sexes the scores decrease during treatment; however, they are still twice as high at the end of the treatment as those of the sample of the reference group.

To describe the psychological situation in more detail a problem score

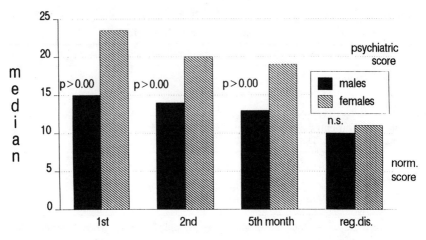

FIGURE 13.1.
Depressiveness (median at various stages of treatment; Depressivitäts-Skala; v. Zerssen, 1976).

has been developed as a predictor for dropout and relapse (see the chapter by Herbst in this volume). Both clients and staff rated for every stage of the treatment

- whether there is an acute problem in the client's life (e.g., learning to become aware of one's feelings, dealing with authorities, clearing up relationship problems, etc.);
- whether the problems were worked on within the last two months of treatment
- whether the problem situation has changed.

Figure 13.2 shows how many acute problems the clients mentioned. Women report more acute problems; above all, becoming self-confident, achieving assertiveness, establishing a real partnership and sexual competence are mentioned. In general, the female clients report more problems on which they are working with the staff. (Figure 13.3).

Figure 13.4 shows the problem improvement. Women start off worse, but at the end of the treatment they state more frequently than the men that their problem situation has improved. A second comparison shows the difference between all clients and the staff: Clients report more positive changes than the staff.

Another important variable is the overall satisfaction with treatment

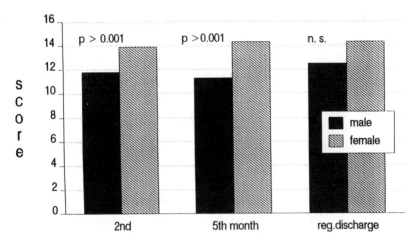

FIGURE 13.2.
Problem situations rated by clients

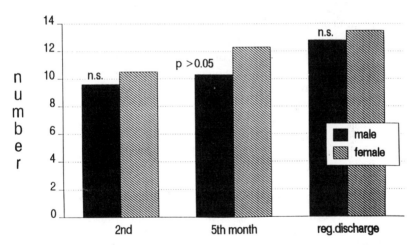

FIGURE 13.3.
Number of treated problems rated by clients

conditions, for example, comfort of the treatment center facilities, leisure time, and organization. Figure 13.5 shows that there is no difference between men and women as far as general satisfaction is concerned. An interesting question is whether women are more satisfied in treatment centers where the sex ratio is about 1 to 1 than in institutions in which they are a minority. The data indicate that there is no difference.

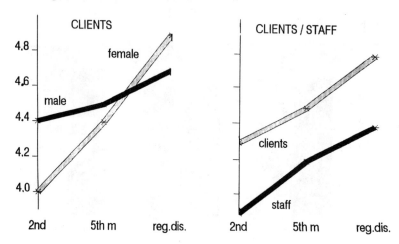

FIGURE 13.4.
Problem-improvement scores rated by clients and staff (Rasch-scaling).

The relation between demographic variables, drug-related variables, and the psychological situation at the beginning of treatment was analyzed. It would be expected that some of the drug-related variables (e.g., the severity of drug dependence) would influence the problem situation scores or the treatment course. But neither the age at first regular opiate use nor the duration of drug dependence influenced the problem situation, depressiveness scores, the time in treatment, or the dropout rate. There is a weak indication that clients with more previous treatment experience do not drop out as often as clients without this experience.

Finally, an unexpected result should be presented: In contrast to the expectation of the staff, the dropout rate between the sexes does not differ; for both it is 57%. But at the beginning of the treatment the staff estimated the women to be significantly more prone to dropping out. They expected that the women would drop out more than twice as often as the men would (52% versus 22%).

CONCLUSIONS

The present study comes to the following conclusions:

• The demographic variables are comparable with the data from other German studies about drug users.

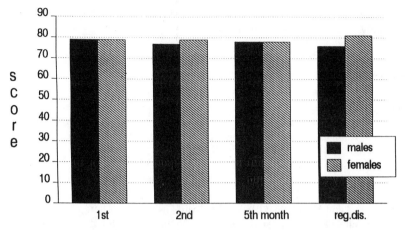

FIGURE 13.5.
Treatment satisfaction scores rated by clients (maximum obtainable score is 110).

- In general, the sample consists of severe drug users who are maladjusted in social relationships and have a low rate of employment.
- The high level of depressiveness suggests the classification as a group with psychiatric symptoms.
- The stimulus for enrollment in the therapeutic community is more often due to legal pressure than to self-motivation.

As shown above, most of the clients have served a prison sentence and thus their expectations and needs differ from those of clients from earlier years, when legal pressure was not the norm; for example, these clients need more motivation strategies at the beginning of the treatment. The discrepancy between client and staff perceptions of problem improvement is remarkable. It is unclear whether there was an improvement and the staff did not notice it or whether there was no improvement but the clients perceived one.

According to an estimate by experts, about one-third of all drug users in Germany are women, but in the residential treatment centers the figure is only 21%. While it isn't possible to equalize the sex ratio in the treatment centers, women should never be placed in a minority. While treated in a institution for both sexes, female clients do not drop out from treatment more often than male clients, but the variety of their problems demonstrates that they need more individualized treatment programs. The starting conditions of women coming into the treatment centers are worse, but they are more willing to try to change themselves.

REFERENCES

Hanel, E. (1989). Drogenabhängigkeit und Therapieverlauf bei Frauen in stationärer Entwöhnungsbehandlung. In *Therapieverläufe bei Drogenabhängigen. Kann es eine Lehrmeinung geben?* Feuerlein, W., Bühringer, G., Wille, R. (eds.), 148–69. Heidelberg: Springer.

Hanel, E., and Herbst, K. (1988). Beschreibung und erste Ergebnisse einer prospektiven Studie zur stationären Nachbehandlung von Drogenabhängigen. *Suchtgefahren* 34: 1–21.

Herbst, K., and Hanel, E. (1989a). Meßbare Größen des Therapieprozesses bei Drogenabhängigen in stationärer Entwöhnungsbehandlung. In *Therapieverläufe bei Drogenabhängigen. Kann es eine Lehrmeinung geben?* Feuerlein, W., Bühringer, G., Wille, R. (eds.), 170–83. Heidelberg: Springer.

Herbst, K., and Hanel, E. (1989b). Verlauf der stationären Entwöhnungsbehandlung bei Drogenabhängigen. *Suchtgefahren* 35: 235–51.

Herbst, K., Hanel, E., and Haderstorfer, B. (1989). Rückfallgeschehen bei stationär behandelten Drogenabhängigen. In *Rückfall und Rückfallprophylaxe*, Cohen, R., Watzel, H. (eds.) Heidelberg: Springer.

Raschke, P., and Schliehe, F. (1985). *Therapie und Rehabilitation bei Drogenkonsumenten.* Düsseldorf: Minister für Arbeit, Gesundheit und Soziales des Landes Nordrhein-Westfalen.

Stosberg, K., Pfeiffer-Beck, M., and Lungershausen, E. (1985). *Wege aus der Heroinabhängigkeit.* Erlangen: Perimed.

Zerssen, D. von (1976). *Depressivitäts-Skala.* Weinheim, Basel: Beltz.

CHAPTER 14

Changes of Personality and Depression During Treatment of Drug Addicts

Heiner Ellgring and Heinz C. Vollmer

INTRODUCTION

The question of to what extent drug addicts can be characterized by specific personality factors is relevant for treatment in various ways. The evidence of specific personality traits would have consequences for therapy indication, the course of treatment, and evaluation of therapeutic effects. For the therapist, prediction of (1) motivation for change, (2) course of therapeutic progress, and (3) risk for relapse on the basis of personality measures would be valuable. Moreover, information on personality aspects could help to further develop hypotheses about the psychological origin of addiction. From these, specifically adapted goals for therapy of the individual could be derived. For patients, knowledge of their personality traits could help them to achieve an integrated view of their own situation and thus reach a better understanding of themselves. The goal of this chapter is to examine stable and variable aspects of personality in drug addicts. With this, the use of commonly applied psychological instruments for treatment evaluation will be investigated.

According to our present knowledge, the question whether there are personality traits which may be considered (1) being especially pronounced or (2) being even specific for addicts can be answered as follows. Various studies, partly covering samples of several thousand individuals, found a tendency in drug addicts for emotional lability, depressive tendencies, and vegetative disorders (Müller-Oswald, Ruppen, Baumann and Angst 1973; Spille and Guski 1975; Bachman and Jones 1979; Sieber 1981; Labouvie and McGee 1986). However, as is also asserted by various authors, these effects can rarely be considered as very strong. Thus Sieber (1981) reports correlations of about r = .20, meaning that only a small proportion of variance (about 4%) is explained by personality measures. Data reported recently by Shedler and Block (1990) from the Berkeley longitudinal study pointed out a tendency for lack of impulse control in 11-year-old subjects who became heavy marijuana smokers later, at the age of 18. Nevertheless, the group differences reported do not allow any individual prediction whether a young individual will become an excessive user of drugs as an adult.

In no case could a valid individual prognosis be warranted on the basis of personality measures. According to Wanke (1987) a valid prognosis of which person will become addicted was not possible at any time. Moreover, "The major conclusion to be drawn from studies of personality variables in heroin addicts is that there is little basis for assuming commonality of such traits among addicts. This is true for such commonly observed traits as psychopathy as it is for more specific traits such as temporal perspective or locus of control" (Platt and Labate 1976). There is little to add to this conclusion, even when the evidence of the recent literature is included. Various questions, however, remain open, given this negative statement:

— Could it be that our clinical experience misleads us when it suggests more commonality than is genuinely present? Are we misled by our perceptual tendencies, selective perception, and biases for categories in assuming characteristic personality traits in addicts where in fact a variety of personalities is present?

— Could it be the case that our instruments used to assess personality are insufficient? Or are our concepts of stable, persisting, and thus predictable behavioral tendencies inadequate?

Rather than searching for the "addictive personality," it could be more fruitful to ask for a development of personality aspects during the process of addiction. Wanke (1987, pp. 33ff.) refers to results indicating that therapists are less able to adequately predict the behavior of drug addicts shortly before relapse. On the other hand, changes in personality become apparent during the progression of dependency. These are, according to Wanke, characterized for drug addicts by a triad of euphoric mood, apathy, and passivity. For alcohol addicts, a reduction in activity and spontaneity, unreliability, loss of critical thinking and responsibility, lack of concentration, and reduced motor skills become predominant. Thus, instead of searching for persisting, predisposing traits for a dependency, attention should be given to changes during the course of dependency and especially those changes occurring contingent upon therapeutic interventions.

This, however, reveals a dilemma: Personality theory and treatment differ with regard to their assumptions about stability and change. Therapy aims at changing behavioral tendencies and cognitive structures, including those covered by personality constructs. Personality theory, in contrast, has to assume a certain stability of personality factors over time. Instead of postulating *either* stability *or* change, the following could be considered: Especially over the course of treatment, stable and changeable components of personality aspects should be differentiated. Thus stable components of neuroticism could describe an individual disposition, whereas its variable components could be tested as criteria for therapeutic effects. Mainly variable components would be targets for therapeutic change.

METHOD

The longitudinal study on the treatment of drug addicts reported here was conducted in a treatment center of the "Prop Alternative Aiglsdorf."* There were 181 drug addicts (79% male and 21% female) treated in two centers of the institution who took part in this study. The average age was 24 years (range: 17–32 years); 98% of the patients were opiate addicts, and 2% amphetamine addicts. Addiction lasted on the average 10 years for "soft drugs" and 8 years for "hard drugs." Seventy-four percent of the patients had their therapy as part of a sentence with legal conditions imposed by the court. Treatment in one of the two centers was behaviorally oriented; in the other center therapy was mainly humanistic (Vollmer, Ellgring, and Ferstl, submitted for publication). A regular release after about 26 weeks (i.e., a planned duration of 6 months of treatment in the therapeutic community), was reached by 81 patients (45%). Thirty-seven patients (21%) had an early discharge from treatment because of disciplinary measures, 63 patients (34%) prematurely terminated treatment on their own.

As measures of personality and psychological state, the Freiburg Personality Inventory (FPI; Fahrenberg and Selg 1978) Forms A and B, an inventory similar to the MMPI (Minnesota Multiphasic Personality Inventory), was repeatedly given at the beginning and end of therapy, as

*The support of the managing director of the "Prop Alternative," Dr. A. Dvorak, is gratefully acknowledged.

FPI Factor (Nr)

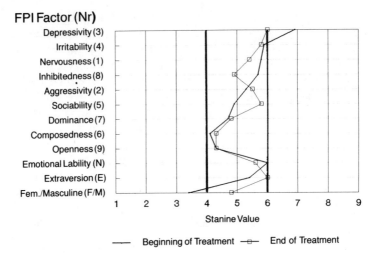

FIGURE 14.1.
Average stanine scores in factors of the Freiburg Personality Inventory (FPI) for drug addicts at the beginning (N = 181) and end (N = 81) of treatment. Bars at stanine scores 4 and 6 indicate the normal range.

was the Beck Depression Inventory (BDI; Beck, Rush, Shaw, and Emery 1981). Only those patients with a regular termination of treatment could be tested at the beginning and end.

RESULTS

From the results reported in this section, the following findings deserve special notice: On the one hand, only *minor deviations from the norm* were found in personality factors for the total group of drug addicts, and this at the beginning of treatment only. On the other hand, regarding individual cases, a considerable number of the patients revealed *extreme stanine values* in single personality factors. Moreover, a factor analysis of *changeable components* within personality factors revealed a number of factors indicating specific effects of treatment. With regard to the initially increased *depression scores*, clear changes in motivational and emotional aspects as well as in self-image became apparent during therapy.

TABLE 14.1

Proportion of Extreme Stanine Values in Factors of the FPI and Their Change during Treatment
Proportion (%) of Stanine Values 7–9 (resp. 1–3*).

| | | Treatment | | Diff. |
| | | Beg. | End | |
FPI Factor (Nr.)		%	%	%
Depressivity	(3)	60	34	−26
Inhibitedness	(8)	40	15	−25
Nervousness	(1)	61	46	−15
Sociability*	(5)	36	23	−13
Irritability	(4)	42	30	−12
Composedness*	(6)	36	30	− 6
Aggressivity	(2)	33	31	− 2
Openness	(9)	29	27	− 2
Dominance	(7)	23	26	+ 3

Deviation from the Norm

In general, only minimal deviations from norm values were found in the average personality profile of drug addicts (see Figure 14.1). At the beginning of treatment, patients had augmented values in depressivity and emotional lability (irritability, nervousness) only. All other averages were located within the norms. It should be noted that the dimensions "extraversion (E)," "emotional lability (N)," and "masculinity/femininity (M/F)" are assembled from items also contained in the first eight FPI factors. Thus the factor "emotional lability" closely resembles "nervousness (1)." Since results from Form B were nearly identical, only those of Form A will be depicted here.

Comparison of these scales from the beginning and end of therapy revealed significant improvements in the following aspects: Patients expressed less depressivity, emotional lability, and composedness as well as increased sociability, extraversion, and masculinity (Wilcoxon-Test: p < .01). Although an error of central tendency has to be taken into account, the significant changes on the basis of minor deviations from the norms were in accordance with therapy goals. These changes also become apparent in the proportion of patients showing extreme values in single factors (Table 14.1). The proportion of patients with extreme stanine values from 7 to 9 (1–3 in factors "sociability" and "composedness") decreases about 25% for the factors "depressivity" and "composedness" and about 15% to 12% for the factors "nervousness," "lack of sociability," and "irritability." There were no significant differences between groups with various forms of treatment termination with regard to these personality measures. Thus, personality measures in our case did not allow for prediction of the regular or irregular course of treatment.

Factors of Change

As can be derived from Table 14.1, personality factors differ considerably with regard to their stability and variability. Since changeable components are especially important for treatment, those items of the FPI were factor-analyzed which were responded to differently by at least 25% of the patients at the beginning and end of therapy. Because of lack of space, a corresponding analysis of stable components cannot be reported here. Items from Forms A and B of the FPI were analyzed together because data from the beginning and end of treatment were available for both. A total of 35 (16%) of the 224 items met the criteria set. A principal component factor analysis with consecutive Varimax rotation produced a proportion of 50% variance explained, given a 7-factor solution. With 12 factors this proportion was 63%. Reliability of the seven factors was at the median $r = .65$.

In general, the resulting factors point to areas of change which are in accordance with the goals of treatment. Emerging out of the different factors, three domains with a potential for change can be described (Item examples with number from Forms A and B of the FPI and their factor loadings are given in parentheses):

1. Action Regulation
Factor I: Pleasure with Activity and Decisions.
(B33: "I am generally able to make firm and fast decisions." $r = .74$).
Factor II: Control of One's Own Activity.
(A85: "I frequently make deliberate remarks which I later regret."$r = .79$).
Factor III: Sociability.
(A99: "I would describe myself as talkative." $r = .82$).
2. Dysfunctional Thinking
Factor IV: Despair and Resignation.
(B24: "Sometimes I feel quite miserable without reason." $r = .61$).
Factor V: Daydreaming.
(B16: "I daydream more often than is good for me." $r = .75$).

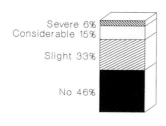 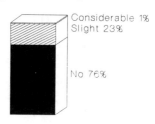

Severe 6%
Considerable 15%

Slight 33%

No 46%

Considerable 1%
Slight 23%

No 76%

Beginning of Treatment   End of Treatment

FIGURE 14.2.
**Proportions of drug addicts with different degrees of depression according to scores
from the Beck Depression Inventory (BDI) at the beginning (N = 181) and end (N = 81)
of treatment.**

3. Psychosomatic Complaints
Factor VI: Bodily Reactions to Arousal.
(A21: "I gasp in arousing situations so that I have to inhale
deeply." r = .73).
Factor VII: Sleep Disturbances
(A83: "I have difficulties in getting to sleep and sleeping all
night." r = .82).

Instead of factors suggested by the FPI on the basis of a validation
with a normal population, these results point to specific problem domains
relevant to drug addicts. They reflect actual problematic aspects of personality.

Depression

Depressive tendencies deserve special attention in drug addicts. There is
a high prevalence for depressive tendencies in drug addicts, with symptoms being similar in European and American cultures (Hendriks, Steer,
Platt, and Metzger 1990). Clear changes during treatment appeared for
the population studied here. The proportion of patients with increased
depression values in the FPI declined from 60% to 34% (See Table 14.1),
and the data from the BDI also reflect clear improvement in the psychological state (Figure 14.2). The proportion of 48% patients with considerable to moderate depression at the beginning of therapy declines to
24% at the end.

At the single-item level, analysis sought to determine which aspects

BDI-Item (Nr)

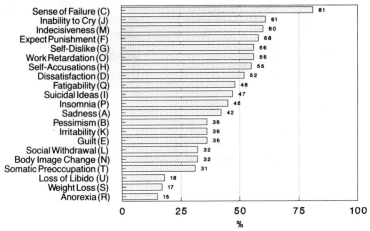

FIGURE 14.3.
Proportions (%) of drug addicts (N = 181) reporting symptoms in Beck Depression In-
ventory (BDI) items.

of depression (1) are especially problematic, (2) change most, and (3) remain problematic even at the end of treatment. An aspect was defined as "problematic" when an individual indicated at least the lowest level of presence of the problem (= 1) on that single item independent of intensity:

1. *Problematic aspects* for more than 50% of the patients at the beginning of treatment are shown in Figure 14.3. These were sense of failure (C = 81%), inability to cry (J = 61%), indecisiveness (M = 60%), expectation of punishment (F = 58%), self-dislike (G = 56%), work retardation (O = 56%), self-accusation (H = 55%), and dissatisfaction (D = 52%). For item J, it is noteworthy that 49% indicated intensity 0, and 56% indicated intensity 3: "I used to be able to cry but now I cannot cry at all even though I want to." Since only 5% had intensity 1, "I cry more now than I used to," one could regard this as a specific emotional/expressive deficit in this population that is different from depressed patients.

2. *Changes* during the course of treatment are shown in Figure 14.4. The differences in the proportion of drug addicts with problematic BDI items between the beginning and end of treatment were determined. Negative values thus indicated a decrease of problems over the time of treat-

BDI-Item (Nr)

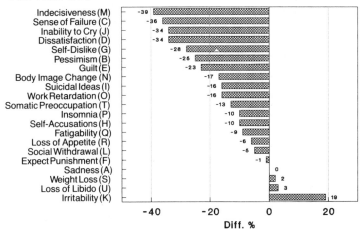

FIGURE 14.4.
Differences between proportions (Diff. %) of drug addicts (N = 81) reporting symptoms
in Beck Depression Inventory (BDI) items at the beginning and end of treatment. Negative values indicate fewer symptoms and thus improvement at the end.

ment. The aspects changing most (i.e., in more than 20% of the patients)
were the following: indecisiveness (M = −39%), sense of failure
(C = −36%), inability to cry (I = −34%), dissatisfaction (D = -34%),
self-dislike (G = −28%), pessimism (B = -25%), and guilt (E = −23%).

3. *Remaining problems:* At the end of treatment, a substantial part of
the drug addicts still reported problematic aspects in the BDI items. Figure 14.5 includes these in respective order. Topics which remain problematic for a substantial part of the patients (>30%) were the following:
self-accusations (H = 49%), irritability (K = 48%), sense of failure
(C = 44%), work retardation (O = 42%). Persisting psychovegetative
problems were fatigability (Q = 47%) and insomnia (O = 33%). The
high proportion of problems with expectation of punishment (F = 63%)
is most probably due to the reality of legal conditions of probation (cf.
description of the sample). It should be noted that a relatively high proportion of drug addicts still reported self-accusations, sense of failure, or
suicidal ideas at the end of treatment.

Comparing the depression data with regard to different kinds of *treatment termination* revealed some interesting trends. Because of the post
hoc analysis, differences will be described without statistical testing. Pa-

BDI-Item (Nr)

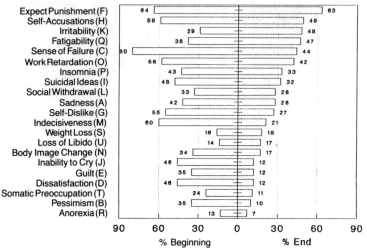

FIGURE 14.5.
Proportions (%) of drug addicts (N = 81) reporting symptoms of depression at the end
of treatment.

tients who prematurely left treatment on their own showed the highest
proportion of problematic values (1 to 3) in 17 out of the 21 items
(Figure 14.6). In contrast, patients who were prematurely expelled from
treatment had the lowest proportion of problematic values in 15 out of
the 21 items, whereas for patients regularly terminating therapy these
proportions were in between. Prematurely leaving patients compared to
expelled ones had more frequent problems with self-dislike (G: +30%),
self-accusation (H: +29%), fatigability (Q: +26%), suicidal ideas (I:
23%), and dissatisfaction (D: +20%). An individual prognosis on the
basis of these differences, however, would be premature. (It could be
argued that expelled patients tend to dissimulate more frequently with
regard to the problems mentioned.)

It appears noteworthy that deficiencies of vital functions, otherwise
prevalent in depression, are comparatively rare in drug addicts: Loss of
appetite (anorexia − R: 15%), weight loss (S: 17%), loss of libido (U:
18%). The young age of drug addicts is probably relevant for this result.
This again points to the problem that concepts of depression as assessed
in the BDI cannot simply be transferred onto this population of drug
addicts. In general, a common concept of "depression" or "depressivity"

BDI-Item (Nr)

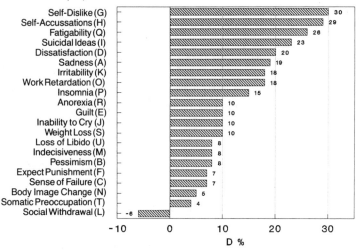

FIGURE 14.6.
Differences of proportions (%) of drug addicts with symptoms in Beck Depression Inventory (BDI) items. Differences between the group of addicts expelled from treatment (N = 37) and the group of addicts prematurely terminating treatment (N = 63). Positive values indicate that addicts prematurely terminating treatment reported more symptoms in all but one item.

is not relevant for drug addicts, but rather specific aspects which also become topics in treatment.

CONCLUSIONS

In accordance with various other studies, the present longitudinal study gave no clues for specific personality variables or traits of drug addicts. Personality factors did not allow a valid prediction of the kind of therapy termination, nor were there clear deviations from the norm. Analyzed as a group, the addicts showed only minor changes that appeared over the course of treatment. These results correspond to data reported on alcohol dependency (cf. Wanke 1987).

A more differentiated picture is gained when stable and changeable components of personality and analyzed separately. Changeable components are of special relevance for treatment. From the current study these were characteristics of action regulation, that is, activation and impulse control, social interaction, and somatic reactions (sleep disorders, bodily reactions to drug deprivation). For relapse prevention, attention should be given to stable, persistent, problematic components. Persistent suicidal ideas turned out to be one such aspect. Like the differentiation between state and trait anxiety, stable and variable components could also be separated for other domains of personality when they are used to describe the course of treatment.

How can personality concepts and instruments for assessment be utilized for treatment? The claim of therapists to predict the outcome of a treatment may be realized for only a delimited period of time. Especially at such critical points as shortly before relapse, a firm prediction might be possible only rarely (Wanke 1987). Lack of predictability could be a warning which, however, can be verified only afterward.

According to the current results, one benefit of personality concepts could be to specify targets of change on an individual basis and thus clarify effects of therapeutic interventions. Personality concepts can help patients to better understand their problems and to recognize changes as well as persistent areas of vulnerability.

REFERENCES

Bachman, J., and Jones, R. T. (1979). Personality correlates of cannabis dependence. *Addictive Behaviors* 4: 361–71.

Beck, A. T., Rush, A. J., Shaw, B. E., and Emery, G. (1981). *Kognitive Therapie der Depression*. München: Urban & Schwarzenberg.

Fahrenberg, J. and Selg, H. (1978). *Das Freiburger Persönlichkeitsinventar FPI*. Göttingen: Hogrefe.

Hendriks, V. M., Steer, R. A., Platt, J. J., and Metzger, D. S. (1990). Psychopathology in Dutch and American heroin addicts. *International Journal of the Addictions 25*, 1051–63.

Labouvie, E. W. and McGee, C. R. (1986). Relation of personality to alcohol and drug use in adolescence. *Journal of Consulting and Clinical Psychology* 54: 289–93.

Müller-Oswald, U., Ruppen, R., Baumann, U., and Angst, J. (1973). Persönlichkeitsaspekte jugendlicher Drogenkonsumenten. Eine repräsentative Umfrage an 6315 neunzehnjährigen Zürchern. *Archiv für Psychiatrie und Nervenkrankheiten* 217: 207–22.

Platt, J. J., and Labate, C. (1976). *Heroin addiction: Theory, research and treatment.* New York: Wiley, pp. 127–54.

Shedler, J., and Block, J. (1990). Adolescent drug use and psychological health. *American Psychologist* 45: 612–30.

Sieber, M. F. (1981). Personality scores and licit and illicit substance use. *Personality and Individual Differences* 2: 235–41.

Spille, D., and Guski, R. (1975). Langfristiger Drogenkonsum und Persönlichkeitsmerkmale. *Zeitschrift für Sozialpsychologie* 6: 31–42.

Wanke, K. (1987). Zur Psychologie der Sucht. In *Psychiatrie der Gegenwart 3: Abhängigkeit und Sucht,* K. P. Kisker, H. Lauter, J.-E. Meyer, C. Müller, and E. Strömgren (eds.), pp. 19–52. Berlin: Springer.

CHAPTER 15

Variations in Behavior Among Narcotic Addicts

David N. Nurco

INTRODUCTION

Our research team at the Department of Psychiatry, University of Maryland and Friends Medical Science Research Center, Inc. has been conducting studies on narcotic addiction for over 20 years. Our work has focused mainly on the heterogeneity of narcotic addicts. An important conclusion emerging from our studies is that, in many respects, not all narcotic addicts are alike. Our research has indicated that addicts differ widely on important dimensions such as criminality (Nurco, Hanlon, Balter, Kinlock, and Slaght, in press; Shaffer, Nurco, and Kinlock 1984), lifestyle (Nurco and Shaffer 1982; Shaffer, Wegner, Kinlock, and Nurco 1983), psychopathology (Shaffer, Kinlock, and Nurco 1982; Shaffer, Nurco, Hanlon, Kinlock, Duszynski, and Stephenson 1988), and attitudes toward narcotic addiction (Nurco, Shaffer, Hanlon, Kinlock, Duszynski, and Stephenson 1987).

Our work involving narcotic addict typologies largely emanated from a reaction to the general tendency in society to regard narcotic addicts as belonging to a homogeneous class. We and others have recognized this view as being harmful from many standpoints, including considerations of etiology, theory, and disposition (treatment, rehabilitation, or incarceration). A consistent theme emphasized by both researchers and policymakers for many years is that narcotic abusers are a very diverse group, and effective approaches to such individuals and their problems must take full cognizance of this diversity (Kleber 1989; McLellan,

Luborsky, Woody, and O'Brien 1980; Strategy Council on Drug Abuse 1973).

The major focus of this paper will be on our studies of addict careers (Nurco, Cisin, and Balter 1981a, 1981b, 1981c). In these studies, we described the variety of ways in which narcotic addicts behave during the first 10 years after the onset of regular narcotic use, or addiction.[1] These descriptions were presented in terms of a typology of narcotic addicts based on the proportion of the addict career[2] spent in each of three statuses: (1) addicted[3]; (2) in the community and not addicted; and (3) in jail or prison and not addicted. The basic objective of these career studies was to increase our understanding of the natural history of events affecting the addict.

Sampling Issues

A frequently encountered problem in the study of narcotic addicts has been the use of samples drawn from "captive" populations, which makes generalization to the total addict population problematic (Gandossy, Williams, Cohen, and Harwood 1980; Inciardi 1986). In many instances, researchers have obtained narcotic addict subjects from either treatment or prison populations. Previous research suggests that subsamples of addicts selected from captive and noncaptive populations may exhibit different patterns of criminal activity and drug use (Pottieger 1981).

Our use of the Baltimore City Police Department roster of narcotic users has minimized the sampling problem mentioned above. Early in our work, we discovered that the Police Department's Narcotic Squad had been keeping detailed records of the drug abusers they had identified (Nurco, Bonito, Lerner, and Balter 1975; Nurco, Wegner, Baum, and Makofsky 1979). Over the years, we have consistently extracted and updated this information in our files. As a result, we have been able to conduct a series of analyses on the demography of the active addict population in Baltimore (Nurco et al. 1975, 1979; Nurco, Wegner, and Stephenson 1982) as well as examine many problems associated with drug abuse, including crime (Ball, Rosen, Flueck, and Nurco 1981, 1982; Ball, Shaffer, and Nurco 1983; Nurco and DuPont 1977; Shaffer, Nurco, and Kinlock 1984), psychopathology (Shaffer, Kinlock, and Nurco 1982), poverty (Nurco and Farrell 1975), and social pathology (Nurco, Shaffer,

1. Narcotic addiction is defined as the nonmedical use of opiates, their derivatives, or synthetics on at least four days a week for a month or more.
2. The addict career is defined as the span of time from the onset of addiction to date of interview.
3. Less than 1% were addicted while incarcerated.

and Cisin 1984). Of greater significance, however, was that these data provided an exceptionally good sampling frame with regard to a communitywide population of male narcotic addicts for our studies of addict careers (Nurco, Cisin, and Balter 1981a, 1981b, and 1981c).

Before our sample was drawn, there was concern over whether the police roster identified most of the narcotic users in Baltimore. In order to be sure of this, we determined whether the names of addicts we ourselves had previously interviewed or identified were on this roster. For example, we originally found that a substantial proportion of narcotic addicts who were patients in mental hospitals were not yet known to the police. Three years later, however, we found that by that time, the police had identified over 90% of these individuals. After interviewing a substantial number of addicts, we determined that it could take as long as five years after the onset of narcotic addiction for the police to identify an individual as a narcotic addict (Nurco et al. 1975). This was particularly true in the 1970s. In the 1950s, the police were able to identify addicts much more quickly (Nurco et al. 1979). Despite this trend, we remain confident that most of the addicts in Baltimore eventually become known to the police.

METHOD

Sampling Procedures

The population of addicts from which our sample was drawn consisted of all males first identified as narcotic abusers by the Baltimore City Police Department from 1952 to 1976, inclusive. From this pool of addicts, we drew 10 white and 10 black males who were initially identified in each of those years. Although the number of blacks on the roster far exceeded the number of whites, equal numbers of blacks and whites were included for each year in order to have enough statistical power to provide projections to both white and black addict populations.

Locating and Interviewing Procedures

Of the 499[4] addicts selected for study, 63 were deceased, two were psy-

---

4. Because only whites were newly listed on the roster in 1956, only white addicts could be included in the sample for that year. Therefore, our total sample consisted of 499 rather than 500 male narcotic addicts.

chotic and could not be interviewed, 8 could not be located, and 24 refused to be interviewed (Nurco, Cisin, and Balter 1981a). Thus, of the original 499 eligible subjects, 491 (98%) were either located or accounted for and 402 (92%) were interviewed.

Interviews were approximately three hours in length. Subjects were told that all information obtained from them would be guaranteed confidentiality under law. In the interview, the subject first described his drug-using behavior prior to the onset of narcotic addiction. After providing the date of the onset of addiction, the subject gave chronological information regarding subsequent addiction periods, nonaddiction periods,[5] and time spent in jail or prison. He then described his behavior and status prior to the onset of addiction with regard to education, employment, social class, and criminal activity. Finally, the subject provided information about his behavior during any subsequent periods of addiction or nonaddiction in the community.

RESULTS

Date of Onset of Narcotic Addiction

Subjects were classified into the following five cohorts according to the year of onset of narcotic addiction: 1937–49, 1950–54, 1955–59, 1960–64, and 1965–72. A disproportionately large number of addicts first became addicted between 1955 to 1959. On subsequent examination (Nurco, Cisin, and Balter 1982), we attributed the increased rates of recruitment into narcotic addiction during this period to the ready availability of liquid codeine. Before 1960, liquid codeine was generally available in drugstores without prescription. During the 1960s, a series of restrictions on its availability was implemented, initially by the Maryland State Department of Health, working in cooperation with pharmacists, and later by a city ordinance. As a result of these restrictions, recruitment rates into the addict population in Baltimore declined.

The Addict Typology

As indicated, the major focus of our addict career studies was to create a typology of narcotic addicts. The purpose of this typology was to pre-

---

5. Periods in which there was no use of narcotics or use on less than four days per week for one month or more.

dict the *kind* of narcotic addict a person became when he became addicted. Since this study dealt exclusively with addicts, it did not address the question of who would or would not become an addict.[6]

There are many dimensions that can be used in describing narcotic addict careers, and these dimensions can be integrated into typologies in a variety of ways. Ultimately, the choice of a particular typology is influenced by the type of data that are available and the orientation of the research staff. In the present series of analyses, an addict's career was viewed as the patterned distribution of narcotic-using behavior over time— specifically, the interaction of any periods addicted and not addicted to narcotics with time spent in jail or prison. This study dealt with the first 10 years of the addiction career, a span of time we considered long enough for individual characteristic patterns of behavior to emerge. Admittedly, this is a restricted view. In theory, an addict's career does not end until the addict dies; therefore, our data were only complete to the point of interview.

The addict career typology under discussion was built on two concepts pertaining to the use of narcotic-addictive drugs: opportunity and motivation. The classification of each addict depended on his degree of involvement with narcotics relative to his opportunity for voluntary abstinence. As a consequence, the typology took into account the proportion of the base period (10 years) spent in the following statuses: (1) addicted; (2) not addicted and out of jail; and (3) in jail or prison. Emphasis was on involvement with narcotic drugs, opportunity to use such drugs as represented by time not spent in jail or prison, and voluntary abstinence. The degree of involvement was defined by that proportion of the base period in which the subject was addicted to narcotics. Opportunity to use narcotics was defined by that proportion of the 10-year period in which the addict was living in the community, as opposed to being in jail or prison. Voluntary abstinence was defined by that proportion of the period of 10 years in which the addict lived in the community but was not addicted. Our formulation assumed that opportunity and involvement are independent at any level of involvement below 100%, and the independent contribution of opportunity becomes more apparent at medium or low ranges of involvement, where choice becomes paramount.

Formation of Addict Types

Since our typology involved the first 10 years of addiction, our classification procedures included only those addicts who had a time span of at

6. This question is being addressed in our ongoing study, "Vulnerability to Narcotic Addiction."

STEP 1. Calculation of the proportion to time spent addicted.

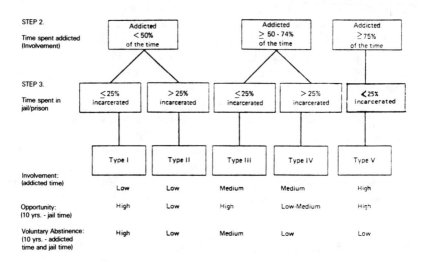

FIGURE 15.1
Selection process resulting in five addict types

least 10 years from the onset of narcotic addiction to the time of interview. A total of 238 addicts (135 blacks and 103 whites) qualified for
inclusion in our analysis of addict careers that emerged. The application
of the concepts of opportunity and motivation to the data pertaining to
these 238 individuals resulted in five clearly distinguished addict types.
Our selection process followed a sequential procedure (see Figure 15.1):

1. Calculation of the proportion of time (months) spent addicted in the
   10-year base period.
2. Division of the sample into three groups based on proportion of the
   10 years spent addicted (under 50%; between 50% and 74%, inclusive;
   and 75% or more). This classified the sample into low, medium, and
   high involvement, respectively.
3. Further division of the sample was based on time spent in jail or prison.

Description of Addict Types

Figure 15.2 shows prototypic case examples of the different types of
addict careers. Compared to the other addict types, Type I addicts did not

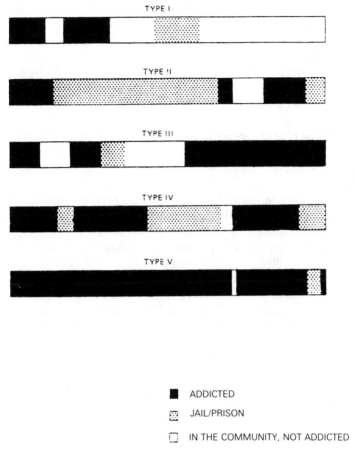

FIGURE 15.2
Characteristic addict careers: the first ten years allocation of time to three statuses.

spend much of their careers either addicted or in jail. These individuals were characterized by the high proportion of time they spent in the community and not addicted. Type I addicts spent more than 7 1/2 years out of 10 nonaddicted in the community, by far the highest proportion of time spent in this status among the addict types.

Type II was similar to Type I in terms of the relatively low amount of time they spent addicted. However, Type II addicts differed from the previous type in that they spent more of the 10-year base period in jail. Because of this incarceration time, they had low opportunity and low voluntary abstinence with respect to narcotic drug use.

Type III addicts were similar to Type I in that they had high opportunity to use narcotics (relatively low jail time). They were distinguished from Type I in that they had more addicted time and less nonaddicted time in the community.

Type IV, similar to Type II, spent more than 25% of their careers in jail. Unlike Type II, however, they spent a high proportion of their time in the community addicted. Very little nonaddicted time was spent in the community.

Type V was distinguished from all other types by the high proportion of their careers spent addicted. These men were addicted more than 75% of the time. Many of these individuals were addicted throughout the entire 10-year period.

In the composition of the five addict types, race was found to be an important variable in several respects. Black addicts had much more addicted time than whites, as well as much more jail time. These racial differences have important implications for public policy and treatment programs which will be discussed later.

Our addict career typology served several functions. First, at a descriptive level, it imposed a simple set of rules which provided a systematic, parsimonious summary of narcotic-using behavior. Second, this typology served to organize and integrate other kinds of data with regard to addict careers and therefore added to our overall understanding of narcotic addiction. This latter method of organizing the data provided the rationale for further analysis of behavioral differences among the various addict types. Our central concern here was with the antecedent correlates of the types rather than the proportion of addicts who made up each specific type. Our purpose in examining these antecedent behavioral correlates was to determine factors which may predict, as stated earlier, the kind of addict an individual would likely become.

Correlates of the Addict Types

Among our most important findings with regard to antecedent behavior, particularly for blacks, was that early onset of addiction was associated with a high percentage of time spent in an addicted status. For the blacks, members of Types III, IV, and V had the earliest onset of narcotic addiction, and they were the ones who were most involved with narcotic addiction. Among the whites, Type V addicts were the only ones who had an early onset age. Social background[7] was also related to addict type. For both blacks and whites, members of Types II and IV, who were most criminal, came from the lowest socioeconomic classes. This finding was consistent among the types despite overall lower social position among blacks. Our results regarding social class and crime were consistent with other findings (U.S. Department of Justice 1983). In addition, we found that Types I and V displayed greater job stability, and this seemed to support a notion of generalized social competence.

Other important findings dealt with differential involvement of the types in juvenile delinquency and criminal activity. Type I addicts were defined as those who were best able to cope with their narcotic addiction, since they had spent most of their careers not addicted in the community. It is surprising that, particularly for whites, the majority of Type I addicts, who spent comparatively little time addicted and who returned to abstinence, were typically those whose preaddiction careers had been quite delinquent and criminal. It appears that their relatively short periods of addiction climaxed a deviant career, and in the 10-year period studied, these individuals were successful in terminating their addiction.

At the other end of the spectrum, we found a different kind of success represented by the Type V addicts, who maintained a virtually uninterrupted narcotic habit during the 10 years reported. They spent little or no time in jail and little or no time off narcotics. It seems that they were the true narcotic careerists, since most of them entered the narcotic scene with virtually no criminal activity and little juvenile delinquency. For these men, narcotic addiction apparently was the beginning, not the culmination, of their deviance, and their greater personal adequacy, as reflected in job stability and lower crime rates prior to addiction, may have helped them to develop skill in avoiding incarceration during a nearly uninterrupted 10-year career.

Trends Across Time

As pointed out earlier, we sampled equal numbers of addicts from each year the police identified individuals as addicted, and therefore we had different sampling fractions for each of the years studied. Because of our concern about changes over time, we weighted the sample accordingly. This new analysis uncovered several important findings. First, the modal group of whites consisted of Type I addicts, the individuals who seem to have moved into addiction as an extension of their acting-out adolescent behavior. For these individuals, addiction had the effect of prolonging their deviance into their middle twenties or up to their thirties, at which

---

7. As defined by parents' occupational status, according to the Duncan occupational rating system (Hauser and Featherman 1977).

point their overall deviance became less pronounced, either as a natural result of aging or because of court pressures or incarceration. From this point on, they tended to stop their use of narcotic-addictive drugs and, because they were from a relatively high socioeconomic stratum, they moved into the working class roles of their fathers.

In more recent years, those white addicts classified as Type II (individuals who were usually either addicted or incarcerated and who spent more time in jail or prison than addicted) have become more numerous. Among these, we have been finding a deviant group of white addicts, who might be defined as "klutzes" or "losers," who are not very stable psychologically.

Among black addicts in our sample, we found that the modal group was composed of Type V addicts, who were addicted throughout most of the 10-year period. Interestingly, this group was never smaller than one-third of the black addict population. During some of the more than 35 years studied, Type V addicts at times accounted for over 50% of the black addict population.

DISCUSSION

The finding that early onset of addiction was associated with a longer and more continuous narcotic career has been reported elsewhere (Lukoff 1974; Nurco, Hanlon, Kinlock, and Duszynski 1988). Also, the finding that addicts from the lowest socioeconomic strata were criminally deviant prior to addiction and spent more time in jail or prison was not unexpected. It was surprising, however, that Type V addicts—those who were involved in addiction for virtually the entire period studied and who avoided jail in the process—were less criminally deviant prior to addiction. These individuals obviously appeared to show an early and continued talent for avoiding trouble.

Some years ago there was a great deal of discussion between Lukoff and McGlothlin that centered on the question of which came first: addiction or crime. In this debate, Lukoff (1974) referred to the results of his study of a population of black addicts in Bedford-Stuyvesant in Brooklyn, New York, and McGlothlin et al. (1978) employed his research findings based on a population of white and Mexican-American addicts in California. The point at issue was whether addicts were criminals before becoming addicted or became involved in crime as a result of addiction. We came to the conclusion that they were both correct, because we found both types of addicts in our career study. Our results also suggested that Lukoff and McGlothlin probably would have found both types as well, if they had classified their subjects in the same way we had. Further, in one of our subsequent studies (Nurco et al. 1988), we classified a sample of 214 narcotic addicts into two groups: those who reported involvement in criminal activity before becoming addicted (N = 108) and those who reported no such activity (N = 106). For the 108 addicts previously involved in crime, addiction was associated with an increase in already established predispositions toward deviance rather than an abrupt change in behavior. In contrast, for the 106 addicts not involved in preaddiction crime, addiction status was associated with a precipitous exacerbation in criminal behavior. Thus, the long-debated issue whether criminal activity committed during periods of narcotic addiction represents a continuation of an already deviant lifestyle or a marked change in behavior is not an either/or proposition but reflects different effects for different types of addicts.

Our results with regard to differences between black and white addicts suggest that blacks are more successful than whites in coping with the problems associated with the maintenance of addiction. The largest proportion of black addicts over time had virtually uninterrupted careers in narcotic drug use (Nurco, Cisin, and Balter 1981c). These individuals were skilled at avoiding jail and apparently were able to function adequately in a lifestyle that involved obtaining income from illegal sources to purchase narcotics, primarily heroin. Whites, on the other hand, appeared to have more difficulty in successfully maintaining addiction careers. Over the years, the proportion of white addicts who were able to maintain addiction careers in the community spent less than half of their 10-year careers addicted, spending most of the remaining time in jail.

Our findings and those of other researchers have suggested that there may be a relationship between ethnicity and psychopathology in the narcotic addict. Since heroin and cocaine are more available in black neighborhoods, their use by whites represents more deviant behavior than their use by blacks (Langrod 1970; Nail, Gunderson, and Arthur 1974; Nurco, Cisin, and Balter 1981c; Waldorf 1973). It has also been reported that while white addicts are more likely than their black counterparts to come from an intact home, earn more money, have more education, have fewer addicted or alcoholic relatives, or be on welfare, they are less likely to report getting along well with their families (Langrod 1970; Waldorf 1973). It is possible that despite their comparatively favorable social position, whites tend to use drugs more as a result of emotional problems or deviance (Langrod 1970; Nail, Gunderson and Arthur 1974; Nurco, Cisin, and Balter 1981c; Waldorf 1973). In line with this reasoning, studies of differences between black and white addicts on the Minnesota Multiphasic Personality Inventory (MMPI) have consistently revealed a greater degree of psychopathology among whites (Dolan, Roberts, Penk, Robinowitz, and Atkins 1983; Hill, Haertzen, and Glazer 1960; Penk, Robinowitz, Woodward, and Hess 1978; Shaffer, Kinlock, and Nurco 1982; Shaffer, Nurco, Hanlon, Kinlock, Duszynski, and Stephenson 1988).

For a number of reasons, our findings appear to have a great deal of relevance for public policy and treatment programs. First, since addicts differ widely with regard to important dimensions such as criminality, lifestyle, psychopathology, and percentage of time addicted, treatment strategies need to be tailored to the individual case. Second, intervention strategies need to take particular cognizance of the demographic backgrounds of clients. This recommendation is based on the findings that white addicts display somewhat greater psychological and social adjustment problems than blacks, many of whom tend to be successful at maintaining addiction and avoiding incarceration and treatment. Third, continued investigation is needed with respect to the process of recruitment into addiction and to variations in the characteristics of newly recruited addicts and the addiction careers they pursue (Nurco, Cisin, and Balter 1981c).

REFERENCES

Ball, J. C., Rosen, L., Flueck, J. A., and Nurco, D. N. (1981). The criminality of heroin addicts: When addicted and when off opiates. In *The Drugs-Crime Connection*, J. A. Inciardi (ed.), pp. 39–65. Sage Annual Reviews of Drug and Alcohol Abuse, Vol. 5. Beverly Hills: Sage.

———. (1982). Lifetime criminality of heroin addicts in the United States. *Journal of Drug Issues* 12: 225–39.

Ball, J. C., Shaffer, J. W., and Nurco, D. N. (1983). The day-to-day criminality of heroin addicts in Baltimore—A study in the continuity of offence rates. *Drug and Alcohol Dependence* 12: 119–42.

Dolan, M. P., Roberts, W. R., Penk, W. E., Robinowitz, R., and Atkins, H. G. (1983). Personality differences among Black, White, and Hispanic-American male heroin addicts on the MMPI content scales. *Journal of Clinical Psychology* 39: 807–14.

Gandossy, R. P., Williams, J. R., Cohen, J., and Harwood, H. J. (1980). *Drugs and Crime: A Survey and Analysis of the Literature*. Washington, D.C.: U.S. Government Printing office.

Hauser, R. M., and Featherman, D. L. (1977). *Process of Stratification: Trends and Analyses*. New York: Academic.

Hill, H. E., Haertzen, C. A., and Glazer, R. (1960). Personality characteristics of heroin addicts as indicated by the MMPI. *Journal of General Psychology* 62: 127–39.

Inciardi, J. A. (1986). *The War on Drugs: Heroin, Cocaine, Crime, and Public Policy*. Palo Alto, CA: Mayfield.

Kleber, H. D. (1989). Treatment of drug dependence: What works. *International Review of Psychiatry* 20: 823–44.

Langrod, J. (1970). Secondary drug use among heroin users. *The International Journal of the Addictions* 5: 611–35.

Lukoff, I. F. (1974). Issues in the valuation of heroin treatment. In *Drug Use: Epidemiological and Sociological Approaches*, E. Josephson and E. E. Carroll (eds.), pp. 129–57. New York: Wiley.

McGlothlin, W. H., Anglin, M. D., and Wilson, B. D. (1978). Narcotic addiction and crime. *Criminology* 16: 293–316.

McLellan, A. T., Luborsky, L., Woody, G. E., and O'Brien, C. P. (1980). An improved diagnostic evaluation instrument for substance abuse patients: The Addiction Severity Index. *Journal of Nervous and Mental Disease* 168: 26–33.

Nail, R. L., Gunderson, E. K. E., and Arthur, R. J. (1974). Black-white differences in social background and military drug abuse patterns. *American Journal of Psychiatry* 3: 1097–1102.

Nurco, D. N., Bonito, A. J., Lerner, M., and Balter, M. B. (1975). Studying addicts over time: Methodology and preliminary findings. *American Journal of Drug and Alcohol Abuse* 2: 183–96.

Nurco, D. N., Cisin, I. H., and Balter, M. B. (1981a). Addict careers: I. A new typology. *The International Journal of the Addictions* 16: 1305–25.

————. (1981b). Addict careers: II. The first ten years. *The International Journal of the Addictions* 16: 1327–56.

————. (1981c). Addict careers: III. Trends across time. *The International Journal of the Addictions* 16: 1357–72.

————. (1982). Trends in the age of onset of narcotic addiction. *Chemical Dependencies: Behavioral and Biomedical Issues* 4: 221–28.

Nurco, D. N., and DuPont, R. L. (1977). A preliminary report on crime and addiction within a community-wide population of narcotic addicts. *Drug and Alcohol Dependence* 2: 109–21.

Nurco, D. N., and Farrell, E. V. (1975). Narcotic abusers and poverty. *Criminology* 13: 389–99.

Nurco, D. N., Hanlon, T. E., Balter, M. B., Kinlock, T. W., and Slaght, E. A classification of narcotic addicts based on type, amount, and severity of crime. *Journal of Drug Issues*, in press.

Nurco, D. N., Hanlon, T. E., Kinlock, T. W., and Duszynski, K. R. (1988). Differential criminal patterns of narcotic addicts over an addiction career. *Criminology* 26: 301–16.

Nurco, D. N., and Shaffer, J. W. (1982). Types and characteristics of addicts in the community. *Drugs and Alcohol Dependence* 9: 43–78.

Nurco, D. N., Shaffer, J. W., and Cisin, I. H. (1984). An ecological analysis of the interrelationships among drug abuse and other indices of social pathology. *The International Journal of the Addictions* 19: 441–51.

Nurco, D. N., Shaffer, J. W., Hanlon, T. E., Kinlock, T. W., Duszynski, K. R., and Stephenson, P. (1987). Attitudes toward narcotic addiction. *Journal of Nervous and Mental Disease* 175: 653–60.

Nurco, D. N., Wegner, N., Baum, H., and Makofsky, A. (1979). *A Case Study: Narcotic Addiction over a Quarter of a Century in a Major American City (1950–1977)*. Rockville, MD: National Institute on Drug Abuse.

Nurco, D. N., Wegner, N., and Stephenson, P. (1982). Female narcotic addicts: Changing profiles. *Journal of Addiction and Health* 3: 62–105.

Penk, W. E., Robinowitz, R., Woodward, W. A., and Hess, J. L. (1978). Differences in MMPI scores of black and white compulsive heroin users. *Journal of Abnormal Psychology* 87: 505–13.

Pottieger, A. E. (1981). Sample bias in drugs/crime research: an empirical study. In *The Drugs-Crime Connection*, J. A. Inciardi (ed.), pp. 207–37. Sage Annual Review of Drug and Alcohol Abuse, Vol. 5. Beverly Hills: Sage.

Shaffer, J. W., Kinlock, T. W., and Nurco, D. N. (1982). Factor structure of the MMPI-168 in male narcotic addicts. *Journal of Clinical Psychology* 38: 656–61.

Shaffer, J. W., Nurco, D. N., Hanlon, T. E., Kinlock, T. W., Duszynski, K. R., and Stephenson, P. (1988). MMPI-168 profiles of male narcotic addicts by ethnic group and city. *Journal of Clinical Psychology* 44: 292–98.

Shaffer, J. W., Nurco, D. N., and Kinlock, T. W. (1984). A new classification of narcotic addicts based on type and extent of criminal activity. *Comprehensive Psychiatry* 25: 315–28.

Shaffer, J. W. Wegner, N., Kinlock, T. W., and Nurco, D. N. (1983). An empirical typology of narcotic addicts. *The International Journal of the Addictions* 18: 183–94.

Strategy Council on Drug Abuse. (1973). *Federal Strategy for Drug Abuse Prevention*. Washington, D.C.: Author.

U.S. Department of Justice (1983). *Report to the Nation on Crime and Justice: The Data*. Washington, D.C.: Bureau of Justice Statistics.

Waldorf, D. (1973). *Careers in Dope*. Englewood Cliffs, N.J.: Prentice-Hall.

PART FIVE

Dropout and Relapse

CHAPTER 16

The Dropout Rate Among Drug Addicts During the First Ninety Days of Residential Treatment*

Heinrich Küfner, André Denis, Irene Roch, and Michael Böhmer

INTRODUCTION

The very high dropout rate of 50% to 75% in drug-free residential treatment is a well-known problem in the treatment of drug addicts (Baekeland and Lundwall 1975; Craig 1985), but it is highly dependent upon the time period one chooses to examine. If one treatment lasts half a year and another is, ultimately lifelong (for instance, as in some programs of methadone maintenance) comparison of the same time intervals is problematic. The problem of high dropout rate should still be analyzed in greater detail. The first basic hypothesis in our study is that dropping out of treatment is in general a negative predictor of treatment outcome. There are many empirical results which affirm this (cf. Baekeland and Lundwall 1975), although some therapists say that in the single case dropping out of treatment may be an important step in the long-term process of moving toward drug abstinence.

Our second basic hypothesis has been controversial in the empirical literature: The longer the addicts stay in treatment before dropping out, the better the treatment outcome. This was affirmed, for example, in a study by De Leon et al. (1982). Within this assumption, the effect of treatment length is an important factor, but the problem is that dropping

*The study was funded by the German Federal Ministry of Health.

out of treatment is presumably a qualitatively different event which may be independent of the effect of treatment length.

From these basic hypotheses the conclusion can be drawn that reducing the dropout rate or lengthening treatment duration improves treatment outcome. Therefore the German Federal Ministry of Health started a demonstration project that first involved 16 treatment centers and later 34 treatment centers. The aim of the project is to reduce the dropout rate by establishing so-called crisis therapists. Crisis therapists should be experienced in the treating of addicts. Their role, function, and interventions are not fixed: each crisis therapist has to determine his or her own role, function, and interventions under the special conditions of the treatment center. Functions of the crisis therapist include, for instance, carrying out interviews at admission, leading special group discussions on the problem of dropping out, offering additional interviews in case of client crisis or when a client wishes to contact somebody other than a therapist. If a client has decided to terminate treatment, he or she can be transferred to another residential or outpatient treatment center or helped to find residence or work. These latter interventions should help to prevent the patient who drops out from going back to the drug scene.

The evaluation of this project by our research group has the following aims:

1. Documentation of the different treatment programs and of the role and interventions of the crisis therapists.
2. Documentation (description) of client variables and of the dropout process.
3. Analysis of the changes in the dropout rates and the relationship between client variables, treatment variables, and dropout.

In the present preliminary analysis the questions are:

1. What is the distribution of dropouts in the course of treatment in the control group of patients before crisis therapists have begun their work?
2. In the present phase of the study, under the condition of the long-term treatment of mostly one year or longer, only the first 90 days in treatment could be analyzed. Therefore, has the dropout rate in the first 90 days of the study group been reduced in comparison to the dropout rate of the control group?
3. On which variables do patients who drop out from treatment in the first 90 days differ from those patients staying in treatment longer?

METHODS

The design of the study is characterized as follows. There are two kinds of treatment centers: one group consists of the old treatment centers (I), because they were the first in the study (1988), and the second includes the new treatment centers (II) which entered the study about a year and a half later. Subsequently, a retrospective control group was formed with patients who were admitted during the two years prior to the creation of the crisis therapist position. With the establishment of crisis therapists, study of the above-mentioned two prospective groups was begun. The data are assessed within the first and second week and, in normal cases, at the regular termination of treatment. Very early dropouts (for example, at the first day) who could not be asked to participate in the study and denials are also assessed, but with only a small set of variables. In the calculation of dropout rates all clients were included. An overview of the different samples is given in Table 16.1.

In the following analysis the client sample of the new treatment centers (II) serves mainly for cross-validation of the results in the old treatment centers (I). Control Group I and Study Group I of the old treatment centers have nearly the same percentage of men (Table 16.2): There are 74% men in the control group of nearly 2,000 addicts and 74% men in the study group of nearly 900 addicts up to now. In relation to age there are some minor differences: men and women in the study group are slightly older than those in the control group.

The assessed variables in the retrospective control group indicate some sociodemographic variables and data about the type of dropout. The variables of the prospective study group were assessed by two questionnaires: one with 40 items answered by the patient and one with 9 items answered by the therapist. The variables should give information about social network, drug consumption and sequelae, psychosocial problems, partner problems, psychopathological disturbances, and about prior treatment for addiction. Another comprehensive questionnaire about treatment variables was developed, but it has not yet been analyzed in the present investigation.

RESULTS

Dropouts in Retrospective Control Group I

The total dropout rate including very early dropouts in the control group of the old centers is 74.5% (Figure 16.1). Dropout was defined as ter-

TABLE 16.1

Overview of the Four Sample Groups in the Demonstration Project

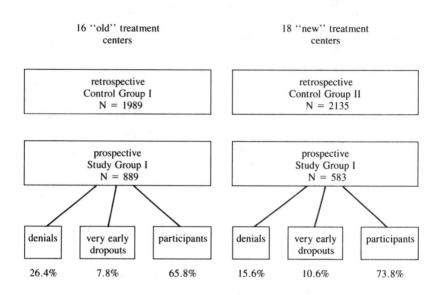

minating treatment before the regular treatment time had passed, whatever the reason. The dropout rates of the different treatment centers vary between about 52% and 88%, thus the maximum difference is 36%. The dropout rate within the first 90 days is important for the present analysis of the study group because until the time of data analysis most patients had not finished the planned treatment period. Sixty percent of all dropouts terminate treatment within the first 90 days. The rank correlation between the dropout rates of the treatment centers within the first 90 days and the total dropout rate is .89. This means that the rank order of centers according to the total dropout rates can be predicted fairly accurately by the dropout rates within the first 90 days.

Control Group I versus Study Group I

In Table 16.3 the dropout rates within the first 90 days of the control groups and the study groups are compared. In Control Group I of the

TABLE 16.2

Control Group and Study Group Compared in Relation to Gender and Age

Variable	Control Group I (N = 1,989)	Study Group I (N = 889)
Sex (men)	(1,475) 74.2%	(657) 73.9%
age (years)	men: M = 26.39 SD = 4.66	men: M = 27.76 SD = 4.95
	Women: M = 24.41 SD = 4.22	women: M = 25.48 SD = 4.26

old treatment centers, the 90-day dropout rate is 44.2%, slightly higher than that of the new treatment centers (40.5%). The broad range of nearly 50% difference in the dropout rates of the individual treatment centers is an important fact because it may be interpreted that, besides differences in the patient samples, there are clear differences between the dropout rates of different treatment centers that are probably dependent on treatment variables. Those differences are the basis for analyzing the relationships between treatment variables and dropout rates.

In both study groups there is a significant reduction of 16% and of 7% in the dropout rates within the first 90 days of treatment. Analyzing the individual treatment centers, one finds a reduction of the dropout rates in 81% of the old treatment centers and in 78% of the new treatment centers. The range of the reduction in all treatment centers was between 0.8% and 47%. The increase was between 0.6% and 14%.

The following data pertain mainly to the results regarding the old treatment centers, because until now we have not analyzed the new treatment centers in all details. In Control Group I men have a slightly higher dropout rate than women (but not significantly), whereas there was the opposite relationship in Study Group I (Table 16.4). After the establishment of crisis therapists, men had a dropout rate of 26.5% in comparison to 33.2% in the women. This is the first clue to a differential effect of the interventions by crisis therapists. The difference in the dropout rates of men and women in the study group is not statistically significant (chi-square test: p = .0621). In both sexes there is a clear reduction of the dropout rates within the first 90 days, but the reduction was stronger in men (men: 26.5% versus 45.2% in Control Group I; women: 33.2% versus 41.4% in Control Group I).

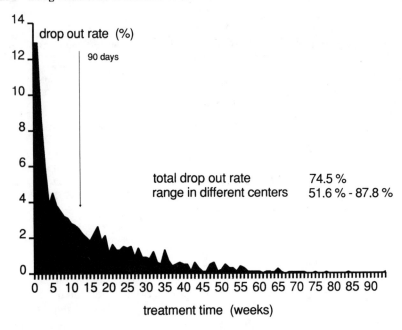

FIGURE 16.1.
Dropouts in course of treatment (Control Group I).

Another goal of the study is to analyze the stability of the reduction in dropout rates in relation to age. Our hypotheses include: (1) younger patients drop out of treatment more frequently than older ones, and (2) the interventions of crisis therapists may mainly help the older clients. In Table 16.4 younger and older groups, separated by gender, were com-

TABLE 16.3

Dropouts within the First 90 Days: Study Groups vs. Control Groups

	dropout rates in	
	"old" treatment centers	"new" treatment centers
control group	N = 1,989(I) 44.2% Range: 27.0%–59.1%	N = 2,135(II) 40.5% Range: 9.7%–54.2%
study group	N = 889(I) 28.2% Range: 5.0%–50.5%	N = 583(II) 33.4% Range: 0–58.8%

Chi-Square-test   p = .000

TABLE 16.4

Age of Clients Who Drop Out within the First 90 Days
(Control Group and Study Group)

age	dropout rate		Chi-Square test
	control group I N = 1989	study group I N = 889	
men:			
≤ 25 years	(313) 47.6%	(70) 29.7%	p = .0000
≥ 26 years	(348) 43.0%	(102) 24.5%	p = .0000
	p = .0860	p = .1748	
women			
≤ 25 years	(141) 43.7%	(53) 44.5%	p = .9536 n.s.
≥ 26 years	(72) 38.3%	(23) 20.7%	p = .0025
	p = .2752	p = .0002	

pared according to the median of the frequency distributions. Comparison of the two groups indicated the following results: First, within the control group the younger men show only a slightly higher dropout rate than the older men. There is no significant difference in the dropout rates between younger and older women, although there is a trend in the same direction. The hypothesis that younger patients drop out of treatment can be affirmed in the control group, but only as a trend. The same is true in the new treatment centers.

In Study Group I the difference in the dropout rates between the older and younger men has diminished and is no longer significant; but the difference between younger and older women strongly increased. The dropout rate of younger women within the first 90 days was not reduced, whereas in older women the dropout rate was clearly reduced. This differential effect can be seen in Figure 16.2. Younger women of an age lower than 26 do not show a reduction in their dropout rate. The same phenomenon is true in the new treatment centers. We have no empirical explanation for this result as yet. An analysis of the relationship between treatment variables and dropout which is planned for the future may lead to some empirically based hypotheses about this problem.

Another topic of this study is related to the type of dropout. We formulated the hypothesis that dropouts by decision of the treatment centers themselves were reduced. In Table 16.5 the different ways or types of dropout are categorized. There is no difference in the frequencies of different types of dropout between the control group and the study group. The same is true again of the new treatment centers. That means that

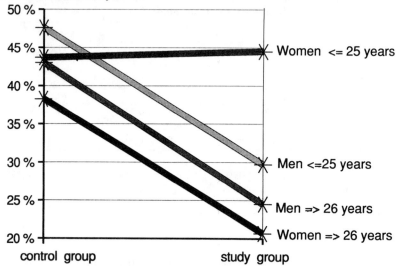

dropout rate
within the first 90 days

FIGURE 16.2.
Dropout rates, sex, and age (Study Group I vs. Control Group I).

the project itself and the interventions of the crisis therapists have not influenced the dropout decisions of the treatment centers. Therefore, the reduction in the number of dropouts cannot be explained by the changed criteria of the treatment centers discharging patients.

Study Group I

The following results are related to Study Group I only, without the denials and the very early dropouts for whom these variables could not be assessed; drug consumption is described and differences between men and women are analyzed (Table 16.6).

Most of the clients take opioids; the frequency of cocaine use is much higher in Study Group II of the new treatment centers. Slightly more than 50% took medication legally or illegally. Men and women show a significant difference in cocaine abuse; more men take cocaine than women. In contrast, more women take legal or illegal medication, as had been expected from other studies. This result is also valid for the new

TABLE 16.5

Different Ways of Dropping Out:
(Study Group vs. Control Group)

way of dropping out	dropouts in			Chi-Square test significance
	control group N = 880		study group N = 251	
own decision	737	83.8%	206 82.4%	n.s.
discharge by treatment center	122	13.9%	38 15.2%	n.s.
other	21	2.3%	7 2.4%	n.s.

TABLE 16.6

Drug Abuse in Study Group I

drug abuse	total 634	men N = 467	women N = 167	Chi-Square test significance
opioids	549 (86.6%)	400 (85.7%)	149 (89.2%)	n.s.
cocaine	272 (42.9%)	213 (46.6%)	59 (35.3%)	p = .0269
other illegal drugs	478 (75.4%)	355 (76.0%)	123 (73.7%)	n.s.
medication	343 (54.1%)	239 (51.2%)	104 (62.3%)	p = .0173
alcohol	293 (46.2%)	221 (47.3%)	72 (43.1%)	n.s.
methadone	80 (12.6%)	47 (10.1%)	33 (19.8%)	p = .0019

treatment centers. The consumption of methadone was surprisingly high, particularly when one considers that substitution programs were prohibited in West Germany until 1988. In the new treatment centers the percentage of methadone consumption for Study Group I is 12.6% and for Study Group II is 23.9%.

In comparing the dropouts from the first 90 days with the patients who stayed in treatment longer, we hypothesized that the dropout group had lower social stability than did those staying in treatment longer. The results indicate only two trends: The dropouts within the first 90 days show a higher rate of unemployment. This relationship is also confirmed by the results in the new treatment centers (dropouts: 79.6% unemployed; longer treatment group: 70.7% unemployed; chi-square test: p = .0969). The results pertaining to partnership ran counter to the hypothesis of social stability. The dropouts more frequently answer that they do have a partnership (dropouts: 52.6% with partner; longer-treatment group: 42.9% with partner; chi-square test: p = .0826). This information may

TABLE 16.7

Drug Consumption: Dropouts within the First 90 Days vs. Clients Staying in Treatment Longer

drug consumption (only significant differences)	dropout within the first 90 days	clients staying in treatment longer	Chi-Square test p-values
medication	651 (42.7%)	282 (57.4%)	.0025
other illegal drugs (without opioids)	95 (66.4%)	383 (78.0%)	.0066
cocaine	51 (35.7%)	221 (45.0%)	.0586

TABLE 16.8

Rating by Therapists: Drop outs in the First 90 Days Compared with Clients Staying in Treatment Longer

	mean score			
Rating by therapists (1 = very good; 6 = very bad)	dropouts within the first 90 days	clients staying in treatment longer	N	U-test
competence for forming relations	4.31 SD = 1.15	4.01 SD = 1.15	395	.0408
competence for communication	4.00 SD = 1.16	3.71 SD = 1.22	395	.0700
coping with stress	4.71 SD = 0.87	4.35 SD = 0.96	395	.0029
motivation for treatment	3.90 SD = 1.19	3.59 SD = 1.16	583	.0073

be ascertained by the way that a client with partner may say, for example, "I do not need the shelter of the treatment center because I am not alone." This result also demonstrates the importance of the addict's partner's involvement in the treatment as early as possible. But this relationship could not be substantiated in the new treatment centers.

Data about drug consumption (only variables with significant differences) are reported in Table 16.7. Dropouts within the first 90 days took medication, cocaine, and other illegal drugs besides opioids less frequently than those staying in treatment longer. These results for cocaine and medication could be confirmed by the data from the new treatment centers. The percentage of multiple drug abuse is lower in the dropouts of the first 90 days. The drug abuse of the 90-day dropouts apparently is not as heavy as that of the clients staying in treatment longer.

TABLE 16.9

Rating by Patients
(Drop outs in the First 90 Days vs. Clients staying Longer in Treatment)

	mean scores			
Rating by patients (1–6)	dropouts within the first 90 days	clients staying in treatment longer	N	U-test significance
Probability for dropping out (1 = very low)	3.02 SD = 1.28	2.43 SD = 1.21	517	.0000
time interval until dropping out (in months)	3.68 SD = 3.12	4.46 SD = 3.19	333	.0057
preparation for treatment by counseling center (1 = very good)	3.73 SD = 1.50	3.37 SD = 1.45	326	.0444

In Table 16.8 the behavior ratings by the therapists show the following differences: The competence to form relationships is rated lower in the group of dropouts, as is the dropouts' competence to communicate with others and the ability to cope with stressful situations. The global treatment motivation was rated lower in the group of dropouts. The interpretation is that therapists do have some idea as to the patients who have a high risk of dropping out of treatment. The poorer competence for communication was affirmed by the results in the new treatment centers, but the variables of coping with stress and motivation for treatment were seen only as trends.

The self-ratings by the patients (Table 16.9) show that the dropouts assess their probability of dropping out as being higher and the time period until treatment termination as being shorter than do the other patients. The preparation for residential therapy by counseling centers is judged as worse by the dropouts. Only the results of the first two variables are also true in the new treatment centers, but the variable regarding counseling centers is not.

Finally, we carried out a multiple regression analysis to assess the prognosis of dropping out of treatment. For the total group the multiple correlation was 0.3. Separated by gender, the multiple correlation for men was R = 0.29 and for women R = 0.35. There is, however, no cross-validation, and some assumptions of regression analysis are not valid; thus these results are preliminary.

DISCUSSION

The high dropout rate of about 74% in the control group before the crisis therapists began their work is comparable to the results of many other studies about premature treatment termination. It must be mentioned that all dropouts, from the first day until the end of treatment, were assessed regardless of the causes of the premature termination. On average, treatment length is about one year, and this long treatment time is connected with higher dropout rates. It is also well known that in first-time treatment the dropout rate is very high; in our study 60% terminated their treatment within the first 90 days. There is a high correlation between the dropout rates after 90 days and the total dropout rate of the treatment centers. Therefore it seems legitimate to use the dropout rate after 90 days to compare different treatment centers.

Regarding the study group, the dropout rate within the first 90 days was reduced after the crisis therapists began their work. This result, of course, may not be interpreted causally without further detailed analysis. Several aspects must be considered:

1. The control group and the study group are not randomized samples. Therefore, one problem is to analyze the comparability of the two samples of clients. For client characteristics, the percentage of men in both groups is the same. In the study group, the clients are on average about one year older than in the control group. Up to now we have had no hints that age is an important predictor of premature termination of treatment.

2. Additionally, the two samples were not surveyed simultaneously, so that changes in the treatment program may have occurred in the interim. We do not have analyzed data thus far in relation to changes in the treatment program. Therefore the question about causal factors of this reduction must remain open.

3. One special explanation could be that treatment centers have changed their way of dealing with clients who had broken treatment rules and who would have been discharged for disciplinary reasons (for instance, if clients had consumed any drugs). In order to reduce the dropout rate, the treatment center could have changed this procedure. Although there was no change in the percentages of the different types of dropouts

(i.e., in the percentage of disciplinary discharges), this explanation still could be valid.

4. Not all treatment centers show a reduction in their dropout rates. In about 20% of the facilities, there is no change at all or even a slight increase. It would be interesting to compare these unsuccessful treatment centers with the successful ones regarding patient variables and especially regarding treatment characteristics. This task will be done in future analyses.

Independent of the causal factors, the reduction of the dropout rate within the first 90 days does mean that at least the time in treatment was extended, although the total dropout rate remains the same. From other studies (e.g., De Leon and Ziegenfuss 1986) we know that the longer the time in treatment the better the outcome. In the group of younger women the reduction of dropout rates could not be found. Possibly, the treatment program is not specialized for younger women, for it seems not to be attractive enough to bind these clients to the treatment. In some treatment centers special groups for women have been established, but the effect of these interventions could not yet be evaluated.

The prediction of dropout is a difficult task, much as it is for predictions in many other domains. Our results show that the therapists' rating of the competence of the clients to get into contact with other persons is a predictor of dropping out. Coming together in the treatment center means that new relationships with other clients or therapists can develop that might reduce the probability of dropout. It was also shown that even at the beginning of treatment, the clients had a certain feeling that they would drop out earlier than other clients who were staying in treatment longer than 90 days.

What do the different patterns of drug consumption as predictors mean? The more frequent consumption of legal and illegal medication, which is more characteristic of women, could imply that this client group has other needs (e.g., for more warmth and shelter in the sense of medical care which is not offered in most of our treatment centers). The more frequent consumption of other illegal drugs besides opioids may mean that the effect and the consequences of these different drugs are not sufficiently considered in the treatment process. Also, it may be that there are different personalities using different drugs and this could not be integrated into the treatment process.

Further analysis of the ongoing study will show whether the predictors could be reproduced in other patient samples. The analysis of the data at the regular discharge of treatment can provide interesting information about treatment factors which may help clients to cope with the crisis of premature treatment termination. Once the effect of patient selections is taken into consideration, the relationships between treatment variables and dropout rates will be most important for improving residential treatment for addicts.

REFERENCES

Baekeland, F., and Lundwall, L. (1975). Dropping out of treatment: A critical review. *Psychological Bulletin* 82: 738–83.

Craig, R. J. (1985). Reducing the treatment drop-out rate in drug abuse programs. *Journal of Substance Abuse Treatment* 2: 209–19.

De Leon, G., and Rosenthal, M. S. (1979). Therapeutic communities. In *Handbook of Drug Abuse*. Dupont, R. L., Goldstein, A., O'Donnell, J., and Brown, B. (eds.), pp. 39–47. Washington, DC: Government Printing Office.

De Leon, G., and Schwartz, S. V. (1984). Therapeutic communities: What are the retention rates? *American Journal of Drug and Alcohol Abuse* 10 (2): 267–84.

De Leon, G., Wexler, H. K., and Jainchill, N. (1982). The therapeutic community: Success and improvement rates 5 years after treatment. *International Journal of the Addictions* 17: 703–47.

De Leon, G., and Ziegenfuss, J. T. (eds.). (1986). *Therapeutic Communities for Addictions: Readings in Theory, Research and Practice*. Springfield, Illinois: Charles C. Thomas.

Holland, S. (1978). Gateway houses: Effectiveness of treatment on criminal behavior. *International Journal of the Addictions* 13: 369–81.

Siddall, J. W., and Conway, G. L. (1988). Interactional variables associated with retention and success in residential drug treatment. *International Journal of the Addictions*: 1241–54.

CHAPTER 17

Factors Influencing Dropout from Drug Abuse Treatment Programs*

André Denis, Heinrich Küfner, Irene Roch, and Michael Böhmer

INTRODUCTION

Many studies in dropout research focus on the personality characteristics of the patients and try to correlate them with the dropout event (Craig 1985). Most of these studies deal with alcoholic and psychiatric patients, and the relevant findings do not explain much of the dropout process. Roback and Smith (1987) propose the analysis of the ongoing process of dropout. This also implies an analysis of the social network of the patient, meaning, for example, that we should examine the interaction between the patient, the treatment group, and the therapists. What we need to explain and predict dropout is a comprehensive description of dropout as a process. One aim of this analysis is to provide such a description; another goal is to formulate hypotheses for further research based on empirical data.

The analysis presented here refers to a part of the study discussed by Küfner et al. in this volume, thus the entire study will not be described here. In order to gather more information on the event of dropout and to produce hypotheses for further research, an analysis of the process from the therapist's perspective was made: First, a classification system was developed to get a widely differentiated representation of the attrition pro-

*This study was funded by the German Federal Ministry of Health.

TABLE 17.1

Category System (Main Categories) for the Analysis of Dropouts

1. external form of dropout
2. events which lead directly to dropout
3. stressful diseases
4. psychopathological symptoms
5. psychosocial problems
6. stressful life events
7. drug-related factors
8. disciplinary factors, not drug related
9. relationships within the facility
10. relationships outside the facility
11. other external factors: money, justice
12. the patient's attitude toward treatment in general
13. treatment process:
    ambivalence over a a long period of time
    beginning of a decisive step in treatment which is interrupted by dropping out
14. crisis interventions by the therapeutic team

cess. Then a quantitative analysis of the therapist's reports was made to detect the most important factors influencing the dropout event.

METHOD

We asked the therapists to describe the precise circumstances of the patient's premature treatment termination. To analyze the answers given by the therapists, the factors and circumstances found in the reports were collected. The next step consisted of looking for "recurring guidelines" in the data and sorting them into categories. Using Patton's (1980) guidelines for developing a classification system, a description and definition was constructed for each category, and then the categories were judged for "internal homogeneity" and "external heterogenity." "Internal homogeneity" corresponds to the extent to which the data seem to be consistent and fit together within one category. "External heterogenity" means the extent to which differences among categories are bold and clear. The last steps in the analysis involved working with both the data and the classification system to verify its meaningfulness, the accuracy of the categories, and the placement of data in categories.

There is not enough space here to present the resulting classification system with all 112 categories in detail, thus Table 17.1 shows only the main categories. The first category is concerned with the external form of dropout, that is, whether the dropout was unexpected and whether it was clandestine. The second category, "events which lead directly to dropout," refers to whether the patient is forced to leave the facility without being responsible for it. The next categories relate to stressful diseases, such as psychosomatic reactions or HIV infection, and to psychopathological symptoms, such as psychotic disorders, compulsions, and depressive disorders. "Psychosocial problems" is a category that includes statements difficult to operationalize, for example, "the patient has a low frustration tolerance." Category 6 concerns stressful life events mentioned by the therapist, such as death of a relative or the experience of imprisonment. The next category deals with all factors directly related to drugs or drug dependency, for example relapse, craving, lack of insight into one's own disease, doubts about the sense in and the ability to achieve a drug-free life.

In connection with interpersonal relationships there are two main categories: relationships inside the facility (9) (partnerships in the sense of heterosexual friendships, relationships to their children, and relationships with other patients or with the therapists) and relationships outside the facility (10), such as partnerships and family relations. Money and legal matters are included in a separate category. Categories 12 and 13 deal with the patient's attitude toward therapy; the former deals with statements about motivation, fears, desire for freedom, and so on, and the latter deals specifically with ambivalence about continuation of therapy over a long period of time. Interruption during the therapy at the beginning of a new, decisive step is another aspect that contributes to the patient's attitude toward the therapy process, and it is a dropout factor. Crisis intervention by the therapeutic team is marked in the last category. The following shows an example of a statement to be rated:

Since the beginning of therapy the patient had great **difficulties in integrating** herself into the community and in **deciding to undergo therapy**. She started **several relationships with men** and was in crisis nearly the whole time. The patient had to be disciplinarily discharged because she **relapsed into inhaling chemical substances**.

The marked main categories and subcategories are:

- ambivalence to the therapy in general over a long period of time
- relationships within the facility:
  - partnership within the facility
  - repeated close relationships with members of the opposite sex
  - relationship to other patients
  - difficulties in integrating in community life, outsider status

TABLE 17.2

Description of the Sample: Type of Dropout

Type of Dropout	Total (142)		Men (93)		Women (49)	
	N	%	N	%	N	%
Sign out against medical advice	113	79.6	71	76.3	42	85.7
Disciplinary discharge	26	20.4	19	20.4	7	14.3
Others	3	2.1	3	3.3	0	0.0

• drug-related factor:
  −relapse
  −inhaling chemical substances

All reports concerning dropouts with a length of treatment of up to 90 days were entered into the analysis. This is the same sample as in the study presented by Küfner et al., excluding those patients who refused to participate in the study and those who left the facilities in the first days of treatment. One hundred and forty-three dropouts remained, but one of these had to be excluded; 142 cases were presented by the therapists and could be analyzed by two raters. Of all ratings made by either of the raters, 84% were marked concordantly and 40% of all cases were rated in exactly the same manner. For each category and subcategory the Kappa-value, which is a measure of interrater reliability, was computed. The Kappa range for the main categories, which will be mentioned in the discussion of the results, varies from .83 to .93. This means that these main categories proved to have high reliability. After the first rating, the cases which had been rated discordantly were discussed by the two raters and a new rating was made which entered into further analysis. The mean number of categories rated for each case was six.

RESULTS

Nearly 80% of the sample of dropouts signed out against medical advice, and 20% were discharged for disciplinary reasons. More women signed out voluntarily (86% of the women versus 76% of the men), and fewer women left due to disciplinary discharge (14% of the women versus 20% of the men), but these differences are not significant (Table 17.2).

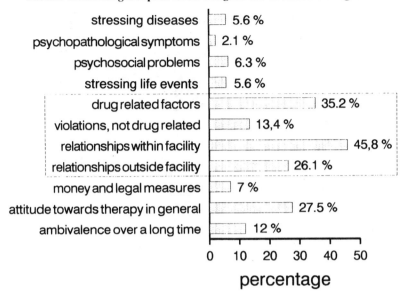

FIGURE 17.1.
Main categories used for the analysis of the therapists' reports about dropouts.

Figure 17.1 shows the main categories concerned: Stressful diseases, psychopathological symptoms, psychosocial problems, and stressful life events are each mentioned in less than 7% of the therapist's reports. The most important factors are marked by a frame in this figure. Drug-related factors play a role in only 35% of the reports; violations of treatment rules which are not drug related occur in 13% of the cases; relationships within the facility seem to be involved in 46% of the cases, and those outside the facility in 26% of the cases. Other factors like money and legal measures are involved in 7% of the cases. The categories "attitude toward therapy in general" and "ambivalence over a long time" are marked in 28% and 12% of the cases, respectively. They include "soft data," that is, data that are difficult to operationalize by the therapists as well as by the raters. Some of the subcategories of these items have an interrater reliability as low as .007, thus these categories will not be included in our discussion. Instead, we shall focus on drug-related and nondrug-related violation and relationship factors.

Figure 17.2 shows the proportion of single and combined main categories involved in dropout. In 14% of the cases none of these categories was involved. We see that the relationship factor alone is found in more than 40% of the cases, in combination with drug problems and nondrug-

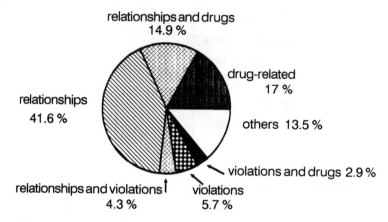

FIGURE 17.2.
Relationships, drugs, and violations (singular and combined).

TABLE 17.3

Drug-Related Factors for Dropouts

Factors	N	%
Drug related (total)	50	35.2
Selected items:		
Relapse	21	14.8
Craving	10	7.0
Instigation of other patients	7	4.9
Doubts about the sense in and the ability to achieve a drug-free life	6	4.2

related violations in over 60% of the dropouts. The drug-related factor alone is present in 17% and the violation factor alone in 6% of the cases.

We would first like to take a closer look at dropouts involving drug-related problems, whether mentioned alone or in combination with other categories. Table 17.3 shows the proportions of some selected drug-related subcategories: In 15% of the sample relapse is involved, craving in 7%, instigation of other patients to drug consumption in 5%, and doubts about the sense in and the ability to achieve a drug-free life in 4%.

Table 17.4 presents the subcategory percentages of the relationship factors: On the left side relationships within the facility are marked in 46% of the cases. The subcategory "Partner relationships" is marked in

TABLE 17.4

Relationship Factors for Dropout

Factor	N	%	Factor	N	%
Relationships within the facility	65	45.8	Relationships outside the facility	37	26.1
Partner	37	26.1	Partner	29	20.4
Own child	3	2.1	Family	13	9.2
Other patients	27	19.0			
Absence of the therapist	5	3.5			
Conflict with the therapist	5	3.5			

26% of the cases. "Partner" in this context means every close relationship with a patient of the opposite sex mentioned in the therapist's report (data on homosexual relationships were not collected). It is remarkable that no friendships with patients of the same sex are mentioned in describing circumstances of dropout. Parent-child relationships played a role in the dropout of three cases (2%) exclusively involving mothers. The relationships to other patients, mostly conflicts or an outsider status, played a role in 19% of the dropout reports. Both absence of the therapist and conflict with therapist were dropout factors in 3.5% of the cases. Relationships outside the facility contributed in 26%, partnerships in 20%, and family relations in 9% of the cases.

Frequencies of all categories rated for the sample were analyzed for significant differences between the sexes. In the left column of Table 17.5 the relevant categories are mentioned; the next column specifies the subsample, as some significant differences were found in the total sample and some only in the group that signed out against medical advice. The first listed item refers to dropouts in which relationships outside the facility were involved, not including drug or disciplinary factors or relationships inside the facility. The significant sex difference of 20% of the women versus 8% of men can be explained by differences of the subsample of dropouts against medical advice (24% of the women versus 9% of the men). The proportion of women dropping out because of partnerships inside the facility is higher than for men: 39% versus 19%. On the other hand, dropouts of men that involve relationships with other patients are more frequent than among women (28% versus 10%), when based on the sample of sign outs against medical advice.

All categories with significant differences between the types of discharge are represented in Table 17.6. On the left side of Table 17.6 the

TABLE 17.5

Significant Gender Differences in Dropout Factors

Factors	Subsamples	Men		Women		p-value
		N	%	N	%	
Relationships outside the facility (not in connection with drug or disciplinary factors or relationships inside the facility)	sign out against medical advice	6	8.5	10	23.8	.0473
	total sample	7	7.5	10	20.4	.0482
Partnerships inside the facility	total sample	18	19.4	19	38.8	.0211
Relationship with other patients	sign out against medical advice	20	28.2	4	9.5	.0354

drug-related factors, violations, and relationship factors are listed; on the right side one can see the percentages of the patients who sign out against medical advice and the patients who were disciplinarily discharged. "Drug related (exclusively)" means that in these cases the dropout is not in connection with relationship factors or violations. Similarly, the term "relationships within or outside the facility (exclusively)" means that there is no connection with drug-related factors or violations.

There are four factors for which the percentage of the ratings is significantly higher among disciplinary discharges than among sign outs against medical advice: Among disciplinary discharges, drug-related categories (1), alone or in connection with other factors, were marked in 58% of the cases. The percentage for exclusively drug related (2) dropout was 35%; relapse (3) was reported specifically in 50% of the discharges. For the violations category (4), the proportion among discharges was 35%.

For four relationship categories the proportion of ratings is significantly higher among sign outs against medical advice. In this group, relationships either within or outside the facility (5) contributed to 69% of the cases. The same factor, but not in connection with drugs or violations (6), is marked in 45% of the cases; relationships outside the facility (7) are marked in 32% of the cases; and partnerships outside the facility (8) are marked in 25% of the cases.

DISCUSSION

In general, social relationships are dominant among the categories reported as circumstances for dropping out (61.3% of the total sample). Drug-related factors play a role in only 35.2% of the cases. In this main category the highest frequencies are reached by the factors of relapse and craving. *External relationships*, which are not connected with drug or disciplinary factors, are more important for women than for men. On the other hand, it seems that for men the *internal (nonerotic) relationships* with the other patients are more important than for women. This significant difference is found in the group that left against medical advice. Concerning erotic or sexual *partnerships* inside the facility, more women than men are involved during the dropout process.

Some of the gender differences probably are because the proportion of men in the facilities is much higher than that of women. At least to some extent this fact could explain that for women more than for men *internal (erotic or sexual) partnerships* contribute to the dropout process. Concerning *external partnerships* there is no sex difference, not even a

TABLE 17.6

Significant Differences Between the Types of Discharge

Factor		Sign out against medical advice		Disciplinary discharge		p-value
		N	%	N	%	
Drug-related	(1)	33	29.2	15	57.7	.0115
Drug-related (exclusively)	(2)	12	10.6	9	34.6	.0055
Relapse	(3)	7	6.2	13	50.0	.0000
Violations	(4)	9	8.0	9	34.6	.0009
Relationships within or outside the facility	(5)	78	69.0	9	34.6	.0023
Relationships within or outside the facility (exclusively)	(6)	51	45.1	3	11.5	.0032
Relationships outside the facility	(7)	36	31.9	1	3.8	.0076
Partnerships outside the facility	(8)	28	24.8	1	3.8	.0357

trend. If further research confirms that for women partnerships inside a facility contribute to dropout, the question arises whether it would be better to separate the sexes in therapy.

The analysis also found some differences in the type of discharge: If the patient leaves of his or her own accord, the dropout is more frequently tied to the relationship factor than if he or she is discharged by the facility. On the other hand, in the case of discharge by the facility there are more drug-related factors, especially relapses and nondrug-related violations that contribute to dropout. We must not forget that in this study the attrition process is described from the therapist's view; meaning that his or her assumptions and beliefs about this process, and about the important and less important factors, influence the analyzed reports. Second, the sample consists of only 142 cases, therefore replication in another study is called for.

One central consequence of these results is to focus research and treatment on relationship factors, in other words, on the interaction between the patient and other patients, the patient and therapist, and the patient's social network outside the facility in order to avoid dropout. For a better understanding of the dropout process it is important to include not only the patient's personality or sociodemographic characteristics but also the ongoing system of relationships within and outside the facility.

REFERENCES

Craig, R. (1985). Reducing the treatment drop out rate in drug abuse programs. *Journal of Substance Abuse Treatment* 2: 209–19.

Patton, M. (1980). *Qualitative Evaluation Methods*. Beverly Hills, London: Sage Publications.

Roback B., and Smith, M. (1987). Patient attrition in dynamically oriented treatment groups. *American Journal of Psychiatry* 144: 426–31.

CHAPTER 18

Prediction of Premature Termination of Therapy in the Treatment of Drug Addicts*

Heinz C. Vollmer, Heiner Ellgring, and Roman Ferstl

INTRODUCTION

The number of addicts on hard drugs in the Federal Republic of Germany is estimated at around 80,000 (Reuband 1989). The most frequent form of treatment for drug addicts in Germany is a course of treatment on a residential basis lasting 6 to 12 months. In the Federal Republic of Germany there are approximately 100 residential treatment centers for drug addicts. Heroin substitutes such as methadone are not prescribed at any of these treatment centers, which only have drug-free treatment programs. The premature termination rate in the residential treatment centers is between 50% and 70% (Herbst and Hanel 1989a; Kunz 1989; Vollmer 1988). Patients who complete a course of therapy according to plan are more likely to live drug-free lives after treatment than those who terminate

*We would like to thank our colleagues and the patients of Aiglsdorf and Baumgarten treatment centers (Dr. A. Dvorak, director) for their support with the collection of the data; Frau Dipl. Inf. H. Pfister and Dr. K. Herbst for advice with the statistics and analysis of the data; and Ms. S. Bollans for the translation into English. This study was financially supported by the Volkswagenwerk Foundation.

treatment prematurely (De Jong and Henrich 1980). In addition, the probability that the patient will lead a drug-free life later on increases with the length of stay (Herbst, Hanel, and Haderstorfer 1989). The number of completed courses of treatment is hence one of several success criteria in the treatment of drug addicts. It is therefore necessary to identify at an early stage patients likely to terminate therapy prematurely in order to improve the treatment programs.

There have been numerous studies investigating the variables by which premature therapy termination might be predicted (Baekeland and Lundwall 1975; De Leon 1984). The results have generally been contradictory, and as yet no clear predictive criteria have emerged. Therapists are thus not in a position to recognize patients in danger of dropping out or being discharged (Vollmer 1989). Early identification of patients who are at risk would make it easier to devise measures to reduce premature termination. The contradictory results in the literature and the wish of the staffs at the two treatment centers to develop measures for the explicit purpose of reducing premature termination of treatment prompted the present study. Potential predictive variables were documented over a long period of time at the two treatment centers, with the aim of forming and testing hypotheses which might help explain the contradictory results in the literature. One hypothesis of this study was thus that predictive criteria vary between treatment centers. Additionally, it was felt that a distinction should be made between various types of premature termination of therapy, such as termination by the patient and premature discharge by the therapist, as suggested by Baekeland and Lundwall (1975). According to Harris, Linn, and Pratt (1980) patients who drop out differ from those discharged for disciplinary reasons with respect to personality, attitudes toward drugs, and certain anamnestic variables. Most studies of premature termination of therapy are conducted without cross-validation, although the authors generally consider this to be necessary. Differences between the individual centers, the different types of premature termination, and the survey periods were taken into account in the design of the following study.

The questions asked in this study were as follow:

1. Which anamnestic variables and personality factors correlate with completion of therapy according to plan independently of the treatment center, the nature of premature termination, and the survey period?
2. Do the predictive criteria of the two centers differ from one another?
3. Are there different predictive criteria for dropout and discharge?
4. Are the results obtained confirmed by cross-validation?

METHOD

Treatment Centers

The study was conducted in two drug-free residential treatment centers. The planned duration of treatment was 6 to 9 months in both centers, with an average duration of eight months. Both centers had very similar admission and discharge criteria. On admission to the center the drug addicts were already detoxified. A counseling center distributed the patients between the centers, usually on a space-available basis.

In Center A the treatment was based solely on behavior therapy. The emphasis was on individual therapy, small groups concentrating on specific subjects (e.g., assertiveness training), and work therapy. The individual therapy was exclusively the responsibility of psychologists; the majority of the therapists at the time the data were collected were male, and the number of therapy places was 16. Treatment Center B operated in accordance with the humanistic paradigm. Here group therapy was more important than in Center A, and occupational therapy and art therapy (dancing, painting) were also offered. Individual therapy was conducted by psychologists and social workers. Most of the therapists were female and the number of therapy places was 12. The two centers did not differ substantially from one another in any other respects.

Data Collection and Measuring Instruments

The most important anamnestic data such as age, sex, previous treatment, nature of drugs consumed, and so forth were collected on the day the patients were admitted. In the first week of treatment all the patients were asked whether they would participate in the survey. Those who agreed to do so completed a personality questionnaire The Freiburger Persön-lichkeitsinventar (FPI/A) and the Beck Depression Inventory (BDI) in the second week of treatment and a parallel form of the personality questionnaire (FPI/B) in the third week. In the fourth week further anamnestic data were collected, including the patients' reasons for registering for treatment, the number and duration of drug-free phases, and the psychological stress caused by previous periods of imprisonment.

The FPI personality questionnaire is comparable with the MMPI. The FPI is used both for recording personality factors and measuring change during and after a course of psychotherapy. Stanine scores were used to standardize the results. Fifty-four percent of the standardized sample had scores which fell in the 4 to 6 range of the individual personality scales.

Table 18.1.

Design of the study. Number of patients admitted to the centres and percentage of patients who agreed to participate in the study

	Survey period I		Survey period II	
	Admissions	Participation	Admissions	Participation
Treatment centre A	129	114 (88%)	43	39 (91%)
Treatment centre B	98	80 (82%)	27	23 (85%)
Total (A + B)	227	194 (86%)	70	62 (89%)
Duration of the survey period	/------------ 39 months -----------/		/------------ 12 months -----------/	

The BDI is a German translation of the questionnaire developed by Aaron Beck, which is now also valid in Germany.

Due to the personal presence of one of the authors of this study in both therapy centers and the high degree of cooperation of the therapists, it was possible to register all the patients admitted to the two centers, even those who terminated treatment after only a few hours or days.

Sample

The study was divided into two successive survey periods. The second period was used to cross-validate the results obtained in the first period (Table 18.1). In the first period a total of 227 drug addicts were questioned in both centers and in the second period a total of 70; 86% and 89% respectively, agreed to participate in the study. The primary diagnosis of most of the patients (94%) according to the DSM-III-R was opioid dependence (304.00), and of the remaining patients amphetamine dependence (304.40), cocaine dependence (304.20), alcohol dependence (303.90), and cannabis dependence (304.30). Almost all the patients also had a record of cannabis abuse. The majority of the patients were from the lower middle class. Only 17% of the patients had a final school qualification higher than Hauptschule (basic secondary-school level). Most patients were under legal obligation to have treatment.

At the beginning of treatment the patients in the two centers differed only with respect to two variables (Table 18.2). In the first survey period

Table 18.2.

Characteristics of Patients on Admission for Treatment and Significant Differences between Groups (Treatment Centre A, B; Survey Periods I, II)

Admission variable	Survey period I						Survey period II						Comparison	p
	Treatment centre						Treatment centre							
	A			B			A			B				
	M	s.d.	N	M	s.d.	N	M	s.d.	N	M	s.d.	N		
Age	25	(2.7)	129	24	(3.2)	98	25	(3.6)	43	24	(2.9)	27		n.s.
First use of opiates, amphetamines or cocaine (age)	18	(2.4)	123	18	(2.8)	78	18	(2.6)	41	17	(2.7)	27		n.s.
First use of cannabis (age)	15	(2)	117	15	(2.4)	78	15	(1.8)	41	14	(1.7)	27		n.s.
Duration of previous courses of treatment terminated prematurely (weeks)	24	(21)	51	13	(15)	35	19	(19)	14	26	(23)	11	period I: A vs. B	<.01
Months in prison	20	(18)	105	24	(19)	63	27	(23)	33	25	(21)	23		n.s.
Expected term of imprisonment (months)	17	(8)	80	16	(7)	48	18	(7)	24	19	(6)	21		n.s.
Reasons for registering for treatment (1=very weak, 6=very strong reason):														
- to give up drug taking	4.8	(1.3)	98	5.3	(1.1)	48	4.7	(1.6)	32	5.6	(0.7)	15	period I, II: A vs. B	<.05
- to avoid imprisonment	4.4	(1.7)	90	4	(1.8)	45	4.5	(1.5)	32	5.3	(1.1)	14	centre B: I vs. II	<.05

	% of Total		N	% of Total		N	% of Total		N	% of Total		N		
Female	23%		129	21%		98	21%		43	30%		27		n.s.
No final school qualification	28%		122	26%		69	10%		42	19%		27	centre A: I vs. II	<.05
No partner	72%		124	62%		68	63%		43	52%		27		n.s.
Partner also on drugs	43%		35	65%		26	81%		16	62%		13	centre A: I vs. II	<.05
No prior treatment periods	57%		124	47%		83	67%		42	59%		27		n.s.
No prior imprisonments	11%		123	7%		82	17%		41	11%		27		n.s.
No legal order	26%		121	27%		82	10%		42	4%		27	centre A, B: I vs. II	<.05
Opioid dependence	97%		124	99%		84	91%		43	70%		27		n.s.

it was seen that the patients in Center B who had prematurely terminated courses of treatment on previous occasions had on average done this at an earlier stage than those in Center A. In both survey periods the patients in Center B gave the item "in order not to take drugs any more" a higher rating as a reason for starting treatment than the patients of Center A. There was no difference between the patients of the two centers at the beginning of treatment with respect to the rest of the data, including the personality factors and the BDI data. There were more differences between the patients of the different survey periods. More of the patients in survey period 2 had a final school qualification (Hauptschule), were under legal obligation to have treatment, and had a partner who was involved with drugs.

According to their personality scores, the patients of survey period 2 were on the whole more balanced at the beginning of treatment than the patients of survey period 1 (Table 18.3). This applies particularly to the patients of Center A, who at the onset of treatment were more stable emotionally, less depressive, had fewer psychosomatic problems, and were calmer and more confident. There were no differences between the patients of the two survey periods with respect to the other variables such as age, length of time drugs had been taken, number of prison sentences, or Beck Depression Inventory scores.

Treatment Termination Criteria

A distinction was made between three types of treatment termination:

1. Discharge according to plan

   All patients who were in the treatment centers for at least 180 days were put in the category of "discharge according to plan." One hundred and eighty days was the shortest normal therapy period possible for the treatment offered in the two centers. A time criterion for defining normal and premature termination of treatment was used in order to avoid classification errors on the part of the therapists and to achieve a better basis for comparison of the two centers.

   Therapy was considered prematurely terminated when the patients stayed in the treatment center for less than 180 days. The therapist on duty when the patient terminated treatment was responsible for classifying this as "dropout" or "premature discharge."

2. Dropout

   This category was designated for patients who made the decision to terminate treatment themselves.

Table 18.3.

Personality Scores of Patients on Admission for Treatment and Significant Differences between Groups

Personality scale (FPI; A, B)	Survey period I Treatment centre A M	s.d.	N	B M	s.d.	N	Survey period II Treatment centre A M	s.d.	N	B M	s.d.	N	Comparison	p
1. Nervousness FPI-A:	6.6	2.0	111	6.5	2.0	70	5.9	1.8	38	6.2	2.7	19	centre A: I vs. II	<.05
FPI-B:	6.0	2.0	105	6.0	2.0	72	4.2	2.3	19	5.7	2.9	10	centre A: I vs. II	<.01
2. Spontaneous aggressiveness	6.0	1.6	110	5.7	1.6	70	5.8	1.7	38	6.0	1.5	19		n.s.
	5.3	1.8	105	5.1	2.0	71	5.2	2.0	19	6.1	1.9	10		n.s.
3. Depressiveness	7.1	1.6	111	6.8	1.9	70	6.3	1.7	38	6.8	1.7	19	centre A: I vs. II	<.05
	6.7	1.7	104	6.4	2.1	71	5.5	2.1	19	6.2	3.2	10	centre A: I vs. II	<.05
4. Excitability	5.9	1.8	111	5.8	2.1	70	5.2	1.8	38	5.7	1.9	19		n.s.
	6.0	1.6	105	5.8	2.1	72	5.6	2.1	19	5.6	2.4	10		n.s.
5. Sociability	4.7	2.2	111	4.4	2.5	69	5.0	1.8	38	4.8	2.2	19		n.s.
	5.3	1.9	105	4.7	2.0	71	5.4	1.5	19	4.4	2.8	10		n.s.
6. Calmness	4.4	1.8	109	4.0	1.6	69	4.4	1.6	38	4.8	1.7	19	centre A, B: I vs. II	<.01
	3.6	1.7	104	3.4	1.5	72	5.0	1.6	19	5.2	2.0	10		n.s.
7. Reactive aggressiveness	5.2	1.8	111	4.9	1.9	70	5.2	1.7	38	5.6	2.0	19		n.s.
	5.3	1.8	104	5.2	2.3	72	5.5	2.2	19	5.8	1.9	10		n.s.
8. Inhibition	5.9	2.0	111	5.9	1.9	69	5.2	1.8	38	4.6	2.0	19	centre B: I vs. II	<.05
	5.5	2.2	105	6.0	1.9	72	4.8	1.8	19	5.2	2.9	10		n.s.
9. Openness	5.5	1.8	111	5.2	2.0	70	5.0	1.9	38	5.3	2.1	19		n.s.
	5.7	1.9	105	5.3	2.1	72	5.0	1.8	19	6.7	2.5	10		n.s.
E. Extraversion	5.3	2.2	111	5.1	2.4	70	5.5	2.2	38	6.0	2.4	19		n.s.
	5.0	2.0	105	4.6	1.7	71	5.9	2.1	19	5.5	1.9	10		n.s.
N. Emotional lability	6.2	1.7	111	6.0	1.9	70	5.6	1.6	38	6.0	2.1	19	centre A: I vs. II	<.05
	6.7	1.7	104	6.5	2.2	71	5.5	1.8	19	5.8	2.7	10	centre A: I vs. II	<.01
M. Masculinity	3.6	2.0	110	3.5	1.8	68	4.2	1.9	38	4.3	1.6	19		n.s.
	4.1	2.1	105	3.4	1.8	72	5.3	2.1	19	4.6	2.5	10		n.s.

Depression score (BDI)	N = 111	N = 69	N = 38	N = 19		p
no depression (≤ 11)	44 %	48 %	55 %	32 %		
slight depression (12 -19)	34 %	32 %	29 %	42 %		
medium depression (20 - 26)	15 %	15 %	13 %	16 %		
severe depression (> 26)	6 %	6 %	3 %	11 %		n.s.

3. Premature discharge
    This category included patients who were prematurely discharged on the instruction of the therapist (e.g., because of drug consumption during treatment or because they left the center without permission).

Evaluation

The anamnesis and personality variables of the patients who had completed therapy according to plan were compared with those of (a) patients who dropped out and (b) patients who were prematurely discharged. Differences in frequency distribution were statistically tested with the chi-square test or, in the case of small samples, with Fischer's test. Comparisons of mean scores were carried out using the Mann-Whitney U test. The statistical tests in survey period I were based on two-tailed tests, and where correlations were found in the cross-validation of survey period I, one-tailed test were used in survey period II. Discriminant analysis of the items on the personality questionnaire was carried out following the "Mahal" method. For all these calculations the SPSS program was used. Duration of stay prior to dropout and premature discharge was examined by K. Herbst using survival analysis methods, data after 180 days in the center being censored. Analysis of duration of stay in the center was based on the generalized gamma-distribution model, using the maximum-likelihood method and the likelihood-ratio test (see Herbst et al. 1989).

Legal Obligation to Undergo Treatment

In the Federal Republic of Germany there are two laws which are frequently applied to drug addicts:

1. According to Section 56 of the penal code (StGB), a drug addict can be ordered to undergo treatment and his sentence can be suspended. In the case of premature termination of treatment, this is not normally followed by further imprisonment. The probation order is only revoked when the patient commits a new crime, for example, when he again consumes illegal drugs.
2. According to Section 35 of the Narcotics Act (BtmG), the sentence can be suspended for the duration of treatment. After successful completion of treatment the remaining sentence is generally suspended.

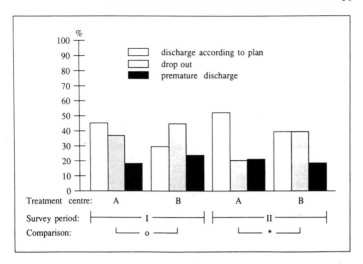

FIGURE 18.1.
Types of treatment termination in two different treatment centers (A, B) at two differ-
ent survey periods (I, II). o = P < .10; * = p < .05; N: (IA = 129; IB = 98;
IIA = 43; IIB = 27).

In the case of premature termination of treatment the patient is usually
rearrested.

The patients are aware of the legal consequences of premature termination of treatment.

RESULTS

Number and Nature of Premature Terminations

Of the total sample (Centers A, B; survey periods I, II), 42% of the
patients completed treatment according to plan. Thirty-seven percent decided to break off treatment themselves and 21% were prematurely discharged by the therapists. More patients completed treatment according
to plan in Center A than in Center B. This difference is significant in
the second survey period and there is a tendency in this direction in the
first survey period (Figure 18.1). There is no significant difference between the two centers with respect to the survival function (Figure 18.2).
The rate of premature termination was highest in the first three months.

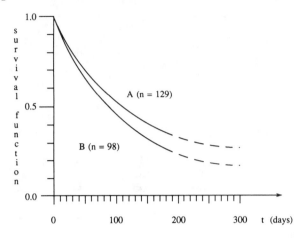

FIGURE 18.2.
Duration of stay in treatment Centers A and B (data after 180 days of treatment are censored).

Only after around 90 days did the survival function curve flatten out (i.e., fewer patients were terminating treatment prematurely).

There also were no differences between the two centers with respect to the risk of dropout or premature discharge. Between these two types of premature termination there were, however, significant differences ($X^2 = 13.15$, df $= 2$, p $< .01$; Figure 18.3). The risk of a patient's terminating treatment decreased slightly in the initial weeks and then remained almost constant during therapy. The risk of premature discharge increased during the first three months in particular. In both centers the risk of patients' terminating treatment was higher than the risk of their being prematurely discharged by the therapists. Cross-validation with respect to the survival and hazard function was not possible on account of the small sample size in the second survey period.

Anamnesis Data and Premature Termination of Treatment

Only one variable, legal orders, correlated in survey period I with premature termination of treatment regardless of center type (Center A or B) and in treatment Center B regardless of the nature of premature termination (dropout or premature discharge) (Figure 18.4). In treatment Center A patients without legal orders were not prematurely discharged more often.

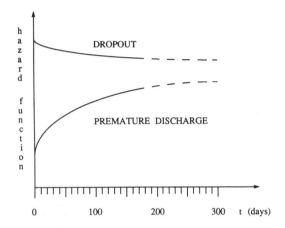

FIGURE 18.3.
Risk of dropout and premature discharge for treatment Centers A + B, N = 227 (data after 180 days of treatment are censored).

Significantly more patients under legal obligation to have therapy completed treatment according to plan than patients who were not under any such obligation. The nature of the legal order did not play any part, and patients with a treatment order according to Section 56 of the penal code completed treatment according to plan as frequently as patients with a suspended sentence according to Section 35 of the Narcotics Act (Figure 18.5). In the second survey period the number of patients without a legal order was too small to conduct a statistical test. In Center B the only patient without a legal order terminated treatment, and in Center A two out of four patients without a legal order terminated treatment.

A second variable that repeatedly correlated with the nature of treatment termination was age (Table 18.4). In survey period I at Center B and survey period II at Center A, more young patients terminated treatment prematurely. In the larger sample, on the other hand (survey period I, Center A), there was no connection between age and premature termination. Other anamnestic variables, such as age at the onset of drug consumption, the last time drugs were taken, or no final school qualification, only had predictive value in connection with the center, the nature of premature termination, and the survey period. The variables that correlated with premature discharge were thus different from those that correlated with dropout. The two centers also differed with respect to the variables that had predictive value. In some cases the results obtained in the two centers and for the different types of premature termination even

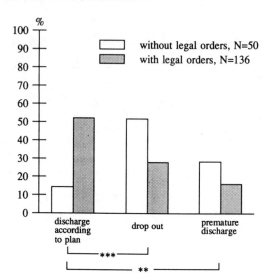

FIGURE 18.4.
Legal orders and treatment termination (** = p < .01; *** = p < .001).

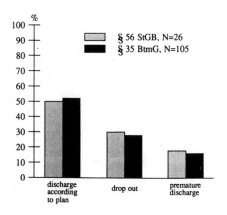

FIGURE 18.5.
Comparison of type of legal order with type of treatment termination.

contradicted one another. In Center A, for example, there was a tendency for more patients to be discharged who had been in prison for a long time (p < .10), but in Center B more patients were discharged who had had shorter periods of imprisonment (p < .10). In no case was the predictive value of a variable confirmed in the second survey period.

Table 18.4.

The Relationship between Intake Variables and Outcome

Intake variable	Treatment centre A				Treatment centre B			
	Survey period I		Survey period II		Survey period I		Survey period II	
	drop out	premature discharge	drop out	premature discharge	drop out	premature discharge	drop out	premature discharge
Age			younger ***	younger •	younger °	younger **		
First use of cannabis			earlier °		earlier *			
First use of hard drugs			earlier *			earlier *		
Length of time cannabis taken			shorter *	shorter °				
Last use of medicaments	shorter *		longer °					
Duration of previous courses of treatment prematurely terminated			shorter *					
Time spent in prison			longer °	shorter *		shorter °		
Stress caused by imprisonment (1=very weak, 6=very strong)	weaker *		weaker **					
Giving up drug taking as a reason for registering for treatment (1=very weak, 6=very strong reason)	stronger *							
Choice of treatment centre on account of individual treatment sessions (1=very weak, 6=very strong reason)						stronger *		
Left school without a final qualification					more frequent *			
No previous treatment terminated prematurely					less frequent *			

^{0} = p < .10; * = p < .05; ** = p < .01; p < .001 < .001

▨ = no statistical test could be carried out

Table 18.5.

The Relationship between Personality Factors and Outcome

Personality factors	Treatment centre A				Treatment centre B			
	Survey period I		Survey period II		Survey period I		Survey period II	
	drop out	premature discharge	drop out	premature discharge	drop out	premature discharge	drop out	premature discharge
Spontanous aggressiveness			more aggressive **	more aggressive °				
Reactive aggressiveness			more dominant *	more dominant *				
Inhibition		more spontaneous *						more inhibited *
Extraversion		more extraverted *						

^{0} = p < .10; * = p < .05; ** = p < .01;   ▨ = no statistical test could be carried out

Personality Factors and Premature Termination of Treatment

The prediction of premature termination of treatment by means of personality factors presented a similar picture to that of prediction on the basis of anamnesis data (Table 18.5). In Center A more extroverted or less inhibited patients were discharged by the therapists in the first survey period. These results, however, were not confirmed in the second survey period. Discriminant analysis of the individual items of the personality questionnaires showed that in Center A (survey period I) 77% of the patients could be classified under the discharge according to plan, dropout, and premature discharge categories by 14 items. These results, however, were not confirmed in the second survey period.

Variables without Predictive Value

Some variables will now be examined which are frequently thought to correlate with the way therapy is terminated, but which allowed no prediction to be made in this study in either survey period or in either of the two centers. Although in the two centers far fewer women are treated than men, female patients completed their treatment according to plan just as often as the male patients. In addition, premature termination of treatment occurred independent of whether the patient had a partner, how long the patient had been addicted, when the patient last consumed hard drugs, how long he or she had to wait before admission to therapy, whether he or she had come to treatment from prison or the drug scene, and the length of sentence expected in the case of premature termination of therapy. Patients who had more extreme scores on the personality questionnaire or the BDI also did not break off treatment more frequently than the patients whose scores were in the normal range.

DISCUSSION

Most of the centers for the treatment of drug addicts in the Federal Republic of Germany were relatively small. The number of therapy places is between 10 and 40. Center A, for example, has 16 therapy places and takes up to 50 patients per year. Center B has 12 places and takes up to 30 patients a year. Prediction criteria are thus only of use to the individual treatment centers if patients likely to terminate therapy prematurely can be identified at an early stage even with such small samples. The sample size of this study in the second survey period was 43 patients in one center and 27 patients in the other. With this sample size it was not possible to find valid predictive criteria in the two centers with the measuring instruments used in the study, with the possible exception of legal orders. Since in the second survey period there were only 5 patients who were not under legal obligation to have treatment, it was not possible to check the connection between legal orders and termination of treatment by cross-validation.

Another variable which produced unexpected results in this study was age. The patients who terminated treatment prematurely, whether they dropped out or were prematurely discharged, tended to be younger. In the data collected at Center A, however, age and termination of therapy were only found to be connected in the second survey period, and in the data for Center B only in the first period. In the larger sample (Center A, survey period I) on the other hand, there was no correlation between age and premature termination of treatment. Various other studies have found that younger patients are more likely to terminate therapy prematurely (Baekeland and Lundwall 1975), and in this study too, younger patients appeared to be at greater risk than older ones. It must be said, however, that younger patients are not automatically more likely to end treatment prematurely.

The other predictive variables followed a similar pattern and different criteria correlated with termination of treatment according to plan depending on the center, survey period, and nature of therapy termination. Although, given the number of variables tested, accidental significance cannot be entirely excluded, there were nevertheless connections that appeared plausible when the two therapy centers were known. It was thus, for example, possible to see where the treatment could be improved on the basis of the predictive criteria found. The following is an example of a predictive criterion that appears reasonable: At the beginning of treatment, patients in Center A rated "motivation to stop taking drugs as a reason for therapy" lower than the patients in Center B. This discrepancy can be explained by the fact that the patients in Center B tended to give the answers desired by the therapists, because in this center there is more emphasis on confrontation and greater pressure is put on the patients who do not appear to be highly motivated than in the other center. In Center A there is greater acceptance of a lower motivation level by the therapists.

In Center A in the first survey period the patients who considered themselves to be more highly motivated broke off treatment more frequently than the less motivated ones. It is possible that the "motivated" patients at Center A were disappointed at the apparently low demands that were made of them by the therapists and at the therapists' acceptance of the "low" motivation of other patients. Based on these results, measures, such as more individually designed therapy, were introduced to improve cooperation in therapy. Against this background, it is easy to see why the correlation between highly rated motivation and termination of treatment only occurred in Center A, survey period I, and not elsewhere. Further examples of individual predictive criteria which appeared plausible occurred at both centers, but it is not possible to deal with them in detail here, because it would require a more precise description of both treatment programs.

In general, the results can be interpreted as follows: There were different predictive criteria for premature termination depending on the center and survey period. A differentiation must also be made between the types of termination. When the treatment programs and the background are known, some variables can be said to be plausible as predictive criteria. While accidental significance cannot be excluded, it is unlikely as the sole explanation for the results of this study. Some of the criteria from the empirical literature such as sex, depression, and extreme personality scores did not correlate with premature termination of treatment in this study. These results suggest that there are very few general predictive criteria and that certain combinations of center, therapist, and patient influence the way treatment is terminated. One would thus expect different patients to terminate treatment prematurely each time, according to whether it is of a more confrontational or nondirective nature or whether the majority of the patients are or are not under legal obligation to have treatment. In the same way changes in the treatment program would lead to changes in the predictive criteria. Different predictive criteria in different studies would thus not only be understandable but also expected. If this hypothesis is true, more importance should be attached to the individual analysis of treatment centers than has previously been the case.

The relationship of premature discharge to length of time in treatment corresponds to other studies (De Leon 1984; Kunz and Kampe 1985). In the first few months the risk of premature discharge is highest and then decreases slowly the longer the patient is in treatment. As also shown in the study by Herbst and Hanel (1989b), there is a significant difference between the relationship of dropout and premature discharge to length of time in therapy. This may be a variable that is independent of the treatment centers and programs. It might reflect decision processes on the part of patients and therapists which should be more closely investigated. Finally, the authors felt that what they had achieved with the publication of this study was to add to the predictive literature a few unimportant and unreliable criteria and yet more unanswered questions! On the other hand, the individual analyses indicated how the two therapy programs investigated might be improved and provided some ideas for improving the methods used in the empirical study of predictive criteria.

REFERENCES

Baekeland, E., and Lundwall, L. (1975). Dropping out of treatment: A critical review. *Psychological Bulletin* 82: 738–83.

Harris, R., Linn, M. W., and Pratt, Th.C. (1980). A comparison of dropouts and disciplinary discharges from a therapeutic community. *The International Journal of the Addictions* 15: 749–56.

Herbst, K., and Hanel, E. (1989a). Meßbare Größen des Therapieprozesses bei Drogenabhängigen in stationärer Entwöhnungsbehandlung (Measurable aspects of the treatment process in drug-dependent individuals participating in residential treatment programs). In *Therapieverläufe bei Drogenabhängigen*, W. Feuerlein, G. Bühringer & R. Wille (eds.), pp. 170–83. Berlin: Springer.

Herbst, K., and Hanel, E. (1989b). Verlauf der stationären Entwöhnungsbehandlung bei Drogenabhängigen (The process of residential treatment of drug addicts). *Suchtgefahren* 35: 235–51.

Herbst, K., Hanel, E., and Haderstorfer, B. (1989). Rückfallgeschehen bei stationär behandelten Drogenabhängigen (Relapse of drug addicts following inpatient treatment). In *Rückfall und Rückfallprophylaxe*, H. Watzl and R. Cohen (eds.), pp. 139–48. Berlin: Springer.

De Jong, R., and Henrich, G. (1980). Follow-up results of a behavior modification program for juvenile drug addicts. *Addictive Behaviors* 5: 49–57.

Kunz, D. (1989). Bedingungen des Therapieabbruchs Drogenabhängiger (Factors influencing the drug-dependent individual's decision to drop out of therapy). In *Therapieverläufe bei Drogenabhängigen*, W. Feuerlein, G. Bühringer, and R. Wille (eds.), pp. 224–44. Berlin: Springer.

Kunz, D., and Kampe, H. (1985). Zum Problem des Therapieabbruchs von Heroinabhängigen (Discharge of drug addicts against therapeutic advice). *Suchtgefahren* 31: 146–54.

De Leon, G. (1984). Program-based evaluation research in therapeutic communities. In *Drug abuse treatment evaluation: Strategies, progress and prospects* F. M. Tims and J. P. Ludford (eds.), pp. 69–87. Rockville: NIDA Research Monograph 51.

Reuband, K.-H. (1989). Illegale Drogen (Illegal drugs). In DHS Deutsche Hauptstelle gegen die Suchtgefahren (ed.), *Jahrbuch '90 zur Frage der Suchtgefahren*, pp. 113–55. Hamburg: Neuland.

Vollmer, H. C. (1988). Die vorzeitige Therapiebeendigung bei der Entwöhnungsbehandlung Drogenabhängiger: Analyse und Interventionen (Premature termination in the treatment of drug addicts: Analysis and interventions). *Suchtgefahren* 34: 65–79.

———. (1989). Motivation und Willensstärke im Urteil opiatabhängiger Patienten (Motivation and willpower as assessed by opiate-dependent patients and their therapists). *Suchtgefahren* 35: 281–88.

CHAPTER 19

Therapeutic Accessibility of Drug Addicts During Treatment in Therapeutic Communities

Dieter Kunz

INTRODUCTION

Therapeutic communities for drug addicts can be seen as planned treatment systems designed for the solution of behavior problems that have been formed in the course of the drug career. Drug-free residential facilities must offer their clients a learning environment that, step-by-step, removes the emotional and cognitive ties with the drug-related lifestyle. Therapeutic communities make great demands upon the clients regarding comprehensive changes in their lifestyle. Many clients avoid solving the resultant problems by dropping out of programs.

The frequencies of regular and premature treatment terminations in therapeutic communities seem to be internationally comparable, as studies by the research groups of De Leon (De Leon and Ziegenfuss, 1986) and Bühringer (1981) show. In Figure 19.1 the cumulated relative frequencies of terminations in three German therapeutic communities are drawn. These graphs show the generally known regularities:

1. During the first three months of treatment, up to 50% of all clients drop out (Baekeland and Lundwall 1975; De Leon and Schwartz 1984; Simpson and Sells 1982; Kunz and Kampe 1985).

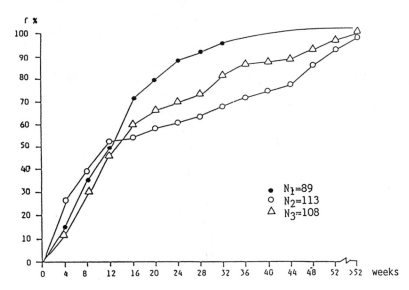

FIGURE 19.1.
Cumulative relative frequencies of treatment terminations in three therapeutic communities (N^1 = 89, N^2 = 113, N^3 = 108; Kampe and Kunz 1983; Kunz and Kampe 1985).

2. The probability of continued retention in treatment increases the longer the clients stay in treatment.

If one regards the expression of an intention to leave the program as an indication of real dropout, one sees comparable characteristics in the course of treatment. According to American and European studies, intent to leave the program is a useful predictor of the client's integration in the psychotherapeutic process and of his or her success or failure in treatment (Brown 1976; Bloch and Crouch 1985; Quekelberghe v. 1979). Figure 19.2 shows the course of probabilities of drop out in relation to the first remark of intention to leave the program (Kunz 1989).

Out of 16 clients, who during the first week of treatment declared their intention to discontinue the program, 15 in fact dropped out at a later stage. If in the first three months of treatment, a client mentions his or her intention to leave the therapeutic community, the therapist must recognize that in 70% of all cases such termination will occur. Remarks that occur after the initial three months indicate dropout in only 20% of all cases.

From these findings the following can be deduced:

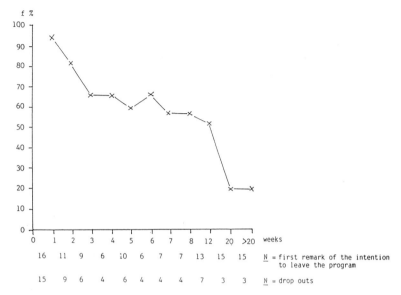

FIGURE 19.2.
Probabilities of dropout after the first remark of intention to leave the program.

1. Dropout intentions that are initially observed at a later stage in treatment, are expressed for reasons different from those voiced at the beginning of treatment.
2. A therapeutic intervention obviously has different effects on the client in advanced stages of therapy than during the initial phase of treatment.

At this point, some theoretical remarks on the importance of therapeutic cooperation for dropping out are briefly outlined. Des Jarlais et al. (1976) found that cognitive-dissonance conflicts and double-avoidance conflicts lead to dropout. Such conflicts are provoked by the high and often unreasonable pressures put on the clients by the therapists. According to these authors, a specific, implicit theory about the addict personality rules the interventions of the therapists. In self-fulfilling prophecies this implicit theory is verified by the therapists. Deissler (1978, 1982) even says that the clients are "driven away" by the therapists. Deissler posits that the psychic abilities of the clients (i.e., problem solving) grow in a process of maturation during rehabilitation. This process is structured in developmental phases. Dropout is a result of therapeutic interventions that are not appropriate to the development of the client.

According to the findings of the Monroe research group (Monroe and Astin 1961; Monroe 1971; Monroe and Hill 1958; Berzins, Ross and Monroe 1970), we must further consider that even at the beginning of treatment there are differences in clients with regard to their self-esteem and their ability to be influenced by therapeutic interventions. (For similar results see Kunz, Kampe, and Kremp 1985.) Results of our own research show that a selection of clients in early dropouts, late dropouts, and succeeders can be observed under conditions of largely the same therapeutic treatment (Kunz and Kampe 1985; Kampe and Kunz 1982). A very important variable complex for the distinction of these different client groups seems to be their different therapeutic accessibility.

In the following section, some of our research results regarding the problem of therapeutic accessibility in connection with dropout of drug addicts are described. These studies were conducted in three German therapeutic communities.

COMPONENTS OF THERAPEUTIC ACCESSIBILITY

The results reported in this section concern studies of the influence of various treatment modalities in a therapeutic community. This therapeutic community was structured according to the principles of a token economy and corresponds to other German drug-free treatment facilities (measured by the SEKT-Questionaire: Henrich and De Jong 1976; Kampe and Kunz 1979). The following observations were made (Kampe and Kunz 1983):

1. Early dropouts, late dropouts, and succeeders all take part in the same way in the treatments offered (for example, group or work therapy).
2. Deviant behavior (i.e., rule-breaking behavior) occurred with comparable frequency in all client groups at the beginning of treatment.
3. Reinforcements of social behavior were applied in the same way to succeeders, late dropouts, and early dropouts by the staff. The late dropouts, who survived the first step of treatment, self-evaluated their behavior in the same way as the succeeders, and they self-reinforced their behavior in the same way.
4. The differentiation of the demands on the social behavior of the clients (more frequent and more specific therapeutic interventions) through a program change led to the following consequences:

a. the rate of early dropouts stayed the same,
b. the rate of the succeeders decreased from 33% to 18%.
c. the rate of late dropouts increased from 21% to 32%.

Obviously, social therapeutic challenges in the changed program—so-called rule system B—were too high for the late dropouts.

The results in Table 19.1 (Kampe and Kunz 1985) indicate that differences in the therapeutic accessibility of the clients become evident when general demands on social behavior are examined. This assumption is also confirmed by more specific observations of social behavior. The social behavior of the clients was rated daily on four dimensions: rule orientation, social maturity and independence, prosocial interpersonal activity and self-control. Figure 19.3 shows the mean values of these dimensions for three groups: Succeeders (D) Late dropouts (S) and Early dropouts (F). These groups were observed at four different times during:

1. the first week in treatment,
2. the last week in Step 1 of the program,
3. the last week in Step 2 of the program and
4. the last week in Step 3 of the program.

According to these results one can assume that at the beginning of treatment, therapists noticed consistent differences among the three groups. As therapists recognized, the behavior changes of the dropouts were less significant than those of the succeeders.

Similar correlations appeared when the clients themselves were asked to rate the therapeutic program, the interventions by the therapists, and their own problems:

1. The therapeutic program is rated by all client groups in a comparably positive way. The group therapy strained the clients more than did other program components. Judgments of the relative importance of treatment effectiveness were related to the length of stay in treatment.
2. Regarding the ratings of the relationship to the therapists (e.g., "I have confidence that therapists help me to solve my problems"), there are clear differences among the client groups. Succeeders, in contrast to dropouts, are significantly better able to accept criticism of their behavior.
3. Succeeders also rate their own skills in interpersonal behavior in a

TABLE 19.1

Dropout Rates and Success Rates of Two Different Therapeutic Program Conditions
(RuleSystem A = RSA; B = RSB)

	RSA N = 52		RSB N = 56		Total N = 108	
	%	(N)	%	(N)	%	(N)
Succeeder (D)	33	(17)	18	(10)	25	(27)
Late dropouts (S)	21	(11)	32	(18)	27	(29)
Early dropouts (F)	46	(24)	50	(28)	48	(52)
Total	100	(52)	100	(56)	100	(108)

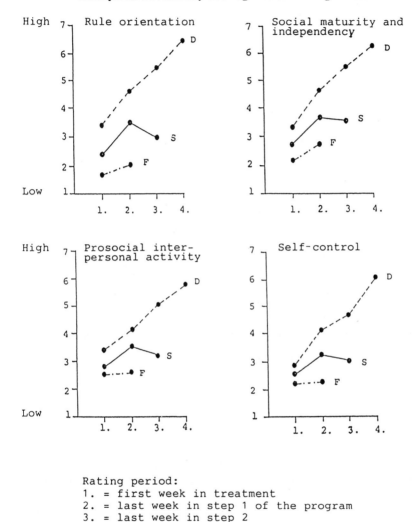

Rating period:
1. = first week in treatment
2. = last week in step 1 of the program
3. = last week in step 2
4. = last week in step 3

FIGURE 19.3.
Behavior ratings on four dimensions of behavior for Succeeders (D), Late dropouts (S) and Early dropouts (F).

more self-critical way than do early dropouts (Kampe and Kunz 1979).

Both the results of behavior ratings by the therapists and the self-ratings of the clients refer to a marked therapeutic accessibility of the succeeders

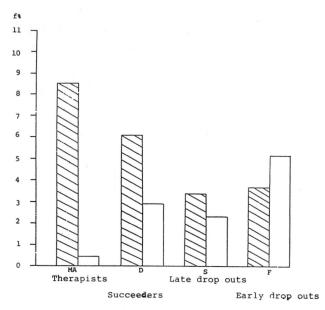

FIGURE 19.4.
Means-end-statements of therapists and different client groups in daily group discussions.
▨ adequate means-end-statements
☐ inadequate means-end-statements

in comparison to the drop outs. The cognitive aspects of therapeutic accessibility related to such behavior ratings are described in the following. A study of verbal behavior in group discussions (taking a sample of 21 clients during 32 weeks), showed differences in verbal abilities among succeeders, late dropouts, and early dropouts (Figure 19.4). The recording system of verbal behavior consists of 10 categories. This study only points out the ability of clients to produce adequate or inadequate reasons for their social behavior. Like Platt (Platt, Scura, and Hannon 1973; Platt and Metzger 1987), we understand, by inadequate means-end-concepts, incorrect justifications for social behavior such as rationalizations, neutralizations, or practical accounts.

Figure 19.4 shows that succeeders produce more adequate means-end-statements than the other client groups. The converse seems to be true for the early dropouts; they produce more inadequate than adequate means-end-statements. In this regard late dropouts form a group between succeeders and early dropouts. Obviously, early dropouts tend to distort social information in the verbal communication. Verbal-cognitive abilities make it possible for the succeeders to cope more adequately with

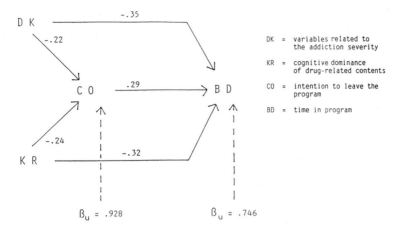

FIGURE 19.5.
Results of a path analysis for the prediction of retention in treatment.

social information, and it may be that they have a better ability to solve social problems (Kampe and Kunz 1981). The analysis of the contents of 148 written life reports of drug addicts indicated the same relationship. While the knowledge of drug usage is available to all client groups in the same frequency (mean value 11% of all words in the life reports are drug slang words), drug-related contents are mentioned by dropouts more frequently in comparison to the succeeders. With the successful clients, school and general educational problems are cognitively emphasized rather than drug problems (Kampe, Kunz, and Kremp 1986; Kunz and Kampe 1985).

In a qualitative follow-up study, it was found that the cognitive dominance of drug-related contents persists with the dropouts over the years (Kampe and Kunz 1984). Cognitive attachments with the drug culture seem to be highly resistant to change. Other results indicate that the cognitive predominance of drug-related themes corresponds with the variables of the drug history of the clients, (i.e., consumption of substitute drugs like alcohol, speed, cannabis; amount of consumed drugs; length of drug taking; integration in the drug market). In comparison to the dropouts, clients who completed treatment had a lower addiction severity index and were cognitively less dependent on the lifestyle of the drug culture (Kunz 1988).

By means of these variables we are able to set up a path-analytic model, which predicts the course and duration of treatment with an explained variance of 43% (Kunz 1988). Figure 19.5 shows this model, which is based on the collected data of 115 consecutively admitted clients who were treated in a therapeutic community during a survey time of three years. The signs of the path-coefficients define the direction of the influence. The results can be summarized as follows:

1. Commitment to treatment—measured by the expressed intention to leave the program—has a direct positive effect on retention in treatment. The earlier a client says that he wants to leave, the earlier he leaves the program. The other two variables in the model have a direct and, via the commitment, an indirect effect on treatment duration.
2. The more problems clients have with their drug career, and the more they are cognitively involved in the deviant drug culture, the earlier they intend to leave the program and the more likely they will drop out.
3. Experiences from socialization, (e.g., life events and the frequency of participation in group therapy), are of no importance in this prediction model.

These results correspond to results that are also known from the American research (e.g., Wexler and De Leon 1977) and can be seen as a summary of our investigations of components of therapeutic accessibility.

THERAPEUTIC ACCESSIBILITY IN THE THERAPEUTIC PROCESS

In the following, the results of investigations of some aspects of the therapeutic process in therapeutic communities are reported. In the first study, the structure of therapeutic intervention is analyzed. To this end we observed the written commentaries of deviant and prosocial behavior in a token economy. Using 12 categories, we examined the therapeutic reasons for spending behavior points of 111 clients over a period of 58 months. Independent variables were defined: positive versus negative behavior points, two different systems of social rules (rule system A, rule system B), and actor/observer difference in the attribution of reasons for the clients' behavior (evaluation through the therapists'/self-evaluation of the clients).

The cluster analysis in Figure 19.6 serves as a summary and illustration of the results, which have been replicated by other statistical methods (Kunz 1984). The main results are as follows:

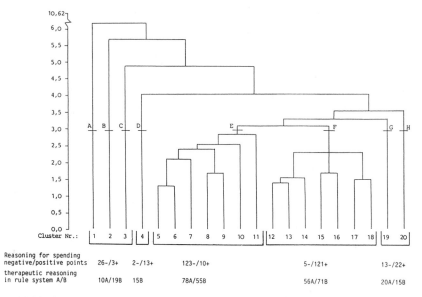

FIGURE 19.6.
Results of a cluster analysis of therapeutic reasoning for spending behavior points in a token economy.

1. There are two main clusters to be distinguished (clusters E and F). In one of them (cluster E) are mostly the categories of reasons for spending negative points; in the other (cluster F) are primarily the categories of reasons for spending positive points.
2. Rule-breaking behavior is justified on a structurally simple level. Reasons for prosocial behavior are given in a more complex way.
3. Only the reasons for spending positive points for prosocial behavior could be changed by altering the system of social rules.
4. In regard to reasons for behavior, no difference was found by the therapists among succeeders and late and early dropouts. Similarly, no difference was found between reasoning by the therapists (observer) and the self-attribution of reasons by the succeeders and the late dropouts (actors).

   The three groups were treated in the same way by the staff, although one has to assume that the accessibility of the clients is variable. According to these results therapeutic interventions are more oriented toward whether behavior is rated positively or negatively than toward specific communication problems of the clients. Because therapeutic interventions vary according to the change in therapeutic rule systems, one must consider the different verbal-cognitive abilities of the clients in the construction of therapeutic programs.

In another study, daily group discussions in a therapeutic community were analyzed over a period of three years. We examined the themes of group discussions and the reactions of the clients to these specific therapeutic confrontations. The data are based on the records of the group discussions of 111 clients during the first four weeks in treatment. Figure 7 shows the frequency distributions of themes and of the cognitive processing of social information in group discussions (Kunz 1988, 1989).

At the beginning of treatment, 74 clients were confronted with predominantly personal and private conflicts; 37 clients were confronted primarily with rule conflicts. We described the cognitive processing with three categories:

- denial; i.e., defense, leaving the group discussion, inadequate means-end-statements, interruptions in verbal communication;
- emotional reaction: i.e., contrariness, aggressiveness, rage, resignation, offense in social interaction;
- negotiation: i.e., information seeking, adequate means-end-statements, problem-solving behavior.

The right column of Figure 19.7 shows which reactions are generally used by succeeders (D) and dropouts (A): 22 dropouts react with denial on personal conflicts, while only 2 succeeders do.

A configuration frequency analysis (Krauth and Lienert 1973) leads to the following conclusions:

1. When succeeders are confronted with private conflicts or rule conflicts, they react mainly by trying to find an adequate solution for their problems. Negotiation here means that these clients tried to negotiate the appropriate problem-solving strategy.
2. Dropouts, on the other hand, react with denial and defensiveness when their personal problems are mentioned or when they are confronted with rule conflicts.
3. These reaction differences exist independently of the themes of confrontations in the group discussions. The emotional reactions of the client groups show no frequency differences.

We interpret these findings as a sign of the cognitive inaccessibility of the dropouts, which may lead to serious communication problems in

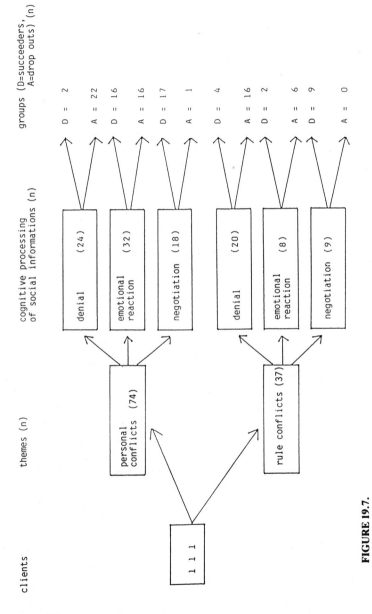

clients   themes (n)   cognitive processing   groups (D=succeeders,
                                     of social informations (n)   A=drop outs) (n)

FIGURE 19.7.
Themes of group discussions and cognitive processing of social information during the first 4 weeks in treatment.

283

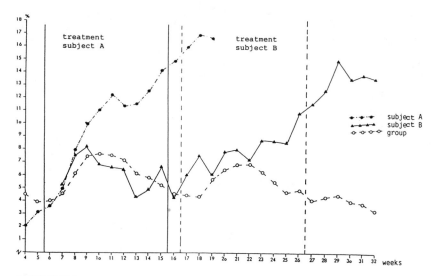

FIGURE 19.8.
Results of a replicated single case study. Improvement of adequate means-end-state-
ments over time.

the therapeutic cooperation. We believe that there could be a relationship
to the special verbal behavior of drug addicts.

In a single case study, we tried to change the clients' verbal behavior
by a training program that resembled role playing. In this paper we report
only the generalized observed effects of one variable in the daily group
discussions, also outside of the training situation itself. Figure 19.8 shows
the improvement in the production of adequate means-end-statements during the different experimental phases (Kampe and Kunz 1981). During
the treatment, the frequencies increased temporarily over the 95% confidence interval and remained at a high level in the posttreatment phase.
The curves also illustrate that behavior changes in the second subject
(B) could be replicated experimentally.

It is important to point out that, due to the changes in verbal behavior,
generalized changes could also be observed in the above-described so-
cial-behavior ratings. The curves in Figure 19.9 show the changes in
behavior ratings on the scale "Prosocial interpersonal activity" (Kampe
and Kunz 1983). These results refer to the fact that in a single case
study some conditions of therapeutic accessibility can be modified by
specific interventions. Considerable therapeutic efforts are necessary; for
example, role playing was carried out with one client and two therapists
in 20 training units over a period of 10 weeks. There is also the question

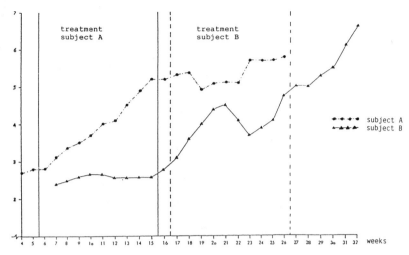

FIGURE 19.9.
Results of a replicated single case study. Behavior rating on the scale "Prosocial Inter-personal Activity."

of how such specific therapeutic intervention programs can be realized in the organization of a therapeutic community on a day-to-day basis.

DISCUSSION AND OUTLOOK FOR FURTHER RESEARCH

In this section, the consequences of our studies will be discussed briefly. In our opinion accessibility itself should be a therapeutic goal. The treatment of therapeutic accessibility of drug addicts requires an individualization of programs within the organization of therapeutic communities. Three levels of individualization seem to be relevant:

1. Treatment programs should be structured differently so that individualization of treatment with the goal of therapeutic accessibility will become possible. The philosophy of treatment and the theoretical premises underlying the interventions by the therapists must take into account the different abilities of drug addicts at the beginning of therapy in the same program.
2. At the level of therapeutic cooperation, therapists' interventions should be differentiated. This, among other things, can be achieved by daily cooperation if, for example, therapy groups are composed according

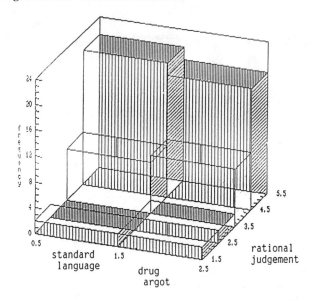

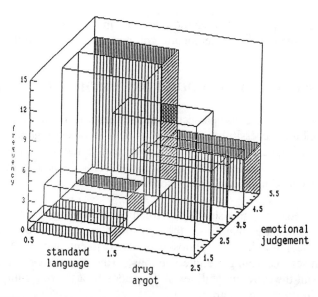

FIGURE 19.10.
Rational judgments of a conflict and emotional judgments of the resolution of a conflict under two conditions: drug argot and standard language.

to the cognitive-verbal abilities of the clients. This approach makes it easier for the therapists to focus on the problem of accessibility.

3. At the level of single-subject therapy, a specific diagnosis of therapeutic accessibility, with its various components, is necessary. In the construction of a goal-attainment scaling, we see one possibility for a dynamic diagnosis of that individual problem.

In further research we attempt to analyze the connections between therapeutic accessibility and drug addicts' specific emotional disturbances. The emotional components of therapeutic accessibility are important but until now have been less comprehensible. In a pilot study we have used an experimental situation in which we confronted drug addicts with a moral conflict. For this confrontation we chose the following conflict situation: "Winni and his girl friend are drug addicts and they need money for drugs. Winni continues to force his girl friend to work as a prostitute although she is HIV infected." These conflicts are presented in two language versions: in the standard language and in the drug argot (Figure 19.10).

The conflict situation should be judged rationally and emotionally. The question to the interviewees was: "Is it right or wrong to force this girl in this situation?" and "How did Winni feel in this situation—good or bad?" Under both conditions the subjects judged Winni's decision as a wrong one, as one can see in the top histogram of Figure 19.10. The emotional judgments changed under the introduced conditions. If the conflict is presented in standard language, Winni has a bad feeling as a result of forcing his girl friend. If we presented the conflict story in drug language, the interviewees were convinced that Winni felt fine, as the bottom histogram shows.

According to these findings, the emotional component in the decision-making process of drug addicts seems to be influenced to a higher degree by the drug language than by the cognitive-rational judgment. In our further investigations of therapeutic accessibility, we try to take into consideration these effects, which are associated with the specific verbal behavior of drug addicts.

REFERENCES

Baekeland, F., and Lundwall, L. (1975). Dropping out of treatment: A critical review. *Psychological Bulletin* 82: 738–83.
Berzins, J. I., Ross W. F., and Monroe J. J. (1970). Crossvalidation of the

Hill-Monroe Acceptability for Psychotherapy Scale for Addict Males. *Journal of Clinical Psychology* 26: 199–201.

Bloch, S., and Crouch, E. (1985). *Therapeutic Factors in Group Psychotherapy.* Oxford: Oxford University Press.

Brown, J. T. (1976). The Relationship of Environment and Stress to Relapse Among Post-addicts in a Therapeutic Community. Unpublished Diss.

Bühringer, G. (1981). *Planung, Steuerung und Bewertung von Therapieeinrichtungen für junge Drogen- und Alkoholabhängige.* München: Gerhard Röttger.

Deissler, K. J. (1978). Das Kübler-Ross-Phänomen, Drogensucht und Rehabilitation. *Schweiz. Ärztezeit.* 47: 2106–2111.

———. (1982). Warum laufen Süchtige während der Rehabilitation weg? *Drogalkohol* 6: 31–40.

De Leon, G., and Ziegenfuss, J. T. (eds.) (1986). *Therapeutic Communities for Addictions. Readings in Theory, Research and Practice.* Springfield, Ill.: Thomas.

De Leon, G., and Schwartz, S. (1984). Therapeutic communities: What are the retention rates? *American Journal of Drug and Alcohol Abuse* 10: 267–84.

Des Jarlais D. C., Knott, A., Savarese, J., and Bersamin, J. (1976). Rules and rule breaking in a therapeutic community. *Addictive Diseases* 2: 627–42.

Henrich, G., and De Jong, R. (1976). *Skala zur Einschätzung des therapeutischen Klimas und des Therapieprogrammes (SEKT). Zielsetzung, Ergebnisse und Interpretationshinweise.* München: Max-Planck-Institut für Psychiatrie.

Kampe. H., and Kunz, D. (1979). Forschungsergebnisse einer von der Deutschen Hauptstelle gegen die Suchtgefahren geförderten Untersuchung eines lerntheoretisch begründeten Behandlungsprogrammes für Deogenabhängige. Frankfurt a. M. (unveröffentlicht).

———. (1980). Über die Rückfälligkeit von Drogenabhängigen. *Suchtgefahren* 26: 165–87.

———. (1981). Sprachliches Interaktionsverhalten Drogenabhängiger als Parameter des therapeutischen Prozesses. In Keup, W. (Hrsg), *Behandlung der Sucht und des Mißbrauches chemischer Stoffe,* 152–164. Stuttgart: Thieme.

———. (1982). Ansätze zur Untersuchung von Selektionsprozessen in der Langzeitbehandlung Drogenabhängiger. In Ladewig, D. (Hrsg), *Drogen und Alkohol,* Bd 2, 115–29. Basel: Karger.

———. (1983). *Was leistet Drogentherapie? Evaluation eines stationären Behandlungsprogrammes.* Weinheim: Beltz.

———. (1984). Integration und Fehlanpassung Drogenabhängiger nach der Behandlung in einer Therapeutischen Gemeinschaft. *Praxis Kinderpsychol. Kinderpsychiat.* 33: 49–55.

———. (1985). Evaluation der Langzeitbehandlung von Drogenabhängigen in einer Therapeutischen Gemeinschaft. *Suchtgefahren* 31: 236–45.

Kampe, H., Kunz, D., and Kremp, M. (1986). Sondersprachgebrauch Drogenabhängiger in ihren Lebensläufen. *Suchtgefahren* 32: 103–11.

Krauth, J., and Lienert, G. A. (1973). Die Konfigurationsfrequenzanalyse (KFA) und ihre Anwendung in Psychologie und Medizin. Freiburg: Alber.

Kunz, D. (1984). Zuschreibungen von Handlungsbegründungen im Behandlungsprozess Drogenabhängiger. Mainz (unveröffentlicht).

Kunz, D. (1988). *Analyse des Therapieabbruches in einer stationären Behandlungseinrichtung für Drogenabhängige. Untersuchung zur Entwicklung eines Bedingungsmodelles mittels multivariater Korrelationsstudien.* Bonn: Universitätsdruckerei Bonn.

———. (1989). Bedingungen des Therapieabbruches Drogenabhängiger. In Feuerlein, W., Bühringer, G., Wille, R. (Hrsg), *Therapieverläufe bei Drogenabhängigen,* 224–44. Berlin: Springer.

Kunz, D., and Kampe, H. (1985). Zum Problem des Therapieabbruches von Heroinabhängigen. *Suchtgefahren* 31: 146–54.

Kunz, D., Kampe, H., and Kremp, M. (1985). Darstellung des Selbstkonzeptes Drogenabhängiger in ihren Lebensläufen. *Praxis Kinderpsychol. Kinderpsychiat.* 34: 219–25.

Monroe, J. J. (1971). The attribution by opiate addicts of characteristics to addict subgroups and to self. *Journal of Social Psychology* 85: 239–49.

Monroe, J. J., and Astin, A. W. (1961). Identification processes in hospitalized narcotic drug addicts. *Journal of Abnormal and Social Psychology* 63: 215–18.

Monroe, J. J., and Hill, H. E. (1958). The Hill-Monroe Inventory for predicting acceptibility for psychotherapy in the institutionalized narcotic addict. *Journal of Clinical Psychology* 14: 31–36.

Platt, J. J., and Metzger, D. S. (1987). Cognitive interpersonal problem-solving skills and the maintenance of treatment success in heroin addicts. *Psychology of Addictive Behaviors* 1: 5–13.

Platt, J. J., Scura, W. C., and Hannon, J. (1973). Problem-solving thinking of youthful incarcerated heroin addicts. *Journal of Community Psychology* 1: 278–81.

Quekelberghe, v., R. (1979). *Systematik der Psychotherapie.* München: Urban & Schwarzengerg.

Simpson, D. D., and Sells, S. B. (1982). Evaluation of drug abuse treatment effectiveness: Summary of the DARP follow up research. NIDA treatment research report, Rockville.

Wexler, H. K., and De Leon, G. (1977). The therapeutic community: Multivariate prediction of retention. *American Journal of Drug and Alcohol Abuse* 4: 145–51.

CHAPTER 20

*Prediction of Dropout and Relapse**

Klaus Herbst

INTRODUCTION

The evaluation and prediction of treatment outcomes still present challenges to the research on drug addiction. Generalizable conclusions can be expected only if the design, conduct, and analysis of the studies are sophisticated. In particular, methodological problems arise with therapy studies if the length of observation time varies in the sample. A considerable variation of the regular time in treatment and of the follow-up period is found even in unicenter studies. Multicenter prospective studies may be useful only if the differences in programs are taken into account. Moreover, it can be shown that the core of statistical information about the stochastic processes of dropouts and relapse is given by functions of time that map the hazards of the critical events. Statistical methods for censored lifetime data allow for both demands.

THE MUNICH MULTICENTER TREATMENT EVALUATION STUDY

Participation in the Munich Multicenter Treatment Evaluation Study (MTES) involved 13 German facilities with drug-free residential programs and 304 clients, i.e., 70% of all admissions to these agencies from fall 1985 to spring 1987. The time period from admission to regular

*The study was funded by the German Federal Ministry of Health. For further details see the chapters by Hanel and Hadersdorfer in this volume.

TABLE 20.1

Basic Statistics of Three Selected Therapeutic Communities from the Munich Multicenter Treatment Evaluation Study

TC	Mean Retention Time (days)			Dropout Rate	N
	all	discharge	dropout		
1	87	118	51	46%	69%
2	183	321	86	59%	58%
3	125	273	64	71%	51%

discharge ranged from 4 to 20 months. Even within the single programs, this period was not constant. Thus, the observed retention time of a client depended not only on his or her persistency but also on the individually planned treatment duration. Clients in long-term programs may be at risk of dropout for a longer time than those in shorter programs. Consequently, neither the mean retention time nor the dropout rate provides meaningful statistics to describe the in-treatment performance of a typical client.

The first of three follow-up inquiries, scheduled for 3 months after regular discharge or dropout from treatment, was actually obtained with delay in many cases, maximally after 10 months. For the most part, this was due to the judicial charges imposed on the clients that were violated by dropout or drug use. Since the probability of relapse is expected to increase with the period of follow-up, the same arguments as before apply here. A meaningful method for predicting dropout or relapse should consider the individually observed time at risk; this can be obtained by a survival analysis.

THE SO-CALLED BASIC STATISTICS OF TREATMENT AND INFERENCE PROCEDURES FOR LIFETIME DATA

To demonstrate the problem, let's take a look at some simple (often called basic) statistics of three therapeutic communities (TCs) from the study (Table 20.1). TC 1 had the least mean time of retention (87 days) but also the lowest dropout rate (46%). In TC 2, the clients stayed longer but more of them dropped out. TC 3 had a medium mean retention time and the greatest percentage of dropout. Is this confusing result an effect of differences in the length of planned treatment time?

In order to answer the question, some statistical requisites are indicated. At first, a failure-time random variable T is defined as the elapsed time in treatment until dropout. From the probability density function of T, f(t), two additional functions can be derived: the survival function S(t), denoting the probability of no failure until time t; and the hazard function h(t). This function is important because it maps the instantaneous rate of failure at time t for those subjects who survived, (i.e., did not drop out), up to that time. In the following analysis, the generalized gamma distribution is used. This is a fairly flexible family of distributions for lifetime data, including as special cases the gamma, Weibull, and exponential distributions; the log-normal distribution also arises as a limiting form. The discrimination among these models and the estimation of parameters for a given data set is done by maximum-likelihood methods (Lawless 1982).

Table 20.1 shows that some clients completed the treatment and did not fail by dropout. They were still at risk when the observation finished, but the critical event did not occur. It is only known that they survived a specified period; their data are labeled censored at the time of regular discharge. Thus, two qualitatively different events are observed: namely, failure by dropout or censoring by regular discharge. With T as time of failure and C as time of censoring, it can be shown that, under some constraints, the likelihood of the individual data is given by the probability density function f(t) if the subject failed, or by the survival function S(c) if the observation was censored. The total likelihood of the sample is set equal to the product over all individual functions.

This framework allows an evaluation of the dropout risk even if the periods of observation are not identical for all subjects. The problem of varying planned treatment durations is solved in a closed form in this model. With respect to relapse, the problem of differing follow-up intervals is handled analogically. In this case, T denotes the time of relapse, and C indicates the time of interview (used if the client remained drug free up to that point).

A look at the survival functions (Figure 20.1) for the three TCs, mentioned above, shows that the probability of retention in TC 1 is estimated to be lower than in TC 2, but higher than in TC 3. The percentage of dropout as well as the mean retention time are affected by the planned time of treatment. This is marked in the figure by rectangles and dotted lines pointing to the arithmetic mean of regular discharge time, and by the extension of the survival curves drawn down to the last regularly discharged client. The spread of discharge time is noticeable, in TC 3 for example, the last client left therapy about seven months after the mean time of regular discharge.

The corresponding hazard functions of the three TCs (Figure 20.2) indicate that the rank order of retention with respect to the dropout risk

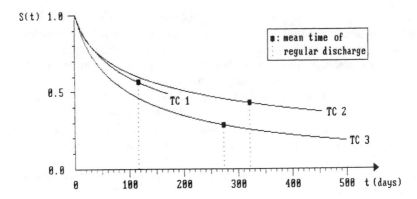

FIGURE 20.1.
Survival functions of dropout for three selected TCs after t days of treatment (dotted lines point to the mean of regular discharge times).

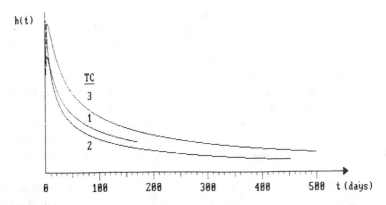

FIGURE 20.2.
Hazard functions of dropout for three selected TCs after t days of treatment.

is TC 2, TC 1, TC 3, in contradiction to the orders (see Table 20.1) given by the mean retention time (TC 2, TC 3, TC 1), as well as by the dropout rate (TC 1, TC 2, TC 3). In any case, the peak of risk is located within the first 10 days of treatment. The survivors of this first attack, however, remained at a considerable risk of therapy disruption for a fairly long time. To some extent, this is due to the increasing danger of a disciplinary discharge from treatment, in consequence of severe violations of institutional rules. We shall now analyze the data from the entire study, as far as they have been investigated by the first follow-up.

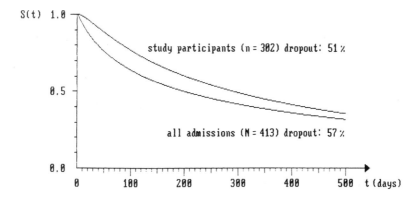

FIGURE 20.3.
Survival functions of dropout for all admissions and for the study participants.

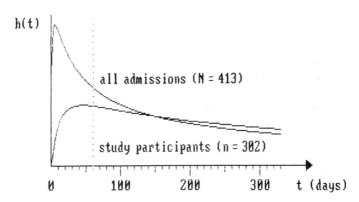

FIGURE 20.4.
Hazard functions of dropout for all admissions and for the study participants.

THE DROPOUT PROCESS AND EVALUATION
OF RISK FACTORS

Figure 20.3 shows the survival curves of dropout for all admissions, as well as for the participants of the prospective study from all 13 facilities. Although the two percentages of dropout are similar, the survival functions are significantly different. The sample of study participants had a higher probability of staying in treatment (i.e., they did not drop out or were not discharged disciplinarily).

The hazard functions (Figure 20.4) indicate that we missed particularly

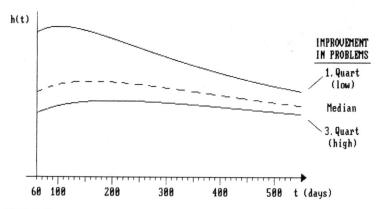

FIGURE 20.5.
Hazard of dropout as a function of the improvement in psychological problems (rated by therapists) after 60 days of treatment.

those clients who dropped out at the beginning of treatment, while after two months the risks are quite similar. In consequence, the data base for prediction is poor with respect to early dropouts but powerful enough to represent clients staying longer than 60 days in treatment; this corresponds to 75% of all admissions.

Up to this point, the sample of clients participating in the study has been analyzed as a whole, without considering distinctive features of the individuals. Extending the statistical model used so far, we define the prediction of dropout, now, as an evaluation of the individual risk dependent on concomitant variables. This can be done on the basis of parametric regression models for lifetime data (Lawless 1982). Using multivariate methods, we tried to establish risk factors of failure. A lot of variables were tested but only a few turned out to have predictive power; all of them can be called treatment process variables. Up to now, we have not found valuable predictors in the large set of sociographic variables, including drug-use history. This may be an effect of the limited sample of this study, but more likely it is a consequence of the very complex structure of the addiction and therapy process.

The sole highly significant predictor variable of dropout is defined by the improvement in psychological problems of the clients during treatment. The scores result from a questionnaire given to their therapists. The parallel self-assessment by the clients yields no significant predictor. Figure 20.5 shows that clients with low improvement scores after 60 days of treatment are at a very high risk of dropout in the next period of evaluation, while clients who profit from treatment have better odds of staying. This effect is preserved when we analyze the dropout and

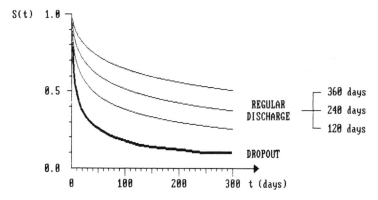

FIGURE 20.6.
**Survival functions of relapse after dropout and after regular discharge from treatment
at different times.**

improvement process after five and eight months of treatment. There is
no statistical difference between subjects who drop out by themselves
and those who are discharged disciplinarily by the facility.

THE RELAPSE PROCESS AND VARIABLES
FOR PREDICTION

The analysis of the relapse process in the first follow-up period after
dropout or regular discharge from treatment is based on data obtained
from 144 clients who had been questioned until December 1987. Relapse
is defined here as a fairly continuous abuse of cannabis, opiates, or opiate
substitutes lasting at least two weeks within the follow-up period. Almost
all clients who relapsed continued to use drugs until the follow-up interview, the time of which varied. Altogether, 62% of the clients interviewed
relapsed to continuous abuse.

The prediction of relapse is governed by the question of whether the
treatment had been completed regularly or not. Clients who dropped out
or had been disciplinarily discharged had very poor chances of staying
drug free. The length of the last treatment had no statistically significant
influence on this process. The fact of dropout has severe consequences;
the point of time at which it occurs makes no great difference. The
regularly discharged clients had better odds than the dropouts and, moreover, they were likely to profit from the duration of treatment. The survival curves (Figure 20.6) show the highly significant gap between

TABLE 20.2

Relapse Rates and Results of Likelihood-ratio Tests for Survival Models in Cases of Dropout from Treatment and of Regular Discharge in Conjunction with Three Additional Therapy Variables (First Follow-up)

Therapy Variable		Relapse Rate	LR-Test
Regular discharge		49%	p < 0.001
Dropout		79%	
Regular Discharge and:			
Improvement	high	38%	p < 0.01
	low	60%	
Treatment time	long	37%	p < 0.01
	short	61%	
Aftercare	yes	33%	p < 0.01
	no	64%	

dropout and regular discharge, as well as the effect of time in treatment on the probability of relapse.

For the regularly discharged clients only, there are two further significant prediction variables of relapse: first, again, the initial improvement in problems during treatment and second, whether the client got immediate aftercare or not. In Table 20.2 the risk factors of relapse in the first follow-up period are depicted. The results of the likelihood-ratio tests, given the multivariate survival model, are compared to the relapse rates by subsets of clients. Once more, it should be pointed out that the percentages of relapse are biased by unequal periods of follow-up. The survival model, however, allows for a valid evaluation of risk factors.

CONCLUSIONS

In this study, the grave risk factors of dropout from treatment and of relapse after treatment are centered on the current treatment process. Data from the history of the drug addicted remain unyielding, insofar as they did not help to predict the future. This may be an effect of sampling but, more likely, it may be a problem of measuring significant features of the addiction careers. The results of the study indicate that a long-term drug-free residential treatment is effective if the clients are able to profit from therapy, do not drop out, and receive aftercare.

There are a lot of questions left open: Who profits from therapy? Are treatment effects cumulative over time, even in cases of dropout? Is the status of the first follow-up period perpetual? We hope that some answers to these questions will be given when the data of the next two follow-up periods (one and two years after the end of residential treatment) have been analyzed.

Statistical methods for lifetime data, like the survival analysis, are unusual in the field of addiction research. It should be recognized, however, that both addiction and treatment have to be conceived as stochastic processes. It has been shown that a failure theory mustn't ignore the length of observation time, and, moreover, that the course of the hazard of failure is in itself of great importance for the evaluation of treatment outcomes.

REFERENCES

Lawless, J. F. (1982). *Statistical Models and Methods for Lifetime Data.* New York: Wiley.

CHAPTER 21

Factors Influencing Relapse and Treatment Dropout

Helmut Kampe and Dieter Kunz

INTRODUCTION

The treatment of drug addicts in therapeutic communities often fails. Many clients drop out of treatment after a few days or weeks of therapy, and even after longer periods of abstinence and treatment, relapse rates are high in these populations. The reduction of relapse risks of abstinent addicts is the most serious and difficult problem of addiction treatment. This article presents some results of several studies of the relapse process and related problems in heroin addicts. The problem of craving as the most important predictor of relapse (Deissler 1977) is the focus of our research interests.

As Washton (1990) stated, a relapse is the process of returning to the use of heroin or other drugs by a person who remained abstinent for a period of time and has made a serious attempt at recovery. In order for a return to drug use to be considered a "relapse," the addict must have at least begun the recovery (change) process (Washton 1990: 115). A similiar approach to the definition of relapse has been proposed by Marlatt and Gordon (1985, p. 36f.). Within this perspective, a distinction has been made between the lapse, the first discrete violation of self-imposed rules or regulations governing the rate or pattern of a selected target behavior (for instance, abstinence), and the secondary effects of a "lapse," in which the behavior may or may not increase in the direction of the original pretreatment base line levels (a full-blown relapse).

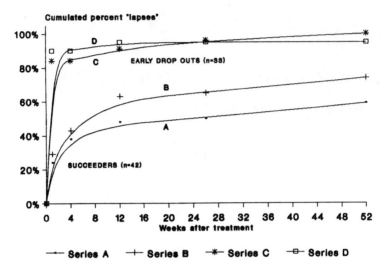

FIGURE 21.1.
Relapse rates of suceeders (n = 42) and dropouts (n = 33) in a follow-up interval of 12 months (Curve A: heroin relapses; Curve B: cannabis/alcohol consumption of succeeders; Curve C: heroin relapses; and Curve D: cannabis/alcohol consumption of dropouts).

SUMMARY OF PREVIOUS STUDIES

Regularities of Recidivism of Heroin Addicts

The description of regularities of the relapse process after treatment in a therapeutic community for drug addicts is relatively simple. In a follow-up study of all 108 treated heroin addicts of a small therapeutic community in Germany, it was possible to interview 75 of the 97 living clients. Figure 21.1 presents the cumulated relative frequency (survival) curves of the first relapses of heroin addicts after treatment (Kampe and Kunz 1983). The following regularities of the relapse process can be specified:

1. The greatest risk of relapse occurs in the first 12 weeks after termination of treatment.
2. Those clients treated for a longer time (more than approximately 12 weeks), here called succeeders, did not relapse at the same rates as the early dropouts. More than 80% of the early dropouts relapsed within the first week after treatment and 100% within the first year

after treatment. Only 24% of the succeeders relapsed in the first week and 60% during the first year. This means that approximately 40% of the succeeders stay opiate free during this period.

3. The relationship between substitute drug taking (cannabis and/or alcohol consumption) and opiate drug taking in the two groups can also clearly be seen in Figure 21.1. The subjects in the early dropout group started cannabis or alcohol and opiate consumption nearly at the same time. Those clients treated for a longer time started substitute drug consumption earlier than opiate consumption. Nearly all clients violated abstinence rules in different forms. In most cases the process of relapse was initiated by substitute drug consumption.

The analysis of heroin consumption after the first relapse makes clear that relapses do not always lead to complete readdiction. Eighty-five percent of the dropouts became readdicted, whereas only 38% of the succeeder group completely readdicted after the first relapse. Fifteen percent of the early dropouts stayed clean or had relapse episodes (less than 20% of follow-up time on drugs); whereas among those clients treated for a longer time than three months, 62% stayed clean or had relapse episodes during the follow-up interval of 12 months. These findings resemble American and other results in this research field (Hunt and Bespalec 1974; Herbst et al. 1989).

The Relapse Process

In contrast to the relatively simple regularities in the description of relapse, the explanation of the relapse process of drug addicts is a relatively complex problem. In order to approach this problem, the relapse processes of all new admissions during one year (n = 21) in a small therapeutic community for heroin addicts were observed. The results can be summarized as follows (Kampe and Kunz 1980): In accordance with Meyer and Mirin (1979), it was found that some addicts seemed more likely to relapse than others—they were more susceptible than others. Twenty-seven percent of the clients stayed opiate free during treatment. Forty percent of the clients relapsed one to two times, thereby accounting for 20% of all relapses. Thirty-three percent of the clients relapsed three to six times, accounting for 80% of the total of 51 relapses observed in the sample. In more than 70% of the situations which preceded the relapses, drug-related behaviors were observed (e.g., talking the drug argot, retreat from social interactions or conflict-orientated and rule-breaking behavior in the therapeutic community). The drugs were consumed mainly in the company of other drug addicts; in only 21% of the observed relapses drugs were taken alone.

Further, we found that the reported drug effects were experienced as positive if the situation of drug taking could be characterized by drug market related stimuli (e.g., the companionship of addicted friends and shooting at locations where formerly drugs were taken). Under these conditions it seems more probable that opiate effects are subjectively interpreted as positive. These results correspond to American results, wherein positive drug effects have been found to affect the speed (shortening the time interval) of the repetition of drug taking in a relapse situation (Chaney et al. 1982; Kampe and Kunz 1980; Kampe et al. 1989).

Meyer and Mirin (1979: 89) explained the difference between those clients who relapsed at lower rates by positing the importance of drug craving to the relapse. They also mentioned as explanations, conditioning processes, behavioral imitation, and cognitive labeling processes in the state of craving for drugs. Meyer and Mirin defined craving in the context of (subjective) drug availability as a complex response pattern which they called the heroin stimulus. The craving complex is, in this perspective, the most important factor in the chain of events ultimately leading to relapse.

Behavioral Changes during the Relapse Phases

The relapse develops in a complex process involving cognitive, emotional, behavioral, and physiological components. This process may be divided into three parts: The prerelapse phase, the drug-taking behavior chain itself, and the postrelapse phase.

In everyday interactions with clients, therapists sometimes noticed behavioral changes some days before and after a relapse occurred. They often got feelings and uncertain impressions that something was wrong with a client. They said, for example: "I do not know what is happening with client A." They could not comprehend the developmental process that leads to craving and relapse. We therefore analyzed the behavior of relapsing clients of the therapeutic community. The behavior of all clients of that therapeutic community was continuously observed with a behavioral rating system on a daily schedule. On several dimensions of this rating system, irregularities in the behavior before and after a relapse occurred could be measured.

Figure 21.2 shows that general arousal increased three days before the clients relapsed. We observed that general restlessness, motor miscoordi-

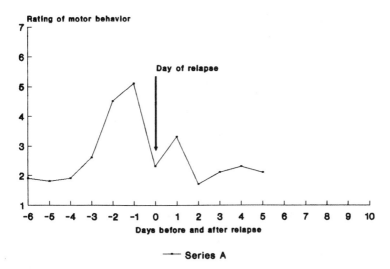

FIGURE 21.2.
Changes in general arousal 6 days before and 5 days after a relapse (n = 9).

nation, and speech disorders functioned as indicators of arousal. At the same time the mood of clients worsened (Figure 21.3). They became irritable, depressed, and inaccessible. Apart from that, a general withdrawal from the standard activities of the therapeutic community could be observed (Figure 21.4). The clients' recovery from this stress burden also took several days. These changes in behavior during the prerelapse phase could not be influenced by behavior consequences in the contingency management system of that therapeutic community. Perhaps this was because the therapists were unable to specify the cognitive and emotional background of these irregularities in behavior (Kampe and Kunz 1983).

Verbal Interaction during the Prerelapse Phase

The verbal behavior of the relapsing clients also changed in the week before a relapse. The observations of verbal interactions in group therapy represent a general cognitive and emotional destabilization in the prerelapse phase. This destabilization is reflected in the loss of connections between the specific verbal interaction behaviors. Figures 21.5 and 21.6 present the significant results of a path analysis modeling this destabili-

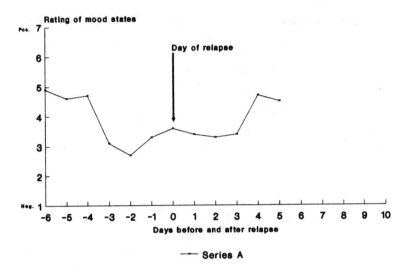

FIGURE 21.3.
Changes in mood states 6 days before and 5 days after a relapse (n = 9).

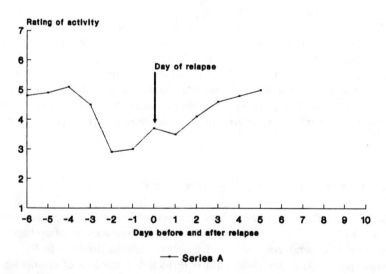

FIGURE 21.4.
Changes in social activity 6 days before and 5 days after a relapse (n = 9).

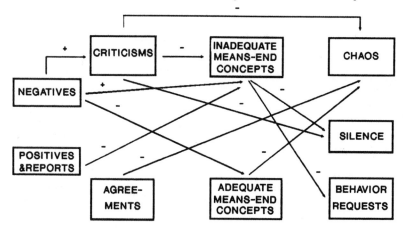

FIGURE 21.5.
Verbal interactional behavior of heroin addicts (n = 15) in an abstinent interval of one week (lines and valences indicate positive and negative significant paths.)

zation (Kampe and Kunz 1981). The daily group therapy sessions were tape recorded over 32 weeks and verbal interaction behavior was observed with the aid of a category system. Every 5 seconds one observation was attributed to 1 of 10 categories.

It is supposed that positive reinforcing utterances (i.e., "hm-hm," "yea-yea," or simple verbal reports; category: positives) and evaluative agreements (i.e., "This is very interesting what you just said!"; evaluative disagreements or elaborated negative comments like, "I can't understand your reasons . . . ; I would have done other things like . . . "; categories: agreements and criticisms) regulate the production of adequate means-end concepts as well as adequate behavior requests. Both are involved in the conceptualization of goals and behavioral means as meaningful social actions in the course of reasoning through social actions and behavior planning. Similarly, it was supposed that disruptive verbal behaviors which suppress and disturb verbal interactions, like interruptions or devaluating criticisms/devaluative arguing (category: negatives), regulate the production of inadequate means-end concepts (i.e., practical accounts or neutralizations/rationalizations; category: inadequate means-end concepts) or the occurrence of parallel talking and silence (categories: chaos and silence; Figure 21.5) in the course of behavior reasoning. It is further supposed that in the state of emotional and cognitive destabilization in the prerelapse phase, positive and negative interactional verbal behaviors lose their regulating functions. One can recognize the diminished com-

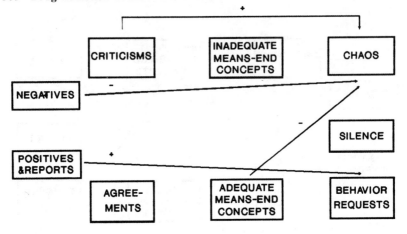

FIGURE 21.6.
Verbal interactional behavior of heroin addicts (n = 15) a week before a relapse (lines and valences indicate positive and negative significant paths).

plexity of the verbal interactional behavior system of the clients in the week preceding a relapse (Figure 21.6).

Other results indicate that the cognitive and emotional changes represented by the verbal behavior of relapsing clients are correlated with the social desintegration of the clients. These changes seem to be mediated by the use of the drug argot (Kampe and Kunz 1984). In an analysis of 146 written life reports, it was found that dropouts used more drug argot words, mentioned more drug-relevant events, and produced less meaningful means-end concepts than clients who successfully terminated their therapy (Kampe and Kunz 1986; Kunz and Kampe 1985).

Comparable findings were reported by Platt (Platt et al. 1973; Platt and Metzger 1987). American heroin addicts seem to be less able to produce adequate cognitive means-end constructions in problem-solving test situations than a control group. Appel and Kaestner (1979) found that with the same test poor problem-solving addicts were more likely to relapse.

These results indicate that large domains of the cognitive and emotional behavior systems of drug addicts change several days before a relapse occurs. This state can be characterized as a general cognitive and affective destabilization. During this state, automized drug-relevant behavior programs (mediated by drug slang usage) seem to become more important. Thus, these programs regulate the social behavior of heroin addicts through drug-oriented behavior leading ultimately to a relapse.

Self-reported Subjective Reasons for Relapse

Conditioned withdrawal symptoms (the conditioned withdrawal syndrome) seem to have very little weight for the relapse process in the framework of Marlatt's relapse theory (Marlatt and Gordon 1985). Apart from this, Marlatt, contrary to many theorists, defines craving as the subjective desire to experience the effects or consequences of a given act. Craving experiences of addicts are mediated by the anticipated gratification of drug consumption and may be the product of conditioning (as a conditioned response elicited by stimuli associated with past gratifications). Therefore Marlatt assumes that addicts report more emotional disturbances and positive expectancies as relapse reasons than physical withdrawal complaints or coercive negative cravings for drugs. Marlatt reported the following rank order of relapse reasons. This scheme explains 79% of all heroin relapses with four reasons: Social pressure to retake drugs (36%); stressing negative emotional states like frustration, anger, fears, anxiety, and tensions (19%); interpersonal conflict situations; (14%) and the desire to experience positive feelings (10%). And, indeed, negative physical states (9%) and craving for drugs (5%) seem to be relatively unimportant factors of the relapse process.

A replication of his investigation (Kampe et al. 1989) led to results that considerably deviate from those reported by Marlatt. In the first position of the rank order of main relapse reasons we found that: 40% reported (exclusively withdrawal-like) negative emotional states as reasons for relapses; 18% reported craving for drugs; and 18% social pressures to retake drugs. Seventy-six percent of all relapses could be explained with these three reasons. The remaining 24% were distributed over positive effect expectations, testing personal control, interpersonal conflicts, and positive effect expectations in social situations (Table 21.1).

Apart from Marlatt, we analyzed the reasons that were reported as second-order reasons by the interviewees. The results reveal a departure from Marlatt's theory and results. Drug addicts recognized and reported the components of the conditioned subclinical withdrawal syndrome as important reasons for the relapse. In addition to the first-order reasons, they most frequently reported drug-associated physical withdrawal complaints (43%) as second-order reasons. Next came social pressure (29%) and subjective craving for drugs (10%) as secondary reasons for relapses. Contrary to Marlatt's theory, the combination of the reported first- and second-order relapse reasons indicate that 68% of the 84 interviewed addicts report conditioned withdrawal symptoms and craving as reasons for the relapse. There was a wide margin between these complaints and negative emotional states (46%; exclusively withdrawal-like affective dis-

TABLE 21.1

Analysis of Self-Reported First- and Second-Order Relapse Reasons (Kampe et al. 1984)

	First-Order Reasons	Second-Order Reasons	Marlatt (1985)
	N = 84	N = 78	N = 129
Intrapersonal determinants			
Negative emotional states	40%	6%	19%
Negative physical states	1%	43%	9%
Positive emotional states	11%	6%	10%
Testing personal control	6%	6%	2%
Urges and temptations	18%	10%	5%
Interpersonal determinants			
Interpersonal conflict	4%	0%	14%
Social pressure	18%	29%	36%
Positive emotional states	2%	0%	5%

turbances) as well as temptations to retake drugs in social pressure situations (44%).

We also found that the interviewed drug addicts were not able to relate their relapse experiences to future involvement with drug-relevant events. Only 33% were able to learn through their relapse experiences and were then able to precisely specify conditions of relapse dangers against the background of their own experiences. The other subjects mentioned relapse dangers in such situations described as "no money, no girls, no apartment" (Kampe 1989). These results support a call for further research in the field of craving as an important factor in the relapse process.

The Conditioned Subclinical Withdrawal Syndrome

It is supposed that the complex response pattern "craving" is learned in withdrawal situations. By classical conditioning processes, this response pattern becomes independent from the drug-induced physiological changes and live on in abstinence. The response pattern "craving" seems to be the most important predictor of relapse (Meyer and Mirin 1979; Gossop 1989; O'Brien and Ternes 1977; Rist et al. 1989).

In the framework of this theory, a distinction is made between negative physical complaints that resemble withdrawal symptoms (for instance, vomiting, bone pain, etc.) and the component of conscious and frequently coercive drug desire (cognitive planning of drug seeking): the craving.

Conditioned positive drug effects are not considered in this relapse model. But self-reported relapse reasons indicate that positive physical sensations that are similar to positive drug effects were sometimes experienced and mentioned as relapse reasons by heroin addicts (McAuliffe and Gordon 1974). Thus it is possible to discriminate among three components of the craving complex which are elicited by stimuli associated with drug-relevant behavior and withdrawal situations: conditioned withdrawal (such as physical complaints), drug craving (the conscious desire to seek or to take drugs), and conditioned physical sensations (which are similar to drug effects). This theoretical orientation goes back to Linde-smith (1937) and Wikler (1980).

A further assumption is important in the framework of this model: during the development of drug dependence, internal changes such as trivial mood changes or slight colds take over the functions of the signaling threats of withdrawal symptoms. Many everyday, trivial complaints resemble the mild withdrawal symptoms. Indeed, abstinent heroin addicts sometimes feel physically ill if they sweat in high summer temperatures.

During abstinence, drug addicts also suffer relatively frequently under dysphoric or hypophoric disorders, depressive ill-feelings, disgust, or boredom. They also remember, with relative frequency, drug-relevant situations and drug-related experiences or events. One important problem seems to be the analysis of the relationships between these hypophoric symptoms, drug-relevant thinking, and drug-related situations as (generalized) conditioned eliciting stimuli, on the one hand, and as the occurrence of the three components of the craving complex on the other hand. Many addicts experience the components of the craving complex without knowing the real reasons for the occurrence of such complaints. They often mention that these complaints occur like lightning out of the clear blue sky. At the same time, we also have to take into account the cognitive processing of external and internal occurrences before and after a relapse and different aspects of psychopathology as setting conditions.

CURRENT RESEARCH ON CRAVING

To investigate these issues in this general theoretical context, the present study addresses the following questions and hypotheses (Kampe and Overbeck-Larisch 1990):

1. What are the frequency rates (and correlates) of the components of the response-pattern craving in a population of addicts in therapeutic communities?

2. What are the determinants of the actual frequencies of the occurrences of the three components of the craving complex? It is hypothesized that the readiness to respond with (conditioned) symptoms of the craving complex to external and internal eliciting stimulus conditions determine these frequencies.
3. Is there any influence of trait anxiety and/or depressive disorders on the readiness to respond to both external and internal stimulus conditions with the craving complex? It is hypothesized that the degree of general arousal and depressive disturbances are psychopathological setting conditions that influence the readiness to respond to internal and external addiction specific stimulus conditions.

Method and Instruments

The investigation of these questions was carried out in four therapeutic communities (TCs) in Germany. All 158 new admissions to these TCs during one year were included. The clients were 26.4 years old (SD = 5.6); they started daily opiate use at an age of 18.5 years (SD = 3.8); and they consumed heroin, other opiates, and drugs for an average of 7.4 years (SD = 4.9). They were drug free for approximately 4.9 months at the time of interview. Seventy-six percent of these clients were male and 24% female.

The clients were personally interviewed with a standardized schedule of questions that followed the guidelines of the standards for follow-up studies proposed by the German Society on Addiction Research. The rating measures of the response readiness were validated in a pilot study (Kampe 1989). For example, readiness to respond to drug-relevant situations with craving and conditioned physical withdrawal symptoms was analyzed using the situations and symptoms proposed by O'Brien and Ternes (1977). The measures of trait anxiety were obtained from the German adoption of the Spielberger State-Trait-Anxiety-Inventory (Laux et al. 1981) and the depressive disorder from a German version of the cognitive component "hopelessness" questionnaire (Beck et al. 1982).

Results

Frequency Rates of the Components of the Craving Pattern

As can be seen in Figure 21.7 (Series 2), 73% of the clients reported that they suffered craving during the last three months, 62% experienced

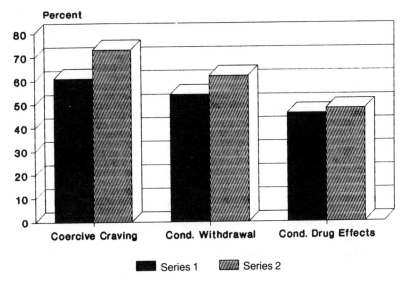

FIGURE 21.7.
Frequencies of the occurrence of the three components of the craving complex in two groups of heroin addicts (Series 1: frequencies after approximately 120 weeks of abstinence [n = 100], Series 2: results of another group after 20 weeks of abstinence [n = 158].)

conditioned withdrawal effects. Series 1 in this figure represents the results of the pilot study. The frequencies of craving and conditioned withdrawal symptoms are significantly lower than the frequencies found in the present study. These variations may be explained by the different times of abstinence. The subjects of the pilot study were abstinent for approximately 120 weeks, whereas the subjects of the present study stayed abstinent for only 20 weeks. Craving and conditioned withdrawal symptoms are negatively correlated with time of abstinence ($r = -.30; r = -.24$). Conditioned effect sensations are not correlated with time of abstinence ($r = -.03$). In this context, one result of the pilot study may be of particular interest. Dropouts of a therapeutic community suffer earlier and more often under the craving response pattern.

The self-reported frequencies of the components of the craving complex are not very highly intercorrelated. The correlations range from about $r = .26$ to $r = .32$. Again, these results closely resemble the results of the pilot study. They also are highly similar to American results (Childress et al. 1984; McLellan et al. 1986).

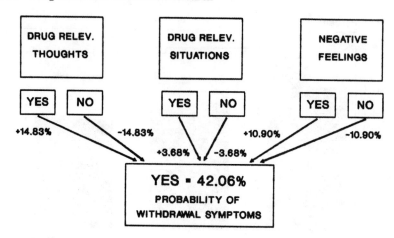

FIGURE 21.8.
Influence of the readiness-to-respond factors on the probability of conditioned withdrawal symptoms.

Readiness to Respond to Drug-related Stimulus Conditions

The next step in the course of investigating the craving response pattern showed that the self-reports of the clients indicated readiness to respond with coercive drug desires, conditioned withdrawal symptoms, and conditioned drug effect sensations to the following generalized stimulus conditions: drug-relevant situations (the same situations investigated by O'Brien and Ternes [1977] and his research group); drug-relevant thinking/thoughts; and addiction-specific negative feelings like disgust, boredom, loneliness, inner emptiness, and other hypophoric feelings. These self-reported triggers of the craving response pattern are relatively highly correlated—the range lies between r = .43 and r = .67. It was also found that the same drug-relevant situations, in approximately the same rank order, trigger coercive desires as well as conditioned withdrawal symptoms (rank correlation r = .93; compare O'Brien et al. 1977). The readiness to respond with coercive drug desires to drug-relevant thinking and situations decreases in the time of abstinence. The seven other readiness variables are not significantly correlated with time of abstinence.

Determinants of the Frequency Rates of the Craving Response Pattern

In order to determine the quantitative effects of the readiness-to-respond variables upon the actual frequency of occurrence of the three compo-

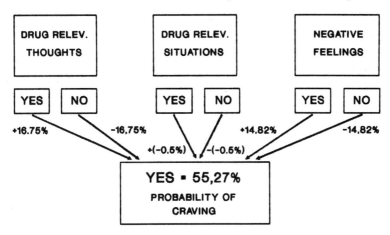

FIGURE 21.9.
Influence of the readiness-to-respond factors on the probability of coercive craving attacks.

nents of the craving complex, the data were analyzed with the categorial data modeling procedures of the SAS statistical computer program (CATMOD; linear model, parameter estimate: WLS). Figures 21.8 and 21.9 indicate the following results: If the interviewed subjects report readiness to respond to drug-relevant thinking, drug-related situations, and negative emotional disturbances with mild withdrawal symptoms (Figure 21.8), then these conditions have a cumulative influence on the reported actual occurrence of conditioned withdrawal symptoms (42.06% + 14.83% + 3.68% + 10.90% = 71.47%). Under these conditions, the probability of self-reported withdrawal complaints during the last three months increases to 71%. In the case of self-reported denial of readinesses to respond, the influence diminishes (42.06% − 14.83% − 3.68% − 10.90% = 12.65%). Under these conditions, the probability of self-reported withdrawal complaints during the last three months diminishes to 13%. The probabilities to report coercive drug desires during the last three months are 86.34% in the case of consent and 24.20% in the case of denial (Figure 21.9).

In general, the results show that the actual frequencies of the occurrences of conditioned withdrawal complaints and coercive drug desires are clearly influenced by two internal stimulus conditions: drug-relevant thinking/thoughts and addiction-specific negative emotional disorders. The influence of drug-relevant situations is, in this statistical model, not significant. Moreover, the analyses have shown that the occurrences of conditioned drug effects could not be explained in the framework of this statistical data modeling procedure.

Further analysis with this statistical method showed that the readiness-to-respond variables are in general not reinforced by trait anxiety/stress burden or by "hopelessness," the cognitive component of depressive disorders regarded as psychopathological setting conditions. There is one exception: A high level of trait anxiety strengthens the liklihood of a conditioned drug effect response to drug-relevant thinking. Nevertheless, this specific readiness to respond is only of negligible importance for the occurrence of actual conditioned-effect sensations.

DISCUSSION

The research results presented here lead to the following conclusions:

1. The craving response pattern seems to be the most important factor in the processes that ultimately lead to relapse. This response pattern was characterized by three components: coercive negative drug desires (drug seeking), conditioned withdrawal symptoms, and conditioned drug effects. In contrast to Marlatt and Gordon's assumptions (1985) with respect to the relapse process, the present results indicate that coercive negative drug desires, conditioned withdrawal complaints, and withdrawal-specific negative emotional disturbances were cited most frequently as relapse reasons by heroin addicts. Positive-effect expectations, anger, or frustration were also mentioned, but they do not seem to have any overwhelming importance for relapse. Temptations in social pressure situations are a bit more important.

2. The craving response pattern seems to be a relatively stable one. Even after long-lasting abstinent periods, a large proportion of addicts suffer coercive desires and/or mild withdrawal symptoms. We observed a significant but relatively low negative relationship between the time of abstinence and coercive drug desires, a weaker negative one to conditioned withdrawal, and no correlation between abstinence and conditioned drug effects. The last result agrees with experimental data which indicate that positive drug effects are difficult to establish and extinguish, and that they are associated with post-injection stimuli (Lynch et al. 1976; Sideroff and Jarvik 1980). Apart from this, the results of an earlier study indicate that dropouts of a TC suffered earlier and more frequently from these complaints than did regularly terminating clients (Kampe 1989).

3. We found that subjectively unexplainable coercive drug desires and withdrawal complaints were strongly stimulated by a readiness to re-

spond to drug-relevant thinking and addiction-specific negative emotions or hypophoric disorders. In general, these variables are not related to time of abstinence. The exceptions reflected a readiness to respond with coercive drug desires to drug-relevant thinking and situations.

The readiness to respond to situational stimulus conditions, as suggested by Wikler's two-factor theory (1980), does not have any significant influence on the occurrence of coercive desires and conditioned withdrawal. This result does not contradict this fruitful theory. We suspect that situational stimulus conditions trigger withdrawal symptoms, coercive drug desires, and, to a lesser degree, conditioned drug effects in actual drug-relevant situations in which, for instance, drugs are offered or consumed. A few interviewed addicts mentioned temptations in social pressure situations as relapse reasons. Therefore, the following conclusion might be correct: that the subjectively unexpainable craving attacks, "occurring like a lightning out of the clear blue sky," are triggered by drug-relevant thinking and negative emotional states, whereas in actual tempting social pressure situations, the craving response pattern fits the criteria of the conditioning model best.

A further result seems worthy of note. Conditioned drug-effect sensations cannot be explained in this statistical model. This result confirms the suggestion that this component of the craving response pattern is of marginal importance to the relapse process. Nevertheless, the interviewed addicts mentioned positive emotional states as relapse reasons, but with a small frequency.

4. Psychopathological disturbances, such as trait anxiety or the hopelessness component of the depressive disorder, do not contribute very much to the explanation of readiness to respond to drug-related or emotional stimulus conditions. Therefore, the craving response pattern seems to be a relatively independent trigger-response system which is psychologically describable. The craving response pattern can be best described as a complex, connected system of internal and external triggers and reactions. This system perhaps maintains its features by self-regulation, as may become clearer and more detailed when the cognitive functions of drug slang usage and imagery are investigated.

REFERENCES

Appel, P. W., and Kaestner, E. (1979). Interpersonal and emotional problem solving among narcotic drug abusers. *J. Cons. Clin. Psychol.* 47: 1125–27.
Beck, A. T., Steer, R. A., and McElroy, M. G. (1982). Relationships of hope-

lessness, depression and previous suicide attempts to suicidal ideation in alcoholics. *J. Stud. Alc.* 43: 1042–46.

Chaney, E., Roszel, D. K., and Cummings, C. (1982). Relapse in opiate addicts: A behavioral analysis. *Addictive Behaviors* 7: 291–97.

Childress, A. R., McLellan, A. T., and O'Brien, C. P. (1984). Assessment and extinction of conditioned withdrawal-like responses in an integrated treatment for opiate dependence. NIDA Research Monograph 55.

Deissler, K. (1977). Der periodische Suchtanfall. *Schweizerische Ärztezeitung* 13: 514–18.

Gossop, M. (1989). Lapse, relapse and continued abstinence among opiate addicts after impatient treatment: A prospective follow-up study of a British sample. In Feuerlein, W., Bühringer, G., and Wille, R. (eds.), *Therapieverläufe bei Drogenabhängigen*, 128–47. Heidelberg: Springer.

Herbst, K., Hanel, E., and Haderstorfer, B. (1989). Rückfallgeschehen bei stationär behandelten Drogenabhängigen. In Watzl, H., and Cohen, R. (eds.), *Rückfall und Rückfallprophylaxe*, 139–48. Heidelberg: Springer. 1989.

Hunt, W. A., and Bespalec, D. (1974). Relapse rates after treatment for heroin addiction. *Journal of Community Psychol.* 2: 85–87.

Kampe, H. (1989). Der periodische Suchtanfall im Therapieverlauf. In Feuerlein, W., Bühringer, G., and Wille, R. (eds.), *Therapieverläufe bei Drogenabhängigen*, 203–23. Heidelberg: Springer.

Kampe, H., and Kunz, D. (1980). Die Rückfälligkeit Drogenabhängiger. *Suchtgefahren* 26: 165–87.

————. (1981). Sprachliches Interaktionsverhalten Drogenabhängiger als Parameter des theapeutischen Prozesses. In Keup, W. (ed.), *Behandlung der Sucht und des Mißbrauches chemischer Stoffe*, 152–64. Stuttgart: Thieme.

————. (1983). *Was leistet Drogentherapie? Evaluation eines stationären Behandlungsprogramms.* Weinheim, Basel: Beltz.

————. (1984). Integration und Fehlanpassung Drogenabhängiger nach der Behandlung in einer Therapeutischen Gemeinschaft. *Praxis der Kinderpsychologie* 33: 49–55.

————. (1986). Sondersprachgebrauch Drogenabhängiger. *Suchtgefahren* 32: 103–11.

Kampe, H., Kunz, D., and Schreck, T. (1989). Der Rückfall Drogenabhängiger als Forschungsproblem. Eine Untersuchung zur Rückfalltheorie von G. A. Marlatt. *Suchtgefahren* 35: 289–99.

Kampe, H., and Overbeck-Larisch, M. (1990). Bedingungen der Rückfälligkeit behandelter Drogenabhängiger. *Querschnitt* 4: 38–55.

Kunz, D., and Kampe, H. (1985). Darstellung des Selbstkonzeptes Drogenabhängiger in ihren Lebensläufen. *Praxis der Kinderpsychologie* 34: 219–25.

Laux, L., Glanzmann, P., Schaffer, P., and Spielberger, C. D. (1981). *Das State-Trait-Angstinventar.* Weinheim: Beltz Testgesellschaft.

Lindesmith, A. R. (1937). *The Nature of Opiate Addiction.* Chicago: University of Chicago Press.

Lynch, J. J., Stein, E. A., and Fertziger, A. P. (1976). An analysis of 70 years of morphine classical conditioning. Implications for clinical treatment of narcotic addiction. *Journal of Nervous and Mental Disorders* 63: 47–58.

Marlatt, G. A., and Gordon, J. R. (eds.). (1985). *Relapse Prevention*. New York: Guilford Press.

McAuliffe, W. E., and Gordon, R. A. (1974). A test of Lindesmith's theory of addiction: The frequency of euphoria among long-term addicts. *American Journal of Sociology* 79: 795–809.

McLellan, A. T., Childress, A. R., Ehrman, R., O'Brien, C. P., and Pashko, S. (1986). Extinguishing conditioned responses during opiate dependence treatment: Turning laboratory results into clinical procedures. *Journal of Substance Abuse Treatment* 3: 33–40.

Meyer, R. E., and Mirin, S. M. (1979). *The Heroin Stimulus: Implications for a Theory of Addiction*. New York: Plenum Medical Book Company.

O'Brien, C. P., and Ternes, J. (1977). Conditioning as a cause of relapse in narcotic addiction. In Gottheil, E. (ed.), *Addiction Research and Treatment: Converging Trends*, 124–281. New York: Pergamon Press.

O'Brien C. P., Testa, T. O'Brien, T. J., Brady, J. P., and Wells, B. (1977). Conditioned narcotic withdrawal in humans. *Science* 195: 1000–1002.

Platt, J. J., and Metzger, D. D. (1987). Cognitive interpersonal problem-solving skills and the maintenance of treatment success in heroin addicts. *Psychology of Addictive Behaviors* 1: 5–13.

Platt, J. J., Scura, W. C., and Hannon, J. R. (1973). Problem-solving thinking of youthful incarcerated heroin addicts. *J. Commun. Psychol.* 1: 278–81.

Rist, F., Watzl, H., and Cohen, R. (1989). Versuche zur Erfassung von Rückfallbedingungen bei Alkoholkranken. In Watzl, H., and Cohen, R. (eds.), 126–38. *Rückfall und Rückfallprophylaxe*. Heidelberg: Springer.

Sideroff, S. J., and Jarvik, M. E. (1980). Conditioned responses to videotape showing heroin-related stimuli. *International Journal of the Addictions* 15: 529–36.

Washton, M. A. (1990). *Cocaine Addiction: Treatment, Recovery and Relapse Prevention*. New York: W. W. Norton.

Wikler, A. (1980). *Opioid Dependence: Mechanisms and Treatment*. New York: Plenum Press.

PART SIX

Treatment and Outcome

CHAPTER 22

Evaluation of a Drug-Free Outpatient Treatment Program for Drug Addicts*

Gabriele Spies, Michael Böhmer, and Gerhard Bühringer

INTRODUCTION

This article reports on a pilot study of an outpatient drug-free treatment program which was carried out from 1983 to 1987. In the early 1980s, the majority of those working in the field of drug addiction in Germany still doubted the effectiveness of outpatient drug-free treatment for severe drug addicts. Long-term residential treatment was seen as the only treatment which promised some success. Even today most drug addicts are treated in residential facilities, as there are few possibilities for outpatient treatment beyond the usual counseling services.

PROGRAM AND METHOD

The treatment is based on a behavioral therapy approach. It is an individualized program carried out in individual therapy sessions. The goals of the treatment are abstinence, social integration, and solution of personal problems. The regular duration of the program is about nine months, but length is dependent on attaining individually defined treatment goals. The

*The study was funded by the German Federal Ministry of Health.

Table 22.1

Demographic Characteristics at Time of Admission (N = 78)

Average age	26y (range 17 to 44 years)

Sex	
Male	64%
Female	36%

Marital status	
Single	85%
Married	9%
Divorced/Living separately	6%

program is planned for people dependent on hard drugs, predominantly heroin and other opiates. Detoxification is not required for enrollment in treatment. The client has to live in or near Munich in order to ensure that he or she is able to come to the therapy sessions. (For more details on the program see Dehmel et al. 1986; Dehmel et al. 1987; Dehmel 1988.)

Client data were collected by standardized questionnaires at the time of admission, at the time of discharge, and 6, 12, and 24 months after treatment. For both ethical and practical reasons no randomized control group was possible. As a first approach to evaluate the results of the program the data of the outpatient program were compared to those collected in residential facilities by the Munich Multicenter Treatment Evaluation Study (MTE-Study; see the chapters by Haderstorfer and Künzel-Böhmer, Hanel and Herbst in this volume).

RESULTS

Sample Characteristics

Altogether, about 100 clients were treated in the outpatient program. Data from 78 clients who were treated after an initial project phase in which the program was developed are presented here. Table 22.1 shows some demographic characteristics at the time of admission. Thirty-six percent of the clients were women, a higher percentage than is usual in residential facilities. Perhaps outpatient treatment better suits the needs of women who are more involved with family and children than are men, and who often are a minority in residential facilities (see the chapter by Hanel in

TABLE 22.2

Education and Employment (N = 78)

Education	
Elementary school, no degree	18%
Elementary school, graduate	18%
High School, no degree	28%
High School, graduate	32%
College education, no degree	4%
Employment	
Unemployed	49%
Employee	14%
Worker	17%
Trainee/pupil and others	20%

TABLE 22.3

Drug Use History (N = 78)

Primarily used drug	
Heroin/other opiates IV	88%
Heroin oral	8%
Other opiates oral	4%
Average time of addiction	
Marijuana/Hashish	8.0y
Illegal hard drugs	6.6y
Average age of first use	
Marijuana/Hashish	15y
Illegal hard drugs	19y

this volume). In comparison to the clients of the MTE-Study, more clients completed at least a high school education: 36% as opposed to 24% (Table 22.2). At the time of admission nearly half of the clients were unemployed; more than 30% had a job.

All clients were opiate users; most of them injected heroin, on average, for more than 6 years (Table 22.3). Fifty-one percent of the clients lived in an apartment, alone or with a partner. In comparison to the residential clients of the MTE-Study, where 33% of the clients lived in their own apartment, this percentage is fairly high. There is a significant difference between the two groups. Accordingly, more of the residential clients (30%) came directly from jail into treatment. Sixty-eight percent of the clients' partners have or had drug problems themselves.

Three-fourths of the clients had a delinquent background; nearly half of them were already in prison, for 15 months on average. Sixty-four percent were referred by court to the outpatient program. These referrals encompass a wide range of situations, including probation, on the one hand, and Section 35 of the German Narcotic Law, on the other. In contrast, almost all clients in residential facilities who are referred by court are in treatment in compliance with Section 35, the reason being that outpatient treatment is often not regarded as treatment according to Section 35 because it imposes less restriction on the clients' lifestyle.

Nearly all clients had several detoxifications before the outpatient treatment; half of them had been in residential treatment, for an average of 28 weeks in total. Under upon their described characteristics, all clients in the outpatient treatment program were severe drug addicts according to DSM III. They differ significantly from clients in residential facilities on the following variables:

- There are more women in the outpatient program.
- A higher percentage of the clients completed high school.
- More clients lived in their own apartment prior to admission.
- Fewer clients were in treatment under Section 35 of the German Narcotic Law.

In regard to drug use variables there were no differences.

Discharge and Duration of Treatment

On average the clients have been in treatment for six months with slightly more than one therapy session per week: in the initial stage the sessions were more frequent; in the end they were less so (Table 22.4). One-third of the clients were routinely discharged, a result which is comparable to residential facilities. Even if abstinence was not required for enrollment, it was required for remaining in the program after an appointed time, depending on the client's individual circumstances. If the clients did not succeed in becoming abstinent, an effort was made to refer them to residential facilities. In this case the outpatient program provided a good opportunity to motivate them to enter residential treatment.

TABLE 22.4

Time in Treatment and Situation at Discharge (N = 78)

Time in treatment	24	weeks
Number of sessions	29	sessions

Type of discharge	
Regular	33%
Dropout by client	31%
Dropout by staff	19%
Referral/arrest	17%

TABLE 22.5

Drug Use at Time of Regular or Premature Discharge (N = 65)

	Regular discharge *(n = 26)*	*Dropout* *(n = 39)*
No drug use	100%	10%
Marijuana/Hashish	—	10%
Opiates	—	80%

Table 22.5 shows the drug use at time of discharge for the regularly discharged and dropouts only. Clients discharged by referral/arrest are not considered here. Eighty percent of the dropouts used opiates. Only 10% were drug free, as opposed to 100% of the regularly discharged clients, as measured by randomized urine analyses.

Follow-up Results; Comparison of Outpatient and Residential Treatment

We collected data from 60 of the 78 clients in the outpatient program six month after discharge (77%). This percentage is tolerably high for studies on drug addicts. The 18 nonresponders differed significantly (p < .05) from the 60 responders with regard to

- age of the clients: responders are younger
- number of detoxifications: responders have fewer than nonresponders
- length of addiction: nonresponders have been addicted for a longer time.

TABLE 22.6

Criteria and Statistics of Matching 60 Outpatient and 60 Residential Clients

	Outpatient	Residential
Age	24.9y	25.4y
Sex (Females)	35%	27%
Education (with degree)	38%	32%
Employment	55%	43%
Prior residential treatment	52%	43%
Duration of addiction	5.9y	5.8y
Follow-up time	193 days	176 days

Relative to the type of discharge there are no differences between responders and nonresponders. In interpreting the results, the differences between responders and nonresponders must always be considered.

In order to compare the follow-up results of the outpatient program to those of residential facilities, we matched a group of 60 clients out of the whole sample of 164 clients on whom the MTE-Study had first follow-up data. The matching of the outpatient sample to a subset of the residential sample was performed by a multivariate statistical procedure. Using the nearest neighbor principle and the variance criterion, the best fitting pairs were found with respect to six basic variables (Table 22.6). Altogether a well-fitting matched group was found. No criterion differed significantly between the two groups.

The following tables show the follow-up results for the outpatient (6 months after treatment) and the residential groups (3 to 6 months after treatment). Each group consists of 60 clients. With regard to the social situation, no significant differences between the groups were found either for the housing situation or for the drug use of the partner (Table 22.7). In the field of employment and financial situation there are significant differences between the two groups (Table 22.8). In the outpatient groups there were more employees and more clients who earned their living by work than in the residential group. Accordingly, more residential clients lived on social support systems, such as unemployment benefit or social welfare.

In both samples only a few clients were convicted of criminal offenses again in the first month after treatment (Table 22.9), but about half of them were still on probation. Statistical differences between the two groups were not found. No differences were found with regard to the following residential treatments. But the outpatient group had significantly more detoxifications after treatment than did the residential group.

TABLE 22.7

Social Situation at Follow-up in 2 Matched Samples (N = 2 × 60)

Housing situation		
	Outpatient	*Residential*
Own apartment		
(alone or with partner)	58%	42%
With relatives	19%	18%
With others	12%	12%
Aftercare facility	—	17%
Hospital, home, or prison	13%	12%

Drug use of the partner		
No drug problems	30%	22%
Drug problems in the past	10%	17%
Drug problems now	23%	33%
No partner	37%	28%

TABLE 22.8

Employment and Income at Follow-up (N = 2 × 60)

Employment		
	Outpatient	*Residential*
Unemployed	31%	42%
Employee	24%	5% **
Worker	18%	28%
Trainee/pupil and others	13%	13%
Others (hospital, homes, or prison)	13%	12%

Income (during the last six months)		
Work	45%	25% *
Relatives/partner	13%	10%
Social support systems	23%	50% **
Illegal	2%	
Others (hospital, homes, or prison)	17%	15%

*Significant at p < .05; **p < .001

TABLE 22.9

Legal Status in Follow-up Period (N = 2 × 60)

Convictions after treatment		
	Outpatient	Residential
Convicted	17%	8%
Imprisoned (at the time of interview)	7%	8%
On probation	45%	55%
Remaining time at probation	25 months	28 months

Table 22.10 shows data on the drug use after treatment. The percentages of those who never used drugs after treatment in the outpatient (18%) and the residential groups (25%) do not differ significantly, but there is a slight trend toward a higher percentage in the residential group. Nearly half of the clients in the regularly discharged group never used drugs after treatment, whereas almost all dropouts relapsed. The time of the first relapse after discharge and the first drug use after discharge are—in a statistical sense—equal for both groups.

DISCUSSION

Prior to this program there have been few experiences in the field of outpatient treatment for drug addicts in Germany. As a result of this pilot study, we can state that outpatient treatment for drug addicts is possible and may not have worse outcomes than residential treatment, contrary to the expectation of many experts in Germany. The clients treated in the program did not differ from those in the residential facilities with respect to the severity and duration of addiction, but there were more women and more socially integrated clients than in residential treatment. Outpatient treatment allows these clients to stay in their social relationships—an important advantage over residential treatment.

Summarizing the results of the follow-up comparison between outpatient and residential clients, we can see that statistical differences have not been found, except in the number of detoxifications after treatment and the source of income. Perhaps this last difference will disappear in further follow-ups, because many of the outpatient clients were never out of work, whereas all of the residentially treated had to find a new job after treatment. On the other hand, there are some indicators that the clients in the residential group are less socially integrated in general. In

TABLE 22.10

Drug Use in the Follow-up Period (6 months; N = 2 × 60)

	Outpatient	Residential
No drug use		
all clients	18%	25%
regular discharge	45%	39%
dropouts	4%	7%
First Drug Used after discharge		
Marijuana/Hashish	35%	29%
Opiates	50%	71%
Cocaine	15%	0%
First relapse after discharge		
Until the end of		
first week	35%	42%
first month	25%	13%
first 3 months	10%	31%
Later than 3 months	30%	13%

this comparison we could only answer a few questions because of the different types of questionnaires used in the two studies and the small number of clients in the several subgroups. A standardized data collection in outpatient and residential facilities over a longer period of follow-ups should provide better comparisons.

Based on this result, further research on outpatient treatment would seem to be worthwhile. Longer follow-up times and more specific research questions are needed. Also, in view of the financial costs, an important issue for further research would be to identify for which clients outpatient treatment is more appropriate and effective than residential treatment. According to the results of the present study, women and clients who are socially more integrated are better suited for outpatient rather than residential treatment. In order to obtain valid information on this topic, it would be necessary to randomly assign the clients to the different types of treatment. This is very difficult in Germany, however, because residential and outpatient treatment are financed in different ways and are not accepted by courts or insurance companies in the same way.

Additionally, the therapeutic program must be further refined and improved. One important objective must be to motivate clients to change their behavior and participate in therapy for a longer time in order to reduce the dropout rate at the beginning of treatment. Another important objective for outpatient treatment is to make it possible for clients to undergo a short-term residential stay when necessary, for example, for detoxification or in times of crisis. At present, the systems of residential and outpatient treatment in West Germany are rather independent and there is relatively little collaboration between them. The outpatient program has shown, however, that there should be more flexibility in the form of day clinics, leisure and work programs for unemployed clients, and short-term residential programs.

REFERENCES

Dehmel, S. (1988). Therapieprozess und Therapieabbruch bei ambulant behandelten Drogenabhängigen. In Feuerlein, W., Bühringer, G., and Wille, R. (eds.) *Therapieverläufe bei Drogenabhängigen. Kann es eine Lehrmeinung geben?*, 75–101. Heidelberg: Springer-Verlag.

Dehmel, S., Klett, F., and Bühringer, G. (1986). Description and first results of an outpatient treatment program for opiate dependents. In Miller, W. R., and Heather, N. (eds.) *Treating Addictive Behaviours: Processes of Change*, 3–27. New York: Plenum Press.

Dehmel, S., Krauthan, G., Kühnlein, I., and Raab, P. (1987). Ambulante Therapie für Abhängige von harten Drogen. In Kleiner, D. (ed.) *Langzeitverläufe bei Suchtkrankheiten*, 279–82. Heidelberg: Springer-Verlag.

CHAPTER 23

Individualized Behavior Therapy for Drug Addicts

Heinz C. Vollmer, Roman Ferstl, and Heiner Ellgring

INTRODUCTION

The main form of treatment for drug addicts in the Federal Republic of Germany is drug-free therapy on a residential basis. Various follow-up studies have shown that, two years after therapy, around 30% to 35% of the addicts are no longer taking hard drugs (De Jong and Henrich 1980; Herbst, Hanel, and Haderstorfer 1989; Klett 1987; Klett, Hanel and Bühringer 1984; Melchinger 1989). It is not possible to say whether this is attributable to the treatment because there have been no controlled studies. It is equally hard to say which parts of the treatment program are effective. From the point of view of a clinical psychologist working with drug addicts, there has been far too little research conducted into therapy, both in the Federal Republic and elsewhere.

An empirical basis for treatment is almost entirely lacking. This is reflected in the theories on the treatment of drug addicts, which sometimes appear irrational and are closer to myths (Reed 1980) than to the understanding of an empirical clinician working in the spirit of the Boulder conference (Kanfer and Phillips 1970; Wilson 1982). It is an overall aim of this study to find and point out ways in which research can be conducted under the conditions of routine clinical practice in order to improve the level of knowledge about the determinants of behavior change in therapy for drug addicts, and to provide the practicing psy-

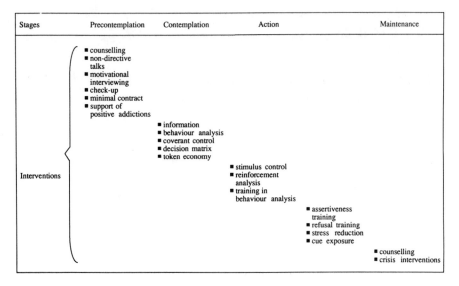

FIGURE 23.1.
Stages of change (Prochaska and Di Clemente 1983) and examples of interventions practiced in a behavior therapy program.

chologist with guidelines for their treatment. The following study was therefore conducted in two centers that provide normal treatment for drug addicts, where the therapy can only be altered for research purposes to a very limited extent.

The publication of Prochaska and Di Clemente's model (1983, 1986) led one of the treatment centers to modify its behavior therapy program. According to Prochaska and Di Clemente, drug addicts may find themselves at different stages of change and different therapeutic interventions are indicated for each stage. It would thus, for example, not be appropriate to carry out refusal training or cue exposure with a patient who is not yet ready to stop taking drugs and is, rather, in need of motivating methods such as motivational interviewing. In Figure 23.1 the individual interventions are allocated to the various stages on the basis of experience with the behavior therapy program described in this study.

The study described in this paper poses the following question: Does a procedure based on Prochaska and Di Clemente's change model (i.e., individualized therapy) lead to an improvement in the treatment of drug addicts? In order to answer this question, an individualized behavior therapy program was compared with two other types of therapy: a standard behavior therapy program and a "humanistically" oriented therapy program. The first hypothesis of the study was as follows:

1. Patients who receive individualized therapy more frequently complete treatment according to plan and remain in treatment for longer periods than patients receiving standard behavior therapy and humanistic therapy.

Should this hypothesis prove true, the following hypothesis was to be examined in order to exclude a worsening in the quality of the treatment in spite of an increased number of patients completing it according to plan:

2. More or at least as many patients who complete individualized treatment according to plan are drug free at the 3-month and 12-month follow-ups in comparison with patients completing a course of standard behavior therapy or humanistic therapy.

METHOD

Treatment Centers

The study was carried out in two drug-free residential treatment centers. The planned duration of therapy was six to nine months in both centers, with an average of eight months. In center A the treatment for many years had been based solely on behavior therapy. The emphasis was on individual therapy, small groups for the purpose of concentrating on specific subjects (i.e., assertiveness training, coping with stress), and work therapy. The individual therapy was exclusively the responsibility of psychologists; the majority of the therapists during the period of the study were male; and the number of therapy places was 16.

Treatment center B operated in accordance with the humanistic paradigm. Here group therapy was more important than in center A, and occupational therapy and art therapy (dancing, painting) were also offered. Individual therapy was conducted by psychologists and social workers. Most of the therapists were female and the number of therapy places was 12. The two centers did not otherwise differ substantially from one another. Both centers had similar discharge criteria.

In the first half year of the study all the patients in center A were treated in accordance with the behavior therapy program (standard therapy) that had been followed there for several years (Figure 23.2). The

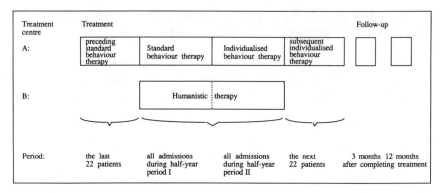

FIGURE 23.2.
Design of the study.

theoretical basis of this behavior therapy program comprised the learning paradigms (Skinner 1953; Pavlov 1927), the self-control approach (Kanfer 1971), the broad spectrum approach (Lazarus 1966), social learning theory (Bandura 1977), the concept of irrational beliefs (Ellis 1977), interactional behavior therapy (Grawe 1980), and the relapse model (Marlatt and Gordon 1985). Among the interventions practiced by the center were behavior analysis (Kanfer and Saslow 1969; Schulte 1974), motivational interviewing (Miller 1983), assertiveness training (Libermann King, De Risi, and McCann 1975; Ullrich and Ullrich 1976), stress inoculation training (Meichenbaum and Jaremko 1983), rational emotive therapy (Ellis 1977), relapse prevention training (Marlatt and Gordon 1985) and token economy (Ayllon and Azrin 1968).

All of the therapeutic sessions were obligatory. In the second half-year, Prochaska and Di Clemente's model (individualized therapy) was added to the therapy program. All of the therapeutic intervention measures were retained; the only change was a broadening of the theoretical basis of the therapy. It was not possible, as with Prochaska and Di Clemente, to determine which patient was at which stage of change. It was therefore left to the patients themselves to set their own goals for treatment and choose which therapeutic measures they wanted to participate in. The introduction of the Prochaska and Di Clemente model had the most effect on the therapy groups. While until then participation in all groups (communication training, relapse prevention, assertiveness training) had been obligatory, after the introduction of the Prochaska and Di Clemente model the patients could decide themselves which group they wanted to participate in. In the individual therapy, the broadening of the theoretical base of the therapy program increased the influence of the patient on the therapy goals. The therapists were instructed to accept the therapy goals of the patients as much as possible and to insist on none of their own goals—on the basis of either behavior analysis or observations of the patients' behavior. After the study, treatment center A continued the individualized behavior therapy program.

Treatment center B served as the control group. The therapy program of treatment center B remained unchanged throughout the entire study.

The therapists of both centers were not informed of the design of the study, with the exception of the clinical psychologist responsible for planning and conducting the study, who himself worked as a therapist in center A. There he looked after 30% of the patients and was convinced that changing the program would lead to an improvement in the treatment. The other therapists in center A had a very critical attitude toward the introduction of Prochaska and Di Clemente's model. The reason it was possible not to inform the therapists of the design of the study was that in both centers studies of termination and relapse had been conducted for several years.

Sample

Both treatment centers had identical admission criteria. The patients were mainly referred to the two centers from drug counseling facilities and social service departments in the prisons. For admission to therapy the patients had to fulfill the following criteria:

1. Dependence on opiates, amphetamines, or cocaine
2. Already detoxified
3. Age between 18 and 35
4. Absence of any acute psychosis or acute danger of suicide
5. No partner or child addicted to drugs being admitted at the same time
6. Agreement already obtained from certain paying authorities to fund the treatment, primarily on the part to the Versicherungsanstalt für Arbeiter (social insurance institution for workers)

Patients who, during or after admission, were discovered not to be in the above age group or to have another addiction nevertheless continued to be treated.

Seventy patients (17 female, 53 male) participated in the study. After an initial evaluation of the data, two more groups of patients were also included: one was a group of patients who were treated immediately before the study began (preceding standard therapy group), and the other was a group of patients who were treated immediately after the study was concluded (subsequent individualized therapy group). These two groups were defined by the number of patients: the "preceding standard therapy" group consisted of the last 22 patients admitted before the study began, and the "subsequent individualized therapy" group was made up of the first 22 patients admitted after the study was completed. The sample thus comprises a total of 114 patients.

Since both treatment centers are only recognized by certain paying authorities, almost all the patients were working class. Most of the patients were under legal obligation to undergo treatment. These patients usually go back to prison if they terminate treatment prematurely or have to begin a new course of residential treatment immediately. Most patients said they had started therapy because they could shorten their sentences by having residential treatment and because, if they completed it according to plan, their sentence would be suspended. Other characteristics of the patients are listed in Table 23.1.

At the beginning of treatment the patients of some groups differed from those of others with respect to individual characteristics. The humanistic therapy patients (survey period I) had, for example, a shorter remaining term of imprisonment than those of survey period II and the standard therapy patients. The individualized therapy patients were older than the standard therapy patients, and the patients of the "subsequent individualized therapy" group were older than the standard therapy patients and the patients of the "preceding standard therapy" group. With the exception of age, none of the characteristics where there were differences between the individual groups (i.e., remaining term of imprisonment, age when soft drugs were first taken) correlated with the way therapy was terminated (Vollmer, Ellgring, and Ferstl 1990). However, age did have predictive value with respect to the way treatment was terminated for a proportion of the sample and must thus be taken into account in the evaluation.

Procedure

Distribution of the Patients

In order to achieve as random a distribution as possible of the patients between the two centers, whichever center had a higher percentage of places available received the next patient. The person responsible for the distribution of the patients was not informed of the design of the study.

Table 23.1.
Characteristics of Patients

| Variable | Behaviour therapy | | | | | | | | Humanistic therapy | | | | Comparison |
| | preceding standard therapy (N=22) | | standard therapy (N=21) | | individualised therapy (N=22) | | subsequent individualised therapy (N=22) | | period I (N=12) | | period II (N=15) | | p |
	M	s.d.	M	s.d.	M	s.d.	M	s.d.	M	s.d.	M	s.d.	
Age	24	3	24	4	26	3	27	4	24	3	25	3	see Table 2
First use of opiates, amphetamines or cocaine (age)	18	2	17	3	18	3	18	3	17	2	17	3	n.s.
First use of cannabis (age)	15	2	15	2	15	2	16	3	15	1	14	2	Ind. vs HII <.05
Months in prison	15	14	26	22	28	24	28	21	17	8	30	25	pSt vs sInd. <.05
Expected term of imprisonment (months)	17	5	20	7	15	7	21	11	11	10	20	5	St vs HI <.05; Ind. vs HII <.05; HI vs HII <.05
	No		No		No		No		No		No		
Sex													n.s.
female	7		6		3		3		5		3		
male	15		15		19		19		7		12		
School qualification													
No final qualification	5		3		2		4		3		2		
Hauptschule[1]	14		17		20		13		9		13		
Mittlere Reife[2]	3		1		0		5		0		0		
Abitur[3]	0		0		0		0		0		0		n.s.
Partner situation													
No partner	12		14		13		10		6		8		
Partner also on drugs	5		4		6		6		1		2		
Partner not on drugs	5		3		3		6		5		5		n.s.
Prior courses of treatment													
0	12		13		15		13		9		6		
1	5		5		5		6		2		7		
>1	5		3		2		3		1		2		n.s.
No legal order	4		2		3		3		1		0		n.s.
Principal diagnosis (DSM III R)													
opioid dependence	20		19		20		19		10		9		
amphetamine dependence	1		1		2		2		0		4		
cannabis dependence	1		0		0		1		1		2		
alcohol dependence	0		0		0		0		1		0		
sedative dependence	0		1		0		0		0		0		n.s.

[1] basic secondary school level, [2] equivalent to 0-levels, [3] equivalent to A-levels. Ind: individualised therapy; sInd: subsequent individualised therapy; ST: standard therapy; pSt: preceding standard therapy; HI: humanistic therapy,period I; HII: humanistic therapy, period II.

Interviews at the Beginning of Treatment

On admission, the patients were interviewed by experienced psychologists or social workers in order to establish whether they were suffering from any psychiatric disorders; they were then classified according to DSM III R. If serious psychiatric disorders were suspected, a structured interview with a psychiatrist took place. On the day of admission, anamnestic data such as age, schooling, and length of time on drugs were collected using a standardized questionnaire.

Follow-up Interview

Three and 12 months after the end of treatment, the patients who had terminated treatment according to plan were visited in their homes by a psychologist for a follow-up interview. The psychologist had taken part beforehand in interview training which consisted of six sessions with video feedback. She was not informed of the purpose and design of the study, and her task was to establish what had caused any relapse and to ascertain whether patients who said they had had no relapse since the end of therapy were in fact free of drugs.

A semi-standardized questionnaire dealing with the relapse process was used for the follow-up interview. Among the details the patients were asked to give were quantity and frequency of drug consumption, type of drug, and the cause of the relapse. They also filled in a questionnaire themselves and answered questions about drug consumption, work situation, etc. The patients who said they had taken no drugs in the last four weeks were asked to provide urine under supervision. The urine was analyzed at the Institute for Forensic Medicine of Munich University; the analysis involved drug screening with TDX, and, in the case of positive findings, a thin-layer chromatography test.

Patients who had terminated treatment prematurely were not visited for a follow-up interview for the following reasons: virtually no patients with legal orders are allowed their freedom by the court so that they can try living without drugs. Most patients go back to prison or are obliged to start another course of treatment immediately. The decision whether the patients stay free, go back to prison, or start another course of treatment is made by the court according to legal criteria (i.e., criminal offenses before the start of treatment) and not from a therapeutic standpoint (i.e., progress achieved so far). The follow-up results of the prematurely discharged patients therefore could not be used to evaluate the treatment. For patients under legal obligation to have treatment, the way the treatment was terminated was, consequently, a crucial success criterion. Almost all the patients who completed treatment according to plan were able to stay free and thus had the opportunity to try living without drugs.

Evaluation

A comparison was made between the outcome criteria (type of treatment termination and duration of stay) of the standard behavior therapy and the individualized behavior therapy, and of survey period 1 and survey period 2 in the case of the humanistic therapy. The frequency distributions were tested for significance with the chi-square test and the mean value comparisons with the t-test or covariance analysis. The level of significance adopted was 5%. The comparison of the success criteria was based on a one-tailed test with the hypothesis that individualized therapy has better results. The other comparisons were based on a two-tailed test. Since the sample size was small, because of the high quota of premature discharges, the follow-up data are presented in descriptive form. The follow-up data of the control group were not taken into account in the evaluation since the sample size was too small to allow any conclusions to be drawn.

RESULTS

Type of Treatment Termination and Duration of Stay

Significantly, more individualized therapy patients than standard behavior therapy patients terminated treatment according to plan (Table 23.2 and Figure 23.3). While there were 8 patients following the standard program who terminated treatment according to plan, in the case of the individualized program patients this figure was 16. Among the individualized therapy patients, the number of patients terminating treatment themselves decreased, as did the number prematurely discharged by the therapists. In the second treatment center, on the other hand, there was no difference between the two survey periods with respect to the number of patients completing treatment according to plan. In both periods, almost the same number of patients terminated treatment prematurely. In the standard therapy group the patients who terminated treatment according to plan were significantly older than those who terminated treatment prematurely, but

Table 23.2.

Statistical Values for Differences between (Preceding) Standard Therapy and (Subsequent) Individualised Therapy

	Differences in age [1] (t-test)		Differences in number of patients: discharge according to plan vs premature discharge [2] (chi square, df=1)		Differences in duration of treatment [2] (analysis of covariance, df=1)			
					main effect: group		covariate: age	
Treatment group	t	P	χ^2	P	F	P	F	P
individualised vs standard	-2.14	.039*	5.23	.011*	2.12	.08	13.48	.001***
subsequent indiv. vs preceding standard	-2.08	.044*	0.82	.183	3.50	.03*	0.002	.963
individualised vs preceding standard	1.64	.109	3.339	.033*	0.34	.28	2.22	1.44
subsequent indiv. vs standard	-2.49	.017*	1.90	.084	9.17	.002**	4.89	.033*

[1] The (subsequent) individualised therapy patients were older in every case.
[2] More (subsequent) individualised therapy patients completed therapy according to plan and they also spent longer in therapy (see Figures 3 and 4).
Significant values are indicated by an asterisk

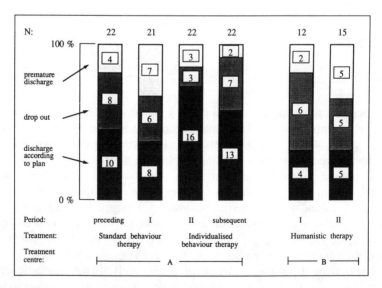

FIGURE 23.3.
Type of treatment termination.

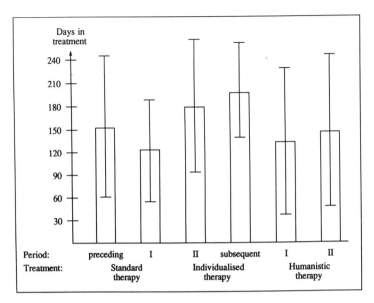

FIGURE 23.4.
Days in treatment.

there was no such age difference in the other groups. The other characteristics where the patients of the individual groups differed did not correlate with the outcome criteria type of treatment termination and duration
of stay. Nor did the patients of the different individual therapists differ
with these two outcome criteria.

It would theoretically be possible to increase the number of patients
completing treatment according to plan by shortening the therapy period.
This did not happen with the individualized therapy patients, who on average spent longer in treatment than the standard therapy patients (Figure
23.4). This applied both to prematurely terminated treatment and treatment completed according to plan. In the humanistic therapy program
there was scarcely any difference between the two groups in duration of
stay. When the characteristic age was partialed out by means of covariance analysis, it was shown that the differences between individualized
and standard therapy patients are due to age and not to the treatment.

There is no difference between the two samples additionally included
in the study (preceding standard therapy, subsequent individualized therapy) with respect to the number of patients terminating treatment according to plan. The "subsequent individualized therapy" patients had

Table 23.3.

Number of Patients Interviewed at 3 month and 12 month Follow-ups

Treatment termination	Contact with patients	3 months follow-up		12 months follow-up	
		standard therapy	individualised therapy	standard therapy	individualised therapy
Discharge according to plan	interviewed	6	9	3	7
	not interviewed because of relapse [1]	0	3	2	4
	not traced	2	4	3	5
premature termination	not interviewed	13	6	13	6
Total		21	22	21	22

[1] Patients with whom no proper interview could be conducted or with whom no interview took place because they were under the influence of drugs.

treatment for significantly longer periods, even when the age factor was partialed out. A comparison of the "subsequent individualized therapy" with the standard therapy showed that the longer periods spent in therapy in the former case were due both to the treatment and to age.

Follow-up

An increase in the number of patients completing treatment according to plan and in the duration of stay could possibly also be achieved by more relaxed, less demanding therapy. This would be reflected in poorer follow-up results. In order to exclude this possibility, there must be at least the same number of successful patients in both the standard therapy and the individualized therapy groups. Three months after treatment had been completed according to plan, it was possible to interview six standard program patients and nine individualized therapy patients (Table 23.3). At the three-month follow-up, more of the individualized therapy patients said they had taken no cannabis, no medication, and no hard drugs in the last 30 days (Table 23.4). The urine checks of the individualized therapy patients also produced more negative results. There were no differences between the two groups in the work situation. In one group, five patients and in the other six patients had regular jobs at the time of the interview; four in one group and five in the other said they had not been unemployed since the therapy ended.

At the 12-month follow-up fewer patients were interviewed in both groups (Table 23.3). The number of patients who could not be inter-

TABLE 23.4.

Use of Psychoactive Substances Recorded at 3-month Follow-up of Interviewed Patients Who Completed Treatment

Psychoactive substances taken in the last 30 days:

Substance: Treatment group:	Alcohol		Cannabis		Medication		hard drugs	
	Standard	Individua-lised	Standard	Individua-lised	Standard	Individua-lised	Standard	Individua-lised
Days: 0	0	0	0	3	4	8	3	7
≤7	1	2	1	1	2	0	2	1
8-14	1	3	0	0	0	0	0	1
>14	4	4	3	5	0	1	1	0

Urine analyses of patients who claimed they had not taken any drugs:

Result	Standard	Individua-lised
drugfree	2	6
Cannabis	1	0
hard drugs	0	0
refused	1	1

viewed because of relapse increased. There was no longer any difference between the standard program and the individualized therapy groups regarding the number of patients who had stopped taking drugs (Table 23.5). More individualized therapy patients had regular jobs at the time of the interview (N = 6 vs. 3) and said they had not been unemployed since the therapy finished (N = 4 vs. 2).

DISCUSSION

As measured by the type of therapy termination and the duration of treatment, more patients in the individualized behavior therapy or subsequent individualized behavior therapy groups than in the standard behavior therapy and preceding standard behavior therapy groups, and the humanistic therapy groups of periods 1 and 2 succeeded in halting their drug consumption. The better results of the patients from the two individualized therapy groups can be explained in three ways: the age of the patients, the change of therapy program, and the individualized therapy.

The attempt to exclude potential confounding variables through the mode of distribution of the patients between the two treatment centers failed as far as the age factor was concerned. The better results of the individualized therapy group are thus in part because the patients involved were older than those of the standard therapy group. The results of the individualized therapy group are not, however, exclusively due to the patients being older, since age does not always have predictive value for the success of therapy and the subsequent individualized therapy group differed significantly from the two standard therapy groups, even when age was partialed out by means of covariance analysis.

A further potential determinant of change is the introduction of something new into the therapy. It may be irrelevant which measure is introduced, provided that the patients react positively to the new measure and it is not contraindicated for the treatment of drug addicts. Occasionally, changing a therapy program, whatever form such a change takes, could thus improve the attention of the patients and their identification with the therapy, and have a positive effect on their willingness to change their behavior. If it is assumed that the novelty value wears off after six months, it is unlikely that the results of the individualized therapy can be explained exclusively by the introduction of something new, because even the results of the subsequent individualized therapy group are better than those of the two standard therapy groups.

The hypothesis of the study, that individualization of the therapy produces better results, could not be tested as conclusively as had been hoped,

TABLE 23.5.

Use of Psychoactive Substances Recorded at 12-month Follow-up of Interviewed Patients Who Completed Treatment

Psychoactive substances taken in the last 30 days:

Substance: Treatment group:	Alcohol		Cannabis		Medication		hard drugs	
	Standard	Individua-lised	Standard	Individua-lised	Standard	Individua-lised	Standard	Individua-lised
Days: 0	0	0	2	2	3	5	3	4
≤7	1	2	0	0	0	1	0	2
8-14	0	1	0	1	0	0	0	0
>14	2	3	1	4	0	0	0	1

Urine analyses of patients who claimed they had not taken any drugs:

Result	Standard	Individua-lised
drugfree	1	2
Cannabis	1	2
Tranquilizer	1	0

but there are various indications that this hypothesis is correct. Thus, on the one hand, the above-mentioned disturbance variables are not sufficient to explain the better results of the patients in the individualized therapy groups, and, on the other hand, some comparisons between the groups indicate that it was the treatment that was having an effect, in particular for comparisons between subsequent individualized therapy and the two standard therapy groups, and for the comparison with the humanistic therapy program, where there was no improvement during the study period.

There are also practical and theoretical considerations which indicate that individualized therapy is superior to standard therapy. If one assumes that drug addicts under legal obligation to undergo treatment are at various stages of change, it does not seem appropriate to apply the same measures to all patients at the same time and with the same intensity. As the patients are treated according to their current stage of change, they are protected from measures that are not indicated and that seem irrelevant to them, and that would also reduce their resistance to the therapy and increase their cooperation. There are various authors who feel that the systematic assignment of patients to different types of treatment is more likely to be successful than uniform treatment, and this has, to some extent, also been empirically proven.

In this study, in addition to treatment according to indication of stage of change, another feature of the individualized therapy and hence a potential determinant of change is the freedom of the patients to make their own decisions about their therapy. Since there were no valid criteria for assigning patients to the various measures, the patients were allowed to decide what they would participate in themselves. Attribution research shows that people's intrinsic motivation increases when they can make their own decisions and are not acting for external reasons (Bandura 1977). It is conceivable that the external control imposed by legal orders, which can have a detrimental effect on patients' willingness to change, is partly offset by the freedom they are granted within the treatment and that their intrinsic motivation to continue with treatment is increased. A greater degree of freedom in therapy carries with it the danger that it will be less demanding, more relaxed, and not as effective, so that a reduction in the rate of termination would occur at the price of the quality of the therapy. The data from the three-month follow-up in particular show that this is not the case. The number of patients no longer on drugs is higher after individualized therapy than after standard behavior therapy.

Standard programs, in particular group therapy, are the norm in the treatment of drug addicts. Many therapists are very skeptical about individualized therapy for drug addicts, and this applied to most of the therapists at the two treatment centers participating in the study and to colleagues at other centers. However, based on the results of this study, it can be said with some certainty that the introduction of individualized behavior therapy did not have a detrimental effect on the treatment of the drug addicts. It can quite probably even be assumed that the patients in the individualized therapy group did better than the standard therapy and humanistic therapy patients. It is not possible to define the determinants of change precisely. Variables that correlate with age, the novelty value of the therapy, and the individualized behavior therapy program may have influenced the results. It is not possible to say here how much the effect of the treatment in individualized therapy is due to treatment according to indication of stage of change and how much to the patients' freedom to decide. This would be an interesting question for further studies.

In this study, the criteria for the success of the therapy were the number of patients who terminated treatment according to plan and the duration of their stay at the center. Normally, the number of patients is too approximate a measure for a comparison of therapy programs. In order for the differences to be significant with a group size of 22 people, even at the lowest level of significance (5%) and with one-tailed tests, 5 to 6 more people must complete treatment according to plan. In the context of everyday therapeutic practice, such improvements are unrealistic. Measuring instruments which are more sensitive to changes regarding the attainment of various therapeutic goals are prerequisite for the identification of determinants of behavior change. The number of days in treatment would seem to be a suitable measure for evaluating types of therapy, because it has predictive value as far as subsequent freedom from drugs is concerned (Bradley 1989, Herbst et al. 1989). The validity of this measure should, however, also be examined more closely. The number of drug-free people at the follow-ups is too approximate a measure, and the number of drug-free days would have been more appropriate. The numbers of drug-free days were not compared on account of the differences in discharge according to plan, which ruled out group comparison at follow-up.

The inclusion in the follow-up of the patients who terminated therapy prematurely would not have made the study more conclusive. It is not possible to form hypotheses about causal connections between treatment and drug situation with these patients because of uncontrollable disturbance variables (i.e., different interpretation of legal orders). The type of therapy termination and the duration of stay are thus important success criteria for the treatment of drug addicts, especially those under legal obligation to have treatment. As long as there are no other valid measuring instruments for the evaluation of the success of therapy, such simple measures as duration of therapy will have to suffice. This is particularly unsatisfactory for practicing clinical psychologists, since these simple success criteria do not do justice to the complexity of the therapy goals and the involved and laborious therapeutic process. On the other hand, they enable the practicing psychologist to carry out empirical studies with a minimum of complication. Nevertheless, on the basis of the authors' experience with this and previous studies, the demand made by some researchers (Wilson 1984) for publications by practicing psychologists is only realistic under certain conditions. It is no problem to incorporate the documentation of data from patients and the systematic variation of interventions into the everyday routine—given a cooperative team and uncomplicated measuring instruments. However, the practicing psychologist is frequently unable to cope with the work involved in evaluating the data.

Without the research institutes mentioned here, the publication of the study would not have been possible. Research institutes, with their better technological and staffing facilities, can help clinical psychologists with the evaluation of the data that have been collected. Close cooperation on an equal basis between therapy and research centers has the advantage of providing a means of mutual control, with one concentrating more on the relevance to practice and the other more on objectivity. In this study, it was possible to show that even in a normal treatment center for drug addicts it is possible to carry out research into the determinants of change of a particular kind of therapy by means of systematic documentation and controlled change. The extent to which the results of this study can be generalized would have to be tested in other treatment centers. The study produced hypotheses for basic research about individual determinants of behavior change in therapy which could be tested under controlled conditions. Given the unsatisfactory level of knowledge about determinants of change in therapy for drug addicts, what is needed, especially from the standpoint of a practicing psychologist, is more practice-oriented and basic research.

Acknowledgments

We would like to thank the following for making this study possible: the patients and colleagues of the Aiglsdorf and Baumgarten treatment centers (director Dr. Alfred Dvorak); Mrs. Dipl. Psych. Angelika Leitner for the follow-ups; Mr. Michael Waadt for advice about the statistics and evaluation of data; Dr. Ludwig von Meyer (Institut für Rechtsmedizin der Universität München—Institute for Forensic Medicine of Munich

University) for the urine analysis; Mr. Phillipp Korintenberg for the graphics and tables; and Ms. Sue Bollans for the translation into English. The data presented in this paper were collected as part of a research project to investigate the relapse process, with financial assistance from the Volkswagenwerk Foundation.

REFERENCES

Ayllon, T., and Azrin, N. H. (1968). *The Token Economy: A Motivational System for Therapy and Rehabilitation*. New York: Appleton-Century-Crofts.

Bandura, A. (1977). Self-efficacy: Towards a unifying theory of behavior change. *Psychological Review, 84*, 191–215.

Bradley, B. P. (1989). Heroin and the opiates. In M. Gossop (ed.), *Relapse and Addictive Behaviour*, 73–85. London: Tavistock/Routledge.

De Jong, R., and Henrich, G. (1980). Follow-up results of a behavior modification program for juvenile drug addicts. *Addictive Behaviours* 5: 49–57.

Ellis, A. (1977). The basic clinical theory of rational-emotive therapy. In Ellis and R. Grieger (eds.), *Handbook of Rational-Emotive Therapy*. New York: Springer.

Grawe, K. (1980). Die diagnostisch-therapeutische Funktion der Gruppeninteraktion in verhaltenstherapeutischen Gruppen (The diagnostic-therapeutic function of group interaction in behaviour therapy groups). In K. Grawe (ed.), *Verhaltenstherapie in Gruppen*, 88–223. München: Urban & Schwarzenberg.

Herbst, K., Hanel, E., and Haderstorfer, B. (1989). Rückfallgeschehen bei stationär behandelten Drogenabhängigen (Relapse of drug addicts following inpatient treatment). In H. Watzl and R. Cohen (eds.), *Rückfall und Rückfallprophylaxe*, 139–48. Berlin: Springer.

Kanfer, F. H. (1971). The maintenance of behavior by self-generated stimuli and reinforcement. In A. Jacobs and L. B. Sachs (eds.), *The Psychology of Private Events*, 39–57. New York: Academic Press.

Kanfer, F. H., and Phillips, J. S. (1970). *Learning foundations of behavior therapy*. New York: Wiley.

Kanfer, F. H., and Saslow, G. (1969). Behavioral diagnosis. In C. M. Franks (ed.), *Behavior Therapy: Appraisal and Status*, 417–44. New York: McGraw-Hill.

Klett, F. (1987). Langzeitverläufe bei Drogenabhängigen bis zu 10 Jahren nach Behandlungsende (Long-term course in drug addicts up to 10 years after treatment termination). In D. Kleiner (ed.), *Langzeitverläufe bei Suchtkrankheiten*, 162–78. Berlin: Springer.

Klett, F., Hanel, E., and Bühringer, G. (1984). Sekundäranalyse deutschprachiger Katamnesen bei Drogenabhängigen (Secondary analysis of German follow-up studies on drug dependents). *Suchtgefahren* 30: 245–65.

Lazarus, A. A. (1966). Broad spectrum behavior therapy and the treatment of agoraphobia. *Behaviour Research and Therapy* 4: 95–97.

Libermann, R. P., King, L. W., De Risi, W. J., and McCann, M. (1975). *Personal Effectiveness.* Champaign, Ill.: Research Press.

Marlatt, G. A. and Gordon, J. R. (eds.). (1985). *Relapse Prevention.* New York: Guilford Press.

Meichenbaum, D.*, and Jaremko, M. E. (1983). *Stress Reduction and Prevention.* New York: Plenum.

Melchinger, H. (1989). Therapie unter Freiheitsentzug: Katamnestische Untersuchungen bei Klienten der Fachklinik Brauel (Court-ordered therapy at a closed facility: A follow-up study of drug-dependent clients at the Brauel Treatment Center). In W. Feuerlein, G. Bühringer, and R. Wille (eds.), *Therapieverläufe bei Drogenabhängigen*, 245–64. Berlin: Springer.

Miller, W. R. (1983). Motivational interviewing with problem drinkers. *Behavioural Psychotherapy* 11, 147–72.

Pavlov, I. P. (1927). *Conditioned Reflexes.* London: Oxford University Press.

Prochaska, J. O., and Di Clemente, C. C. (1983). Stages and processes of self-change of smoking: Toward an integrative model of change. *Journal of Consulting and Clinical Psychology* 51: 390–95.

———. (1986). Toward a comprehensive model of change. In W. R. Miller and N. Heather (eds.), *Treating addictive Behaviors*, 3–27. New York: Plenum Press.

Reed, Th. (1980). Challenging some "common wisdom" on drug abuse. *The International Journal of the Addictions* 15: 359–73.

Schulte, D. (1974). Ein Schema für Diagnose und Therapieplanung in der Verhaltenstherapie (A guide for diagnosis and treatment planning in behavior therapy). In D. Schulte (ed.), *Diagnostik in der Verhaltenstherapie*, 75–104. München: Urban & Schwarzenberg.

Skinner, B. F. (1953). *Science and Human Behavior.* New York: Free Press.

Ullrich. R. and Ullrich, R. (1976). *Das Assertiveness-Training-Program* (The assertiveness training program). München: Pfeiffer.

Vollmer, H. C., Ellgring, H., and Ferstl, R. (1990). Prediction of Premature Termination of Therapy in the Treatment of Drug Addicts. Manuscript submitted for publication.

Wilson, G. T. (1982). Clinical issues and strategies in the practice of behavior therapy. In C. M. Franks, G. T. Wilson, Ph. C. Kendall, and K. D. Brownell (eds.), *Annual Review of Behavior Therapy*, vol. 8, 305–45. New York: Guilford.

Wilson, G. T. (1984). Clinical issues and strategies in the practice of behaviour therapy. In C. M. Franks, G. T. Wilson, Ph. C. Kendall, and K. D. Brownell (eds.), *Annual Review of Behavior Therapy*, vol. 10, 291–320. New York: Guilford Press.

CHAPTER 24

The Munich Multicenter Treatment Evaluation Study: Results of the First Follow-up*

Barbara Haderstorfer, and Jutta Künzel-Böhmer

The prospective treatment evaluation study (MTE-Study) has been conducted in Munich since November 1985. Data were gathered from 302 clients of 13 residential drug-free therapeutic communities located throughout the former Federal Republic of Germany.

FOLLOW-UP METHOD

The clients were interviewed 3, 12, and 24 months after regular discharge or dropout. Six clients were still in therapy at the time of the data analysis, so 296 clients were asked by letter to take part in the first follow-up interview. A standard questionnaire was used. Three follow-ups, including urine analysis, were scheduled for each client. It was difficult to reach the clients after they left the treatment facility because many of them had changed their addresses or disappeared. The response rate of all three follow-ups was 72%. Only four clients, that is 1.5% of

*The study was funded by the German Federal Ministry of Health. For further details see also the chapters by Hanel and Herbst in this volume.

TABLE 24.1

Response Rate and Characteristics of the Follow-up Sample

Response Rate

All 3 follow-up interviews	72%
First follow-up (n = 177)	60%
Selected sub-group (n = 164)	55%

Time Between Discharge and First Follow-up Interview
(cumulative percentages)

< 3 months	9%
− 6 months	70%
− 9 months	96%
Range 6 weeks−11 months	

Characteristics of the Follow-up Sample

	Follow-up (n = 164)	Total sample (n = 296)
Time in Treatment		
< 3 months	20%	23%
− 6 months	31%	28%
− 12 months	31%	34%
− 18 months	15%	14%
range: 6–635 days		
Discharge		
Regular discharge	57%	47%
Dropout	43%	51%
Other	0%	0%

the total sample, expressly refused to participate in the follow-up interviews (Table 24.1).

At first follow-up 60% (n = 177) of all clients were reached for an interview. There were 13 clients who were alcohol dependent or had a nonmedical use of medication, and they were excluded from the sample. Thus the first follow-up sample includes data on 164 clients (55%). The majority were interviewed within nine months after their individual date of discharge. In comparison to the total sample, this follow-up subgroup does not differ significantly on basic variables including distributions for duration of treatment, age, and type of discharge. As expected, there are more interviews for clients who were routinely discharged. Six clients died in the 3.5 years of the study.

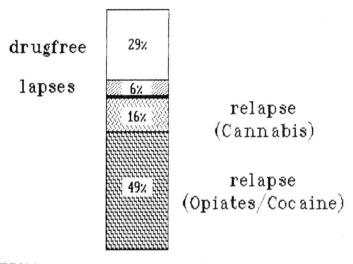

FIGURE 24.1.
Patterns of relapse during first follow-up period (m = 5 months after discharge; N = 164).

RESULTS

Pre- and Posttreatment Drug Use

The major outcome data for the treatment evaluation are described below. Client relapse, as depicted in Figure 24.1, is defined as a positive urine analysis or client admission of relapse during the follow-up period. Fourteen percent (n = 23) refused to take part in the urine test; we categorize them as relapses. Only five clients who denied any drug use had positive opiate screening results. Twenty-nine percent of the 164 interviewed clients remained drug free, as defined above, throughout their entire first follow-up interval. Six percent (n = 10) had a "lapse." A "lapse" is defined as use of illegal drugs for no longer than 14 days, and staying drug free for the remainder of an interval. A total of 65% of the clients relapsed, 16% of whom used only cannabis. Those who had relapsed were asked whether they took drugs continuously or whether they had drug-free periods in between. The analysis shows that 45% of them used drugs daily (n = 52). Thirty five percent had long-lasting episodes of drug use and another 21% only consumed drugs for a short period of time.

Seventy-one percent of the clients took illegal drugs at least once after discharge. The main drugs used after treatment were cannabis and opiates.

TABLE 24.2

**Self-Reported Pre- and Posttreatment Drug Use by Drug Type
(Multiple Responses)**

Drugs	Pretreatment (n = 164)	Posttreatment (n = 164)	Use at first relapse (n = 111)*
Heroin	76%	36%	29%
Cocaine	56%	14%	4%
Other Opiates	40%	20%	6%
MJ/Hash.	82%	78%	32%
LSD/Halluc.	25%	4%	1%
Amphetamines	37%	10%	3%
Inhalants	4%	2%	—
Sedatives	40%	18%	2%
Sleep. Pills	43%	11%	1%
Analgesics	23%	26%	—
Alcohol	71%	69%	17%

*53 clients gave no information

Cocaine and amphetamines were used less frequently. Forty-six percent of all clients mentioned use of pills, especially sedatives and pain killers, but only a small number admitted nonprescription pill use.

The pre- and posttreatment drug use ("pretreatment" is the six-month period before treatment) by drug type is described in Table 24.2. Additionally, the types of drugs that were used at first relapse are shown in the last column. Sixteen clients (10%) reported that they have never used any drugs, pills, or alcohol after treatment. Quite a few clients reported that they never wanted to stop using cannabis, because they consider it as a harmless recreational drug. This explains why most of these clients still take marijuana/hashish and alcohol. Regarding heroin there is a reduction in the percentage of users from 76% before treatment to 36% after treatment. A reduction is also found in the use of other types of drugs. At first relapse most of the clients took cannabis or heroin or both together.

Legal Status

After treatment, 78% of the interviewed clients had no new contact with the law. More than two-thirds were on probation, significantly more men than women (Table 24.3). Twenty-three men and three women (16%)

TABLE 24.3

Legal Status after Treatment

	Men n = 126	Women n = 38	Total n = 164
No new conflict with the law after discharge	75%	87%	78%
On probation/parole*	75%	55%	71%
New charges following treatment	18%	8%	16%
– drug related	12%	8%	16%
Convictions following treatment	7%	0%	6%
Imprisonment/custody following treatment*	12%	0%	10%

*significant difference between men and women: p < 0.05

reported new, mostly drug-related charges during their follow-up period. Seven percent of the men interviewed had already been convicted at the time of the interview. Only one of these convicted clients was referred for treatment at the time of conviction. Fifteen men (12%) were put in prison for some time during the first follow-up period.

Employment Status

One very important factor in rehabilitation is the client's chance of getting a job after discharge. But the labor market in Germany is quite disadvantageous, especially for former drug addicts. Thirty-eight percent could not find a job at all and 46% had at least one job after discharge (Table 24.4). Only 12% (n = 18) of the clients kept their job during treatment or had found employment before they left the treatment facility. It was found that half of those who had a job (40 out of 77 clients) worked after treatment and more than 80% had a full-time job. This is an interesting outcome in regard to the clients' motivation to change their lifestyle and to become socially integrated.

The clients' professional standing after treatment shows that, in comparison to their pretreatment status, many former employees and independent businessmen had to do unskilled labor. The percentages listed in the table are with reference to their first place of work. It is expected that these results will change in the second and third follow-up toward better positions commensurate with the clients' skills. As a result of their poor employment status, many clients are on some sort of welfare or get financial support from their relatives. Only eight clients admit to an illegal income after discharge. The financial situation of quite a few clients

TABLE 24.4

Employment and Financial Situation

Employment Status

Employed throughout follow-up time	12%
One short-time job or more	34%
Unemployed during entire follow-up time	38%
Longer lasting imprisonment	7%
Reentry in residential treatment facilities	7%
Housewife	1%

Professional Standing

	Pretreatment	*Posttreatment*
Unskilled worker	29%	49%
Skilled worker	39%	37%
Employee	21%	11%
Independent businessman/woman	12%	3%

Financial Situation

Main Source of Income:		
Work	23%	33%
Social support systems	32%	45%
Relatives	10%	12%
Illegal income	35%	5%

is of concern: 37% are at subsistence level, that is, they have an income of less than DM 500 per month and another third (32%) report that they have an income of less than DM 1000 per month, which is just enough to live on in Germany. Only about 40% are free of debts. There are 14% who have to pay off debts totaling DM 20,000 or more.

Emotional Status

In order to analyze the client's risk for relapse, a modified version of the Situational Confidence Questionnaire developed by Annis (1985) was used. This self-report questionnaire is designed to assess Bandura's concept of self-efficacy (1977) in relation to a client's perceived ability to cope effectively with high-risk drug-taking situations. The 70 items are descriptions of high-risk drug-taking situations based on the work of Marlatt. Figure 24.2 shows that, on average, the total scores at the time of

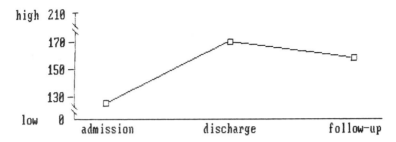

FIGURE 24.2.
Self-efficacy scores (median) before and during treatment and at follow-up (N = 144).

discharge are significantly better than those at the beginning of the treatment, but at follow-up the scores are lower again. The realities of life outside of the therapeutic community appear to have reduced the clients' self-confidence with high-risk relapse situations.

During the follow-up interview, the clients were asked to describe the specific situation at the time of their first relapse and to name individual problems that could lead them to use drugs again. Analyzing these answers and the most frequently marked items of the Situational Confidence Questionnaire, we found that there are four factors of primary importance: First, the clients' social situations, in particular their contact with drug-taking friends; second, their loneliness; third, a negative emotional state; and finally, the lack of any assistance when they have problems.

Table 24.5 shows the relevant variables of the clients' social situation and living conditions. Forty-three percent are without a partner or just have temporary partnerships. Twenty-six percent of those clients who live in their own apartment lived alone during the entire follow-up period. This is interesting considering that loneliness is one of the self-reported high-risk factors for relapse. According to the analysis of the actual situation at the first relapse, the most frequently reported reason to start using illegal drugs again is contact with other drug users, mostly old friends from the drug scene. More than two-thirds of the clients are still in contact with opiate or cocaine users and even more with people who consume cannabis (see "Scene Involvement" in Table 24.5). Moreover, 30% have a partner who is addicted or at risk for addiction. Consequently, it should be an essential goal of therapeutic work to increase the clients' awareness of this risk factor.

Figure 24.3 demonstrates the mean scores for the clients' depressiveness at the beginning and end of treatment and at the first follow-up

TABLE 24.5

Relationships and Living Conditions

	Pre-treatment	Post-treatment
Relationship Status		
Single	22%	25%
Committed partnership	49%	57%
Temporary partnership	29%	18%
Scene Involvement		
Contact to Opiate/Cocaine users	94%	73%
Contact to Marijuana/Hashish users	96%	77%
Partner addicted/at risk	52%	30%
Lodging		
Own apartment	34%	42%
With parents/relatives	21%	18%
In homes/hospital/prison	33%	21%
Of no fixed abode	2%	2%
Other	10%	17%

interview. It is assessed by Zerssen's Depression Inventory (1976). The median score for the clients is significantly higher than that for healthy normals at any time. The score of the women found at admission (20.5) meets the criterion of a psychiatric disorder. The difference between men and women at the beginning of treatment is highly significant ($p < 0.001$). Interestingly, the depressiveness of the women constantly decreases, in contrast to the findings in the male group. The men's scores at first

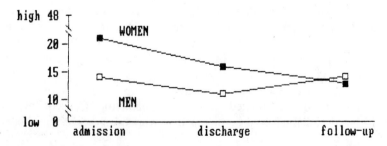

FIGURE 24.3.
Depressiveness scores (median) before and during treatment and at follow-up time (N = 164).

TABLE 24.6

Aftercare in the First Follow-up Period (N = 164)

Aftercare	
Participation in some kind of aftercare	56%

Aftercare Agencies: (multiple responses)	
Drug counseling center	87%
Aftercare facilities	24%
Self-help groups	14%

New Treatment	
Withdrawal at home	16%
Detoxification	7%
Drug-free residential treatment	7%

follow-up are slightly higher than at admission and they approach the women's scores. The high degree of the posttreatment depressiveness should be taken into account when clients contact aftercare agencies. It is well known that the continuous provision of support for ex-addicts after discharge is very important for increasing the effectiveness of residential treatment. Even those clients who are highly motivated to remain abstinent need certain kinds of help to cope with the problems they have to face after they leave the shelter of the treatment facility. Fifty-six percent of the follow-up sample took part in some kind of aftercare (Table 24.6). Most of them went to a drug counseling center and 7% (n = 12) had already decided to reenter a drug-free residential treatment within the first follow-up period.

Sexual Behavior and AIDS

About 10% of all AIDS cases are intravenous drug users. Data on AIDS surveillance in thirty-two European countries published by the World Health Organization (as of 30 September 1990) show that Germany's IV drug users (n = 661) rank fourth behind Italy (n = 4993), Spain (n = 4474), and France (n = 1804) with respect to number of AIDS patients within this population.

A total of 115 clients of the first follow-up subgroup were questioned. The results are described separately for the HIV-seronegative and sero-

TABLE 24.7
Sexual Behavior (N = 111)*

Sexual Behavior	HIV NEG	HIV POS
women	(n = 22)	(n = 5)
(male partners):		
– no partner	9% (2)	—
– 1 partner	55% (12)	40% (2)
– 2–4 partners	36% (8)	60% (3)
men	(n = 76)	(n = 8)
(female partners):		
– no partner	7% (5)	43% (4)
– 1 partner	28% (21)	14% (1)
– 2–5 partners	59% (45)	29% (2)
– 6–10 partners	7% (5)	14% (1)
Change of Sexual Behavior		
– women	23% (5)	100% (5)
– men	47% (36)	50% (4)

* Missing data: 4

positive clients. This last group consists of only 13 clients (8 men and 5 women), of whom 2 men and 1 woman already suffer from symptoms (1 ARC, 2 CDC-AIDS). The most relevant risk behaviors were the clients' sexual and injecting behaviors. Thirty-five percent of the HIV-negative and 30% of the HIV-positive injecting drug users still share needles.

With respect to heterosexual contacts, the men in general are more promiscuous than the women. All of the seropositive women and half of the HIV-infected men report that they somehow changed their sexual behavior after they found out that they were infected (Table 24.7). In the HIV-negative group this finding is reversed.

Table 24.8 shows selected data concerning high-risk conduct in regard to sexual activities. There were only 5 men who reported having sexual contact with male partners, but no man said that he had exchanged sex for money or drugs. The 5% indicated in the table who had sex in exchange for money or drugs are all women, and 2 women admitted to intercourse without condoms while engaging in prostitution. In comparison to the men, more women in both groups stated that they had intercourse with an HIV-infected partner.

Table 24.9 evaluates the effects of AIDS prevention efforts undertaken

TABLE 24.8

Sexual-Risk Behavior Concerning HIV Transmission (N = 115)

Sexual-risk behavior	HIV-NEG (n = 102)		HIV-POS (n = 13)	
Male homosexual or bisexual	5%	(5)	0%	
Exchange of sex for money or drugs	5%	(5)	0%	
– always using a condom	75%	(4)	0%	
– sometimes using a condom	25%	(1)	0%	
Intercourse with HIV-infected partner				
– women	20%	(5)	80%	(4)
– men	13%	(10)	38%	(3)

TABLE 24.9

Risk Reduction Behavior in Order to Avoid HIV Transmission

	HIV-NEG (n = 102)		HIV-POS (n = 13)	
Total abstinence from sexual activity	4%	(4)	23%	(3)
Compliance with recommended risk reduction behavior	5%	(5)	15%	(2)
Use of protective measures	(n = 88)		(n = 13)	
– never	58%	(51)	17%	(2)
– sometimes/often	20%	(18)	17%	(2)
– always	22%	(19)	67%	(9)
Self-reported preventive behaviors	(n = 48)		(n = 13)	
– use of condoms	65%	(31)	62%	(8)
– safer sex	3%	(2)	8%	(1)
– monogamy	11%	(5)	8%	(1)
– avoidance of HIV POS partners	19%	(9)	—	
– frequent HIV testing	2%	(1)	—	
– avoidance of receptive sex	—		22%	(3)

by public health programs and the therapeutic staff to encourage risk-reduction behavior. The only "absolute" protection from sexually transmitted infection is abstinence or a completely monogamous relationship and there are nine clients in the HIV-negative group who are in this category. Against all expectations only 5% of this group follows commonly recommended risk-reduction behavior. The remaining 95% still share needles and have unprotected intercourse (i.e., never use condoms or safe sex). This confirms the results of some American studies reviewed by Kelly and St. Lawrence (1988) that show that most drug users do not engage in safer sex practices and that it is difficult to produce substantial reductions in needle sharing among addicts, particularly when a supply of new needles is unavailable (Des Jarlais et al. 1988; Flynn et al. 1987).

Especially alarming is the fact that a third of the seropositive clients report that they do not always use protective measures. This could be interpreted either as negligence or as a lack of information that the exchange of semen even between HIV-positive partners should be avoided because of the risk of further infections. The self-reported preventive behaviors shown in the last part of Table 24.9 result from an open question about the kind of methods the clients choose to use in order to prevent HIV transmission. Some of them, like "avoidance of infected partners" or "frequent HIV testing," are ineffective actions in practice.

COMMENTS

The major outcome data show that in regard to pre- and posttreatment drug use the clients' consumption of heroin and cocaine diminished, but there was no reduction in the use of cannabis and alcohol. More than half of the clients of the first follow-up sample participated in some kind of aftercare, and most of them received outpatient treatment in drug counseling centers. In regard to legal status, two-thirds of the clients were on probation and only 16% were charged again after treatment. Forty-six percent of the clients had at least one job following treatment, but 45% lived on social support.

Some of these results seem to be discouraging, especially those concerning the relapse rate. Nevertheless, a relapse after discharge does not mean that the treatment was a total failure. The majority of the clients believed treatment helped them to somehow change their lifestyle. Only 19% said that the treatment was not useful at all. Fifty-eight percent of those who dropped out regretted having left treatment before their planned termination. When asked about their positive experiences and skills they learned during treatment, many clients reported that one of the best experiences they had was the new feeling that they could be happy without taking drugs. They also felt that they increased their self-confidence and their competence to cope with problems. As it is known from studies on the length of drug careers, a residential treatment is *one* appropriate step for an individual with a long history of drug use. Additional interventions seem necessary to completely bring his or her addiction problem under control.

In general, the findings concerning compliance with recommended risk-reduction behavior to avoid HIV transmission are not promising. Certainly more health education efforts must be undertaken. The provision of specific prescriptive advice during treatment should be the goal of prime importance, particularly when one considers that, in this sample of clients treated between 1986 and 1988, there were still 39% who said they were not well informed about the AIDS issue by the therapeutic staff.

REFERENCES

Annis, H. M. (1985). Situational confidence questionnaire. In W. R. Miller and N. Heather (eds.), *Treating Addictive Behaviors: Process of Change*. New York: Plenum.

Bandura, A. (1977). Self-efficacy: Toward a unifiying theory of behavioral change. *Psychological Review* 84: 191–215.

Des Jarlais, D. C., Tross, S., Abdul-Quader, A., and Friedman, S. R. (1988). Intravenous drug users and the heterosexual transmission of AIDS. In J. A. Kelly (chair), *Outcomes of AIDS Prevention Programs: What Works Best with Whom*. Symposium conducted at the American Psychological Association Annual Meeting, Atlanta, GA.

Flynn, N. M., Jain, S., Harper, S., Bailey, B., Anderson, R., and Acuna, G. (1987). Sharing of paraphernalia in intravenous drug users: Knowledge of AIDS is incomplete and doesn't affect behavior. Paper presented to the III International Conference on AIDS, Washington, D.C.

Hanel, E., and Herbst, K. (1988). Beschreibung und erste Ergebnisse einer prospektiven Studie zur stationären Nachbehandlung von Drogenabhängigen. *Suchtgefahren* 34, 1–21.

Herbst, K., and Hanel, E. (1988). Verlauf der stationären Entwöhnungsbehandlung bei Drogenabhängigen. *Suchtgefahren* 35: 235–51.

———. (1989). Meßbare Größen des Therapieprozesses bei Drogenabhängigen in stationärer Entwöhnungsbehandlung. In Feuerlein, W., Bühringer, G. und Wille, R. (eds.). *Therapieverläufe bei Drogenabhängigen*, 170–183. Heidelberg: Springer.

Herbst, K., Hanel, E., and Haderstorfer, B. (1989). Rückfallgeschehen bei stationär behandelten Drogenabhängigen. In R. Cohen and H. Watzl (eds.), *Rückfall und Rückfallprophylaxe*. Heidelberg: Springer.

Kelly, J. A., and St. Lawrence, J. S. (1988). Aids prevention and treatment: Psychology's role in the health crisis. *Clinical Psychological Review* 8, 255–84.

World Health Organisation. (1990). AIDS—Surveillance in Europe. WHO-Report Nr. 27, *AIDS-Forschung* 2, 78–99.

Zerrssen v., D. (1976). *Depressivitätsskala (D-S)*. Weinheim: Beltz.

CHAPTER 25

Therapeutic Community Research: Recent Studies of Psychopathology and Retention

Nancy Jainchill and George De Leon

Therapeutic community (TC) research has focused primarily on the issues of outcome and psychopathology. The first studies on retention established the direct relationship between time in program and outcome: clients who remained in residential therapeutic community treatment for at least one year were significantly better at follow-up than clients who had less than one year's time in the program (e.g., see De Leon 1984; De Leon and Jainchill 1981–82; Simpson and Sells 1982). These findings highlighted the need for efforts to identify factors that would increase the likelihood of client retention in treatment.

Most investigators have attempted to distinguish client characteristics that relate to remaining in treatment. However, recent studies in the United States have evaluated the influence of treatment parameters on retention. In particular, modifications to traditional therapeutic community protocols were introduced, and their effects on retention rates were studied, to assess the relationship between specific treatment components and client retention in treatment (De Leon 1988, 1989). As reported elsewhere (De Leon 1988), changes in treatment protocol, such as the introduction of increased individual counseling sessions, affected retention rates positively.

A primary objective of TC research has been to understand the interaction between client characteristics and treatment parameters. In this regard, a series of related studies by the authors have addressed the issue of psychopathology, focusing on the assessment of psychiatric diagnoses among admissions to drug-free residential treatment (therapeutic communities). This chapter reports the main findings from these studies centering on two questions: (1) what is the extent and type of psychopathology and psychiatric disorder that occurs among admissions to residential treatment; and (2) what is the role of client disposition to outcome—specifically, what is the relationship between diagnosis and retention?

STUDY 1: THE CHANGING PROFILE OF ADMISSIONS TO THE THERAPEUTIC COMMUNITY

This study examined trends in the psychological profiles of individuals entering therapeutic community treatment. Data were analyzed from two sources: a single large urban therapeutic community, and a consortium of seven TC programs. The urban therapeutic community is an example of a traditional TC. It has been in existence for over 20 years and has diversified to offer a range of residential and nonresidential services, including aftercare and short-term residential programs. It processes over 1200 admissions annually and maintains a drug-free residential population of approximately 700; several hundred clients are served in aftercare and special services.

The consortium sample consisted of seven programs that belong to a national organization, Therapeutic Communities of America (TCA). They were not necessarily a representative sample of all TCs, nor did they reflect the regional or geographic distribution of therapeutic communities nationally. All were voluntary participants in an earlier research project, the objective of which was to train program-based evaluation capability. Each program was described by respective executive personnel as a long-term therapeutic community in terms of philosophy, treatment goals, structure, process, staffing pattern, and essential therapeutic tools. The programs, however, varied in size (40–160 beds) and in period of existence (6–15 years). Overall, the TCA sample was not statistically representative of the TC modality, so that generalization of results to the residential drug-free modality must be limited.

Instruments

Measures of psychopathology included the Beck Depression Inventory (Beck et al. 1961), the Shortened Manifest Anxiety Scale (Bendig 1956), and the Shortened Schizophrenia Scale (Clark and Danielson 1956). These scales have been validated in the literature as indices of psychopathology.

Self-esteem was assessed utilizing the Tennessee Self-Concept Scale (TSC; Fitts 1965), a standardized test for measuring self-esteem and psychological disturbance. Norms and scores from various comparison groups have been published, and it has demonstrated sensitivity for detecting psychological change over time.

These instruments were chosen because each has established reliability and validity data, straightforward instructions that make administration in a group setting manageable, and all have been used with drug-abusing samples in previous studies.

Procedures

1. *The 1974 Cohort*: Clients admitted to the urban therapeutic community between July 1, 1974 and Feburary 1, 1975 were administered psychological testing within the first five days of entry into treatment. Measures of psychopathology and self-esteem were obtained.

2. *The 1984 Cohort*: Data were collected on all new entries into the urban residential treatment program between October 1, 1984 and December 31, 1985. Within the first four days of admission the new client was administered the full battery of psychological tests, usually in a group setting. Psychological information was obtained on over 1,000 admissions to treatment during this period.

3. *The 1979 Cohort (TCA Consortium)*: The TCA data set was developed during a two-year demonstration project undertaken to establish self-evaluation capability in the seven participating residential treatment programs (De Leon 1980). Intake information and psychological data were obtained by program-based research assistants who were full-time staff trained by the project staff in interview and data recording.

The Samples

Data sets were developed on two cohorts of all admissions (1974 and 1984) to the single urban TC. The two cohorts were similar in their demographic characteristics. Both had a majority of males (75–80%) and blacks (50–60%), but the 1984 cohort was somewhat older. There were differences in the distribution of the clients' self-reported primary drug: among the 1974 cohort a majority were primary opioid abusers (39%), compared with the 1984 cohort, the majority of whom self-reported primary cocaine abuse (43%).

The TCA client sample consisted of all admissions to the consortium between February 1 and August 15, 1979. Consortium admissions were mainly male (78%), white (58%), and aged 19–26 years. There were approximately equal proportions reporting primary drug use of pills or opiates (about 35%); see Table 25.1.

Results

Analyses focused mainly on a comparison of the 1974 and 1984 cohorts, since this minimized variance arising from program differences. However, the tables and figures include the data on the 1979 TCA cohort, and statistical comparisons were completed for the three data sets.

As shown in Table 25.2, there were some differences among the demographic profiles of the three cohorts. There were fewer females in the 1974 cohort, which might reflect a concerted effort by TC programs in more recent years to encourage women to enter treatment. The racial/ethnic differences obtained between the metropolitan TC and the consortium reflect regional differences. There is a significant change in the distribution of reported primary drug of abuse, reflected in increased cocaine use and decreased use of heroin and alcohol, most evident between the 1974 and 1984 cohorts.

Psychological profiles: Tables 25.3 and 25.4 show that on the symptom scales, the 1984 cohort reveals worse scores than either of the two earlier cohorts, particularly on depression. The largest differences are between the 1974 and 1984 cohorts. Although there are significant differences in IQ across the three cohorts, the decline in scores may be largely artifactual, attributable to the lower norms of the revised Beta II IQ tests.[1]

STUDY 2: DUAL DISORDERS AMONG ADMISSIONS TO THE TC

Until recently, most studies have reported psychopathological profiles utilizing such measures as the MMPI, the Tennessee Self-Concept, and symptoms scales such as the Beck Depression Inventory and the Shortened Manifest Anxiety scale. In part, these measures were used because the problem of substance abuse was not considered a "psychiatric" problem; in fact, drug addicts had been treatment failures within the medical-psychiatric treatment system. But additionally, the existence of a functional, descriptive nosological system to classify disorders (i.e.,

---

1. The 1974 cohort was administered the Beta I, while the 1979 and 1984 cohorts were administered the Beta II test. The 1979–1984 IQ differences are therefore not artifactual.

TABLE 25.1

Demographic and Primary Drug of Abuse Characteristics of Admissions to the 1974, 1979, and 1984 Cohorts

	Phoenix House 1974 Cohort		Consortium 1979 Cohort		Phoenix House 1984 Cohort	
	N	%	N	%	N	%
Sex						
Male	444	83.5	762	77.9	828	78.5
Female	88	16.5	216	22.1	227	21.5
Total	532	100.0	978	100.0	1055	100.0
Ethnicity						
Black	322	60.5	338	35.0	544	51.6
Hispanic	90	16.9	60	6.2	278	26.4
White	117	22.0	557	57.7	226	21.4
Others	3	0.6	11	1.1	7	0.7
Total	532	100.0	966	100.0	1055	100.0
Age						
< 19	94	18.6	206	21.3	233	22.1
19–26	248	49.1	466	48.2	440	41.8
27+	163	32.3	294	30.4	380	36.1
Total	505	100.0	966	100.0	1053	100.0
*Primary Drug**						
Marijuana	113	26.4	132	14.1	165	15.8
Cocaine	18	4.2	62	6.6	445	42.7
Opiates	166	38.8	320	34.2	283	27.1
Alcohol	108	25.2	85	9.1	57	5.5
Others	23	5.4	336	35.9	93	8.9
Total	428	100.0	935	100.0	1043	100.0

* A polydrug group was excluded from comparison since this category was defined only in the 1974 cohort. However, the majority of clients in all cohorts were multiple drug users.

TABLE 25.2

Summary of Chi-Square Results For the Comparison of Three Cohorts On Demographic Variables and Primary Drug 1974, 1979, 1984

Demographic Variables	Cohort Comparisons		
	1974 vs. 1984	*1974 vs. 1979*	*1979 vs. 1984*
Sex	5.51*	6.59**	0.10
Ethnicity	18.82***	186.74***	325.00***
Age	7.57*	1.60	9.65**
Primary Drug	248.63***	187.46***	433.81***

*Significant at the .05 level
**Significant at the .01 level
***Significant at the .001 level

Summary of differences between cohorts:

Sex	**Age**	**(Cont.) Primary Drug**
Female	19–26	Alcohol
1984 > 1974	1984 < 1974	1984 < 1974
1979 > 1974	1984 < 1979	1984 < 1979
	27+	
	1984 > 1979	1979 < 1974
Ethnicity	*Primary Drug*	
Hispanic	Marijuana	*Others*
1984 > 1974	1984 < 1974	1984 < 1979
1984 > 1979	1979 < 1974	1979 > 1974
1979 < 1974		
Black	Cocaine	
1984 > 1979	1984 > 1974	
1979 < 1974	1984 > 1979	
White	Opiates	
1984 < 1979	1984 < 1974	
1979 > 1974	1984 < 1979	

DSM-III) and structured instruments to obtain such diagnoses are relatively recent developments.

Study 2 described the psychiatric profiles of over 350 clients admitted to a large metropolitan area therapeutic community. Also, the psychiatric profiles of admissions to long-term residential treatment are compared with those of individuals entering short-term or outpatient treatment, and

TABLE 25.3

**Means and Standard Deviations on Four Measures of Psychopathology and
Beta IQ for Three Cohorts: 1974, 1979, and 1984**

Scale	1974 (N = 492)		1979 (N = 736)		1984 (N = 949)	
	Mean	SD	Mean	SD	Mean	SD
Beck Depression	16.3	9.5	16.0	9.2	19.6	8.7
Anxiety	9.5	4.5	10.0	5.0	10.3	4.6
Schizophrenia	7.2	4.1	7.8	4.3	7.9	4.1
*Socialization	26.1	5.5	—	—	25.9	5.4
			(N = 657)		(N = 899)	
Beta IQ	91.2	14.7	86.7	13.8	82.9	13.1

*The Socialization Scale was not obtained on admissions to the 7 programs of the
1979 TCA Consortium.

TABLE 25.4

**Summary of Significant Differences between Cohorts on 4 Measures of
Psychopathology and Beta IQ**

	1974, 1979, and 1984		
	Group Comparisons		
	1974 vs. 1984	1974 vs. 1979	1979 vs. 1984
Scales	t test	t test	t test
Beck Depression	6.43***	0.54	−8.25***
Anxiety	2.97**	1.89	−1.18
Schizophrenia	3.46***	0.68	0.68
Socialization	−0.61	—	—
Beta IQ	−10.64***	−5.23***	5.52***

Note: The t-test for independent samples was used to assess group differences.

***p < .001
**p < .01
*p < .05

with two groups of individuals who were not in treatment: nonadmissions (persons denied admission) and "pendings" (persons awaiting a bed or who do not return for further assessment).

Instruments

The Diagnostic Interview Schedule (DIS, Version 3A; Robins and Helzer 1985) was utilized for the clinical diagnostic studies in the present research. The DIS was developed for use in a national epidemiological study to assess prevalence and incidence of psychiatric disturbance in the general population. This instrument has a structured format, and the interview can be conducted by trained lay people as well as by psychiatrists or psychologists. The interview is read verbatim to the respondent and covers 43 DSM-III categories. The criteria for selection of diagnostic categories were based on expected prevalence rates in the general population, severity and clinical importance of treatment needs, and research interest (Myers et al. 1984). The presence of symptoms are recorded and severity is differentiated. Symptoms that exist at a subclinical level, that is, do not meet severity criteria, are coded accordingly. Codes are also used to distinguish nonpsychiatric attributions of symptoms, such as medical illness or drug/alcohol use. A historical summary of psychiatric disturbance is obtained, in which age of onset and age of most recent occurrence is ascertained for each positive diagnosis.

Issues of the reliability of psychiatric diagnosis, particularly with respect to establishing an accurate DSM-III diagnosis, have been noted in the psychiatric literature. For discussions of reliability and validity issues related to the DIS see, for example, Robins et al. (1981). Data collected in the present research help to clarify the validity of the DIS for use with drug-abuse samples.

The DIS was administered by trained research assistants to a subsample (N ≈ 350) of admissions to obtain DSM-III diagnoses. The interviewing was conducted between December 1984 and mid-1987.

Sample

Data were collected on a sample of admissions to the long-term residential urban TC described in Study 1. Admissions (N = 358–368) were ran-

---

2. Proportionately more females were interviewed to develop a large enough sample to permit statements about diagnostic distributions and to allow statistical comparisons.

TABLE 25.5

Current and Lifetime Diagnoses

	Lifetime Diagnoses		Current Diagnoses	
	Num.	%	Num.	%
Any Diagnosis	349	97.21	286	79.67
Substance Only	53	14.76	121	33.70
Psychiatric Only	15	4.18	44	12.26
Substance and Psychiatric	281	78.27	121	33.70

Note:
$N = 359$

domly selected. The sample differed from the usual residential population in that it contained a higher proportion of females[2] and fewer clients under 19 years of age (the DIS is recommended for individuals 18 years or older).

Results

The incidence of disorders among long-term residential admissions was first examined in terms of whether individuals obtained a substance abuse/dependence diagnosis only,[3] a psychiatric (nonsubstance) diagnosis only, or both a psychiatric and substance diagnosis. Over 95% of the sample received at least one diagnosis in their lifetime, and among this group, 78% obtained a psychiatric diagnosis in addition to drug abuse/dependence at some time in their life. Thus, less than 20% of the sample were diagnosed with a substance abuse/dependence disorder only, and almost half the sample received more than two diagnoses (see Table 25.5).

Recency of psychiatric disorder was assessed and, as expected, not all individuals who are symptomatic at some time in their life are symptomatic in the month just prior to treatment. Notably, however, almost 80%

3. Unless indicated, the term "substance" refers to all drugs, including alcohol. In DSM-III (APA 1980), abuse and dependence are distinguished for opioids, marijuana, barbiturates, amphetamines, and alcohol. These criteria do not apply for cocaine and hallucinogens. The abuse and dependence distinctions have been substantially modified in DSM-III-R (APA 1987).

received a diagnosis proximal to treatment, and 45% obtained a psychiatric (nondrug) diagnosis alone or in combination with a substance abuse/dependence disorder (Table 25.5). Thus, almost half of the individuals entering treatment for substance abuse problems also manifested other psychiatric symptomatology severe enough to yield DSM-III diagnoses. There were no differences among demographic and primary drug of abuse groups in the prevalence rates of psychiatric and substance disorders, lifetime and current.

The distribution of separate lifetime DSM-III disorders is shown in Table 25.6. The most commonly occurring nonsubstance diagnoses are, in order of frequency: Antisocial Personality, Psychosexual Dysfunction, Generalized Anxiety, Phobias, Dysthymic Disorder, and Major Depression. The distribution of substance disorders reflects the self-reported primary drug groupings.

Differences by demography and primary drug of abuse (not shown): A number of differences were obtained between males and females. Proportionately more females had Major Depressive Disorder, phobic disorders and Psychosexual Dysfunction, while more males were diagnosed with Antisocial Personality. Also, males more often had alcohol, barbiturate, opioid, or marijuana diagnoses.

There were no ethnic differences on any of the psychiatric disorders; however, all of the drug disorders except Cocaine Abuse yielded different prevalence rates for blacks and non-blacks. Non-blacks, compared with blacks, revealed a significantly higher incidence of use of all drugs other than cocaine.

Among the primary drug groups, heroin abusers had a higher incidence of phobic disorders. The distribution of drug disorders indicates that the majority of the sample included frequent users of more than one drug. There were a number of differences in the distribution of the drug disorders among the primary drug groups. Clients who stated cocaine to be their primary drug of use revealed a generally lower incidence of other drug use. Of those who claimed that marijuana was their main drug, a greater proportion obtained a diagnosis of Cocaine Abuse (79%), rather than Marijuana Abuse or Dependence (55%). Primary opiate/heroin abusers had the greatest incidence of barbiturate or amphetamine disorders.

Comparison with other modalities

The samples from the short-term residential and outpatient modalities were not randomly drawn, but no sources of bias were evident. DIS interviews were carried out regularly, almost daily, for approximately nine

TABLE 25.6

**Distribution of DSM-III Diagnoses among Admissions
to Residential Drug Treatment**

Diagnosis	Number	Percent
Organic Brain Syndrome		
Definitely Mild ·	9	2.51
Could be severe, mild, or absent	5	1.39
Affective Disorders		
Manic Episode	7	1.96
Major Depression	43	12.32
Dysthymia	59	16.91
Bipolar Disorder	1	0.28
Atypical Bipolar Disorder	8	2.29
Schizophrenic Disorders		
Schizophrenia	9	2.51
Schizophreniform	0	0.00
Anxiety Disorders		
Obsessive Compulsive Disorder	19	5.32
Phobic Disorders	99	27.73
Agoraphobia	57	15.97
Simple Phobia	55	15.41
Social Phobia	38	10.64
Panic Disorder	9	2.51
Generalized Anxiety	107	34.19
Other		
Antisocial Personality	156	44.07
Somatization Disorder	0	0.00
Anorexia	0	0.00
Pathological Gambling	22	6.20
Psychosexual Dysfunction	141	39.83
Bulimia	1	0.31
Posttraumatic Stress	25	10.59
Ego-dystonic Homosexuality	5	2.14
Transsexualism	1	0.77
Substance Abuse/Dependence Disorders		
Alcohol	141	39.28
Abuse	45	12.53
Dependence	13	3.62
Abuse and Dependence	83	23.12
Barbiturates	51	14.21
Abuse	4	1.11
Dependence	22	6.13
Abuse and Dependence	25	6.96

TABLE 25.6 (cont'd.)

Diagnosis	Number	Percent
Opioids (Heroin)	98	27.30
Abuse	3	0.84
Dependence	20	5.57
Abuse and Dependence	75	20.89
Cocaine Abuse	284	79.11
Amphetamines	36	10.03
Abuse	6	1.67
Dependence	16	4.46
Abuse and Dependence	14	3.90
Hallucinogen Abuse	32	8.91
Marijuana	143	39.83
Abuse	57	15.88
Dependence	34	9.47
Abuse and Dependence	52	14.48

Note:
$n = 349$ to 359 for all but the following diagnoses:
Generalized Anxiety, $n = 313$
Bulimia, $n = 320$
Posttraumatic Stress, $n = 236$
Ego-dystonic Homosexuality, $n = 234$
Transsexualism, $n = 130$

Cocaine and Hallucinogens: DSM-III has no Dependence diagnosis.

months. The sample size for the short-term (N = 88) and outpatient (N = 100) modalities constitutes more than 70% of admissions to those modalities during the data collection period. There were two samples of individuals who were not in treatment: nonadmissions (N = 96; those who were excluded from treatment); and pendings (N = 59; those awaiting admission or who did not return for a second evaluation). These constituted approximately 50% and 30% samples of the respective classification during the data collection period.

Results

As shown in Table 25.7, there were some differences in the demographic profiles of admissions to short-term residential and outpatient settings compared with long-term residential admissions, "pendings," and nonad-

TABLE 25.7

Demography by Modality of Treatment for the DIS Sample*

	Totals (N = 711) %	Non-Admits (N = 96) %	Pendings (N = 59) %	Outpatient (N = 88) %	Short-term Res. Tx (N = 100) %	Long-term Res. Tx (N = 368) %
Totals	100	13.5	8.3	12.4	14.1	51.7
Sex						
Males	68.3	63.5	83.0	83.3	92.0	57.1
Females	31.7	36.5	17.0	16.7	8.0	42.9
Ethnicity						
Black	53.8	54.2	55.2	40.9	41.4	60.0
Hispanic	13.0	15.6	12.1	12.5	10.1	13.4
White	32.2	29.2	32.7	44.3	48.5	25.5
Other	1.0	1.0	0.0	2.3	0.0	1.1
Age at Entry						
< 19yrs.	4.4	6.3	0.0	1.1	0.0	6.5
19, 20	12.0	16.7	10.2	10.0	5.1	13.4
21–26	37.5	43.8	42.4	20.0	31.3	41.0
> 26	46.1	33.2	47.4	68.9	63.6	39.1

* Primary drug is not shown here; see Table 25.6 for diagnoses of drug abuse/dependence.
Where there are missing data, percentages are based on total sample size excluding the missing cases.

missions. Among the former groups, there were proportionately more whites and the clients were older.

Over 93% of the clients across all groups had at least one diagnosis, and most (71.5%) obtained multiple diagnoses. Proportionately fewer outpatient clients yielded substance and psychiatric diagnoses (51%), followed by long-term residential admissions and pendings (70%–75%), short-term clients and nonadmissions (80%–83%; not shown).

Tables 25.8, 25.9, and 25.10 show the prevalence of all diagnoses. There are notable modality differences: (1) the outpatient groups show a lower proportion of phobias and antisocial personality disorders compared with short- and long-term residential modalities, as well as fewer diagnoses of drug abuse/dependence; (2) clients in short-term residential treatment had significantly higher proportions of alcohol and cocaine abuse even when compared with long-term residential clients; (3) long-term residential clients showed a higher prevalence of psychosexual dysfunction.

Among the nonadmissions, there is a significantly higher prevalence of most diagnoses. The range and severity of psychiatric disorder among the nonadmissions far exceeds that of the admissions. Of particular note is the prominence of Organic Brain Disorder (13%), Schizophrenia (18%), Major Depressive Disorder (27%), and other depressive disorders (18%).

STUDY 3: PSYCHIATRIC DISORDER AND RETENTION IN TREATMENT

Data taken from the sample of long-term admissions described in Study 2 were used for the third study. The effect of type and severity of psychiatric disorder on retention was examined among clients in long-term residential treatment. A major problem for residential drug treatment programs is that of retaining clients in treatment long enough to be helped. Recommended length of stay is 18 months to two years, and the highest rate of "dropout" (a term generic to the therapeutic community that refers to individuals who leave treatment against clinical advice) occurs within the first 30 days of treatment; 25–30% of all admissions have left after one month (see De Leon 1988, De Leon and Schwartz 1984).

The relationship between psychiatric status at admission and three months' retention was examined. The decision to identify three months' time in the program as a focus of study was based on several considerations. First, three months allows the individual enough time to interact with peers and staff and to participate in house activities, allowing proper

TABLE 25.8

DSM-III (Nonchemical) Diagnoses in Several Modalities

	Not in Treatment		Treatment Modalities			
Diagnosis	Non-Admissions (N = 96) %*	Pending (N = 59) %	Long-term Res. (N = 368) %	Short-term Res. (N = 100) %	Out-patient (N = 88) %	Total Tx (N = 556) %
Organic Brain Disorder	13.2	3.4	3.0	0.0	1.1	2.2
Mania	7.4	0.0	1.4	4.0	2.3	2.0
Major Depressive Disorder**	27.1	11.9	9.5	18.0	13.6	11.7
Dysthymia	5.2	3.4	11.1	9.0	8.0	10.2
Bipolar Disorder	5.3	0.0	0.3	2.0	1.1	0.7
Atypical Bipolar Disorder	7.3	3.4	1.6	3.0	0.0	1.6
Schizophrenia	17.9	0.0	2.2	0.0	0.0	1.4
Schizophreniform	1.1	0.0	0.0	1.0	0.0	0.2
Obsessive Compulsive Dis.	10.0	3.4	3.8	4.0	4.6	4.0
All Phobias	31.3	16.9	25.0	24.0	14.8	23.2
Somatization Disorder	2.1	0.0	0.0	0.0	0.0	0.0
Panic Disorder	1.1	0.0	0.8	3.0	2.3	1.4
Antisocial Personality	45.7	42.4	40.5	49.0	27.6	39.9
Anorexia Nervosa	0.0	0.0	0.0	1.0	0.0	0.2
Generalized Anxiety***	24.0	23.7	24.2	35.0	28.7	27.2
Posttraumatic Stress	19.8	14.3	10.5	17.0	9.8	11.7
Bulimia	2.2	0.0	0.3	1.0	1.1	0.6
Pathological Gambling	3.3	3.4	2.4	5.0	2.3	2.9
Psychosexual Dysfunction	41.8	25.4	32.9	14.0	12.6	26.3

*Percents are based upon full samples; however, clients may have multiple diagnoses.

**includes Depression: single episode and recurrent

***Total N for the long-term residential sample for Generalized Anxiety = 289; for Posttraumatic Stress Syndrome = 238; for Bulimia = 287.

TABLE 25.9

DSM-III (Chemical) Diagnoses in Several Modalities

	Not in Treatment		Treatment Modalities			
	Non-Admissions (N = 96)	Pending (N = 59)	Long-term Res (N = 368)	Short-term Res. (N = 100)	Out-patient (N = 88)	Total Tx (N = 556)
	%	%	%	%	%	%
*Drug Abuse/ Dependence Disorder**	85.4	88.2	82.1	90.0	73.5	82.0
Barbiturates	19.8	10.3	14.7	20.0	19.5	16.4
Opioids	30.2	24.1	27.4	40.0	21.8	28.8
Cocaine	72.0	76.3	77.7	81.0	64.4	76.1
Amphetamines	14.6	12.0	10.3	19.0	14.8	12.6
Hallucinogens	21.5	11.9	9.0	12.0	10.3	9.7
Cannabis	47.9	37.3	40.2	55.0	40.2	42.8
Alcohol	43.8	38.0	39.3	62.0	49.4	45.0
Tobacco	72.6	64.9	67.4	67.0	55.7	65.5

* Drug Abuse/Dependence Disorder does not include alcohol or tobacco, and includes abuse only, dependence only, and both abuse and dependence; the DSM-III classification excludes dependence for cocaine and hallucinogens.

TABLE 25.10

Statistical Summary: DSM-III Diagnoses in Several Modalities

Groups/Comparisons	X^2	
Non-Admits vs. Pending		
on Major Depressive Disorder	5.05*	NA >
on Psychosexual Dysfunction	4.21*	NA >
Non-Admits vs. Long-Term Residential		
on Schizophrenia	36.04***	NA >
on Major Depressive Disorder	20.59***	NA >
on Posttraumatic Stress	5.16*	NA >
Non-Admits vs. Short-Term Residential		
on Psychosexual Dysfunction	18.8***	NA >
Non-Admits vs. Outpatient		
on Major Depressive Disorder	5.07*	NA >
on Posttraumatic Stress	4.20*	NA >
Pending vs. Long-Term Residential	n.s.	
Pending vs. Short-Term Residential	n.s.	
Pending vs. Outpatient	n.s.	
Long-Term Residential vs. Short-Term Residential		
on Generalized Anxiety	4.38*	LT <
on Psychosexual Dysfunction	13.66***	LT >
on Alcohol Abuse/Dependence	16.69***	LT <
on Major Depressive Disorder	5.64*	LT <
Long-Term Residential vs. Outpatient	n.s.	
Short-Term Residential vs. Outpatient		
on Antisocial Personality	9.30**	ST >
on Drug Abuse/Dependence	9.43**	ST >

NA = Non-Admits; LT = Long-Term Residential; ST = Short-Term Residential;
> = more diagnoses; < = less diagnoses;
*p < .05
**p < .01
***p < .001

assessment by clinical staff. Second, three months is seen, clinically, as the first personal milestone.

Results

The study population was divided into two groups: those who remained in treatment less than three months ($n = 151$) and those who were in the program for at least three months ($n = 208$). There were no demographic or primary drug differences between the two groups.

The incidence of current and lifetime diagnoses for the two retention groups was examined. The distribution of type of diagnosis, lifetime (i.e., psychiatric, substance, substance and psychiatric), was significantly different between the two retention groups ($X^2 = 10.942[3]$; $p < .01$; not shown). Clients who remained in treatment less than three months more often had a psychiatric diagnosis only, while those in treatment for at least three months had a higher percentage with substance disorders only.

There is no difference in the distribution of type of psychiatric disorders between the two retention groups. However, there were some differences with respect to the substance disorders; those in treatment less than three months had a higher percentage diagnosed with a Marijuana disorder, and overall, more of the early dropouts obtained combined Abuse/Dependence diagnoses.

Six variables which assess severity of psychological disturbance across all of the psychiatric disorders were computed and compared between the two retention groups. (For further discussion of the statistical techniques utilized see Jainchill 1989). Differences were obtained on Number of Psychiatric Symptoms and Number of Lifetime Diagnoses: those in the longer term retention group yielded more psychiatric symptoms and a greater number of lifetime diagnoses (These two variables were also more highly correlated than the other items).

To more directly investigate whether those who remain in treatment less than three months can be differentiated from those who remain beyond three months, a discriminant analysis was performed. Fourteen variables assessing psychiatric status entered into the discriminant analysis. The selection of the variables was based on two criteria: the general meaningfulness of the item and the correlation of the item with the retention variable (group classification). A fuller description of procedures is provided in Jainchill (1989). Demographic and primary drug of abuse variables were partialed out. The standardized coefficients and the structure coefficients are contained in Table 25.11. The Wilks Lambda of

TABLE 25.11

Discriminant Analysis

Item	Structure Coefficient	Standardized Coefficient
Drug diagnosis only	.108	.604
Psychiatric diagnosis only	−.666	−.333
Psychiatric and Drug Diag.	.354	.540
Antisocial Pers. (DIS)	−.024	−.325
Depression Factor		.173
Childhood Antisocial Personality Factor	−.043	−.107
Adult Antisocial Personality Factor	.348	.466
Lifetime Diagnoses	.449	.381
Current Diagnoses	.320	.057
Drug/Alcohol Symptoms	−.011	−.261
Physical Symptoms	−.219	−.255
Symptoms–Medical Attention	.198	.137
Beck Depression	.291	.263
Short. Schizophrenia	.129	−.131

Note:

$n = 328$; missing data on Beck Depression and Shortened Schizophrenia scales.

9196 was significant, although its magnitude indicates that the two groups do not differentiate optimally on the measures (F [14,309, $n = 328$] $= 1.93, p < .05$). The structure coefficients were used to interpret the nature of the function and to identify the primary discriminators, since they are not affected by correlations among variables or by sample-specific variability. A greater number of lifetime diagnoses and Adult Antisocial Personality are positively associated with retention. However, psychiatric disturbance without an accompanying drug disorder (psychiatric diagnosis only) is negatively related to retention.

DISCUSSION

The results point to a worsening of the psychological profile among admissions to therapeutic community treatment, particularly among the most recent entries. The findings reveal that among admissions to traditional residential therapeutic community treatment, the majority obtain psychiatric diagnoses in addition to drug/alcohol abuse. This has been corroborated by an increase in behavioral indicators, for example, self-

reported incidence of suicide, psychiatric hospitalizations, and violent behaviors among admissions, to the TC over four consecutive years (1983–
1986; see De Leon 1988).

One hypothesis concerning the worsening trend is that it reflects the
"enculturation" of drug use in the last decade, the effect of which may
be evidenced in the psychological functions of substance abusers entering
treatment. Operationally, enculturation is evidenced by three facts: (1)
the spectrum of drug abusers has widened across all socioeconomic
classes; (2) the variety of drug use has increased; and (3) the age of
onset of regular use has steadily declined since 1974 (De Leon 1989).

The worsening psychological picture emerges from the direct effects
of drug use during the developmental years of early and middle adolescence; the indirect effects of problems of adjustment resulting from increased social dysfunction and confusion which accompany drug use;
and the pandemic nature of the enculturation process itself, whereby individuals who formerly would have been self-excluded from drug use
become a part of the experience.

The relationship between psychopathology and substance abuse contains implications for diagnosis and treatment. We must incorporate the
capability to better differentiate among individuals seeking treatment in
mental health and drug treatment settings. In particular, at least three
subgroups of substance abusers should be distinguished: (1) those whose
primary problem is substance abuse without accompanying psychopathology; (2) those whose primary problem is substance abuse with accompanying psychopathology; and (3) those whose primary problem is
psychopathology, but who also present difficulty with substance abuse.
Logically, there is a fourth category, those whose primary problem is
psychopathology but without accompanying substance abuse, but we are
less likely to see these individuals in residential drug treatment. The distinction between recent and historical symptomatology must also be clarified.

The third group, probably represented by the nonadmissions in Study
2, show a range and severity of psychiatric disorder which far exceeds
that of the admissions. This finding is not unexpected since a main ex-
clusionary criterion for the therapeutic community in the present study
is frank, clinical psychiatric disorder and/or history of serious psychiatric
disorder. These findings underscore the fact that a significant number of
substance abusers who appear for drug treatment present a picture of
severe psychiatric disorder in addition to their chemical abuse. Indications
are that these same clients cannot be managed in the existing mental
health treatment facilities. They appear to be the group that "falls between

the cracks" of the two systems, drug abuse treatment and mental health care.

Therapeutic communities, historically, have excluded the most severely psychiatrically impaired who seek admission. The appropriateness of the TC for the clients in the nonadmission group can be enhanced if it adapts its model and methodology while retaining its self-help perspective and community dynamic. However, TC workers must sharpen their diagnostic skills to assess the type, duration, and severity of psychopathological history. Some modification in treatment procedures may also be required, which could involve special staff training, changes in the maximum planned duration of stay, use of modified encounter groups, and so forth.

A better and more complete understanding of the relationship between retention and type of psychiatric disorder is also needed. Clients with a psychiatric diagnosis only tend to leave treatment within three months, supporting the idea that the traditional therapeutic community approach needs to be modified if such programs service individuals whose symptomatology is primarily psychiatric, but with accompanying substance use. Of particular note is that individuals with adult onset Antisocial Personality Disorder are more likely to remain at least three months, while those with childhood onset tend to leave early, suggesting at least two types of Antisocial Personality. This hypothesis is elaborated in a forthcoming paper by the authors.

New residential treatment models based upon an integration of concepts, staff and method from the drug treatments systems, particularly those developed in therapeutic communities, and mental health, are needed to serve the changing composition of substance abusers. Increased clarity as to the psychological types presenting for admission, both in drug treatment and mental health settings, will facilitate the adaptation of a treatment model which respects these differences, and which can retain the self-help perspective and community dynamic of the therapeutic community while incorporating needed modifications to treatment procedures.

REFERENCES

American Psychiatric Association. (1980). *Diagnostic and Statistical Manual of Mental Disorders* (3rd ed.). Washington, D.C.: Author.

———. (1987). *Diagnostic and Statistical Manual of Mental Disorders* (3rd ed. revised). Washington, D.C.: Author.

Beck, A. T., Ward, C. H., Mendelson, M., Mock, J., and Erbaugh, J. (1961). An inventory for measuring depression. *Arch. Gen. Psychiatry* 4, 561–571.

Bendig, A. W. (1956). The development of a short form of the Manifest Anxiety Scale. *J. Consulting Psychology* 20(5), 384.

Clark, J. H., and Danielson, J. R. (1956). A shortened schizophrenia scale for use in rapid screening. *J. Social Psychology* 43, 187–190.

De Leon, G. (1976). *Psychologic and socio-demographic profiles of addicts in the therapeutic community.* Final report of project activities. (NIDA Grant # DA-00831).

———. (1980). Therapeutic communities: Training self evaluation. Final report of project activities (NIDA Grant No. 1H81-DAO [1976]). Rockville, M.D.: National Institute of Drug Abuse.

———. (1984). *The therapeutic community: Study of effectiveness* (DHHS Publication No. (ADM)84-1286). Washington, D.C.: U.S. Government Printing Office.

———. (1988). *The therapeutic community: Enhancing retention in treatment.* Final report of project activities. (NIDA Grant # R01-DA03617). Rockville, M. D.: National Institute of Drug Abuse.

———. (1988). *Therapeutic communities: Psychopathology and Substance Abuse.* Final report of project activities. (NIDA Grant # R01-DA03860). Rockville, MD: National Institute on Drug Abuse.

———. (1989). Psychopathology and substance abuse: What is being learned from research in therapeutic communities. *J Psychoactive Drugs* 21(2), 177–88.

De Leon, G., and Jainchill, N. (1981–82). Male and female drug abusers: Social and psychological status two years after treatment in a therapeutic community. *Am. J. Drug. Alcohol Abuse* 8(4), 467–97.

De Leon, G., and Schwartz, S. (1984). The therapeutic community: What are the retention rates? *Am. J. Drug Alcohol Abuse* 10(2), 267–84.

Fitts, W. H. (1965). *Manual for the Tennessee Self-Concept Scale.* Counselor Recordings & Tests. Nashville, TN.

Jainchill, N. (1989). The relationship between psychiatric disorder, retention in treatment and client progress among admissions to a residential drug free modality. Ph.D. dissertation, New York University.

Myers, J. K., Weissman, M. M., Tischler, G. L., Holzer, C. E., Leaf, P. J., Orvaschel, H., Anthony, J. C., Boyd, J. H., Burke, J. D., Kramer, M., and Stoltzman, R. (1984). Six-month prevalence of psychiatric disorders in three communities. *Arch. Gen. Psychiatry* 41, 959–67.

Robins, L. N., and Helzer, J. E. (1985). *Diagnostic Interview Schedule (DIS), Version 3A.* St. Louis, MO: Dept. of Psychiatry, Washington University School of Medicine.

Robins, L. N., Helzer, J. E., Croughan, J., and Ratcliff, K. (1981). National Institute of Mental Health Diagnostic Interview Schedule. Its history, characteristics, and validity. *Arch. Gen. Psychiatry* 38, 381–89.

Simpson, D. D., and Sells, S. B. (1982). Effectiveness of treatment for drug abuse: An overview of the DARP research program. *Advances in Alcohol and Substance Abuse,* 2 (1), 7–29.

CHAPTER 26

Pharmacological Treatment of Opioid Dependency

Mary Jeanne Kreek

INTRODUCTION

It is now generally accepted in the United States that we need to improve existing pharmacological treatment programs and to develop new ones as well. We also need to combine pharmacological treatment with the best elements of drug-free treatment for those patients who have multiple drug dependencies. The Director of the National Institute on Alcoholism and Alcohol Abuse, Dr. Enoch Gordis, published an outstanding article in the NIAAA *Alcohol Alert* in the summer of 1988; there, he addresses the urgent need to combine methadone maintenance treatment with AA (Alcoholics Anonymous) groups and self-help treatment for alcoholism when these two addictive diseases are present concomitantly (Gordis 1988).

It has been estimated by various federal and state surveys that, in the United States, two million persons have used heroin at some time and approximately 500,000 are "hard-core" heroin addicts (defined as persons who use heroin multiple times daily for one year or more, with development of tolerance, physical dependence, and drug-seeking behavior) (Kreek 1987a). There are at least another half-million persons who use heroin on a regular basis, although they do not meet the criteria for "addiction" described. It has been estimated that there are 22 million persons who have used cocaine at some time in the United States (Kreek 1987a), and that some 6 million persons in the United States have used cocaine recently (approximately 800,000 now use cocaine regularly). Of these,

20% use cocaine by an intravenous route, in those regions where the freebase or so-called crack form of cocaine is not yet available. Apparently, cocaine is arriving in increasing amounts in the Scandinavian countries and along the Mediterranean coast of Europe, although the prevalence of cocaine use in Europe has not been determined. In Scandinavia, amphetamine abuse has been common for over 20 years. Amphetamines are increasingly used illicitly in the western part of the United States but this practice is not yet common in the East. Use of a freebase form of methamphetamine (so-called ice), is now becoming more common in Hawaii and on the West Coast. These figures can be compared and contrasted with the size of the alcohol abuse problem in the United States; about 6 million persons have a severe alcohol abuse problem (Kreek 1987a).

The National Institute of Drug Abuse sponsors the DAWN Network system, which collates data gathered from emergency rooms and from medical examiners regarding drug-related emergency room visits and deaths due to drug abuse. Recently, the numbers of persons coming into emergency rooms and those dying with a cocaine-induced problem have increased significantly. Alcohol in combination with other drugs has dropped to the second most common cause of drug-related emergency room visits and deaths from drug abuse. Heroin-induced problems and deaths are the third most common type (Kreek 1987a).

Opiate addiction begins with chronic opiate use, which is soon followed by the development of tolerance, that is, the need for ever-larger amounts of opiates to achieve the desired goal of the addict—euphoria, or that of the pain patient—analgesia. Physical dependence then develops, characterized by a well-defined group of physiological signs and symptoms upon abrupt withdrawal of the narcotic: the so-called abstinence syndrome. Protracted abstinence has been described and studied by many investigators and has been found to persist with measurable signs and symptoms for at least six months following cessation of regular heroin use. Persistent "drug hunger" is also a major problem, the biochemical basis of which has yet to be determined, just as does the biochemical basis of tolerance and physical dependence, both of which are clinically and experimentally well-established and accepted phenomena. This persistent drug-hunger contributes to the opiate addicts' reversion to opiate use.

EARLY EFFORTS

It is interesting to consider the first data collected from the U.S. Public Health Service facility for treatment of opiate addiction, at Lexington, Kentucky (Pescor 1943). From 1936, when Lexington first opened, to the end of 1940, around 4,700 males had been admitted to Lexington; most were prisoners sent there by the criminal justice system; some were volunteer patients, primarily health care personnel. All of these opiate addicts were treated with the best drug-free approaches available at that time, including group treatment and individual psychotherapy. When discharged persons were followed up from six months to five and a half years later, with a mean of around three years, less than 13% remained abstinent from opiate drugs (Pescor 1943). Pharmacological treatment was attempted in some cases, but there were at that time no pharmacological agents suitable for the treatment of opiate addiction. The only opiates available were short-acting opiates such as heroin, morphine and meperidine. Therefore, with the best drug-free treatment available, 13% of the opiate addicts treated at Lexington remained abstinent, 7% had died, and 40% had relapsed to use of opiate drugs; the status of 40% could not be completely determined, but were assumed either to have relapsed, died, or been incarcerated (Pescor 1943).

In 1964 I had the privilege of joining Professor Vincent Dole and the late Dr. Marie Nyswander at The Rockefeller University (then called the Rockefeller Institute for Biomedical Research), at the very beginning of the studies on possible pharmacological treatment for opiate addiction. At the time, Dr. Dole and I began our work by talking to addicted patients and visiting all the available treatment resources. Marie Nyswander was our mentor; she had worked at the USPHS Hospital in Lexington and at Bellevue Hospital in New York City for many years, as well as on the streets of inner-city New York. During our initial clinical research studies at The Rockefeller Hospital, we began to formulate concepts and hypotheses which are still valid today (Dole, Nyswander and Kreek 1966; Kreek 1987b). The research in my own laboratory in large part is based on addressing these and subsequently formulated, related hypotheses, not only with respect to opiate addiction but also to alcoholism and, more recently, cocaine dependency. We hypothesized that there is a metabolic basis for addiction and that this metabolic basis must be taken into account when one plans treatment approaches; at the same time, one must consider various social, psychological, and environmental factors. Genetic factors perhaps involving alleles of multiple genes which together control or modulate host responses to opiate effects or to the effects of any other addictive drugs, may be central to this metabolic basis of addiction, although it is unlikely that a single gene would lead to an "inborn error" of metabolism and thus cause addiction. Intersections between the pharmacology of the abused drug and the physiology of the individual exposed to the drug undoubtedly play a crucial role. If drug addiction were due to pharmacological actions alone, once the addictive drug was completely cleared from the body and successful rehabilitation had been achieved, one would not expect to see a relapse rate to opiate dependency of over 70%. This rate has been seen repeatedly in our American studies and in studies from other parts of the world, including the results concerning relapse to opiate addiction after drug-free treatment in the careful German studies presented in this book. Clearly, the variable outcomes will depend on multiple factors that alter host responses, in addition to genetic factors.

Multiple injections of heroin each day are needed for the heroin addict to achieve his or her desired goal: a "high" or euphoric state (Dole, Nyswander and Kreek 1966; Kreek 1987b). Later, with the development of increasing tolerance, the same number of injections may be needed just to prevent narcotic withdrawal symptoms. If no heroin is self-administered, there will be a rapid fall-off in the addicted person's blood levels and in the specific opiate receptor levels of the drug; opiate withdrawal symptoms will ensue that can be prevented or reversed only by readministration of the opiate drug.

METHADONE TREATMENT

Methadone, a synthetic organic compound, is now used worldwide for a variety of purposes, including for treatment of chronic pain. Heroin is a synthetic diacetylated compound derived from the natural opium alkaloid product morphine. Heroin, morphine and methadone bind equally well to the specific opioid receptors. However, when methadone, as compared to heroin, is given to patients who are tolerant and dependent on opioids, profound differences in both pharmacokinetics and pharmacodynamics take place. Heroin, like morphine, must be given intravenously to achieve full systemic bioavailability; the onset of action after intravenous administration of heroin is immediate. The duration of action and the pharmacodynamic effects of heroin persist for three to six hours. Euphoria (if in fact the degree of tolerance has been exceeded) will persist for one to two hours. Withdrawal symptoms will begin to occur after three to four hours. Methadone taken orally is effective, with 70% to 90% systemic bioavailability, after administration. The time to onset of action after oral administration is 30 minutes.

The duration of action of methadone is 24 to 36 hours. No euphoria is perceived by the tolerant patient if the dose is carefully selected for that individual to provide opiate action less than the degree of tolerance developed by that person. This last point is very important: individualized dose selection at the beginning of methadone maintenance treatment is essential. When a physician tries to treat pain with an opiate drug, the degree of tolerance developed by the individual must be exceeded by the amount of opiate administered; when a physician attempts to manage opiate addiction, the degree of tolerance developed by the individual must not be exceeded by the amount of methadone given at any one time. Over the first 4 to 8 weeks of methadone treatment, the dose of methadone should be slowly increased from the dose administered at the start of treatment (usually 20 to 40 mg/d) up to an adequate maintenance treatment dose (usually 60 to 100 mg/d) (Kreek, 1990a). If the increase in dosage is gradual, no euphoric effects will be perceived and no withdrawal symptoms will occur in most patients during the 24-hour oral dosing interval.

In our early 1964 clinical research studies at The Rockefeller Hospital, we maintained patients on 80 to 100 mg. each day; clinically, patients appeared to be stabilized, neither experiencing any narcotic effects after dose administration nor any narcotic withdrawal symptoms (Dole, Nyswander and Kreek 1966). At that time, there was no gas chromatographic or mass spectrometric technology sufficiently sensitive and specific to measure either morphine levels (the major metabolite of heroin) or methadone levels in human blood. Therefore, when we chose methadone as a potential treatment agent, we had to rely upon observations of clinical symptomatology in planning dosages. When we selected methadone as a drug for experimental use in the chronic maintenance treatment of opiate dependency, we wanted a drug that was orally effective and long acting clinically with respect to preventing opiate abstinence symptoms. The only opioid drug that seemed to meet these requirements clinically was methadone. Adverse effects, including respiratory depression, had been found by pain researchers where multiple doses of methadone had been administered daily to attempt to control acute postoperative pain. This finding provided a clinical clue that there was accumulation of methadone although the acute pain relief was very short lived. When we maintained former heroin addicts on methadone, after having increased the dose slowly to 80 to 100 mg., we saw neither a euphoric or narcotized state following the oral administration of methadone, nor did we observe symptoms of narcotic withdrawal (Dole, Nyswander and Kreek 1966).

We then performed a sequence of opiate cross-tolerance studies that followed a double-blind, random-order study design. When the code of the study was broken at the end of the sequence of studies, we found indeed that the patients could not perceive subjectively, nor could we measure objectively, any opiate-like effects of morphine, dihydromorphone, methadone or saline, each administered intravenously on separate days against a background of daily oral dosing with 80 to 100 mg. of methadone. When morphine was administered intravenously, a "pins and needles" sensation was perceived by the subjects, but then no high or euphoria ensued (Dole, Nyswander and Kreek 1966). The study subjects would ask, "Where is the high? It feels like morphine but I do not feel anything else, no rush, no sleepiness!" There was no such pins and needles sensation perceived after heroin administration. Additionally, no adverse reactions of any kind, including no respiratory depression, were observed when these short-acting opiates were administered acutely to methadone maintenance patients. We thus learned that the opiate tolerance developed during sustained high-dose methadone treatment would prevent any euphoria or other reinforcing opiate-like effects from being experienced, if heroin was used illicitly by methadone maintenance patients. Furthermore, no adverse or narcotic overdose effects would occur in that setting (Dole, Nyswander and Kreek 1966).

Several years later, when we had developed gas-liquid chromatographic and chemical-ionization mass spectrometric methods for measuring methadone and its metabolites in plasma, urine and feces, we found that the plasma level curve of methadone was essentially superimposable on the much earlier pharmacodynamic response curve drawn from clinical observations of our early methadone-maintained patients (Dole, Nyswander and Kreek 1966; Dole and Kreek 1973; Kreek 1973a; Kreek et al. 1976). When the opiate-dependent patient is maintained on 80 to 100 mg a day of methadone, relatively stable, sustained plasma levels of methadone persist over the 24-hour dosing interval (Dole and Kreek 1973; Kreek 1973a; Kreek et al. 1976; Hachey, Kreek and Mattson 1977; Kreek, Hachey and Klein 1979; Nakamura et al. 1982). The peak plasma levels of methadone occur 2 to 4 hours after an oral dose, and there is barely a doubling of plasma levels from the nadir or sustained levels. This plasma concentration time curve is sharply contrasted with the plasma concentration time curve for morphine or heroin, or that of any of the other short-acting narcotics administered to humans (Dole and Kreek 1973; Kreek 1973a; Kreek et al. 1976; Hachey, Kreek and Mattson 1977; Kreek, Hachey and Klein 1979; Nakamura et al. 1982).

HEROIN ADDICTS AND PREGNANCY

We have received numerous inquiries from Germany regarding the optimal management of pregnant heroin addicts. We have studied patients who entered methadone maintenance treatment prior to becoming pregnant and who then had a desired pregnancy. These patients were usually maintained on a steady dose of methadone throughout pregnancy. Throughout the pregnancy, repeated successive studies of plasma levels of methadone in the same pregnant females showed a successive lowering of levels at every time point studied; this finding was coupled with a decreased area under the plasma concentration time curve during the third trimester of pregnancy. The lowering of plasma levels of methadone is primarily due to the metabolic biotransformation of methadone by the placenta and the accelerated biotransformation of methadone by the liver because of the high levels of progestins which predominate during the third trimester of pregnancy. These progestins may enhance hepatic drug metabolism (Kreek 1979; Pond et al. 1985).

By these clinical research studies, we were able to obtain pharmacokinetic proof of what we had clinically seen and heard, that is, women's complaints of withdrawal symptoms during the third trimester of pregnancy. These pregnant methadone-maintained patients were not suffering from symptoms due to pregnancy per se, as was the usual formulation given by the medical staff; rather, they were suffering from narcotic withdrawal symptoms. We now know that it is imperative that doses of methadone not be reduced late in pregnancy. There have been no significant problems related to methadone maintenance treatment during pregnancy for the woman or the baby when no polydrug abuse and no alcohol had been present, other than modest symptoms of narcotic withdrawal in the neonate after the birth which, in some cases, required short-term management with an opiate compound such as paregoric for a brief period of time (Gordis and Kreek 1977; Finnegan et al. 1982; Kreek 1982; Kreek 1983a). However, there have been serious problems at delivery and during the postpartum period for both the mother and the baby when the pregnant women is a polydrug or alcohol abuser; thus it is imperative to provide concomitant treatment for drug abuse or other addictive problems (Kreek 1979a; Pond et al. 1985; Gordis and Kreek 1977; Finnegan et al. 1982; Kreek 1982; Kreek 1983a).

METHADONE MAINTENANCE

Heroin administered intravenously to humans has a plasma half-life of one to two hours; its major metabolite, morphine, has a half-life of four to six hours. Less than 30% of heroin (or morphine) is systematically bioavailable after oral administration. Methadone administered orally to humans has a 24-hour half-life for the racemic mixture, which is used clinically. (The racemic compound is the one synthesized that yields an equal amount of d- and l-enantiomers.) The half-life of the active l-enantiomer of methadone, measured by stable isotope studies in our laboratory, is around 48 hours (Hachey, Kreek and Mattson 1977; Kreek, Hachey and Klein 1979; Nakamara et al. 1982).

An adequate dose of methadone is essential to accomplish the goals of methadone maintenance treatment (Kreek 1987a; Dole, Nyswander and Kreek, 1966; Kreek, 1990a; Kreek 1973a; Dole 1988). In recent studies reported by Dr. John Ball of the NIDA intramural research program, six independent methadone maintenance clinics in different cities participated in an anonymous special data collection project. It was found that, in those patients for whom the daily dose of methadone was 5 to 50 mg per day, a high number supplemented their methadone dose with illicit heroin; when the daily dose of methadone was 60 to 100mg per day, less than 6% of the patients used illicit heroin, a finding very similar to those made by our Rockefeller University group and others in the 1960s and 1970s (Kreek 1987a; Kreek 1991; Dole 1988). In studies of methadone treatment during pregnancy, our group and others in Philadelphia, Detroit, San Francisco and New York found that, when the constant daily methadone dose was reduced to very low levels (less than 30mg. per day) during pregnancy and with good intentions on the part of the therapist, many women would use other drugs, including heroin, to self-medicate symptoms of drug hunger and opiate abstinence (Kreek 1979a; Pond et al. 1985; Gordis and Kreek 1977; Finnegan et al. 1982; Kreek 1982; Kreek 1983a).

REGULATIONS AND IMPLICATIONS

The first federal regulations concerning methadone maintenance in the United States were released in 1973. Before that time, methadone maintenance was conducted with local institutional, ethical and peer-review scrutiny in individual municipalities where treatment was ongoing. The first consecutive, unselected, maintenance patients admitted to methadone maintenance treatment in New York City from 1964 onward, prior to the first federal regulations, numbered 1,230. They were followed by the Columbia University School of Public Health (an independent evaluation group) for four to eight years after entry to treatment; 66% were retained in treatment voluntarily for that period of time (Kreek 1987a). After their discharge from methadone maintenance treatment, however, 80% of these patients relapsed to heroin use and addiction within two years or more.

Following the release of the first federal guidelines, the time of voluntary retention in treatment dropped sharply. Before the revision of the guidelines in the 1980s (and revocation of any suggested duration of methadone maintenance treatment), continued maintenance treatment for more than two years was officially discouraged. Today, the rate of voluntary retention in methadone maintenance treatment for more than two years after admission ranges from 45% to 80%, with good programs sharing the longest voluntary retention rates. In well-constituted programs, only 5% to 10% of the patients show any continuing heroin abuse after stabilization in methadone treatment for six months or more.

Important variables in addiction treatment programs are the quality and length of service of the clinical staff and medical administrative director. If we could measure the "good" factor or high quality factors of any clinical staff (including not only the directors, physicians and nurses, but all staff members), we would probably understand what constitutes a "good" treatment program. These "good" factors include indices which we have not yet learned how to quantify, but which pertain to humane care and the combination of both scientific and clinical knowledge.

PAIN MANAGEMENT DURING METHADONE MAINTENANCE

There are considerable misunderstandings concerning the effects of methadone, even among physicians. Methadone maintenance prevents opiate withdrawal symptoms and drug-hunger, and it blocks the euphoric effects of illicitly superimposed short-acting opiates (Dole, Nyswander and Kreek 1966; Kreek, 1991; Dole 1988). Methadone maintenance treatment does not, however, prevent a patient from having pain due to any etiology which causes pain in opiate-naive persons. A methadone-maintained patient feels pain just as does an opiate naive person. After patients are stabilized in methadone maintenance treatment, a short-acting narcotic must be given at doses and at dose intervals that will allow the analgesic drug to exceed the degree of opiate tolerance and cross-tolerance that has been developed by the methadone treatment, thus allowing pain relief. Short-acting opiate, analgesic drugs may be used at the upper limits of doses used in the narcotic-nontolerant persons; however, repeated doses may need to be given more frequently to exceed the degree of tolerance developed by the patient.

Doses of methadone should not be increased in an attempt to achieve analgesia; if this is done, the peak plasma levels of methadone will remain only modestly higher than original steady-state levels, and acute pain will not be relieved. The maintenance dose of methadone, however, should not be lowered in an attempt to decrease the degree of opiate tolerance;

such an attempt will not be successful in the short time during which analgesia is required.

METHADONE AND ADDICTION TREATMENT

Methadone is a long-acting narcotic that provides steady-state plasma levels and steady-state perfusion of opioid receptors, primarily at mu opiate receptor subtypes, so that normalization of many physiological functions disrupted by heroin abuse can occur. Alternative treatments for opiate addiction available in this country include opioid antagonist treatment; however, only around 15 to 20% of unselected heroin addicts do well in antagonist treatment. "Drug-free" treatment is effective in around 20 to 30% of heroin addicts. Accordingly, one of the biological questions we are now addressing is, "Are these heroin addicts who do well in drug-free treatment different in some way, biologically and/or psychologically, from the majority who revert to illicit opiate use"?

Methadone maintenance is successful in 45 to 80% of the heroin addicts so treated. However, the other addictive diseases and medical problems of the opiate addict who enters treatment of any of these types do not go away. Hepatitis B infection is chronic, as is delta-agent infection causing hepatitis. Alcohol and cocaine abuse remain chronic problems unless special measures are undertaken to manage these problems. HIV infection and AIDS are also chronic and relentlessly progressive; it has been suggested, however, (although data are not yet available) that the rate of progression form HIV infection to AIDS may be slowed by effective methadone maintenance treatment (Beverly et al. 1980; Cushman and Kreek 1974b; Des Jarlais 1989; Des Jarlais et al. 1984; Kreek 1973b, 1978, 1979. 1983b, 1984, 1988, 1989, 1990b; Kreek and Hartman 1983; Kreek et al. 1983, 1984, 1986, 1989, 1990; Novick et al. 1981, 1985, 1986; Novick, Khan and Kreek, 1986). Immunological abnormalities are present in over 75% of the heroin addicts, as well as altered neuroendocrine function, including abnormalities of the stress-responsive hypothalamic-pituitary-adrenal axis and the reproductive hormones of the hypothalamic-pituitary-gonadal system (Cushman and Kreek 1974a, 1974b; Des Jarlais et al. 1989, Hartman et al., 1983; Kreek 1973a, 1973b, 1979, 1988, 1989, 1990a, 1991, c; Kreek et al. 1972, 1983, 1991; Novick et al. 1981, 1985; Ochshorn 1989). Of great importance, with respect to general health is the fact that both immunological function and neuroendocrine function become normalized in long-term, steady-dose methadone maintenance patients (Cushman and Kreek 1974a,b, 1974b; Des Jarlais et al. 1989; Hartman et al. 1983; Kreek 1973a, 1973b, 1979b,

1987a, 1987b, 1988, 1989, 1990a, 1990c, 1991; Kreek et al., 1983, 1990; Novick et al. 1981; 1986; Ochshorn, 1989).

OPIATE ADDICTION AND STRESS

One of the working hypotheses of our research group is that opiate addiction, and possibly some components of other addictive diseases, are due to abnormal responses to stress, such as those to which we are all subjected; and, in part, these abnormal responses involve the endogenous opioid system. Acutely, opiates profoundly affect neuroendocrine function in humans; the directions of the effects are not identical to those in rodent models. In humans, acute opiate administration will cause inhibition of ACTH and beta-endorphin release, with resultant impaired release of cortisol and flattening of the normal circadian rhythm of hormone release. Inhibition of the release of LH, with resultant lower levels of testosterone, also occurs, along with increased release of vasopressin and prolactin. In the chronic methadone-maintained patient, normalization of each one of these neuroendocrine indicies occurs. However, responsiveness of prolactin release to peak levels of methadone persists, though without hyperprolactinimia or any prolactin levels beyond upper limits of normal; only partial tolerance or adaptation is therefore developed to this effect.

The hypothalamic-pituitary-adrenal axis is the major stress-responsive system in humans. Corticotropin-releasing factor from the hypothalamus causes processing and release of the proopiomelanocortin-derived (POMC) peptides, ACTH and beta endorphin. These peptide hormones circulate peripherally: ACTH acts on the adrenal cortex to effect cortisol production, which in turn exerts negative feedback control on peptide hormone release, acting both at the hypothalamus and at the anterior pituitary. Heroin addicts, while using heroin, have lower levels of release of beta endorphin and ACTH; the opposite pertains during acute narcotic withdrawal. Methadone-maintained patients have normal levels of beta endorphin and ACTH, and normal circadian rhythms of release of these hormones (Kreek et al. 1972; Kreek 1973b; Kreek 1973c; Cushman and Kreek 1974b; Novick et al. 1981; Hartman et al. 1983; Novick et al. 1985). In addition, the response to the chemically induced stress of the metyrapone test (a test of hypothalamic-pituitary reserve), is abnormal, with hyporesponsive release of peptide hormones in heroin addicts, yet it becomes normal in methadone-maintenance patients (Kreek 1973b; Kreek 1973c; Cushman and Kreek 1974b; Hartman et al. 1983; Kreek et al. 1983; Kreek 1990c).

When we have had the opportunity to study completely drug-free former heroin addicts or drug-free former methadone-maintained patients (a study which is still ongoing)—all of whom are former addicts who are not using alcohol and who do not have any ongoing polydrug abuse—we have observed a hyperresponsivity to the metyrapone provocative test. The metyrapone test is like a chemically induced stress in that it cuts off the normal negative feedback control by cortisol of hypothalamic and pituitary hormones; it thus causes in healthy subjects a modestly enhanced release of both ACTH and beta-endorphin (a normal stress response). This hyperresponsiveness to metyrapone observed in drug-free, formerly narcotic-dependent persons may be related to the frequent behavioral concomitant observed in such drug-free former heroin addicts, which is persistent drug hunger with resulting drug-seeking behavior. More than 70% of the drug-free former heroin addicts (or former methadone-treated patients, once medication-free) relapse to opiate addiction.

In long-term, steady-dose methadone-maintained patients, we have observed normalization of T cell numbers, T cell subsets, B cells, NK cells, and normal natural killer cell activity, all of which are disrupted during cycles of heroin addiction. This normalization may be due primarily to the patients' cessation of unsterile needle use, which results in their decreased exposure to diverse chemicals and diseases. It is now well known, however, that many of the elements of neuroendocrine function mentioned (the stress-related hormones cortisol, ACTH, and beta endorphin; androgens, estrogens and prolactin), all modulate immune function. The levels and release of these hormones are disrupted during cycles of heroin addiction. When neuroendocrine function becomes normalized during methadone maintenance treatment, that normalization may in turn contribute to the normalization of immune function (Des Jarlais et al. 1989; Kreek 1988; Kreek 1989; Kreek 1990b).

In 1984 we performed a study in which we reexamined patients who had been fortunate enough and/or motivated enough to get into methadone maintenance treatment prior to the AIDS epidemic (which reached New York City in 1978) and to remain in treatment. In that group we found that less than 10% were HIV positive at a time when, on the streets of New York, 50 to 60% of the intravenous drug abusers were HIV positive (Novick et al. 1988; Novick et al. 1989; Khuri et al. 1984; Des Jarlais et al. 1984).

These are compelling findings which I think we have to recognize and address as a worldwide public health issue (Novick et al. 1988; Novick et al. 1989; Khuri 1984; Des Jarlais et al. 1984; Kreek et al. 1986; Kennedy et al. 1990). We must work together and with our potential patients in order to solve the problems of worldwide drug abuse and the spread of AIDS.

ACKNOWLEDGMENTS

This work was supported in part by: the New York State Division of Substance Abuse Services; HHS-ADAMHA-NIDA Specialized Research Center Grant No. 1-P50-DA05130; Research Scientist Award (from HHS-ADAMHA-NIDA) to Dr. Kreek, No. DA-00049; the NIH-DRR grant for use of the PROPHET computer system at The Rockefeller University; the NIH-DRR grant to the Rockefeller University Hospital General Clinical Research Center, No. RR00102.

REFERENCES

Beverly, C. L., Kreek, M. J., Wells, A. O., and Curtis, J. L. (1980). Effects of alcohol abuse on progression of liver disease in methadone-maintained patients. In *Problems of Drug Dependence, 1979, Proceedings on the 41st Annual Scientific Meeting of the Committee on Problems of Drug Dependence*, L. S. Harris, (Ed.) *NIDA Research Monograph Series.*, Rockville, MD: DHHS Publication No. (ADM) 27:399–401.

Cushman, P., and Kreek, M. J. (1974a). Methadone-maintained patients. Effects of methadone on plasma testosterone, FSH, LH and prolactin. *N.Y. State Journal of Medicine* 74: 1970–73.

Cushman, P., and Kreek, M. J. (1974b). Some endocrinologic observations in narcotic addicts. In *Narcotic and the Hypothalamus*, E. Zimmerman and R. George, (eds.), New York: Raven Press, 161–73.

Des Jarlais, D. C., Friedman, S. R., Novick, D. M., Sotheran, J. L., Thomas, P., Yancovitz, S. R., Mildvan, D., Weber, J., Kreek, M. J. Maslansky, R., Bartelme, S., Spira, T., and Marmor, M. (1989). HIV I infection among intravenous drug users in Manhattan, New York City, 1977 to 1987. *Journal of the American Medical Association* 261:1008–12.

Des Jarlais, D. C., Marmor, M., Cohen, H., Yancovitz, S., Garber, J., Friedman, S., Kreek, M. J., Miescher, A., Khuri, E., Friedman, S. M., Rothenberg, R., Echenberg, D., O'Malley, P. O., Braff, E., Chin, J., Burtenol, P., and Sikes, R. K. (1984). Antibodies to a retrovirus etiologically associated with Acquired Immunodeficiency Syndrome (AIDS) in populations with increased incidences of the syndrome. *Morbidity and Mortality Weekly Report* 33:377–79.

Dole, V. P. (1988). Implications of methadone maintenance for theories of narcotic addiction. *Journal of the American Medical Association* 260:3025–29.

Dole, V. P. and Kreek, M. J. (1973). Methadone plasma level: Sustained by a reservoir of drug in tissue. *Proc. Natl. Acad. Sci.* 70:10.

Dole, V. P., Nyswander, M. E., and Kreek, M. J. (1966). Narcotic blockade. *Arch. Intern. Med.* 118:304–9.

Finnegan, L. P., Chappel, J. N., Kreek, M. J., Stimmel, B., and Stryker, J. (1982). Narcotic addiction in pregnancy. In *Drug Use in Pregnancy*, J. R. Niebyl, (ed.), Philadelphia, Pa.: Lea & Febiger, 163–84.

Gordis, E. (1988). Methadone maintenance and patients in alcoholism treatment. In *NIAAA Alcohol Alert* 1:1–4.

Gordis, E., and Kreek, M. J. (1977). Alcoholism and narcotic addiction in pregnancy. *Current Problems in Obstetrics and Gynecology* 1:1–48.

Hachey, D. L., Kreek, M. J., and Mattson, D. H. (1977). Quantitative analysis of methadone in biological fluids using deuteriumlabeled methadone and GLC-chemical-ionization mass spectrometry. *J. Pharm. Sci.* 66:1579–82.

Hartman, N., Kreek, M. J., Ross, A., Khuri, E., Millman, R. B., and Rodriguez, R. (1983). Alcohol use in youthful methadone-maintained former heroin addicts: Liver impairment and treatment outcome. *Alcoholism: Clin. and Expt. Res.* 7:316–20.

Kennedy, J. A., Hartman, N., Sbriglio, R., Khuri, E., and Kreek, M. J. (1990). Metyrapone-induced withdrawal symptoms. *Brit. J. Addict.* 85: 1133–40.

Khuri, E. T., Millman, R. B., Hartman, N., and Kreek, M. J. (1984). Clinical issues concerning alcoholic youthful narcotic abusers. *Advances in Alcohol & Substance Abuse* 3:69–86. New York: The Haworth Press.

Kosten, T. R., Kreek, M. J., Swift, C., Carney M. K., and Ferdinands, L. (1987). Beta-endorphin levels in CSF during methadone maintenance. *Life Sciences* 41:1071–76.

Kreek, M. J. (1973a). Plasma and urine levels of methadone. *N.Y. State J. Med.* 73:2773–77.

Kreek, M. J. (1973b). Medical safety and side effects of methadone in tolerant individuals. *J. Amer. Med. Assn.* 223:665–68.

Kreek, M. J. (1973c). Physiological implications of methadone treatment. *Proceedings of the Fifth National Conference of Methadone Treatment.* NAPAN II-NIMH, 824–838.

Kreek, M. J. (1978). Medical complications in methadone patients. *Ann. N.Y. Acad. Sci.* 311:110–34.

Kreek, M. J. (1979a). Methadone disposition during the perinatal period in humans. *Pharmac. Biochem. Behav.* 11, Suppl.:7–13.

Kreek, M. J. (1979b). Methadone in treatment: Physiological and pharmacological issues. In *Handbook on Drug Abuse*, R. L. Dupont, A. Goldstein and J. O'Connell, (eds.), NIDA-ADAMHA-DEW-ODAP-Executive Office of the President, 57–86.

Kreek, M. J. (1982). Opioid disposition and effects during chronic exposure in the perinatal period in man. In *Advances in Alcohol and Substance Abuse*, 1:21–53. B. Stimmel, (ed.), New York: The Haworth Press, Inc.

Kreek, M. J. (1983a). Discussion of clinical perinatal and developmental effects of methadone. In *Research in the Treatment of Narcotic Addiction: State of the Art*, J. R. Cooper, F. Altman, B. S. Brown, and D. Czechowicz, (eds.), National Institutes of Drug Abuse Monograph, DHHS Pub. no. (ADM) 83-1281, 444–453.

Kreek, M. J. (1983b). Health consequences associated with use of methadone: Acute and chronic effects. In *Research in the Treatment of Narcotic Addiction: State of the Art*, J. R. Cooper, F. Altman, B. S. Brown, and D. Czechowicz, (eds.), National Institutes of Drug Abuse Monograph, DHHS Pub. no. (ADM) 83-1281, 456–482.

Kreek, M. J. (1984). Opioid interactions with alcohol. *Advances in Alcohol & Substance Abuse* 3:35–46. New York, NY: The Haworth Press.

Kreek, M. J. (1987a). Multiple drug abuse patterns and medical consequences. In *Psychopharmacology: The Third Generation of Progress*. H. Y. Meltzer, (ed.), 1597–1604 New York: Raven Press.

Kreek, M. J. (1987b). Tolerance and Dependence—Implications for the pharmacological treatment of addiction. In *Problems of Drug Dependence, 1986; Proceedings of the 48th Annual Scientific Meeting of The Committee on Problems of Drug Dependence*, L. S. Harris, (ed.), 76:53–61. *NIDA Research Monograph Series*, Rockville, Md.: DHHS Publication no. (ADM) 87-1508.

Kreek, M. J. (1988). Opiate-ethanol interactions: Implications for the biological basis and treatment of combined addictive diseases. In *Problems of Drug Dependence, 1987; Proceedings of the 49th Annual Scientific Meeting of the Committee on Problems of Drug Dependence*. L. S. Harris, (ed.), 81:428–39. *NIDA Research Monograph Series*, Rockville, Md.: DHHS Publication No. (ADM) 88-1564.

Kreek, M. J. (1989). Immunological approaches to clinical issues in drug abuse. In *Problems of Drug Dependence, 1988; Proceedings of the 50th Annual Scientific Meeting of the Committee on Problems of Drug Dependence*. L. S. Harris, (ed.), 90:77–86. *NIDA Research Monograph Series*, Rockville, MD DHHS Publication No. (ADM)89-1605.

Kreek, M. J. (1990a). Drug interactions in humans related to drug abuse and its treatment. *Modern Methods in Pharmacology* 6: 265–82.

Kreek, M. J. (1990b). Immune function in heroin addicts and former heroin addicts in treatment: pre/post AIDS epidemic. In *Current Chemical and Pharmacological Advances on Drugs of Abuse Which Alter Immune Function and Their Impact upon HIV Infection*, Pham, P. T. K., and Rice, K. (Eds.), 96:192–219. *NIDA Research Monograph Series*, Rockville, MD.

Kreek, M. J. (1990c). Methadone maintenance treatment for heroin addiction. In *The Effectiveness of Drug Abuse Treatment*, Platt, J. J., Kaplin, and C., McKim, P. (eds.). 275–93 Melbourne, FL: Krieger.

Kreek, M. J. (1990d). HIV infection and parenteral drug abuse: Ethical issues in diagnosis, treatment, research and the maintenance of confidentiality. In *Proceedings of the Third International Congress on Ethics in Medicine—*

Nobel Conference Series, P. Allebeck, B. Jansson, (eds.). 181–87 New York: Raven Press.

Kreek, M. J. (1991). Using methadone effectively: Achieving goals by application of laboratory, clinical, and evaluation research and by development of innovative programs. In *Improving Drug Abuse Treatment*, Pickens, R., Leukefeld, C., Schuster, R. (eds.), 245–66 *NIDA Research Monograph Series* Rockville, MD.

Kreek, M. J., Des Jarlais, D. C., Trepo, C. L., Novick, D. M., Abdul-Quader, A., Raghunath, J. (1990). Contrasting prevalence of delta hepatitis markers in parenteral drug abusers with and without AIDS. *J Infect Dis* 162: 538–41.

Kreek, M. J., Dodes, L., Kane, S., Knobler, J., and Martin, R. (1972). Long-term methadone maintenance therapy: Effects on liver function. *Annals of Internal Medicine*, 77: 598–602.

Kreek, M. J., Gutjahr, C. L., Garfield, J. W., Bowen, D. V., and Field, F. H. (1976). Drug interactions with methadone. *Annals of the N.Y. Academy of Sciences* 281: 350–70.

Kreek, M. J., Hachey, D. L., and Klein, P. D. (1979). Stereoselective disposition of methadone in man. *Life Sciences* 24: 925–32.

Kreek, M. J., and Hartman, N. (1982). Chronic use of opioids and antipsychotic drugs: Side effects, effects on endogenous opioids and toxicity. *Annals of New York Academy of Science*, 398: 151–72.

Kreek, M. J., Khuri, E., Fahey, L., Miescher, A., Arns, P., Spagnoli, D., Craig, J., Millman, R., and Harte, E. (1986). Long term follow-up studies of the medical status of adolescent former heroin addicts in chronic methadone maintenance treatment: Liver disease and immune status. In *Problems of Drug Dependence, 1985; Proceedings of the 47th Annual Scientific Meeting of The Committee on Problem of Drug Dependence*, Harris, L. S., (ed.), 67:307–09, *NIDA Research Monograph Series* Rockville, MD. DHHS Publication No. (ADM) 86-1448.

Kreek, M. J., Khuri, E., Flomenberg, N., Albeck, H., and Ochshorn, M. (1989). Immune status of unselected methadone maintained former heroin addicts. In *International Narcotics Research Conference 1989 (INRC)*, Quirion, R., Jhamandas, K., Gianoulakis, C. (eds.), 445–48. New York: Alan R. Liss. 1989.

Kreek, M. J., Raghunath, J., Plevy, S., Hamer, D., Schneider, B., and Hartman, N. (1984). ACTH, Cortisol and beta-endorphin response to metyrapone testing during chronic methadone maintenance treatment in humans. *Neuropeptides* 5: 277–78.

Kreek, M. J., Wardlaw, S. L., Hartman, N. Raghunath, J., Friedman, J., Schneider, B., and Frantz, A. G. (1983). Circadian rhythms and levels of beta-endorphin, ACTH, and cortisol during chronic methadone maintenance treatment in humans. *Life Sciences*, Sup. I, 33: 409–11.

Nakamura, K., Hachey, D. L., Kreek, M. J., Irving, C. S., and Klein, P. D. (1982). Quantitation of methadone enantiomers in humans using stable isotope-labeled $^2H_3$, $^2H_5$, $^2H_8$ methadone. *J. Pharm. Sci.* 71: 39–43.

Novick, D. M., Des Jarlais, D. C., Kreek, M. J., Spira, T. J., Friedman, S. R., Gelb, A. M., Stenger, R. J., Schable, C. A., and Kalyanaraman, V. S. (1988). The specificity of antibody tests for human immunodeficiency virus in alcohol and parenteral drug abusers with chronic liver disease. *Alcoholism: Clinical and Experimental Research* 12: 687–90.

Novick, D. M., Enlow, R. W., Gelb, A. M., Stenger, R. J., Fotino, M., Winter, J. W., Yancovitz, S. R., Schoenberg, M. D., and Kreek, M. J. (1985). Hepatic cirrhosis in young adults: Association with adolescent onset of alcohol and parenteral heroin abuse. *Gut* 26: 8–13.

Novick, D. M., Farci, P., Croxson, S. T., Taylor, M. B., Schneebaum, C. W., Lai, E. M., Bach, N., Senie, R. T., Gelb, A. M., and Kreek, M. J. (1988). Hepatitis delta virus and human immunodeficiency virus antibodies in parenteral drug abusers who are hepatitis B surface antigen positive. *Journal of Infectious Diseases* 158: 795–803.

Novick, D. M., Farci, P., Karayiannis, P., Gelb, A. M., Stenger, R. J., Kreek, M. J., and Thomas, H. C. (1985). Hepatitis D virus antibody in HBsAg-positive and HBsAg-negative substance abusers with chronic liver disease. *Journal of Medical Virol.* 15: 351–56.

Novick, D. M., Gelb, A. M., Stenger, R. J., Yancovitz, S. R., Adelsberg, B., Chateau, F., and Kreek, M. J. (1981). Hepatitis B serologic studies in narcotic uses with chronic liver diseases. *American Journal of Gastroenterology* 75: 111–15.

Novick, D. M., Khan, I., and Kreek, M. J. (1986). Acquired immunodeficiency syndrome and infection with hepatitis viruses in individuals abusing drugs by injection. *United Nations Bulletin on Narcotics* 38: 15–25.

Novick, D., Kreek, M. J., Des Jarlais, D., Spira, T. J., Khuri, E. T., Raghunath, J., Kalyanaraman, V. S., Gelb, A. M., and Miescher, A. (1986). Antibody to LAV, the putative agent of AIDS, in parenteral drug abusers and methadone-maintained patients: Abstract of clinical research findings: Therapeutic, historical, and ethical aspects. In *Problems of Drug Dependence, 1985; Proceedings of the 47th Annual Scientific Meeting of The Committee on Problems of Drug Dependence*, Harris, L. S., (ed.), 67: 318–20. *NIDA Research Monograph Series.*, Rockville, MD. DHHS Publication No. (ADM)86-1448.

Novick, D. M., Ochshorn, M., Ghali, V., Croxson, T. S., Mercer, W. D., Chiorazzi, N., and Kreek, M. J. (1989). Natural killer cell activity and lymphocyte subsets in parenteral heroin abusers and long-term methadone maintenance patients. *Journal of Pharm Exper Ther.* 250: 606–10.

Novick, D. M., Trigg, H. L., Des Jarlais, D. C., Friedman, S. R., Vlahov, D., and Kreek, M. J. (1989). Cocaine injection and ethnicity in parenteral drug users during the early years of the human immunodeficiency virus (HIV) epidemic in New York City. *Journal of Medical Virol.* 29: 181–85.

Ochshorn, M., Kreek, M. J., Khuri, E., Fahey, L., Craig, J., Aldana, M. C., and Albeck, H. (1989). Normal and abnormal Natural Killer (NK) activity in methadone maintenance treatment patients. In *Problems of Drug Depen-*

dence, 1988; Proceedings of the 50th Annual Scientific Meeting of the Committee on Problems of Drug Dependence, Harris, L. S. (ed.), 90:369. *NIDA Research Monograph Series,* Rockville, MD. DHHS Publication No. (ADM) 89-1605.

Pescor, M. J. (1943). Follow-up study of treated narcotic drug addicts. *United States Public Health Rep* Suppl 170.

Pond, S. M., Kreek, M. J., Tong, T. G., Raghunath, J., and Benowitz, N. L. (1985). Altered methadone pharmacokinetics in methadone-maintained pregnant women. *Journal of Pharm. & Exper. Ther.* 233: 1–6.

PART SEVEN

Drug Abuse, Delinquency, and Compulsory Treatment

Drugs and Delinquency: Some Results of a Current Self-Report Study of University Students and of Recent In-Depth Interviews with Drug Addicts

Arthur Kreuzer, Ruth Römer-Klees, and Hans Schneider

INTRODUCTION

Several studies relating to drug problems on a criminological-empirical basis have been carried out since 1970 (Kreuzer 1972–1990). Above all the following issues have come to the fore: the increase in use or abuse of legal and illegal drugs; reflections on both the structure and the development of the drug scene from a subcultural point of view; structural differences between detected and hidden delinquency; the influence on drug use and delinquency exercised by styles of control and drug policy; the relationship between drug careers and delinquency careers; and the complex relationship between drug use, drug addiction, and delinquency and their implications for law enforcement, treatment and rehabilitation.

Two courses of methodology were used: in the first, anonymous quantitative self-report studies were carried out by means of representatively selected samples of young people (pupils from all branches of the educational system, see Kreuzer 1975, 1975a) as well as from specific groups (e.g., soldiers likely to perform military service, Kreuzer 1980);

freshmen at Giessen University (Kreuzer 1980, 1986, 1988; Kreuzer et al. 1990, 1990a). The second method employed qualitatively and biographically orientated in-depth interviews with drug addicts (Kreuzer 1974, 1975, 1987; Kreuzer et al. 1982, 1988, 1991). There are methodical as well as practical reasons for this dual approach of research: Data collection by questionnaires carried out anonymously in large samples is feasible only within the normal population. Information about drug addicts is more effectively collected by detailed interviews of single cases. The combination of quantitative and qualitative data completes and corrects the existing knowledge. Our studies can, for instance, correct the theory according to which hashish is the gateway drug for heroin addiction, whether shoplifting marks a crook's entry into a career of crime, and if the wearing of masks and disguises at demonstrations marks the first step toward terrorism. Observations made in connection with extreme groups cannot easily be transferred to normal populations; for example, almost every heroin addict began with hashish, but prior to that had abused alcohol and nicotine; in contrast, only a small portion of those experienced in using hashish switch to hard drugs and hard use, but still show other psycho-sociological disorders.

SOME FINDINGS IN THE RECENT SELF-REPORT STUDY

Method

This year the annual interviewing on delinquency conducted with students in the first semester at Giessen University has been considerably varied and improved in both method and substance (Kreuzer et al. 1990, 1990a). The study was primarily intended to investigate the differences between the sexes in regard to experience, perception and processing of life events and developmental disturbances. The hypothetical framework was as follows: Women experience emotional disturbances within the immediate social sphere with more intensity; they process these disturbances in a strong internally oriented manner (symptoms which may become apparent in abuse of pills, suicidal tendencies, psychical disturbances, retreat and anorexia). Men, however, process disturbances in a more intensely outward oriented fashion (for instance in peer groups, by acts of violence and illegal conduct or by abuse of alcohol and drug abuse).

Thus far, in these studies, law students and economics students had been interviewed, but in 1988/89 the students of all faculties were given a questionnaire at the beginning of their studies. Whereas, in the past, the students had been interviewed in groups during lectures by means of standardized questionnaires, this time we gave preference to the anonymity of individual questioning by mail. When interviewed by questionnaire in groups, the participation amounted to nearly 100%. Interviews by mail resulted in about 60% participation which can be considered a comparatively good response. Of the 1,640 questionnaires, 938 were filled out by female and 694 by male students and they were evaluated together.

The sociodemographic data of these two comparable subgroups were almost identical. However, the average age of the male participants was 21.5 years and was thus one year older than the females. The reason for this is that most of the males had already performed their military or alternative service before enrolling in classes. The higher number of females is primarily because there were more female freshmen that year. As expected, the number of females willing to participate in the interview was also slightly higher. Possible explanations for this tendency might be that women have a greater tendency to reflect on themselves, that they were more open to this specific type of questioning, or that they were more conscientious about questioning by mail. Among the economists, one group of 150 students had been questioned in groups first, whereas the others were interviewed by mail. By this means a methodical problem, which hitherto has never been sufficiently investigated, can be examined: whether those questions that are more troublesome will be answered in a somewhat more reserved way due to the influence of social contacts inside the group as opposed to the situation of being unobserved when interviewed individually. Early findings imply that both the willingness to answer and the reliability of the statements are not reduced by the group situation (Kreuzer et al., 1990b). There are no significant discrepancies between the comparable groups (questioned in groups or individually by mail) as far as delinquent behavior and the consumption of drugs or attitudes toward, for example, the death penalty or life events, are concerned. Only the values gathered from the information on former criminal arrests seem to have decreased slightly in group questioning; this issue seems to be affected adversely by the social rapport within the group.

Juvenile Delinquency in the Sense of "Normality" and "Ubiquity"

As is well known there are comparatively trivial criminal offenses mentioned in the self-reports of the normal population. The more serious offenses, however, can hardly be questioned this way. Yet a greater number can be found in the official record of delinquency. Furthermore, one must consider that students who belong to the middle class show less

TABLE 27.1

Self-Reported Delinquency among Students (freshmen, age approx. 20 years)
at Giessen University in 1988/89 (life-time experience, round figure percentage
terms)

Self-reported behavior (examples)	male (N = 694)	female (N = 938)
Traveling without ticket	78%	74%
Driving without licence	51%	41%
Any theft	86%	75%
Shoplifting	45%	36%
Vandalism	30%	9%
Having beaten someone	36%	12%
Having been drunk	85%	61%
Having been drunk under age fourteen	11%	2%
Having been drunk within the past two months	40%	18%
Having been drunk within the past two months more than five times	5%	1%
Driving while intoxicated	62%	30%
Having obtained an offer to use illegal drugs	58%	44%
Having used illegal drugs	26%	20%
Current drug use	7%	4%
Having delivered illegal drugs	7%	3%

delinquency overall; yet they probably will admit delinquency more
frankly and define it on a larger scale, hence reporting petty offenses
sooner than do, for instance, prison inmates (the latter associating major
events with corresponding questions only).

To illustrate the results of the latest interviews, some patterns of delinquency relating to the subjects' "general delinquency" and "use of
alcohol and illegal drugs" will be reported in Table 27.1.

Apart from a decrease in the abuse of alcohol there are no significant
changes found in the long run. As for some offenses, the data concerning
women are drawing close to those of men. In any case women are involved to a lesser degree, particularly in regard to more serious offenses
linked with aggression and in categories of frequency. Alcohol use is on
the decrease, but is still linked to "masculinity": whereas smoking can
be said to be distributed about equally between the sexes. The interview
confirms that the majority of young people commit offenses occasionally,
that committing offenses is a normal occurrence within every social class
and in all regions; and such offenses decrease after adolescence (in general see, e.g., Kaiser 1988, pp. 341, 356, 499). One can conclude from
these results that there is no need for drastic penalties in order to prevent

long-term criminal activities. In this respect even the estimated number of unreported cases gives no cause for worry. For instance only 5.4% of all male and female students who have shoplifted faced public prosecution; only about 1% of the shopliftings reported had been discovered; and from the students experienced in narcotic drugs only 3% of the males and 2% of the females had been picked up by police.

Addiction, Escape, and Delinquency Symptoms

If we report here on correlations between certain forms of socially deviant behavior, we will, of course, not show exclusive connections nor necessarily causal connections. Such correlations which appear in a small number of the test sample as syndromes can be shown with the help of Table 27.2:

1. We notice a cumulative usage of different drugs, here represented by data for the use of alcohol, nicotine, illegal drugs and pharmaceutical drugs. This might indicate on the one hand a nonspecific drug affinity that might be part of the personality and a result of early socialization. On the other hand, youthful traits, love of experimentation, and taking risks as well as conforming to behavior patterns of peer groups might play a part. Among other factors, early use of alcohol and nicotine proves to have initiative functions for later experimentation with illegal drugs. (Table 27.3).

2. Strong correlations between drug use and forms of escapism could be established. For operationalization, we used symptoms of such attitudes: serious consideration of suicide, frequent instances of truancy, early absenteeism at night. For a small number within the sample this can be understood not only as sporadic episodes, but also as a consistent behavior pattern—as one form of dealing with life.

3. Close connections become apparent between the intensity of alcohol consumption and experience with illegal drugs on the one hand, and delinquency on the other. The intensity of delinquency was measured according to the frequency and severity of a selection of self-reported offenses for each person tested. According to the results of the measurement, the total sample was divided into three groups of intensity. The correlation was confirmed by both the self-reported delinquency and delinquency recorded by the police. In this context it is noteworthy that police arrests following offenses are correlated primarily with the frequency and severity of the actual (meaning, in this context, self-reported) delinquency. This ought to be noted as a further contribution toward weakening the more extreme "labeling approach." It

TABLE 27.2

Addiction, Escape, and Delinquency

(Freshmen at Giessen University 1988/89, sample: male N = 694, female N = 938, age approx. 20 years)

		male female	Exper. illegal drugs	Alcoh. consi-derable	Nicot. consi-derable	Proximity medical drugs	Consi-dered suicide seriously	Attempt. suicide	Frequent truancy	Absenteeism at night	Police arrests	Delin-quency high
Illegal drugs	yes	M 182		49	47	15	29	4	65	47	25	54
		F 190		16	46	30	40	10	57	33	12	29
	no	M 509		11	10	11	18	2	27	20	8	16
		F 742		2	11	20	24	2	24	11	4	6
Alcohol	high	M 149	61		41	14	27	3	54	38	26	51
		F 41	73		59	37	45	13	83	42	17	56
	medium	M 439	21		17	12	20	2	35	28	9	21
		F 525	27		25	22	31	5	34	20	6	10
	low	M 105	2		6	14	19	4	18	11	10	11
		F 365	4		4	20	21	2	19	8	4	7

		N										
Smoking	high	M	140	62	44	/	16	24	2	63	46	24	49
		F	171	52	14	/	32	38	10	54	32	12	23
	medium	M	98	34	21	/	13	21	3	37	32	14	26
		F	158	28	4	/	23	32	4	38	21	5	12
	none	M	436	14	15	/	11	20	2	29	20	9	20
		F	609	10	2	/	19	23	2	23	10	4	7
Police arrests	yes	M	86	54	45	38	14	33	6	58	45	/	50
		F	52	45	14	39	40	33	8	50	31	/	44
	no	M	603	23	18	18	12	20	2	33	24	/	23
		F	883	19	4	17	21	27	4	30	15	/	9
Delinquency	high	M	183	55	42	37	17	28	4	62	45	24	/
		F	104	56	22	39	33	53	15	61	37	22	/
	medium	M	418	20	16	16	12	21	2	31	24	9	/
		F	516	24	4	21	22	28	4	36	18	5	/
	low	M	93	0	9	7	9	10	0	12	6	4	/
		F	318	4	0	8	19	19	1	14	5	2	/

(data in round figure percentage terms, in relation to section of sample being shown in respective line, sexes distinguished)

TABLE 27.3

Age of Initiations in Use of Alcohol, Regular Smoking, and Use of Illegal Drugs
(Freshmen in Giessen in 1988/89; males: N = 694, females: N = 938) and 100 in-depth interviews with IV drug addicts in Hesse 1988/89

	Being drunk for the first time		Regular smoking		First use of illegal drugs		First use of hard drugs	
	males	*females*	*males*	*females*	*males*	*females*	*males*	*females*
Students: Subsample not having used drugs	(N = 408) 15.5 y.	(N = 396) 16.0 y.	(N = 98) 16.1 y.	(N = 151) 16.2 y.	/	/	/	/
Students: Subsample having used drugs	(N = 184) 14.6 y.	(N = 177) 15.3 y.	(N = 132) 15.9 y.	(N = 150) 16.0 y.	(N = 182) 17.3 y.	(N = 190) 17.0 y.	/	/
Sample: 100 IV drug addicts	(N = 64) 12.3 y.	(N = 36) 12.8 y.	(N = 64) 14.1 y.	(N = 36) 13.7 y.	(N = 64) 14.5 y.	(N = 36) 15.5 y.	(N = 64) 18.5 y.	(N = 36) 18.4 y.

should be remembered that the sample represents a section of a general population. It is common in such self-report studies that the bottom strata of society as well as persons with extreme forms and intensity of delinquency are underrepresented.

SOME FINDINGS OF RECENT IN-DEPTH INTERVIEWS WITH HEROIN ADDICTS

Methods

In the periods 1972–1974 (Kreuzer 1975), 1978–1980 (Kreuzer et al. 1981) and 1988/89 (Kreuzer et al. 1991) we carried out biographically oriented, intensive interviews with drug addicts. Developments in the drug addict population, the drug scene, and drug-related delinquency were investigated. In contrast to American criminological research (see especially Ball et al. 1983; Inciardi 1986 pp. 115, with further references; Johnson et al. 1988; Nurco et al. 1988, 1988a; Shaffer et al. 1987, Strug et al. 1984), we have placed emphasis on qualitative aspects. It is more complicated in the Federal Republic to carry out criminological interviews with drug addicts, because of more extensive stipulations in the law concerning data protection. In the course of the current investigation, 100 heroin addicts were interviewed who were in the first stage of drug-addiction withdrawal treatment in therapeutic institutions in Hesse, either in private hospitals or in correctional institutions. The interviews took 3 to 4 hours on average. The average age of the interviewees was approximately 27 years. The majority were IV-heroin addicts who abused numerous other drugs and medical drugs concurrently or at intervals. They were interviewed in their roles as delinquents, victims, and informers. Some observations can be made regarding quantitative aspects, particularly as to the delinquency rate (in this respect, comparison to the American investigations by Inciardi can be made).

Patterns and Intensity of Delinquency

The delinquency rate of drug addicts was measured in numerous large-scale American studies (see, for instance, the above-mentioned studies). The interviews are normally standardized and brief. The measured time period of delinquency is either lifetime, the past year, or the past 36 hours. Samples are selected from medical (methadone maintenance) institutions or from the public drug scene. These methods are not applicable in Germany for several reasons: the local drug scenes are less massive, data protection is stricter and scarcely allows similar approaches, addicts in the drug scene are not as willing to be interviewed for fear of data transmission by research scientists (research scientists do not have the privilege of refusing to give evidence); and furthermore, funds for large-scale studies are restricted. On the other hand, quality oriented intensive interviews are preferred in studies for scientific reasons. The extensive study performed in the early 1970s (Kreuzer 1975) was the first one of this kind in Germany.

The present study measures delinquency rates of 64 male and 36 female IV drug addicts who have been interviewed intensively. Lifetime experiences and delinquency within the last 12 months at liberty were studied. Thirty-eight patterns of delinquency were taken into account. Table 27.4 summarizes 18 of the most important patterns classified according to the sexes and relating to the last 12 months. The data reveal the following aspects: percentage of those admitting to have committed an offense within the 12-month period; average number of offenses committed by each person; total number of offenses committed; percentage of cleared offenses and prosecuted offenses according to the information given by the questioned persons; percentage of cleared offenses computed accordingly; patterns of delinquency specific to the sexes; and ranks of patterns. The main drug-related crimes (acquisitive patterns) are, for both sexes: dealing drugs, especially with small quantities, and smuggling drugs; shoplifting and other forms of theft; check forgery and obtaining loans by fraud; receiving stolen goods. Obtaining medical prescriptions by fraud and illegal acquisition of medications in the drug scene must be added to the list. Obtaining medical prescriptions by fraud is partly made possible by uncontrolled substitute programs: they are mainly misused, they enhance accident hazards and iatrogenic addictions, and half of the drug addicts also supply other people with drugs in this way. Approximately one-third of the prescribed medications are resold on the illegal market.

The number of burglaries in pharmacies and prescription offenses are decreasing compared to results of former studies. Men mainly commit the following offenses: theft of vehicles, burglary, robbery. Prostitution prevails within the female group. In all, the delinquency rate of male drug addicts is significantly higher primarily for serious offenses and violent crimes. Robbery does not occur as often as in the United States. It occurs more often within the drug scene than without. Outside the drug scene, robbery and other offenses are more frequently reported by the victim but are hardly ever reported or prosecuted within the drug scene. This failure to report is a consequence of the victim-offender relationship and the corresponding refusal of a victim to turn in a peer

TABLE 27.4

Selected Patterns and Intensity of Delinquency among Drug Addicts
(In-Depth Interviews with 100 IV Drug Addicts in Hesse, 1988/89)

Selected patterns of delinquency	males (n = 64)			remarkable discrepancy	females (n = 36)			total number (n = 100)		
	rank	% of subsample involved	offenses per person on average (n = 64)		offenses per person on average (n = 36)	% of subsample involved	rank	number of offenses	number of cleared up offenses	quota of cleared up offenses
Drug sales	1	100%	744		624	92%	1	70,091	368	0.53%
Shoplifting	2	77%	234		326	67%	3	27,324	276	1.0%
Prostitution	13	9%	5.5	↑	386	56%	2	14,250		
Theft from vehicle	3	39%	125	↓	34	19%	4	9,220	117	1.27%
Stolen goods	4	39%	77		11	33%	8	5,328	2	0.04%
Other Theft	7	57%	25		17	53%	5	2,171	3	0.14%
Check forgery	6	30%	25		17	19%	6	2,276	123	5.4%
Burglary, housebreaking	5	58%	31	↓	3	19%	13	2,047	91	4.5%
Con games, fraud	9	48%	17		16	58%	7	1,674	63	3.74%
Procuring	8	14%	18		0	0%	18	1,135	10	0.9%
Smuggling	11	34%	8		5	42%	10	727	13	1.8%
Robbery within the drug scene	10	27%	9	↓	2.7	3%	12	681	1	0.15%
Vehicle theft	12	31%	8	↓	0	0%	17	506	22	4.53%
Prostitute theft	16	8%	1.2	↑	8.8	31%	9	396	4	1.01%
Assault, bodily harm	14	52%	4.3		0.7	19%	14	296	20	6.76%
Forgery of prescriptions	15	14%	2.8		3	6%	11	277	12	4.33%
Burglary into pharmacies	18	11%	1		0.3	8%	15	74	4	5.4%
Robbery	17	23%	1.1	↓	0.1	11%	16	72	11	15.3%

to the police. Drug addicts often are delinquents but are just as often victims of violent crimes and they have a very high victim tolerance. They do not denounce one another out of fear, habit, and self-protection. The police must carry out their own investigations. Thus delinquency inside the scene can only be estimated. This explains why there are considerable differences between the structure of hidden (i.e., self-reported) delinquency and officially recorded delinquency. The percentages of actually cleared-up (solved) crimes thus vary widely from those of crimes cleared up in criminal statistics compiled by police. The percentages of cleared-up, self-reported delinquency range from about 0% (in, e.g.; receiving stolen goods, robbery inside the scene, obtaining prescriptions by fraud) and 15% (robbery in public).

All in all, aggressive delinquency is widespread inside the drug scene as an earlier study proved for the first time (Kreuzer 1974). It is due to predelinquent experiences many drug addicts had to the variety of mixed criminogenic milieus inside the drug scene, to the aggression-enhancing effects of certain drugs, and to the inherent rules of the illegal market as well as to the effects of crime prevention. The conclusions based on the "aggression-reduction thesis" were not supported by this finding. This thesis was based on the idea that the delinquency of drug addicts was primarily not aggressive but motivated by utilitarian aspects. The thesis was substantiated by comparisons of the delinquency structure of drug addicts and nondrug-addicted delinquents, based on criminal statistics and prison populations (see e.g., Blum 1969, Cockett 1971, Lidberg 1971). The factors that enhance aggressive delinquency but also veil criminal statistics were not considered; no attention was paid to the structural descrepancy of hidden versus recorded delinquency. For this reason, studies performed by physicians also provided misleading results; they only collected data on recorded delinquency (i.e., prosecuted delinquency) during the case history.

The delinquency rates seem very high, especially in comparison to the results of American studies. This is shown in Table 27.5 by a comparison of our new findings and an earlier study performed by Inciardi (1986, p. 127). In both studies the sample consists of approximately one-third women. Almost all of the compared delinquency patterns were reported by an equal number of subjects of the comparable subgroups in both studies for the last 12 months. But as far as the reported frequency is concerned, the rates are significantly higher in our study. In reality, the delinquency rate of American drug addicts should exceed that of Germans because of milieu-specific particulars, especially since comparable racial problems and the lack of education do not exist. The reporting of more petty offenses in Germany is a consequence of the applied method. During intensive interviews using our method, the subject's memory is refreshed

TABLE 27.5

Comparing Delinquency Rates of Drug Addicts in the United States and in Germany (573 interviews with IV drug addicts in Miami, Florida, 1978–1981; 100 in-depth-interview with IV drug addicts in Hesse, 1988/89)

Selection of the most important patterns of delinquency	USA (n = 573)		FRG (n = 100)	
	percent. of involved persons	average rate of offenses per person	percent. of involved persons	average rate of offenses per person
Drug sales	83.9%	143.9	97%	700.9
Robbery	37.7%	9.3	19%	0.7
Shoplifting	62.1%	43.7	73%	273.2
Burglary	52.7%	11.6	44%	20.5
Theft from vehicle	28.1%	6.5	32%	92.2
Vehicle theft	19.4%	1.5	20%	5.1
Stolen-goods offenses	53.4%	30.1	37%	53.3
Prostitution	22.2%	45.5	26%	142.5
Prostitute theft	15.9%	7.1	16%	4.0
Procuring	24.1%	12.4	9%	11.4

American data from J. Inciardi, *The War on Drugs*, Palo Alto, California, 1986, p. 127.

on a higher degree, unclear questions can be clarified, and it is easier to prevent understatements and exaggerations. All in all, there seems to be a higher delinquency rate than the one obtained by the methodical approach of the short, highly standardized interviews. Independent of the specific methodical approach, serious offenses—especially robberies— do not occur as often and are more unusual, and so they should be defined as well as remembered and reported in an equal way and extent.

There is a significantly higher number of these offenses in the United States. This should also be the case for more serious and less frequently committed offenses—such as manslaughter—which cannot be asked about either here or in the United States. But if serious crimes do occur more often in the United States, then this should apply to other offense as well, and thus also for the overall delinquency rate. On the other hand, shoplifting is admitted to more often during intensive interviews because frequency of shoplifting hampers perception, memory and thus reporting. Memory can be refreshed to a point where it is remembered that theft was committed more than once on certain days or that not just one vehicle was broken into but several. Some differences in the reported frequency are not a consequence of the method of questioning but of the different circumstances: in Germany, the theft of radios or vehicles, for instance, is more popular than in the United States because these items are more expensive here. However, procuring is more popular in the United States because prostitution is still criminalized and female prostitutes are thus dependent on the procurement of customers by men to a higher degree.

Need for Drugs and Financing

We have attempted to assess the drug consumption of IV drug addicts, including financing, in an earlier study (Kreuzer et al. 1981, p. 218) Serious problems are connected with the assessment. Nevertheless, the most important factors were worked out and they are opposed to the prevailing misconceptions in public opinion. The most important uncertainties were caused by the wide range of active agents in drugs which are hard to identify objectively and subjectively. The questioned persons indicated daily needs of heroin from 0.5 to 2.5 grams of average street quality (e.g., the heroin is mixed to an certain extent with other substances). The expenses were assessed the same for both sexes as an average of 250 DM (about $110) a day. The numerous periods during which drugs were not used or supply was insufficient or substitute drugs were taken were disregarded. In addition, drugs are not only bought but also acquired by dealing, theft, and other actions, so that money is not essential. Data on drug-free periods are shown in Figure 27.1. For the measured period of the last year they constituted 18.6 weeks for male addicts and 13.5 for female addicts, on average. Detention and therapy are included in these numbers, as well as voluntary periods of withdrawal and periods of insufficient supply.

Figure 27.2 allows us to approximately assess the financing structure, as that information was given by the intervees. According to it, about 1/5 is financed legally, 1/9 by prostitution, 1/3 by drug dealing, almost 1/3 by committing other offenses, of which only a part—even if it is a bigger one—can be classified as offenses committed, to provide drugs indirectly. Men commit more drug-related crimes for money for buying drugs, while women turn instead to prostitution. In all, the net sum actually needed by a drug addict daily is estimated to be DM 100–150 ($60–100) on average.

Careers in Drug Addiction and Delinquency

One difficulty posed by the drug problem and, indeed, by treatment, is understanding whether the drug addict is ill or delinquent or both, or neither of the two. The mere consideration of the biographical correlation

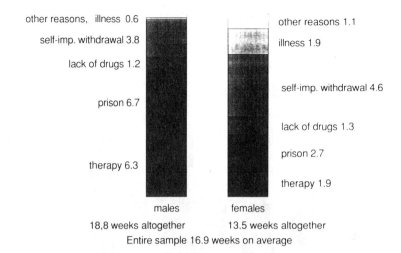

other reasons, illness 0.6

self-imp. withdrawal 3.8

lack of drugs 1.2

prison 6.7

therapy 6.3

other reasons 1.1

illness 1.9

self-imp. withdrawal 4.6

lack of drugs 1.3

prison 2.7

therapy 1.9

males   females
18,8 weeks altogether   13.5 weeks altogether
Entire sample 16.9 weeks on average

FIGURE 27.1.
Drug-free phases during the last year (weeks on average; in-depth interviews with 100 IV drug addicts 1988/89).

between drug use development and the development of delinquency demonstrates the complexity of the problem.

For the first time in a study we attempted to draw a parallel between the course of delinquency and drug dependency in a retrospective, longitudinal biographical view. The question is whether delinquent developments precede or follow a drug career. If drug use or drug prohibition were the decisive presuppositions of delinquent development, delinquency would have to follow drug use (for similar typologies see e.g., Nurco et al. 1981 and Schaffer et al. 1987). Figure 27.3 summarizes typologically the results obtained during the former three studies. The time of first drug use (alcohol use was not considered) was determined as the biographical turning point in this table; cannabis normally served as the initial drug. Only the behavior of drug addicts exceeding "normal" delinquency and not covered by the legal definition of drug use (such as acquisition and possession of illegal drugs) is relevant to the "career in delinquency" within this context.

Figure 27.4 makes it even more evident that predelinquent experiences are decisive in regard to the extent of delinquency in the course of a drug career. In this figure the first use of hard drugs, such as heroin, was determined as the relevant biographical turning point. This assumption is substantiated by the thesis that drug dependency or addiction does not usually begin prior to this point, and it stimulates the need for committing

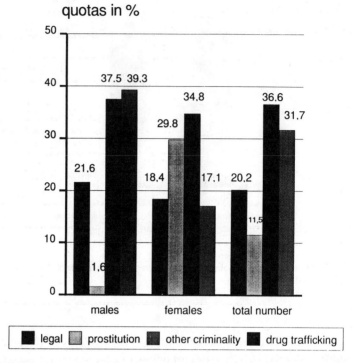

FIGURE 27.2.
Structure of financing drugs (in-depth interviews with 100 IV drug addicts 1988/89).

drug-related crimes to obtain illegal drugs. Our last study enabled us to differentiate this course of drug abuse career. Four-fifths of the male and two-fifths of the female drug addicts went through significant delinquent development before they used hard drugs for the first time. In these cases, drug addiction reinforced a delinquent career but did not trigger it.

Almost every intravenous drug addict exhibits a career of delinquency that is parallel to a drug career. In this respect, mere acquisition and possession of illegal drugs are not included because drug abuse itself is illegal by statute. The interrelations between the two careers are manifold. For one group of drug addicts it seems to be that either the criminal or the drug abuse career starts off concurrently or the drug abuse behavior precedes the delinquent behavior. Within a second group of drug addicts of considerable size the drug abuse behavior starts after the beginning of delinquent behavior. The drug abuse stands for a symptom of general antisocial development which is in the beginning interchangeable with

Biographically-oriented in-depth-interviews with i.v. drug addicts 1972,1978,1988

Type	phase prior to first drug use	phase after first drug use	description	males N=147	females N=70	total N=217
I			drug career without previous or accompanying career in delinquency		1%	0.5%
II		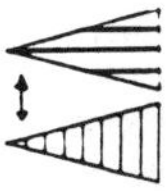	drug career with accompanying career in delinquency	48%	64%	53%
III			drug career in the further course of a moderate career in delinquency reinforcing this career in delinquency	26%	29%	27%
IV	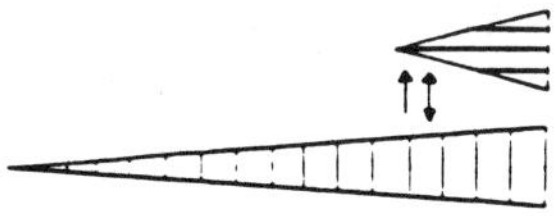		drug career in the advanced course of a career in delinquency being already manifested significantly	26%	6%	19%

drug career

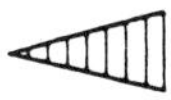

career in delinquency

FIGURE 27.3.
Careers in drug addiction and delinquency (1)

other antisocial behaviors, but which later on determines the further social development. For this second group of drug addicts with a primary delinquency, it is obviously absurd to treat them only as ill people. In these cases treatment is even more complicated; it must be planned comprehensively and punishment cannot often be dismissed. Nevertheless the conceptions relating to careers are not supposed to be understood in a one-way development or to end in resignation. Many drug careers and

Biographically-oriented in-depth-interviews with i.v. drug addicts 1988

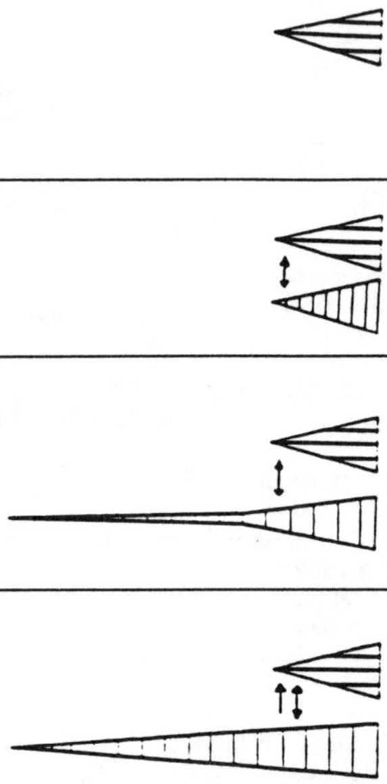

Type	phase prior to first hard drug use	phase after first hard drug use	description	males N=64	females N=36	total N=100
I			drug career without previous or accompanying career in delinquency			0%
II			drug career with accompanying career in delinquency	5%	17%	9%
III			drug career in the further course of a moderate career in delinquency reinforcing this career in delinquency	16%	44%	26%
IV			drug career in the advanced course of a career in delinquency being already manifested significantly	80%	39%	65%

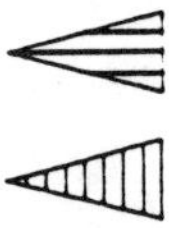

drug career

career in delinquency

FIGURE 27.4.
Careers in drug addiction and delinquency (2)

careers of delinquency are regressive; with growing age, they pass into a maturing-out phase.

Figure 27.5 shows the degree to which predelinquent experiences and orientations influenced the intensity of the delinquency that accompanied a drug career: The more extensive the preaddiction delinquency, the higher the delinquency rate measured during the last 12 months of drug addiction. Violent crimes before and after drug addiction show the same correlation. Most exclusively drug addicts who committed violent crimes

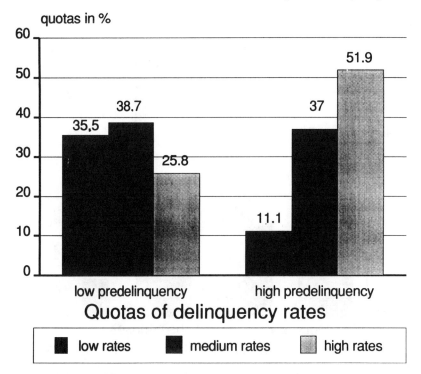

FIGURE 27.5.
Correlating overall preaddiction delinquency and delinquency rates within the last 12 months (in-depth interviews with 100 IV drug addicts).

during their preaddiction phase also developed considerable violent delinquency during the later period.

Figure 27.6 illustrates the complexity of the addiction-crime nexus. The figure correlates former unusual stressful educational situations and significant delinquency during the last 12 months of drug addiction. The biographical interviews distinguish according to whether or not evident, objectifiable significantly stressful situations occurred during childhood (e.g., upbringing by stepmother, changes in educational establishments or orphanages, changes in teachers). These situations form only one indicator of serious disturbances in early childhood. They also indicate the risk of subsequent maladjustment during adolescence. The study shows that the higher the delinquency rates during a drug career, the more sig-

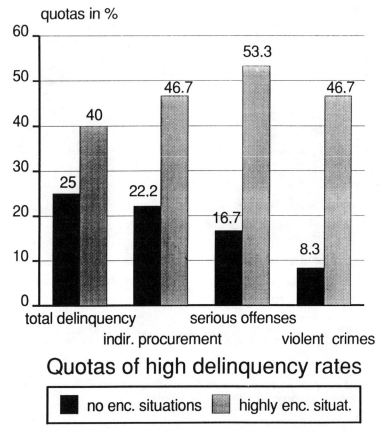

FIGURE 27.6.
Correlating early encumbering educational situations and high delinquency rates
within the last 12 months (in-depth interviews with 100 IV drug addicts).

nificant the educational loads during childhood. This correlation is particularly true in regard to subsequent violent crimes.

For methodical and practical reasons, only two behavioral patterns were
incorporated into the biographical analysis: drug addiction and delinquency. The complexity could be further deepened: in particular, considerations of early defective mental dispositions within the biographical
analysis are suggested. This way, some unanswered questions in therapy
could perhaps be answered better. It is, for instance, still unknown whether significant preaddiction delinquency affects drug treatment adversely.

According to some studies this is not the case. The reason might be that drug addiction is often only an added but erasable form of defective behavior in highly predelinquent persons; nevertheless, the drug career of many less predelinquent drug addicts could have been influenced to a greater extent by early defective mental dispositions or even by mental illnesses, drug treatment is bound to fail here unless the underlying psychosis is diagnosed and also treated.

CONCLUSIONS

The findings concerning the complex nexus of drugs, drug addiction and delinquency can be outlined finally by means of hypotheses only:

1. Apart from the statutory classification, there is no drug per se that leads to delinquency.
2. Addiction careers and careers of delinquency are not inevitable. There are, for instance, those who use heroin regularly without becoming dependent on it; there are users of hard drugs who constantly vary the types of drugs in order to avoid becoming dependent. The spontaneous giving up of drug abuse is seen as well as a gradual reduction. This is especially the case when drug addicts leave the developmental stage of young adults which is often characterized by extreme living habits.
3. Both juvenile delinquency and addiction-related research tell us that everyday theories on the development of careers prove to be misleading, as, in particular, does the gateway theory. Most people who take legal or illegal drugs occasionally in their early years cease to do so later on, and that occurs without any intervention of criminal law or treatment. One cannot draw conclusions that equate extreme conduct with normal conduct.
4. Within the extreme group of noticeably delinquent drug addicts, we can find a wide range of biographical correlations between drug careers and careers of delinquency. One will find the primary drug addict at one pole, while at the other pole there is the secondary drug addict. It is possible that even the latter could exhibit delinquent conduct by committing either petty offenses or even more severe ones, regardless of how dependent he or she is on drugs at all.
5. The relationship between drug use and delinquency during a career is essentially determined by the following factors: (a) personality of the drug addict; (b) preceding and attendant conditions and disturbances of socialization; (c) previous experiences with delinquency; (d) age

and social context (peer group) at the beginning of the drug career; (e) dynamics of a drug dependence career; (f) dynamics of the milieu and the subcultural lifestyle within the drug scene; (g) influences of controlling strategies and tactics with regard to drug policy. For instance, more vigorous police enforcement can serve to reduce criminal acts related to drug seeking on the one hand, while on the other hand, such enforcement can reduce the availability of drugs and strengthen the pressure toward treatment.

REFERENCES

Ball, J. C., Shaffer, J. W., and Nurco, D. N. (1983). The day-to-day criminality of heroin addicts in Baltimore—A study in the continuity of offense rates. *Drug and Alcohol Dependence* 12, 119–142.

Blum, R. (1969) *Drugs and violence.* A consultant's report prepared for the National Commission on the causes and prevention of violence. Stanford/Calif.

Cockett, R. (1971). *Drug abuse and personality in young offenders.* London: Butterworths.

Inciardi, J. A. (1986). *The war on drugs.* Palo Alto: Mayfield.

Johnson, B., and Anderson, K. (1988). A day in the life of 105 drug addicts and abusers: crimes committed and how the money was spent, *Sociology and Social Research* 72, 185–191.

Kaiser, G. (1988). *Kriminologie*, 2. Auflage. Heidelberg: C. S. Müller.

Kreuzer, A. (1972). Kriminologische, kriminalpolitische und strafjustizielle Aspekte des Drogenwesens in der Bundesrepublik. In H. Schäfer (ed.) *Grundlagen der Kriminalistik* Bd.9, 243 ff., Hamburg: Steinfor.

Kreuzer, A. (1974). Aggressionsdelinquenz im Zusammenhang mit Drogenmißbrauch. *Recht der Jugend und des Bildungswesens*, 22, 81–92.

Kreuzer, A. (1975). *Drogen und Delinquenz.* Wiesbaden: Akademische Verlagsgesellschaft.

Kreuzer, A. (1975a). Schülerbefragungen zur Delinquenz. *Recht der Jugend und des Bildungswesens*, 23, 229–44.

Kreuzer, A. (1980). Weitere Beiträge aus Gießener Delinquenzbefragungen. *Monatsschrift für Kriminologie und Strafrechtsreform*, 63, 385–96.

Kreuzer, A. (1980a). Suchtmittel und Delinquenz bie jungen Soldaten. *Suchtgefahren*, 26, 49–67.

Kreuzer, A. et al. (1981). Drogenabhängigkeit und Kontrolle, *BKA-Forschungsreihe Bd.* 14, Wiesbaden: Bundeskriminalamt.

Kreuzer, A. (1986). Cherchez la femme? Beiträge aus Gießener Delinquenzbefragungen zur Diskussion um Frauenkriminalität. In H. J. Hirsch et al. (eds.) *Gedächtnisschrift für Hilde Kaufmann*, 395–408. Berlin, New York: De Gruyter.

Kreuzer, A. (1986a). Kriminologische Grundpositionen einer Drogenpolitik. *Bewährungshilfe* 33, 395–409.

Kreuzer, A. (1987). *Jugend—Drogen—Kriminalität*. 3. völlig neubearbeitete Auflage. Neuwied: Luchterhand.

Kreuzer, A., Gebhardt, C., Maassen, M., Stein-Hilbers, M. (1981). Drogenabhängigkeit und Kontrolle, *BKA-Forschungsreihe* 14, Wiesbaden: Bundeskriminalamt.

Kreuzer, A., Hürlimann, M., Krämer, K., Schneider, H. (1990). Umgang mit Suchtmitteln und anderes abweichendes Verhalten—geschlechtsspezifische Befunde einer Delinquenzbefragung aller Erstsemester der Universität Gießen. In Deutsche Hauptstelle gegen die Suchtgefahren DHS (ed.), *Abhängigkeit bei Frauen und Männern*, 279–92, Freiburg: Lambertus.

Kreuzer, A., Römer-Klees, R., Schneider H. (1991). Beschaffungskriminalität Drogenabhängiger. *BKA-Schriftenreihe*, Wiesbaden: Bundeskriminalamt.

Kreuzer, A., Krämer, K. Römer-Klees, R., Schneider, H. (1990a) Auswirkungen unterschiedlicher Erhebungsverfahren auf die selbstberichtete Delinquenz. Paper presented at the Tagung der Sektion "Soziale Probleme und soziale Kontrolle" der Deutschen Gesellschaft für Soziologie, Köln.

Kreuzer, A., Wille, R. (1988). *Drogen- Kriminologie und Therapie*. Heidelberg: v. Decker und C. S. Müller.

Lidberg, L. (1971). Abuse of central stimulans and its effects on criminal behavior in Sweden. Pharmakopsychiatrie, *Neuropsychopharmakologie*, 212.

Nurco, D. N., Cisin, J. H., and Balter, M. B. (1981). Addict Careers I, II, III, *International Journal of the Addictions*, 16(8), 1305–72.

Nurco, D. N., Hanlon, T. E., Kinlock, T. E., and Duszynski, K. R. (1988). Differential criminal patterns of narcotic addicts over an addiction career. *Criminology 26*, 407–23.

Nurco, D. N., Kinlock, T. W., Hanlon, T. E., and Ball, J. C. (1988a) Narcotic drug use over an addiction career—a study of heroin addicts in Baltimore and New York City. *Comprehensive Psychiatry 29*, 450–59.

Shaffer, J. W., Nurco, D. N., Ball, J. C., Kinlock, T. W., Duszynski, K. R., and Langrod, J. (1987). The relationship of preaddiction characteristics of the types and amounts of crime committed by narcotic addicts. *International Journal of the Addictions 22*, 153–65.

Strug, D., Wish, E., Johnson, B., Anderson, K., Miller, T., and Sears, A. (1984). The role of alcohol in the crimes of active heroin users. *Crime and Delinquency* 30 (4), 551–67.

CHAPTER 28

Criminal Law and the Treatment of Drug Addicts

Rudolf Egg

INTRODUCTION: DRUG-RELATED CRIMES AND SANCTIONS IN WEST GERMANY

In the Federal Republic of Germany in 1988 almost 85,000 violations of the Narcotic Drugs Act were registered by the police.[1] In most cases (about 64%), these concerned general violations (consumption and possession of drugs), in about one-third (32.6%) dealing and smuggling, and in almost 3% of the cases importation of so-called considerable quantities. The different types of drugs registered in the police statistics are headed by cannabis (56.7% of the violations), followed by heroin (30.3%). Cocaine plays a minor role (5.2%), but already the cases of dealing and smuggling as well as the quantities[2] confiscated show a clearly rising tendency, so that in the future an increasing number of offenses due to cocaine use can be expected.

The number of persons convicted of violation of the Narcotic Drugs Act amounts to 20,000 annually (Figure 28.1). In about half of these cases the convictions results in a fine or in other sanctions; in the second half, in which a prison sentence is pronounced, about 3,500 cases are not accorded probation. Many of those convicted are drug addicts. Added to the list should be a rather large, but difficult to determine number of

1. See Bundeskriminalamt (BKA), *Polizeiliche Kriminalstatistik 1988*, (Wiesbaden, 1989), p. 159 ff.
2. In 1988 German police confiscated 537 kg. of heroin and 496 kg. of cocaine.

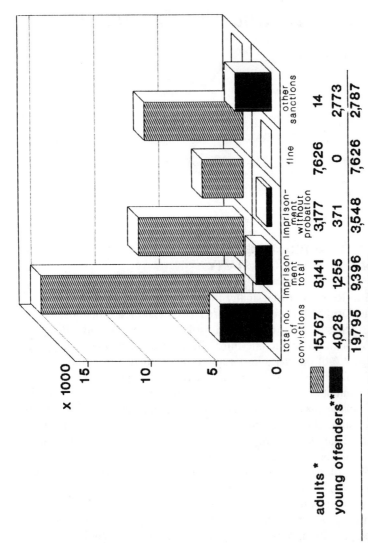

	total no. of convictions	imprison-ment total	imprison-ment without probation	fine	other sanctions
adults *	15,767	8,141	3,177	7,626	14
young offenders**	4,028	1,255	371	0	2,773
	19,795	9,396	3,548	7,626	2,787

x 1000

*   *persons convicted according to general penal law*
**   *persons convicted according to penal law for young offenders*

FIGURE 28.1.
Drug Related Convictions 1987.

people who, due to their drug addiction, commit other offenses such as larceny, robbery, or fraud and are convicted.

Of all drug addicts heroin addicts are considered to be the most difficult group. Estimates of the number of heroin addicts range from about 50,000 to 80,000, or a maximum of 100,000 in Germany. Even considering a fairly large grey area regarding drug offenses, most of the drug addicts have at least occasionally had encounters with the police and the justice system, many of them even repeatedly and with substantial consequences. Effectively addressing the needs of these drug-addicted offenders is difficult for several reasons:

1. Offenses connected with drug addiction, are, like other offenses, forms of social deviance, but are also the manifestations and results of a severe health disturbance, that is the drug addiction.
2. This disease implies—independent of any penal provision—considerable handicaps and dangers for those concerned and can lead to death from overdose intoxication.
3. In the last few years, the danger of AIDS infection has become an additional problem. Especially concerned are heroin users, due to so-called needle sharing, and drug-addicted women who live by prostitution.

Faced with these and other problems, various parties in West Germany have been asking for some time now to apply "treatment instead of penalty" to this group. At the least, strong efforts should be made to motivate drug addicts to undergo suitable therapy, and if they agree to it this treatment should be made available. No penalty should stand in the way of treatment. In the Federal Republic of Germany, drug-addicted offenders have several possible ways of entering into treatment (Figure 28.2). Besides the difficult and rarely practiced therapy within a regular prison are the following three regulations which can be considered as "classical measures":

1. Treatment on condition of probation (Section 56, General Penal Code). The suspended sentence must not exceed two years in these cases.
2. Treatment on condition of parole after the partial completion (one-half to two-thirds) of term of a prison sentence and suspension of the remaining sentence (Section 57, General Penal Code).
3. Treatment in connection with imprisonment in special governmental institutions ("Maßregelvollzug," Section 64, General Penal Code).

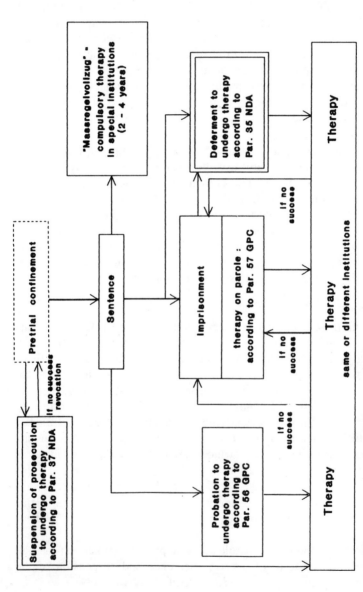

FIGURE 28.2.
Criminal law and the therapy of drug addicts in the Federal Republic of Germany

436

The first and second regulations always depend on a *favorable social and legal prognosis*, i.e., there must be strong indications that the convicted person will commit no further offenses. This expectation, however, cannot be applied to most drug addicts. The third regulation takes into account the converse situation, relating to the high probability that the convicted persons will continue to commit rather *serious offenses* due to their drug addiction. Apparently this negative prognosis is rarely made, since practice shows that the application of this regulation is restricted to a limited number of cases of drug addicts (about 50 cases per year) and is often considered as a last resort by the judge. Such "compulsory therapy" generally lasts from two to a maximum of four years.

In order to give a larger number of drug addicts the chance of rehabilitation with treatment, two more measures were introduced at the 1982 reform of the German Narcotic Drugs Act (NDA): One measure concerns the possibility of a *suspension of prosecution* as defined in Section 37 NDA. This preliminary suspension of prosecution can be applied in cases in which the accused has already been undergoing a drug therapy treatment for at least three months and in which rehabilitation, as well as a penalty not exceeding two years of prison sentence, can be expected. Due to these rather closely defined prerequisites, this form of entry into therapy is rarely practiced (about 100 cases per year).

The second and much more frequently applied newly introduced measure is the *deferment of execution* of sentence according to Section 35 NDA. This regulation gives the law enforcement authorities the opportunity to defer the execution of a prison sentence for a maximum of two years for those offenses committed due to drug addiction. The same is valid for a corresponding remaining sentence concerning offenders convicted to longer terms of imprisonment. The deferment implies that the convicted person will be released from prison or does not even have to go to prison provided he or she participates in a treatment program instead. This deferment is not dependent on a favorable prognosis for successful therapy, which in most cases would present too much of an obstacle. It is sufficient if the convicted person agrees to undergo suitable treatment program. Naturally its start and realization must be granted, i.e., the convicted must have a place for treatment available and its financing must be settled.

If the therapy, once begun, is interrupted, the authorities revoke the deferment of execution of sentence; the convicted person must go or return to prison. Important is that in any case the time spent in treatment is credited to the total prison term. If a new treatment program is commenced, a further deferment of execution of sentence can be accorded.

If everything takes a positive course, the still remaining sentence (maximum one-third of the original penalty) can be suspended on paroles for three or four years. This deferment of execution of sentence according to Section 35 NDA applied to about 860 persons in 1984 and amounted in 1988 to more than 1,500 convicted persons with a tendency to rise.

Of course, these regulations are not undisputed.[3] Critics to some extent refer to certain debatable details in the provisions, for example, to the convicted person's compulsory registration by treatment institutions when the therapy is abandoned. Very often it is judged wrong to force imprisonment as a way to motivate addicts to undergo treatment. In spite of numerous arguments and statements, up to now a precise scientific analysis of these regulations and their results is still lacking.[4]

TREATMENT INSTITUTIONS FOR DRUG-ADDICTED OFFENDERS

Therapy, according to Section 35 NDA is defined as a long-term, mainly in-house program with the objective of teaching the addict to lead a life free of drugs. These measures do not take place in governmental institutions like the above-mentioned "Maßregelvollzug," but in treatment centers founded by private charitable organizations. In the Federal Republic of Germany presently about 130 of such therapy centers exist.[5] Their approximate locations are shown on the map of Figure 28.3, where a higher concentration near big cities such as Berlin and Frankfurt, which are also centers of the drug scene, can be recognized, as well as in Northrhine-Westphalia, which represents a special problem area due to its high population density and its proximity to the Netherlands.

In 1988 our institute made inquiries among these treatment institutions (Egg and Kurze 1989). The results show that the random sample that was examined can be roughly divided into four categories of therapy centers:

• medical institutions, psychiatric hospitals
• psychological/psychotherapy institutions
• flat-sharing groups for therapy purposes
• self-help groups (under/not under expert supervision).

---

3. See, e.g., Kreuzer and Wille (1988: 109 ff.).
4. For a topical discussion of these and related subjects and for an extensive bibliography, see Egg (1988).
5. For a comprehensive description of these institutions see Egg and Kurze (1989).

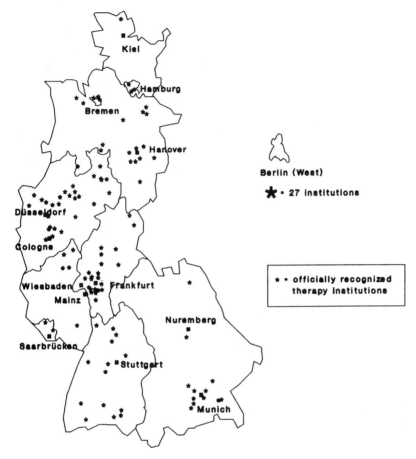

FIGURE 28.3.
Locations of the therapy institutions officially recognized by the government in the Federal Republic of Germany. (end of 1988, 133 institutions).

Numerically the largest part is represented here by the therapeutic community treatment (40% of all institutions), followed by psychological-psychotherapy institutions (roughly 30%), while the more traditional medical institutions come up to about 20% and the self-help groups (especially Synanon), which work without professional personnel, to about 10% of all institutions.[6] A similar situation can be seen when the number of available therapy places in the therapeutic institutions are compared

6. All figures according to the sample of our inquiry (Egg and Kurze 1989)

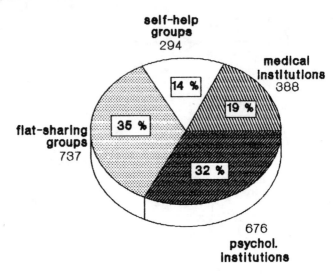

N = 2095 therapy places in 77 therapy institutions

FIGURE 28.4.
Number of therapy places in government recognized therapy institutions

(Figure 28.4); here also psychotherapy institutions and therapeutic communities predominate.

About 75% of these institutions follow the principle of the therapeutic community described by Jones (1968) and others. The length of the sojourn in therapy institutions varies between 6 and 18 months, frequently followed by a sojourn in a halfway house or in outpatient treatment. All institutions require strict renouncement of drug use. In many cases, therefore, before being accepted into a therapeutic community, the client has to undergo a clinical detoxification. The main objectives of the treatment are lasting drug abstinence, physical health, and the professional and social integration of the clients.

The actual therapy is generally divided into several *stages* or *phases*, each of which have specific therapeutic objectives and which increase the demands on clients from stage to stage. This system is gradual for both therapist and client and indicates the corresponding progress made. A transfer into the next stage therefore represents a confirmation of what has already been achieved. The *entrance stage* is intended to stabilize the motivation for treatment and should help the addict to develop realistic perspectives concerning the future course of the therapy. Within the community the client still occupies a relatively limited position. The main focal point for clients is concentration on themselves and their own problems. This also implies an extensive isolation from the external world as well as an interdiction of things which could recall the drug scene (jewelry, hairdo, music, etc.).

The *main* or *treatment phase* forms the central part of the therapy program. According to the institution this phase is subdivided into two or three minor phases. The emphasis is directed to the community life of the group, the respecting of community regulations, the active participation in various work, leisure, and therapy groups as well as the step-by-step confrontation with the demands of reality. The final *leaving stage* introduces the step-by-step transition into the external world. Direct therapeutic interventions are reduced to a minimum, as are the restricting regulations (house rules) of the community, while the self-responsibility of the client becomes the focus. The end term comprises the search for work and housing as well as a new start or the stabilization of those social contacts which—beyond the drug scene—can assure the client's permanent success in everything achieved in therapy.

Therefore the concept of these institutions can as a whole be characterized as social therapy, in which elements of traditional psychotherapy play a minor role. This program is completed—according to the specific organization—by sports activities, spiritual care, physical measures (baths, massages, breathing exercises, autogenous training, etc.) as well as by work and creative exercises. The latter accomplishes, for one, therapeutic objectives (getting used to professional activity, testing the handling of different materials), but also serves the additional function of providing autonomous means for the therapy institution with agricultural products or income from craft shops. The high costs for stays in such a treatment institution are mainly supported by public health insurance and social security (exception: self-help groups based on the principle of autonomous financing). None or only little costs are charged to the drug addicts or their families generally.

EMPIRICAL PART: CONCEPT AND FIRST RESULTS OF AN EVALUATION STUDY

Design

The Kriminologische Zentralstelle, a criminological research and documentation center founded by the Federal Republic of Germany and the federal states,[7] presently conducts an investigation which shall contribute to practice and confirmation of the above-mentioned new therapy regulations for drug-addicted offenders in Germany. The center of the investigation constitutes the analysis of records of a large random sample of all convicted persons during one year. In order to analyze aspects of development, we did not select this year nor the last year, but 1984. Sentence, imprisonment, therapy, and probation are investigated retrospectively.

Since the data collection of the main part of the study, the analysis of records, is still in operation, no definite results are yet available. Instead a preliminary study will serve to explain the extent of the measures investigated as well as the general procedure. As mentioned before, the group we are investigating is a random sample of those persons convicted in 1984 whose execution of sentence was deferred. For the entire population we analyzed the records in the Federal Register of Convictions. In spite of the fact that the data stored there are restricted to very few aspects only, determinations as to which people and offenses are concerned in particular and how the move to therapy works in principle can be achieved.

Description of the Population

The number of convicted persons with deferment of execution of sentence in 1984 totals N = 862, of which 721 (83.6%) are male and 141 (16.4%) female. The quota of women in this population is a little higher than of all persons convicted in 1984 for drug offenses (portion = 14%). The *dispersion of age* ranges from 15 to 46 years (see Figure 28.5); the mean is 26.6 years; and the standard deviation is 3.98 years. The highest accumulation is found in the group of 24- to 26-year-olds. If the *gender* of the convicted person is considered in this dispersion, two important points can be seen:

- The range of the dispersion for women is smaller than for men (18 to 38 years versus 15 to 46 years). The same can be recognized in the somewhat smaller standard deviation (s = 3.46 versus s = 4.4).
- The average age of the women is a little less than that of the men: 25.4 to 26.8 years. In spite of these differences a general comparison of these two groups is possible. The small portion of juveniles and

7. See Jehle and Egg (1986).

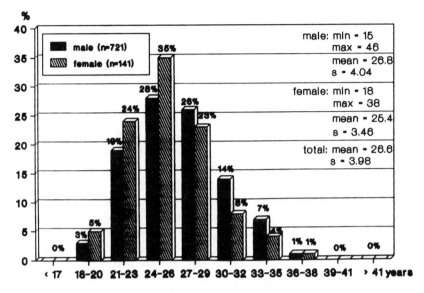

FIGURE 28.5.
Dispersion of age separated by gender—total sample 1984 (N = 862)

young people (age under 21 years) in the respective populations is
striking.

Offenses and sentences

The *offenses* which led to the conviction were divided into three groups
according to the combination of offenses found:

1. "Pure" drug offenses
   These offenses concern persons whose sentences exclusively mention
   violations of the Narcotic Drugs Act.
2. Drug offenses and others
   In this mixed group the entries refer to stipulations contained in the
   first group as well as to offenses outside the Narcotic Drugs Act and
   relating to the General Penal Code. To these belong especially theft
   and embezzlement as well as forgery of documents and other offenses

involving property, robbery and blackmail, traffic violations, and other offenses play a less important role.

3. Exclusively other offenses

   This group consists of those who have not been convicted of a drug offense, but rather—according to the above-mentioned specifications—of offenses committed to finance drug use. In practice, convictions for such offenses usually result in a deferment of execution of sentence. This corresponds to the intention of the legislator who does not limit this provision to drug offenses. The only requirement is that the offense(s) were committed on grounds of drug addiction, no matter what offense was committed.

As expected, in the 1984 population, group 1 (drug offense) was the most represented: N = 570 (68%). The mixed groups 2 and 3 are represented with 17% (N = 189) and 15% (N = 126) respectively.

If the convicted persons are separated by gender it can be stated that women definitely commit more purely drug-related offenses than men (Figure 28.6). While group 1 constitutes 80% of the cases, group 3 is reduced to about 7%. The main reason for this phenomenon probably is that drug-addicted women are able to make money by prostitution. Therefore offenses committed to finance drug use (such as theft) occur less often among women than among men of the same population.

Analysis of the sentences demonstrates that in almost 19% of the registered cases the penalty imposed was suspended on probation. Only after these probations were revoked could the other sentences be executed, and only then was the deferment applied. This especially is true for young convicted users, and for women. It becomes clear that this deferment in practice is really applied to a rather large extent for drug addicts who could not, or could only partially, undergo treatment within the probation period because the suspension of sentence on probation was revoked—for whatever reason. This new ruling provides for a reasonable completion rate of treatment.

EVALUATION AND DISCUSSION

To the questions what are the results of these measures, and, what is the conduct of the addicts of this population, we can only give some preliminary answers, which refer to the settlement of the corresponding penalties. We also have to consider that the 1984–1987/88 time period for observation is rather limited. Figure 28.7 shows the details: In our popu-

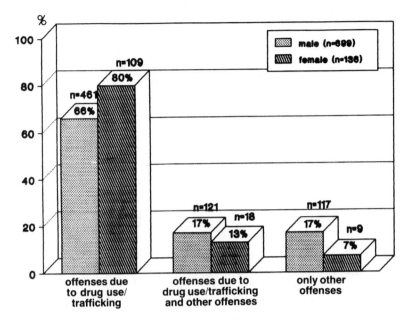

FIGURE 28.6.
Types of offenses according to judgment (by gender)

lation we found that, in 41.7% of the cases (N = 348), the first accorded deferment of execution of sentence was revoked immediately. From a positive point of view this means that in almost 60% of the cases treatment was begun, was not interrupted, and the convicted person did not need to go back to prison. For the majority of this "successful" group—about 85% of the cases (N = 413)—the remaining sentence was suspended on parole after the time spent in therapy was credited. To date this deferment was not revoked in about 86% (N = 353) of the cases. To these "positive" cases can be added another 29 persons who succeeded in the described way after a second deferment. The result is that for 382 persons (353 + 29), that is, almost 46% of a whole year, the option to undergo treatment instead of serving a term of imprisonment has proved to be reasonable and successful.

Naturally, it cannot be concluded now that all these people will live without drugs and without further conviction in the future. Critics may claim that even then more than 50% of the cases temporarily were not successful. But whoever is familiar with the difficult field of drug treat-

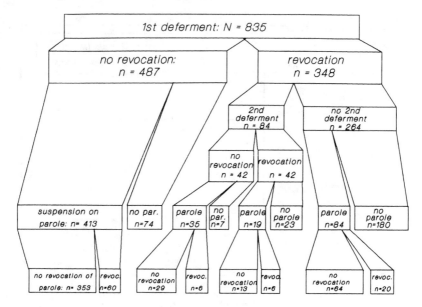

FIGURE 28.7.
Deferment according to Par. 35 Narcotic Drugs Act (1984)

ment knows that progress generally is lengthy and complex. Easy success is rare; interruptions and new starts are the rule. Therefore a high degree of patience, endurance, and motivation is necessary for a lasting positive end result. The legal regulation of deferment (of execution of sentence) in favor of a treatment could be one way to better master this field of problems. The data we collected so far encourage us to continue in this direction. We also expect further explanations from the above-mentioned report analysis for about one-third of the population.

But here problems already occur: The legal authorities of the respective federal states are responsible for granting permission to inspect the records. The authorities welcome our project in principle, in terms of content; but they also are concerned with maintaining the records according to data protection laws.[8] It is rather easy for us in those cases where only a few restrictions exist concerning the storing and processing of the data. It becomes much more complicated when specially determined records, or parts of records, (for example, psychological reports) are with-

8. For details referring to German data protection laws and research in criminology see Jehle (1987).

held from inspection. Some states hand over to us only records in cases where the convicted person agreed to the analysis. This is a very difficult demand because the convicted individuals do not know about these records themselves and very likely have little interest in acceding to our request.

The records themselves constitute a further problem. This collection of documents was created to serve only a practical purpose and was not intended to enable research at a later date. Therefore the records comprise a lot of information we do not need; on the other hand, there are important details missing, since they have very rarely or never been registered. For these reasons we are also confronted with problems of missing data.

The third problem concerns the fact that we cannot directly compare the group we examine with another group, particularly under experimental conditions. The main reason for this is—as mentioned before—that (the measure of) deferment can be applied to a great number of people. This total population cannot be ascertained from the penal register or from any other statistical records. It will therefore be difficult to state the success of deferment in form of a comparison of recidivism of the convicted with other persons. However, the focal point of our evaluation study regards the analysis of the process of deferment, that is, the kind of interaction, reaction, and operation pattern applied by different authorities. According to the definition, that can only be examined within our random sample itself.

It would be too simple to state at this point that a study with a limited possibility of definitive conclusion is better than no study. Instead we would like to emphasize how difficult it is to do evaluation research in the social field, which should meet methodological standards as well as practical needs, especially if only one source of information is available.

REFERENCES

Eberth, A. (1982). *Betäubungsmittelrecht: Kommentar und Anleitung für die Praxis*. München: Eckhard Müller Verlag.

Egg, R. (ed.). (1988). *Drogentherapie und Strafe: Kriminologie und Praxis*. Vol. 3. Wiesbaden: Schriftenreihe der Kriminologischen Zentralstelle e.V. (KrimZ).

Egg, R., and Kurze, M. (1989). *Drogentherapie in staatlich anerkannten Einrichtungen. Ergebnisse einer Umfrage*. Wiesbaden: Kriminologische Zentralstelle. Berichte, Materialien, Arbeitspapiere; Heft 3.

Jehle, J.-M. (eds.). (1987). Datenzugang und Datenschutz in der kriminologischen Forschung. *Kriminologie und Praxis*. Vol. 2, Wiesbaden: Schriftenreihe der Kriminologischen Zentralstelle e.V. (KrimZ).

Jehle, J.-M., and Egg, R. (eds.). (1986). Anwendungsbezogene Kriminologie zwischen Grundlagenforschung und Praxis. *Kriminologie und Praxis.* Vol. 1. Wiesbaden: Schriftenreihe der Kriminologischen Zentralstelle e.V. (KrimZ).

Jones, M. (1968). *Beyond the Therapeutic Community.* London: Yale University Press.

Körner, H. H. (1985). *Betäubungsmittelgesetz: deutsches u. internationales Betäubungsmittelrecht.* München: Beck Verlag.

Kreuzer, A., and Wille, R. (1987). *Drogen—Kriminologie und Therapie.* Heidelberg: C. F. Müller Verlag.

CHAPTER 29

Compulsory Treatment: Results of a Follow-Up Study of Drug Addicts*

Heiner Melchinger

INTRODUCTION

More than 50 years ago, a paragraph added to the German penal code made it possible for a judge to order compulsory treatment for a person who became criminal as a result of drug dependency and who was likely to commit serious crimes in the future as a result of this drug dependency. This paragraph was originally devised for alcoholics. In the early seventies, the courts were confronted more and more frequently with young drug-dependent criminals and there was a sense of helplessness about how to deal with these people. There was a consensus that the traditional alcoholic ward of a psychiatric hospital would not be a place where young drug-dependent clients could be treated in an effective way. At this time, a paragraph was inserted in the German law governing juvenile court proceedings that prescribed court-ordered therapy for young people to be carried out in a treatment center where specific therapeutic and social aids could be applied.

By the beginning of the eighties, two residential treatment centers were founded to comply with this paragraph: the Brauel Clinic and the Parsberg Clinic. These treatment centers, which are sponsored by the Federal Ministry of Health, have the character of model clinics. Therefore evaluation research to examine their effects was also funded by the Federal Ministry.

*The data presented in this paper were collected as part of wider studies funded by the German Federal Ministry of Health (Melchinger 1986, 1988; Schulzke and Holler 1989).

At the same time, the German law concerning narcotics was reformed. The altered paragraphs concerning drug-dependent clients are geared toward the maxim "treatment instead of penalty." In essence, the laws indicate that the sentence of detention can be suspended if the delinquent is willing to participate in a residental treatment program. The situation at that time became complex and confusing, for the following reasons:

• There were new legal means of dealing with drug-addicted criminals (court-ordered therapy on the one side of the continuum and voluntary treatment on the other).
• Judges had limited experience in dealing with drug addicts and their problems.
• There was a controversy about the relative effectiveness of the growing number of alternative treatment methods and institutions.

The above-mentioned treatment centers were founded at this time. It was predicted that their capacity (a total of about 140 treatment slots) would be exhausted in a short time. But the opposite was the case: they had large staffs of well-motivated therapists, but very few clients. On the other hand, the jails were full of drug-dependent prisoners and the jails' administrators were unable to handle them. Against the background of this development, it was decided to extend the legal basis of admission to these treatment centers for drug-dependent prisoners. For this to apply, a prisoner had to express willingness to undergo residental drug therapy, and the jail's medical director had to be willing to refer the prisoner to the treatment center if convinced of the prisoner's true motivation to become abstinent.

CHARACTERISTICS OF THE SUBJECT SAMPLE

At the Brauel Treatment Center, there are clients admitted by court order as well as prison clients who were admitted more or less voluntarily. At the point of admission clients in the study group (N = 316) are between 16 and 30 years old, with an average age of about 21 years. Eighty percent of the clients are male, 20% female. Thirty-three percent have no school graduation certificates, 84% either did not start or did not finish any vocational training.

As shown in Figure 29.1, there are virtually equal numbers of clients admitted by court order and clients referred from jail. The proportion of clients whose treatment was terminated prematurely is relatively high: 56% of all clients referred from jail were referred to jail again after some

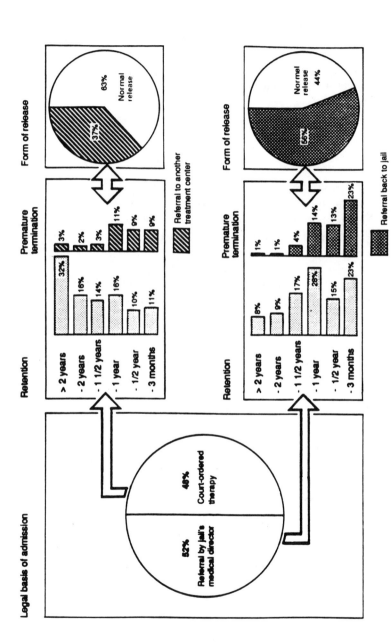

FIGURE 29.1.
Brauel Treatment Center: Clients differentiated according to legal basis of admission, retention and form of release (N = 316).

months of treatment; 37% of the clients admitted by court order were referred to other treatment centers, in most cases to a forensic ward of a psychiatric clinic, where more secure conditions could be guaranteed. The dropouts were caused by continued drug relapses, delinquency, or escapes. These varying dropout rates, however, reflect less the different characteristics of the clients than the different legal bases for referral: the referral to jàil is an easy procedure to effect, whereas client referral to a psychiatric hospital is a much more complicated process.

STUDY DESIGN

The study included follow-up studies of clients 1.4 and 3.5 years after release. Members of the research group tried to establish personal contact with the clients, normally at their homes but in some cases in prison or at a treatment center. This procedure was succesful in 75% of all cases. In addition to personal interviews, information was collected from the Bundeszentralregister. This is a register, managed by the General Federal State Prosecutor, in which the sentences of all German criminal courts are recorded. There is a legal right of access to these registrations for scientific research. Thus information on the criminal records of all clients was provided.

Success was defined by clients meeting the following criteria:

• drug abstinence,
• legal probation,
• structured time use (i.e., social routines and habits),
• integration in a drug-free social context.

When there was no valid evidence about the development of clients they were defined as relapses.

RESULTS

The study included 130 clients: 49% were discharged according to treatment plan, 51% were dropouts. After a follow-up period (1.4 years) of the treatment completers there were 25% successes and 54% failures. The proportional success rates of all admissions dropped to 12% and the failure group rose to 78%. Figure 29.2 presents these results graphically. It is important to note that some of the clients who had relapses were admitted in very poor physical condition. Against this background, the

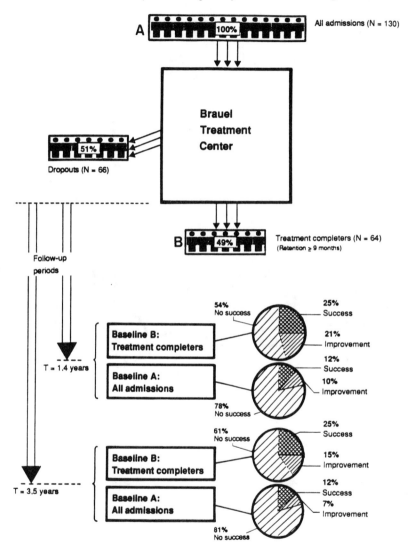

FIGURE 29.2.
Brauel Treatment Center: Success rates referred to different base lines (N = 130).

fact that they are still alive can be seen as a positive treatment effect, even if they are continuing their drug abuse.

The results correspond very closely to those from a follow-up study of clients of the previously mentioned Parsberg Treatment Center, conducted by a research group of the University of Erlangen (Stosberg et

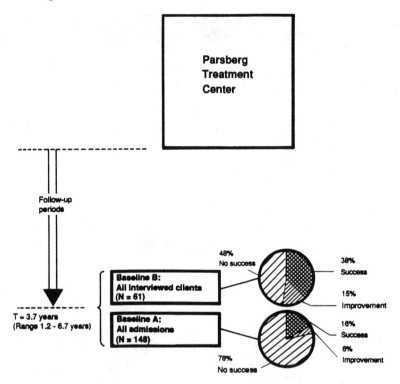

FIGURE 29.3.
Parsberg Treatment Center: Success rates referred to base lines (N = 148).

al. 1988). As shown in Figure 29.3 16% of the clients in this study
were defined as successes and 78% as relapses (the rates referred to total
population of admissions).

Three and a half years after release, the success rates were nearly the
same as before, but there are important subsequent shifts in client behavior. Forty-one percent of all clients were now classified in a different
way than they had been before, 1.4 years after release. This fact is illustrated in Figure 29.4. Three quarters of the clients initially classified
as successes did not relapse again. Nearly all clients classified as improvements did relapse. On the other hand, some of the failed clients
were now found to be free of drugs and delinquency.

Furthermore, it was tested whether there was a relationship between
retention and treatment outcome. In the follow-up study 1.4 years after
release, there was absolutely no relationship (Figure 29.5). The same

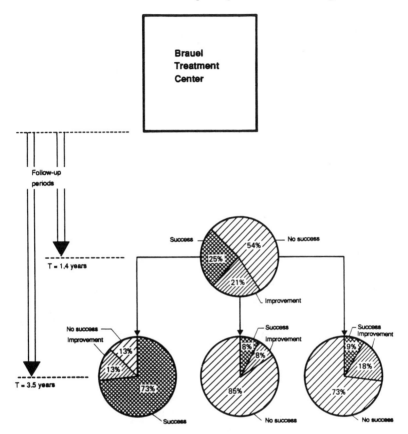

FIGURE 29.4.
Changes in the posttreatment status of clients (N = 64)

findings were reported by the Erlangen research group (Stosberg et al. 1988).

Interestingly, a relationship is apparent if one analyzes the results of the follow-up study 3.5 years after release (Figure 29.6). Here, a curvilinear trend between retention and success can be seen: successes after a retention of less than 12 months are no more frequent than after a retention of more than 24 months, with fewer relapses after intermediate periods. These findings correspond very well with the clients' retrospective appraisal of their experiences during treatment: they confirm that treatment lasting more than two years can produce destructive effects.

As in other studies, pretreatment delinquency proves to be a predictor

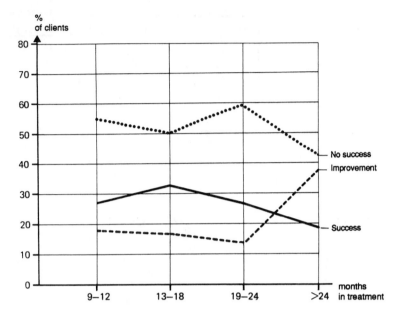

FIGURE 29.5.
Relationship between retention and posttreatment status of clients (1.4-year follow-up study)(N = 64).

of treatment outcomes. When one compares the pretreatment criminal careers of treatment completers and dropouts, the following differences are found: the dropouts are characterized by more criminal trials and by more serious crimes such as robbery, extortion, battery, and homicide. It can also be derived from the follow-up study that there is an association between the status of clients and their pretreatment criminal career. As shown in Figure 29.7, there is a relationship between frequency of pretreatment criminal trials and the clients' status 3.5 years after release. It is apparent that the more trials the less the likelihood of successful rehabilitation. The same tendency is evident if one examines cumulative detention in jails as a predictor of treatment outcome. As illustrated in Figure 29.8, the longer the detention experience the less the chance of a successful rehabilitation.

It appears that, when we compare dropouts and completers on the criterion of achieving legal probation, dropouts get involved more often in repeated delinquency (78% vs. 49% of completers). Furthermore, it appears that the crimes of delinquent dropouts are more serious: 92% of all delinquent dropouts were sentenced to detention of more than a half

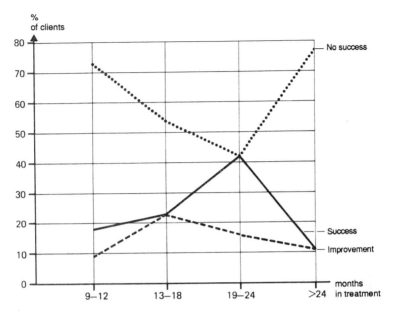

FIGURE 29.6.
Relationship between retention and posttreatment status of clients (3.5-years follow-up study) (N = 64).

year (up to six years and more), compared with 50% of the delinquent completers. If one considers the status of clients admitted by different legal means (clients treated on a compulsory basis and clients treated on a voluntary basis), it becomes evident that there are fewer successes among the voluntary group, i.e., the presumably more motivated clients (17% vs. 29%). In considering this result, it is important to remember that the dropout rate of clients referred from jail is greater, a fact that should lead to a more rigorous selection of clients on the basis of their treatment motivation. This result is further evidence that there is no empirical support for the often formulated thesis that free personal decision is a precondition for treatment success. At least, the result shows that one must treat constructs like voluntariness and treatment motivation cautiously.

In a further analysis, it was shown that there is a relationship between treatment outcome and the age at which clients become regular users of hard drugs. In the follow-up study 1.4 years after release, clients who became regular users of hard drugs at an early age were unlikely to respond well to treatment. Two years later, this relationship disappeared.

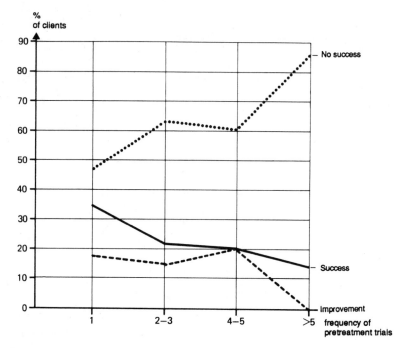

FIGURE 29.7.
Relationship between frequency of pretreatment trials and posttreatment status of clients (3.5-years follow-up study) (N = 64).

Now a relationship between status and the age at which clients became regular users of drugs in general (in most cases these were not hard drugs) can be found. The younger the clients were when they started using drugs on a regular basis, the less likely the treatment success becomes. Exactly the same findings were reported by the Erlangen research group (Stosberg et al. 1988). Clients who became regular users of drugs at a very early age are usually characterized by serious deficiencies in socialization (and even in biological development) which cannot be compensated for by two years of treatment in a social setting dominated by drug-subculture behaviors and values and by overt or covert drug abuse. In some cases young people became even more involved with drug abuse during treatment.

The results, then, can be summarized as follows: Treatment under conditions of legal compulsion can be successful. Such treatment, however, is not appropriate for clients who became regular users of drugs at a

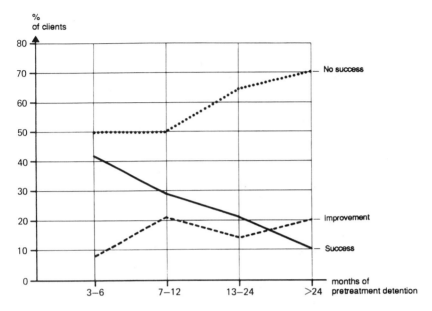

FIGURE 29.8.
Relationship between pretreatment detention experience (cumulative retention) and posttreatment status of clients (3.5-years follow-up study) (N = 64).

very early age, nor for clients who have had a career of serious crimes. Furthermore, it can be seen that treatment in a residental facility over a period of more than two years runs the risk of producing destructive effects.

INQUIRY OF JUDGES AND STATE PROSECUTORS

Parallel to the follow-up study, a representative inquiry was conducted into the attitudes and experiences of German judges and state prosecutors who dealt with drug-addicted criminals. The main findings included the following: There is an extremely wide diversity of opinions among judges and state prosecutors about the right way to deal with drug-addicted criminals. Some judges' sentences can be classified as treatment oriented, while others' sentences are penalty oriented. There are judges who generally prefer court-ordered treatment for their presumed educational value, and there are judges who regard the sentence of a court order as a last resort, to be applied only when all other attempts at therapeutic intervention have not succeeded.

Nevertheless, the majority of judges and state prosecutors have a critical attitude toward court-ordered treatment of drug-dependent clients. Most of them believe that the probability of treatment success in a state residental treatment center would be less than in a therapeutic community. Where the facilities of the German law governing narcotics (treatment instead of penalty) cannot be applied (for example, when voluntary treatment in the past has not been successful or when a client has committed serious crimes), the majority of judges and state prosecutors were more likely to sentence detention than court-ordered treatment. They believe that the search for opportunities to offer therapy during detention (referral to a treatment center or granting suspension of sentence on probation with the obligation to undergo therapy) is more promising. So far they do not show a high level of acceptance of court-ordered therapy at a state residental center.

In this context it is useful to consider the experiences reported from another model program funded by the Federal Minstry of Health which was conducted at 53 locations. In this program, drug-dependent prisoners were offered advice and counseling by drug counselers. An essential aspect of the program was that, because drug-dependent prisoners are mistrustful of any members of the staff, the drug counseler should be a member of an external therapeutic institution.

The experiences in this program were positive. In many cases, it was possible to encourage the clients to undergo therapy and subsequently to arrange for treatment in a state-certified therapeutic community (Holler and Knahl 1988). The findings reported of a covariation between treatment success and detention, strongly suggest that prisoners be offered this form of counseling at an early stage of their detention.

REFERENCES

Holler, G., and Knahl, A. (1988). Aufsuchende Sozialarbeit für betäubungs-mittelabhängige Straftäter. In R. Egg (ed.), *Drogentherapie und Strafe.* Wiesbaden: Kriminologische Zentralstelle.

Melchinger, H. (1986). *Wissenschaftliche Begleitung der Fachklinik Brauel, 1.* Zwischenbericht. Hannover: Institut für Entwicklungsplanung und Strukturforschung.

————. (1988). Therapie unter Freiheitsentzug: Katamnestische Untersuchungen bei Klienten der Fachklinik Brauel. In W. Feuerlein et al. (eds.),

Therapieverläufe bei Drogenabhängigen. Berlin, Heidelberg, New York, and Tokyo: Springer.

Schulzke, M., and Holler, G. (1989). *Wissenschaftliche Begleitung der Fachklinik Brauel*, 2. Zwischenbericht. Hannover: Institut für Entwicklungsplanung und Strukturforschung.

Stosberg, K., Ingenleuf, H., and Bratenstein, B. (1988). *Wissenschaftliche Begleitung der Bezirksklinik Parsberg II*, Abschlußbericht. Erlangen: Universität.

PART EIGHT

Drug Abuse and AIDS

CHAPTER 30

HIV-Infection Rates in Intravenous Drug Abusers in Federal Republic of Germany*

Dieter Kleiber

PURPOSE OF THE STUDY

The following study, conducted in 1988–89 for the German Ministry of Health, focused on intravenous drug abusers in West Germany and West Berlin. The main purpose of the survey was to establish the (true) HIV-prevalence rates in intravenous drug addicts in a sample as representative as possible. Second, information was to be gathered on the differential risks of HIV infection (needle sharing and sexual behavior, social factors) in order to estimate the importance of these factors with regard to the infection. Third and finally, information-gathering concentrated on the extent to which the addicts have changed their behavior, since they are so frequently accused of not heeding appeals for prevention, being low in compliance, and showing little ability or inclination to learn.

METHOD AND DESCRIPTION OF THE SAMPLE

In a multicenter design we conducted detailed one- to two-hour structured interviews with 630 intravenous drug addicts. The structure used for the

*The study was funded by the German Federal Ministry of Health.

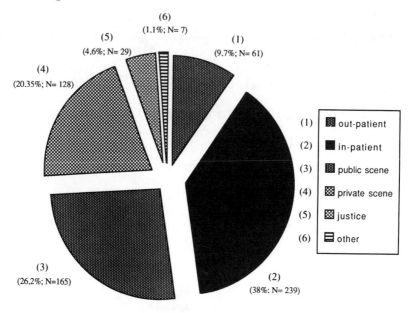

FIGURE 30.1.
Sampling structure according to scene

interviews was elaborated by the author together with counselors and therapists of drug addicts, AIDS-Hilfe (AIDS support centers) and others, and included more than 300 questions on the subject's addictive and sexual histories, life situations and socialization, changes in behavior as a reaction to AIDS, "social support," and daily hassles. A major aim was to reach drug addicts in all of the spheres which they frequent. This was necessary in order to obtain a sample which would be as representative as possible and reflect the reality of the drug scene, thus avoiding the limitations of studies previously conducted in the Federal Republic of Germany, most of which have included only a highly selected clientele. It can be seen from Figure 30.1 that 9.7% (n = 61) of our interviewees were outpatients (most were being seen at counseling centers) and 38% (n = 239) of them were hospitalized. Frequenters of both the public and even the private spheres were also well represented (26.2% [n = 165] and 20.35% [n = 128], respectively), whereas the penal sector is underrepresented. This is partly because we went to great lengths to ensure that the subjects' participation in the study should be voluntary, the data be collected anonymously, and that "situations of coercion" should not be exploited to obtain information. We were of the opinion that this self-imposed restriction on the scope of our study was necessary for ethical reasons. It meant that we undertook to interview addicts involved in judicial proceedings only if we could guarantee that we alone would collect all data (that is, by persons not in the penal system) and that we would not be subject to any obligation to disclose them to the prison administration or physician.

As a rule subjects were not informed of the results of the HIV test. Exceptions were made in cases in which they had expressly requested it in the context of detailed counseling on the services provided by the AIDS-Hilfe System. The interviews were generally conducted by trained interviewers of the same sex as the subject. Subjects could request to have an interviewer of the opposite sex if they wished. The interview (most of which was standardized) was structured in such a way that a combination of counseling and interviewing was possible. In several treatment facilities the questionnaire has now been adopted for general use in taking case histories, evidently with great success. We consider such a combination of research and counseling to be a prerequisite of a "street epidemiology," which must start from the premise that trust is of the utmost importance in research and a necessary precondition for good compliance. Trust was also particularly important because we are not paying our subjects for reasons connected with research ethics and basic principles.

For the sample in this study we have interviewed 32.2% women (n = 203) and 67.8% (n = 427) men. The age distribution showed a mean age of 26 years and a median of 28 years (Figure 30.2). Our sample should therefore be roughly representative of the population of intravenous drug addicts in the Federal Republic of Germany.

RESULTS

Prevalence Rates of HIV in Drug Addicts

For the total sample we have found a prevalence rate of 20.1%. Recently, a commission of enquiry on AIDS in West Germany estimated the HIV-prevalence rates among intravenous drug addicts in the Federal Republic to be between 30% and 60%. Since our sample should be more representative than others and is also relatively large, previous estimates should be reduced on the basis of our data. In our view the prevalence rates have been so frequently overestimated in the past because no surveys have yet been carried out in certain regions, particularly in rural areas

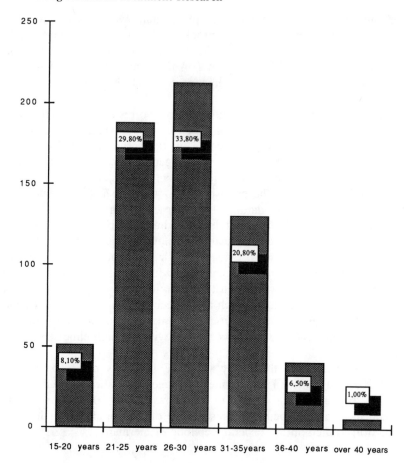

FIGURE 30.2.
Sampling structure according to age (N = 630; x = 26 y.; median = 28y.).

(where the prevalence rates are lower than in big cities such as Berlin and Frankfurt).

We have found a HIV-prevalence rate of 22.1% for female intravenous drug addicts and one of 19.1% for the men. The differences between the two groups are not statistically significant. We found highly significant differences between the prevalence rates in the different geographical regions in which we conducted our survey. In Berlin, where there are 6,000 to 9,000 drug addicts, we found the highest prevalence rate of 26% (Table 30.1). In Frankfurt, where conditions are probably similar, we

TABLE 30.1

Prevalence Rates According to Geographical Regions and City Size

Geographical regions	HIV positive	
Berlin	26.0%	
North Germany (rural)	15.7%	
North-Rhine Westfalia	16.2%	(Chi square; $p \leq .01$)
City size		
Under 50,000	11.6%	
50,000–100,000	14.8%	
Over 500,000	25.8%	(Chi square; $p \leq .0005$)

have as yet been unable to obtain any data. In northern Germany, in the rural areas, 15.7% of those interviewed were positive for the HIV, and in North-Rhine Westphalia (NRW) 16.2% of the active heroin addicts tested HIV positive. The gap between the urban and rural districts, which uncontestably exists, becomes even more evident when we subdivide the addicts taking part in the survey according to the size of the town or village in which they live. Then we see that the prevalence rates increase with the size of the town or community, which means that infection with AIDS is at present a problem mainly encountered in the cities and that the epidemiological development will be subject to a time lag in the rural areas.

The addicts infected with the HIV virus have been divided into age groups. Both with the age groups and also with regard to the number of years of intravenous drug abuse we found that the prevalence increases with increasing age and thus on the average with longer duration of addiction. In the group of 15 to 20-year-old addicts about 6% were HIV positive (Figure 30.3). The percentage among the 31- to 36-year-olds was as high as nearly 30%. While the over-36-year-old men showed a lower prevalance rate than the 31- to 36-year-olds, the percentage among the over-36-year-old women addicts was as high as 33%.

We determined the prevalence rates in the various subpopulations and came to the extremely interesting results shown in Figure 30.4. All the differences between mean prevalence rates for the different yes/no alternatives are highly significant (1–0.1% level). The risk of infection with AIDS is, as the diagram shows, distributed unequally among different social spheres. The prevalance rates were higher in cases of low social integration ("prison," yes/no), poorer social background ("home," yes/

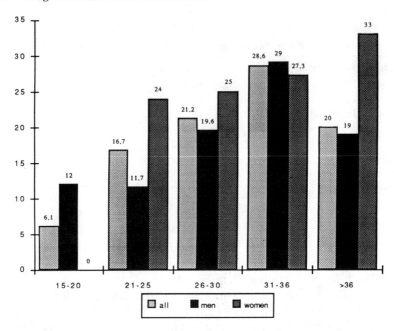

FIGURE 30.3.
Age and HIV-prevalence-rates

no), a lower level of education (special or grade school vs. junior high school or high school), and poorer (or uncompleted) training (vocational training not completed vs. completed).

It is conspicuous that 13% of the group who were not in prison at the time of the interview were positive for the HIV, while the prevalence of HIV in the group that had been or were in prison was almost twice as high (24%). We split the group of those having been in prison at some time, who showed a total prevalence of 24% in 1988, according to the criterion of whether they reported taking drugs during their time in prison. This applied to as many as 40% of intravenous drug addicts in prison, a fact which has not been readily publicized. We found that every third addict of those who reported having been on intravenous drugs in prison (32%) was found to have HIV antibodies, while in the group of those who had not been on intravenous drugs in prison "only" every fifth (20%) was HIV positive.

Promiscuity, prostitution, and previous venereal disease were also clearly associated with HIV infection. However, it is not possible at this stage to establish whether promiscuity is a causal factor in its own right

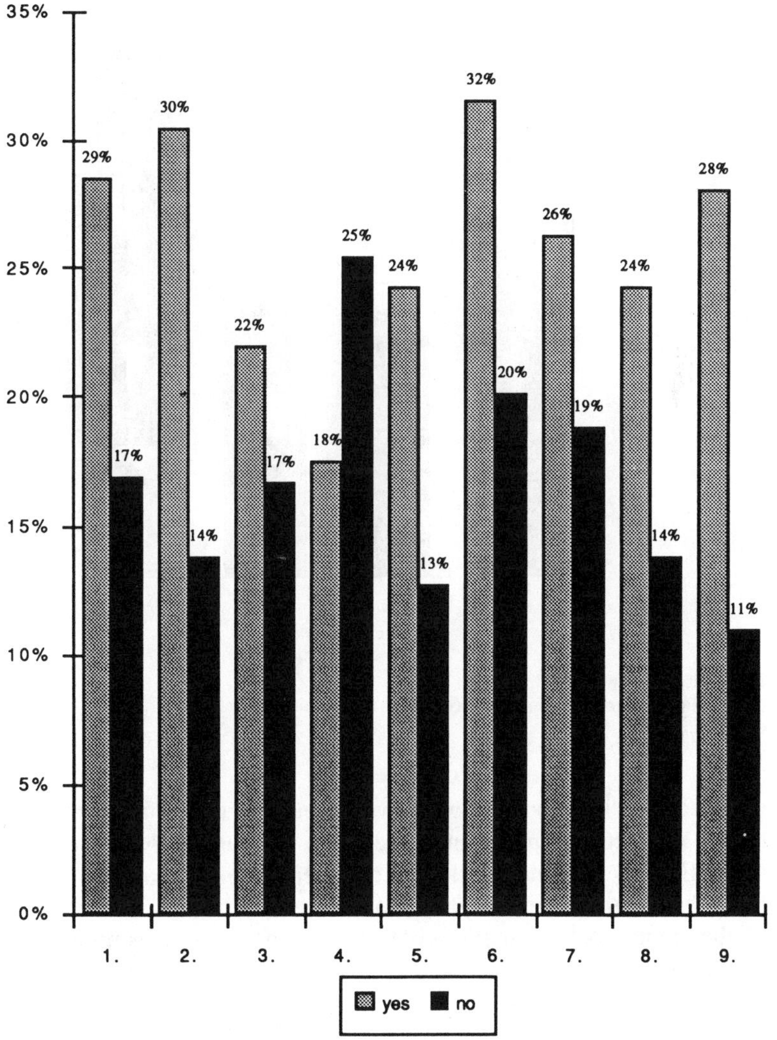

FIGURE 30.4.
HIV prevalence rates in subpopulations

Legend:
1 = prostitution (yes/no)?
2 = veneral diseases in earlier times (yes/no)?
3 = elementary school vs. middle/high school
4 = profesional training (yes/no)?

5 = inprisoned in earlier times (yes/no)?
6 = injected in prison (yes/no)?
7 = home (yes/no)?
8 = promisc (yes/no)?
9 = hepatitis in earlier times (yes/no)?

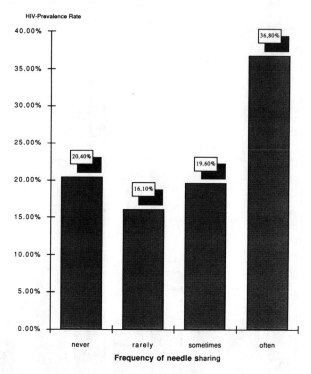

FIGURE 30.5.
Needle sharing and HIV-prevalence rates (Chi square; p ≤ .01)

or whether it is associated with overall higher risk behavior (e.g., with higher drug consumption among addicts who are involved in prostitution). For the present it will suffice to bear in mind that the differences found between the subgroups cannot necessarily be taken as an indication of the importance of sexual contact as a mode of transmission of the infection.

Differential Risks of HIV Infection

Two issues were given priority, namely needle sharing and sexual behavior and their respective significance. Figure 30.5 gives an overview of needle sharing as obtained from over 300 responses to the question: "How often did you share your needle during the past year?" If we ask such a question in connection with HIV status we have to deal with the difficult

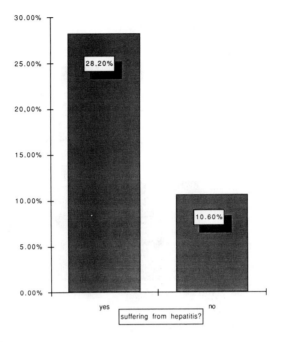

FIGURE 30.6.
HIV-prevalence rates and former hepatitis

problem that to obtain a reliable reply we must limit ourselves to a period which the addicts can more or less remember, so this period must be relatively short. However, it is often quite unrelated to the time of infection. Preventive behavior by anti-HIV-positive persons, for example, leads to a reduction in needle sharing and thus behavior parameters are not good indicators of HIV prevalence. Nevertheless, it evidently does have an effect. More than 35% of the addicts who had frequently employed used needles within the last half year, 20% of those who reported never having shared needles during this time, and as few as 16% of those who reported rarely having employed used needles were infected (Figure 30.5).

Two other parameters, namely a previous hepatitis B infection (which is mainly transmitted by blood-to-blood contact), and a history of venereal disease as a clear indicator of sexual activity, also show a distinct connection with HIV-prevalence rates. Drug abusers who reported not having had hepatitis had a prevalence rate of 10.6% (which was half the rate found in the total sample). By contrast, 28.2% of the addicts who had had hepatitis were HIV positive (Figure 30.6). The picture was similar

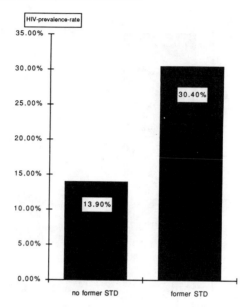

FIGURE 30.7.
HIV-prevalence rate and former STD (N = 610; p ≤ 001)

with regard to previous venereal disease (Figure 30.7). Nearly 14% of the subgroup of addicts who had never had venereal disease (according to their own reports) had HIV antibodies, whereas 30.4% who had had venereal disease were positive for HIV. This replicates a result from research on heterosexual transmission of the HIV virus, according to which inflammations due to infectious diseases such as gonorrhea and syphilis and by trichomonas and chlamydia infections increase both the risk of HIV infection and that of passing on the HIV virus (AIDS-Zentrum des Bundesgesundheitsamtes, 1988, p. 14).

To recap, we have now shown how these two factors are related to one another by creating four subgroups. First we differentiated between addicts with no previous history of hepatitis and those who had had hepatitis B. Then the two subgroups were subdivided again on the basis of the criterion "previous venereal disease: yes/no." Figure 30.8 shows the HIV-prevalence rates in each of these four groups. For addicts who had had neither hepatitis nor venereal disease we found a prevalence rate of 6.6%. In the subgroup who had never had hepatitis but had previously had some kind of venereal disease 18.8% were already HIV positive. The prevalence rate in the subgroup having had hepatitis but *no* venereal dis-

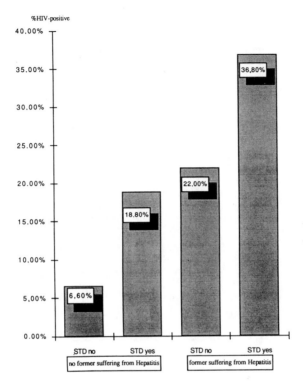

FIGURE 30.8.
HIV-prevalence rates, STD, and hepatitis

ease was 22%, and thus significantly higher. The highest rate (36.8%) was found for the subgroup having had both hepatitis and venereal disease. These results suggest that the hepatitis factor, which we have taken as an indicator for "frequent needle sharing," is dominant.

We also investigated the histories of hepatitis and venereal disease in the subgroups of addicts involved in prostitution. This applies to 54% of the women (in Berlin as many as 80%) and roughly 20% of the men (see Figure 30.9). In addicts practicing prostitution who had not had hepatitis during their drug-using career we even found a comparatively low prevalence of 14.3%. The subgroup of drug abusers who neither practiced prostitution nor reported having had hepatitis showed an even lower risk (HIV-prevalence rate of 9.4%). The rate in the subgroup of those who had had hepatitis but were not prostitutes was much higher (23.8%), while the highest rate (39%) was found in the group of addicts

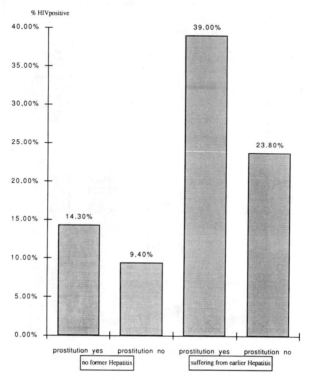

FIGURE 30.9.
Hepatitis and experience in prostitution: HIV prevalence rates

who did practice prostitution and had previously had hepatitis B. From this we conclude that needle sharing over an extended period is probably the dominant mode of transmission, even if the influence of sexual behavior on the rate of HIV infection cannot be overlooked. As far as preventive strategies are concerned the achievement of the goals of "reduction of needle sharing in drug addicts" and "raising the acceptance of condoms by intravenous drug users particularly among addicts who practice prostitution must be given greater priority.

Changes in Behavior as a Reaction to AIDS

It has frequently been claimed that intravenous drug addicts are not capable of learning and will not change their behavior. It has been one of the additional aims of this study to examine this assumption, which has

TABLE 30.2

Changes in Behavior in Reaction to AIDS

	All i.v. DA	HIV+	HIV−	Prostitution	No Prostitution
Change of needle sharing habit (yes)	59.2%	76.0%	56.0%	65.0%	55.8%
Change of sexual behavior (yes)	48.2%	71.1%	47.6%	61.6%	48.8%
Frequency of drug injection					
More frequent under threat of AIDS	2.6%	9.0%	1.0%	3.4%	2.3%
No change	35.0%	23.3%	37.3%	31.8%	35.0%
Sexual behavior					
No change	34.2%	23.3%	37.3%	46.7%	34.2%
Condom use					
Always	12.0%	21.0%	9.8%	12.5%	11.5%
More frequent	26.2%	42.0%	23.0%	44.3%	18.7%
No change	61.6%	36.0%	67.0%	43.2%	69.2%

often been the starting point for repressive policies on AIDS. Clear changes in behavior as a result of AIDS were found among the intravenous drug users in the sample investigated in 1988 (n = 630). Nearly 60% of intravenous drug abusers have already altered their needle-sharing behavior (since the middle of 1986), and about 48% have also changed their sexual behavior to include more AIDS-preventive measures (Table 30.2). These figures are remarkable, although there is no reason for complacency. The changes in behavior in the two subgroups, that is, the addicts identified as HIV positive and the male and female addicts practicing drug-related prostitution, were more pronounced than in the overall population. Seventy-six percent of those positive for HIV stated that their behavior was completely socially responsible as far as needle sharing was concerned (most of the others pay attention to the order when sharing needles and make sure that they use the needles or syringes last) and 71.1% reported changes in sexual behavior.

With regard to needle sharing, which is still being practiced, behavioral changes are reported by all subgroups: 27.6% reported that they now use their own injection equipment only, a further 22.3% that they used equipment which was not their own less often, and 14.4% that they cleaned their equipment more often or always. However, as many as just over a third of the respondents stated that they had not changed their behavior with regard to the use of injection equipment. Investigation of the accessibility of syringes revealed the following picture: 41.8% of the respondents said that they never had any difficulty in obtaining clean syringes and 29.4% that they seldom had any difficulty. Seventeen percent reported sometimes having difficulty and 11.1% that they often or very often had difficulty. The difficulties described by the addicts interviewed were lack of money, reduced activity level as a result of withdrawal effects, fear of being caught with syringes, which are sometimes only sold in packs of 100, and problems at night or on weekends. To what extent structural or situational and/or subjective barriers can act as a hindrance to the use of clean syringes cannot be definitively established from the self-reports of the respondents.

Analysis of the changes in sexual behavior of the intravenous drug users reveals that education and counseling are still greatly needed. It seems to be easier for many to have fewer sex partners or to sleep with one exclusive partner than to use condoms. Only 12% reported using condoms always, and while 26% do use them more often than before, 61% reported no change in the frequency with which they used condoms since they had known about AIDS.

AIDS and Prostitution

Figure 30.10 shows the frequency of condom use in relation to drug abuse-related prostitution. Of the 147 respondents who answered questions on this issue, 23.8% said that they never used condoms when working as prostitutes, 12% that they used them in 50% of cases, and 63.9% that they used them often or always. A working group at our institute (Gersch et al. 1988) drew attention in a study on "Drug-Addicted Prostitutes and their Customers" to the fact that the women are frequently put under pressure by their customers. In the absence of an effective antiviral treatment or prophylactic immunization, AIDS prevention can only consist of behavioral prevention at present, that is, it must be aimed at influencing activities in potentially dangerous situations. Thus the use of condoms assumes a decisive AIDS-preventive function, particularly in prostitution, since it can reduce the epidemiological risks to a minimum. To quote Dr. M. Koch, the head of the German AIDS Zentrum: "In this connection we must keep promoting condoms again and again, I believe this is very important. But I sometimes have the impression that German men consider that to drive on the Autobahn [highway] at 180 km per hour and to have intercourse without condoms are two of their basic rights."

Male and female prostitutes are at a particularly high risk of infection

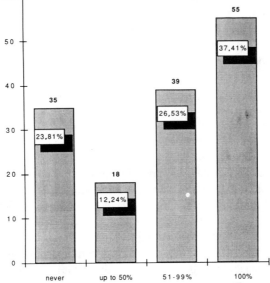

FIGURE 30.10.
Use of condoms during prostitution

if they do not use condoms as a result of the large number of different sexual partners they have. In addition, as the prevalence of the HIV among prostitutes rises, they are increasingly also endangering their customers if they refuse to use condoms or force or blackmail them to perform intercourse without protection. The rate of condom use among customers of prostitutes (male customers of female prostitutes) is distinctly lower in West Germany than in other countries (20%), despite the awareness of the risk of infection. Maiworm (1988) reported from the perspective of a brothel owner that in clubs run by him in which a "catalogue of self-protective measures" is "adhered" to with the aim of supporting prostitutes so that they can withstand the pressure of customers who want to have intercourse unprotected, thus benefiting both, the use of condoms has fallen again in the last few months. Since the risk of transmission of the AIDS virus to the heterosexual population is particularly high in prostitution, and particularly in drug-related prostitution, it is urgent to exert influence on customers of prostitutes to change their behavior, since they not infrequently demand intercourse without condom protection and offer more money for it (Deutscher Bundestag 1988, p. 124). Evidently only a negligible percentage of prostitutes' customers

480 Drug Addiction Treatment Research

wish to use condoms during intercourse, and a further small percentage does not resist the desire or demand of the prostitute to have intercourse unprotected—despite AIDS (Maiworm 1988). To date very little is known about the psychodynamic, lifestyle-related, social, and other reasons for this behavior.

Approaches based on preventive behavior, which shift the responsibility for the use of condoms in prostitution to the prostitutes alone, fail to take into account that prostitutes do have a vital interest in using condoms, but that as a result of several factors they are frequently unable to or do not insist on doing so:

- Drug-addicted prostitutes, in particular, have such a restricted scope for acting and making decisions owing to their addiction that they are easily blackmailed, particularly when they have to get money quickly because of withdrawal symptoms. Their customers often exploit such situations (Gersch et al. 1988). Süssmuth (1987) has rightly pointed out that many customers of prostitutes exert considerable financial pressure on prostitutes, particularly those who are drug addicts. "Strong pressure must be put on men who go to prostitutes to use condoms, so that they infect neither the prostitute, themselves, nor their own partner" (p. 91).
- Since in prostitution, as with many other sectors, the willingness to provide the service is dependent on the price, the women's willingness to take risks will increase the more is paid if she can compensate for loss of income (including that resulting from a general scare associated with AIDS) only by this means.
- Evidently the proportion of high-risk situations (unprotected sexual intercourse) varies in relation to the settings (street prostitution, brothels, bars and saunas, call girls, etc.) in which prostitution takes place. Whereas in street prostitution in New York sex with penetration occurs in 20% to 30% of the cases with a rate of condom use of 50% to 80%, the corresponding percentage of high-risk sexual practices by prostitutes in New York brothels is much higher. It could therefore be expected that forcing a reduction in street prostitution would be counterproductive as far as AIDS prevention is concerned (Wallace et al. 1988).

ACKNOWLEDGEMENTS

To date (1990) our sample includes 1253 IV drug addicts. The actual HIV-prevalence rate in this total sample is 19.4%. I owe my thanks to many people in different areas for their help and support. I am particularly grateful to Dieter Sawalies, Dipl.-Psych., and Jörg. U. Schlender, Dipl.-Psych., who organized the interviews in West Germany and also to my collegue and coworker, Doris Velten, Dipl.-Psych., Dirk Enzmann, Dipl.-Psych. and the other colleagues at my institute, the Sozialpädagogisches Institut Berlin (spi).

REFERENCES

AIDS-Zentrum des Bundesgesundheitsamtes (ed.). (1988). *AIDS-Nachrichten,* 3.

Deutscher Bundestag (ed.). (1988). *AIDS: Fakten und Konsequenzen.* Zwischenbericht der Enquete Kommission des 11. Deutschen Bundestages. Bonn.

Gersch, C. et al. (1988). *Drogenabhängige Prostituierte und ihre Freier.* Berlin: Sozialpädagogisches Institut.

Maiworm, H. '1988). Diskussionsbeitrag über AIDS-Prävention bei weiblichen Prostituierten. In *AIDS-Forschung* 8 (August) 432–41.

Süssmuth, R. (1987). *AIDS: Wege aus der Angst.* Hamburg: Hoffmann and Campe.

Wallace, J. I., Mann, J., and Beatrice, S. (1988). *Survey of Streetwalkers in New York City for Anti-HIV-1 Antibodies.* Unpublished manuscript.

CHAPTER 31

Evaluation of an HIV-Prevention Program for Drug Addicts: The APP*

Eva-Maria Fahrner, Iris Bowman, and Ingolf von Törne

INTRODUCTION

Preventive strategies are less likely to succeed in the population of drug users than in other groups. The main reasons are: the difficulties counselors face in reaching and educating them; the problems associated with illegal drug use; and the drug users' irrational behavior, unstructured living patterns, and preoccupation with obtaining drugs. The dependency behavior controls any other behavior; therefore, special efforts are necessary (Fahrner 1989).

In Germany, the "Aids-Hilfe" (a federally funded organization developed from a self-help model), public institutions, and, primarily, addiction counseling centers are in charge of HIV prevention for drug addicts. Prevention concerning HIV infection is almost exclusively educational. Psychological research, however, indicates that increasing the clients' knowledge does not necessarily lead to changes in attitudes and behavior. Prevention of HIV infections necessitates a long-term and durable shift in high-risk sexual and drug-use behavior by drug addicts. In general, drug users are sufficiently informed about transmission routes and HIV-prevention methods. However, the special characteristics of this popula-

*The project is funded by the German Federal Ministry of Health. Dedicated to Alexander Tutsek on his 65th birthday.

tion, such as external attributions, lack of stress management behavior, inadequate role models, and their social environment combine to form unfavorable conditions for durable change in risk behavior.

Residential and outpatient treatment facilities are possible resources for effective HIV prevention in drug users. There, for a period of time, counselors and therapists have contact with drug users and are therefore able to conduct effective counseling and interventions in the sensitive area of AIDS. The estimated number of persons addicted to hard drugs in Germany (this number includes not only heroin addicts but also consumers of opiate substances, opiate surrogates, or cocaine) ranges between 50,000 and 120,000. Generally, a number between 60,000 and 80,000 is assumed. Reuband (1989) bases his assumptions on the 91,000 consumers of hard drugs who have been registered by the police between 1970 and the end of 1988. During this same period, just over 6,000 drug addicts have died, leaving approximately 85,000 still living.

The evaluation of the German demonstration project entitled "Care of HIV-infected Drug Addicts in Outpatient Treatment Centers" shows the prevention efforts of the therapeutic staff in treatment facilities. Not only do they provide information to clients but, through counseling, they pursue desired attitudinal behavioral changes in the areas of sexuality and needle sharing (Fahrner et al. 1989). Nevertheless, many of the counselors and therapists feel overwhelmed because they lack the necessary training, especially in sex education.

In this article, a comprehensive program for HIV prevention, including preliminary results, will be presented. The program, which has been developed in a research project since 1989, has three goals:

1. To develop a therapeutic HIV-prevention program for drug addicts, including a manual for therapists.
2. To test this HIV-prevention program in established drug treatment facilities.
3. To analyze the effectiveness of the program.

METHOD

Drug addicts in residential and outpatient substance abuse treatment are offered the chance to participate in an additional therapy group based on a therapy manual that contains certain AIDS-related issues. Changes in attitudes and behavior are evaluated by pre- and posttreatment tests. The evaluation is based on HIV-antibody tests, questionnaires, and qualitative interviews. The measures are repeated 6, 12, and 24 months after the end of the therapy, using self-report data (questionnaires and interviews) and additional medical examinations that test if former HIV-negative drug addicts have since been infected. Behavioral changes in terms of avoidance of high-risk situations are also assessed. HIV-positive clients who have tested positive when they entered the treatment are assessed in follow-ups to ascertain whether their behavior has decreased the infection risk for third persons (i.e., sexual-risk behavior, needle sharing).

For comparison, a waiting-list group is assessed with the same instruments; strict random assignment to treatment versus control group was not possible because of ethical considerations. A pilot study preceded the development of the prevention program, including detailed interviews with experts and drug users as well as behavior analyses.

THE AIDS-PREVENTION PROGRAM (APP)

Theoretical Underpinning

The prevention of HIV infections must focus on two goals: (1) Use of sterile syringes or, ideally, abstinence from drug use and (2) Use of condoms during sexual intercourse. For the majority of drug addicts, both goals require a change of established behaviors. Building new behavior, and in our case, changing already established behavior sequences, requires a complex interaction of different factors. The routes of infection define the areas of behavior that should be influenced.

It is known from several studies that few drug addicts experience success in changing their risk behavior (e.g., Kleiber 1992, Arnold and Frietsch 1988). Based on our current knowledge, the special difficulties of target-group prevention become clear in regard to the factors that impact on the efficiency of preventive efforts.

According to Kelly (1988), in order for individuals to give up health-risk behavior it is necessary that they:

- have sufficient cognitive knowledge concerning the health risks of their behavior and effective means of protection;
- have the ability to estimate the level of risk associated with their behavior;
- have expectations that behavior change efforts can be successfully undertaken;
- have strategies to cope with antecedents that trigger health-risk behavior;
- have reminders and prompts to maintain risk-reducing changes;
- have models that illustrate and sanction the desirability of behavior change;

- have environmental and social supports that encourage health-related behavior and discourage health-threatening behavior.

According to the health belief model (Rosenstock 1966, 1974), important factors for the execution of health-promoting behavior are the perceived threat by the illness ("perceived severity"), perceived costs and barriers, as well as the benefits of the behavioral change. Bühringer (1990) names three presuppositions for behavior change:

- motivation for behavior in regard to subjectively anticipated and subsequently experienced advantages,
- surrounding conditions that support behavior change,
- knowledge, attitudes, and behavior competencies regarding the pursued changes.

Beyond these factors, the AIDS-specific locus of control appears to play a major role in prevention-related behavior. According to Lohaus (Lohaus et al. 1988), persons who score high on an internal locus of control are more inclined to seek information and protect themselves. Figure 31.1 gives an overview of different factors that influence HIV-preventive behavior and which are considered in the APP.

Content of the AIDS Prevention Program (APP)

The AIDS Prevention Program (APP) is presented in a manual that is divided into five major therapeutic blocks, each related to certain AIDS issues. The contents of the building blocks concern "Basic Information," "Coping with Fear," "Safer Sex," "Safer Use," and "Women and AIDS." The blocks include a formulation of learning goals and didactic instructions on their implementation. Suggested exercises, home assignments, and written materials are also incorporated (Figure 31.2). Already existing prevention programs in the United States and Germany were considered in the development of the program (National Capital Systems, 1988; Palacious-Jiminez and Shernoff 1986; Deutsche AIDS-Hilfe 1988). The manual is primarily based on cognitive and learning paradigms, reflections on the learning conditions of drug users that have been found in the pilot study, as well as on initial experiences with the HIV-prevention groups.

The previously mentioned therapeutic components of the APP are described in detail below.

Cognitive

- ◆ knowledge

- ◆ ability to estimate self risk

- ◆ locus of control, self-efficacy

- ◆ intention to change risk behavior, attitudes, beliefs, group norms

Emotional

- ◆ concerns, fear of HIV

Behavioral

- ◆ competence to practice safer sex

- ◆ self-management techniques

- ◆ communication and assertiveness skills

Cofactors

- ◆ alcohol and drug use

- ◆ health status

FIGURE 31.1.
Factors that influence HIV-preventive behavior

Basic Information

First, the APP provides therapists with basic information on AIDS and covers the following issues: epidemiology; the immune system and HIV; the stages of HIV infection; the fight against HIV; and the influence of drugs on sexual behavior. Initial interviews indicate that therapists have

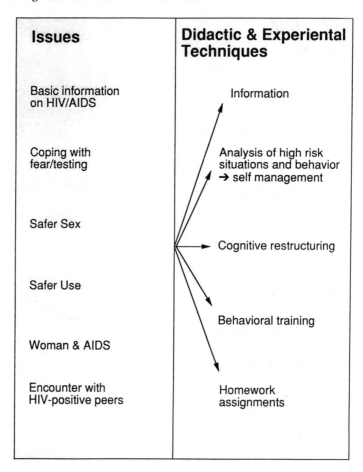

FIGURE 31.2.
Components of the AIDS Prevention Program APP

knowledge deficiencies and desire more information. For example, only a few therapists were knowledgeable about needle desinfection. After the therapists have been introduced to the information, they receive instructions on how to convey the educational messages to clients (e.g., through the use of flash cards or a quiz).

Coping with Fear

The second therapeutic block of the APP deals with the HIV-antibody test and high-risk situations. This block provides information on tests and introduces strategies to cope with the fear of infection and of the test results. Cognitive techniques such as reattribution, self-talk modification, and problem solving help to control irrational though patterns and reinforce health-maintaining intentions. Stress management techniques to reduce the stress resulting from testing and the confrontation with a possible positive test result are introduced. The goal is to achieve an early cognitive confrontation with risk situations and to obtain discriminant stimuli that make it possible to maintain preventive behavior even under stress. Furthermore, counseling and support on the decision of HIV testing is provided to each client.

Safer Sex

In the "Safer Sex" block, specific information about high-risk and low-risk sexual practices enable clients to increase their risk awareness. Practical exercises are employed to help clients acquire a positive attitude toward protection, increase their competency in the safe use of condoms, and initiate positive experiences. Particularly important is the social-skills training, which seeks to help the client resist their sexual partners' pressures to engage in risky practices. An analysis of individual risk behavior is crucial for the adoption of safer sex activities. In this block, clients learn to explore their own risk situations, to recognize internal and external triggers of risk behavior, and to develop effective strategies to cope with the situations or to avoid them. Role playing, practical exercises, and homework assignments are suggested as therapeutic tools. Based on previous therapeutic experiences, purely verbal instruction is insufficient for bringing about changes in attitudes and behavior.

Safer Use

The block "Safer Use" informs clients about ways intravenous drug users can protect themselves from infections from HIV-contaminated needles. Since most drug users in Germany are not familiar with effective methods of disinfection, a detailed description of the procedures are presented, and the process of "bleaching" is illustrated as a practical example. This topic is also recommended for residential treatment, although workers in residential facilities, who regard it as contradicting the goal of abstinence, fear the risk of provoking relapse. Safer use education is important, however, because a large percentage of clients will relapse. The relapse situation is a special risk situation, because it is generally not planned, clean syringes are not available, and in addition, drug addicts find themselves in an emotionally difficult situation. It is thus crucial, especially in these situations, that methods of protection are taught. In residential facilities, the demonstration of the disinfection procedure is restricted to paper and pencil illustrations. In contrast, outpatient treatment clients should have the opportunity for practical training in safer use (i.e., role playing).

Women and AIDS

The block "Women and Aids" plays an important part in the target group of intravenous drug addicts. The majority of HIV-infected women in Germany are heroin addicts. Like heroin-addicted men, they are at risk of infecting themselves through needle sharing, unprotected sexual contacts with other drug users, or through prostitution. Many aspects of prevention, especially in the area of sexuality, are different for women than for men.

Many drug-dependent women find it difficult to assert their wishes for HIV protection against male sexual partners. Others mask their difficulties by citing disgust as a reason for not using condoms. Prostitution or unassertiveness are not the only behaviors associated with this attitude. The female intravenous-drug users' dependence on their partners and their attempts to fulfil the expectations of unconditional love also lead to unprotected activities. In contrast to male intravenous drug users, female drug users often acquire the money for drugs through prostitution. This introduces an additional problem, for they have to insist on condom use even though customers prefer prostitutes who submit to unprotected intercourse. The block "Women and AIDS" discusses the consequences of HIV infections for family planning. The main focus is on training in assertion skills which allow clients to deal with resistance from male partners. Role playing and specific exercises serve as aids.

Practical Implementation

Implementation of the APP requires 6–8 two-hour sessions. Following a basic orientation on AIDS, the sessions focus on risk situations, beginning with sexual risk behavior. Thereafter, safer sex activities and the use of condoms are introduced, continuing with issues of couple relationships. "Safer Use" is generally discussed at the end of the program. A block on "Women and AIDS" is only applicable if there is female group members' participation.

The order and length of the therapy blocks depend on the base-line knowledge of the group and the individual needs of the participants. The group size should be between four and eight clients. Especially for practical exercises and role playing, a large group inhibits effective learning, while very small groups do not offer sufficient opportunities for identification. Since the APP is based on individual needs, the group size determines the length of time that each client has for dealing with his or her specific problems.

The use of written material, work papers, and video films as well as individual home assignments and role playing have been found effective. The use of various work methods and materials is in line with the idea that purely cognitive information has only limited effect on the attitude and behavior of a person. A new experience that is self-experienced and self-reflected is more likely to promote behavior changes than would any good explanation abut what is wrong and what should be done differently. The first HIV-prevention groups' experiences and the feedback from clients confirm this assumption.

FIRST RESULTS

Description of the Sample

Presently, the sample consists of 38 drug addicts: 23 were assigned to the treatment group, which means that they participated in the prevention program, and 15 belong to the waiting list control group. The following results stem from measurements that were conducted prior to and after the prevention program. According to these time intervals, the waiting list group was tested without having received any treatment. Follow-up data are only available from a few persons and therefore will not be included in the present data processing. In interpretation of the data, one must consider that the sample is still relatively small. Consequently, only trends will be discussed.

There were no differences in sociodemographic data between the treatment group and waiting list group. The total sample consists of 30 men and 8 women who received residential drug-free therapy at the time of the survey. Their average age is 28.5 years (SD 4.9) and they consumed illegal drugs since, on average, 11.5 years (SD 5.5). More than half of them have a stable couple relationship (55%), 31% have no steady partner, and 13% have frequently changing relationships.

TABLE 31.1

Drug-Use Behavior (Pretreatment test, N = 38)

Number of persons who shared needles (in the last 6 months prior to entering residential treatment)	19 (50%)
Number of persons who are insufficiently informed about needle hygiene	20 (40%)

TABLE 31.2

Sexual Behavior (Pretreatment Test, N = 38)

Number of persons who frequently have sexual contacts under the influence of drugs	23 (61%)
Number of persons who practice unprotected vaginal intercourse	31 (82%)
Number of persons who practice, at least occasionally (1–11 times a year) unprotected anal intercourse	14 (37%)
Number of persons who never use condoms	30 (79%)

Knowledge, Attitudes, and Behavior regarding AIDS (Pretreatment Test)

The results of the first test show clearly that the drug addicts have uncertainties in knowledge, attitudes, and behavior regarding AIDS prevention. At the moment, there are no differences between the treatment group and the waiting list group. Thus, the results will be presented for the total group. In the areas of drug use and sexuality, which are illustrated in Tables 31.1 and 31.2, the results show that many drug addicts engage in high-risk behavior. Forty percent of the addicts surveyed are not sufficiently informed about the possibilities of needle disinfection. Half of the sample report that they have shared their syringes in the last half-year before they entered the residential facility. Sixty-one percent of the surveyed addicts frequently had sexual contacts while under the influence of drugs; 79% reported no use of condoms.

Most of the clients (75%) engaged in unprotected vaginal intercourse before they entered treatment, and over a third (37%) occasionally engaged in unprotected anal intercourse. These are remarkably high percentages. The question whether these results are a consequence of the drug use or whether it can be explained by prostitution cannot be answered at present. When the clients were asked about their future risk

TABLE 31.3

High-Risk Attitudes in the Area of Sexuality (Pretreatment Test, N = 38)

Number of persons who do not use condoms because they destroy pleasure	28 (74%)
Number of persons who do not use condoms with unfamiliar sexual partners	28 (74%)
Number of persons who do not talk about AIDS with a new sexual partner	24 (63%)

behavior, 32% reported that they do not care about protection during sexual intercourse. The remaining 60% intend to use protection in the future. Deficiency in knowledge and in attitudes can be considered reasons for high- risk behavior. It became obvious that the same number of persons who underestimated the risk of transmitting HIV also overestimated the risk (each 33%).

Seventy-four percent of those surveyed report that they do not use condoms because they could destroy the sexual pleasure. Seventy-four percent would not insist on them even if they were becoming involved with an unfamiliar sexual partner. Sixty-three percent do not talk about AIDS with a new sexual partner (Table 31.3). Despite these problematic attitudes and behaviors, 71% of the surveyed show interest in learning more about protection. Altogether, these results confirm the hypothesis that a prevention program should focus on changing attitudes and on training in alternative behavior in high-risk situations.

Results of the Prevention Program

Evaluation by the Clients

After each therapy session, the participants of the prevention program use ratings (1–6) to evaluate different aspects of the session. Moreover, they were asked about their assessment of the effectiveness of the training after treatment (posttreatment test). Comparing the means of the ratings for the therapy sessions in the five treatment groups, it is apparent that there are only very small differences among the groups. This indicates consistency in terms of the contents and the facilitation of the program. The following figures illustrate the means of five groups that have been implemented up to the present. The group atmosphere was evaluated over-

494 Drug Addiction Treatment Research

all as "good" or "average." There is a striking change concerning the ratings of the participants on the scales "personal ability to change one's own behavior" and "applicability of the learned content in reality" (Figure 31.3). The graph illustrates that the participants were rather skeptical about the usefulness of the training in the first sessions and that their evaluation changed in the positive direction clearly toward the end of training. This result is not a consequence of social desirability: If we regard the results of the scale "group atmosphere" and of other scales not presented in Figure 31.3, there were no essential changes during the course of the training.

The overall evaluation of the prevention program after the last session shows that the clients enjoyed the program and perceived it as helpful. They believed they have gained a more favorable attitude toward behavior change and that their behavior has already been changed by the program (Table 31.4).

Changes between Pre- and Posttreatment Tests

The presented results show that the prevention program can be applied in drug clinics and is accepted by clients. To what extent the newly learned behavior is put into practice can only be tested with the follow-up data, which are only available from a small sample of clients at present. However, some changes can already be noticed at the end of the prevention program. Clients after therapy demonstrate a better capability to talk about AIDS with a new sexual partner as compared to before therapy (Paired Samples T-Test, $p < 0.1$). Clients who completed treatment would also insist on condoms more frequently than before (Paired Samples T-Test, $p < 0.1$). In comparison to the waiting list group, they are significantly more convinced that they will succeed in changing their behavior in order to protect themselves efficiently from HIV infection (Paired Samples T-Test, $p < 0.1$). The results of a questionnaire on AIDS-specific locus of control (Lohaus 1988) show a change in the same direction. After the end of the prevention program, clients express a significantly stronger internal attribution ($p < 0.1$). This means that they take on more responsibility for a possible infection and, on the other hand, perceive more possibilities to protect themselves efficiently.

CONCLUSIONS

If we summarize the preliminary results of the project, the following hypotheses are supported:

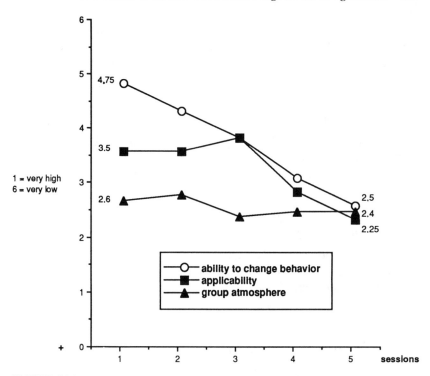

FIGURE 31.3.
Clients' ratings on the APP during different group sessions (means of five treatment
groups, N = 38).

TABLE 31.4

**Evaluation of the Treatment Program by the Clients of Five Therapy Groups
(Posttreatment Test, N = 23)**

Enjoyed participating	2.3
Thought the program was helpful	2.7
Have gained a more favorable attitude toward behavior change	2.15
Have changed their behavior based on the program	2.0
Were satisfied with therapist	1.6

1 = very much
6 = very poor

Need for Prevention

The surveyed clients have deficiencies in knowledge and are at risk for infections due to risky sexual behavior and needle sharing. They have attitudes which prevent protective behavior.

Acceptance of the APP

A short-term behaviorally oriented treatment program for HIV prevention (APP) is well accepted by clients and evaluated as positive. The staff of the facilities also feel the program is necessary.

Improvements by the APP

The first clients who have been treated with the APP show a clear improvement in knowledge; their attitudes toward protection became more positive; and their behavior competencies for dealing with HIV-risk situations have improved.

Importance of Practice

The behavioral elements upon which the APP is based (i.e., role playing), seem to be more relevant for success than does the information.

Implementation

Implementation of the APP in clinical facilities has to overcome certain conceptual barriers. A next step in the project will be to develop and test a therapy manual that will serve to train therapists.

REFERENCES

Arnold, T., and Frietsch, R. (1988). AIDS-Problematik und Drogengebrauch— zur Sichtweise der betroffenen Drogenkonsumenten. *Suchtgefahren* 34, 303– 15.

Bühringer, G. (1990). Drogenabhängige: Spielball der Gesundheitspolitik. *Das Parlament 10 (October)*.

Deutsche AIDS-Hilfe e.V. (eds). (1988). *AIDS*. Weinheim: Beltz.

Fahrner, E.-M. (1989). Prevention of HIV transmission in IV drug users: Problems and proposals. *Paper read at the European Symposium on AIDS and Drug Abuse, Stockholm*.

Fahrner, E.-M., Schumann, J., Niemeck, U., and Vogt, H.-J. (1989). *Beschreib-*

ung und Tätigkeiten der Einrichtungen im Modellprogramm "Drogen und AIDS": Ergebnisse der ersten Befragung. München: IFT-Berichte Bd. 50.

Kelly, J. A. (1988). Psychology's role in the health crisis. *Clinical Psychology Review* 8, 255–84.

Kleiber, D. (1992). HIV-infection rates in intravenous drug abusers in the Federal Republic of Germany. In G. Bühringer, and J. J. Platt (eds.), *Drug Addiction Treatment Research: German and American Perspectives.* Malabar, Florida: Robert E. Krieger Publishing Company (this volume).

Lohaus, A., et al. (1988). Kontrollüberzeugungen und AIDS-Prophylaxe. *Zeitschrift für Klinische Psychologie.* Bd. XVII, Heft 2, 106–18.

National Capitol Systems (Ed.) (1988). *Substance abuse counseling in the age of AIDS: Human sexuality.* Falls Church, VA: The Center for AIDS and Substance Abuse Training.

Palacious-Jiminez, L., and Shernoff, M. (1986). *Facilitators Guide to "Hot, Horny & Healthy."* New York: Chelsea Psychotherapy Associates.

Reuband, K.-H. (1989). Illegale Drogen. In Deutsche Hauptstelle gegen die Suchtgefahren (eds.), *Jahrbuch '90 zur Frage der Suchtgefahren.* Hamburg: Neuland, 113–55.

Rosenstock, J. M. (1966). Why people use health services. *Milbank Memorial Fund Quarterly* 44, 94–127.

————. (1974). The health belief model and preventive health behavior. *Health Education Monographs* 2, 354–86.

CHAPTER 32

The Harlem AIDS Project: Description of an AIDS Outreach Project*

Sherry Deren

INTRODUCTION

The Harlem AIDS Project (HAP) is funded by the National Institute on Drug Abuse (NIDA) as part of an extensive network of more than 50 AIDS demonstration and research projects funded throughout the United States. These projects vary by type of outreach conducted (e.g., in treatment programs, street outreach), the targets of the outreach efforts (e.g., intravenous drug users (IVDUs), sex partners, prostitutes), and the type of intervention provided. All projects administer a base-line instrument provided by NIDA, and all plan to conduct follow-up interviews to assess the impact of their interventions.

The target populations for the HAP project are intravenous drug users (IVDUs) and their sex partners in the Harlem community. Clients will be recruited, through outreach in the street and in the obstetrical/gynecological (OBS/GYN) clinics of Harlem Hospital, to participate in an interview and in AIDS risk-reduction group sessions. Two project sites have been established, in Central and West Harlem. The Harlem community, the home of many renowned educational, historical, and cultural

*This project was funded by the National Institute on Drug Abuse Grant R18 DA05746, "Harlem AIDS Outreach Counseling and Demonstration Project." Any opinions expressed in this paper do not necessarily represent the views of NIDA or NDRI.

institutions, also has a wide range of human service needs. The community has some of the highest indicators of poverty and substance abuse, with more than one-third of the population receiving some public assistance and with one of the highest infant mortality rates in the United States (New York City 1989). Because of this high need for services, a referral service component (briefly described in the next section) was developed as part of the intervention.

Data on AIDS cases in Harlem indicate the need for AIDS risk-reduction outreach efforts targeting IVDUs and their sex partners. Table 32.1 provides a summary of the AIDS cases, by sex, for Harlem and New York City as of December 1988. At that time, there were approximately 80,000 AIDS cases nationally, and New York City accounted for about 18,000, or more than 22% of the total cases. Harlem had 7% of all New York City cases. Table 32.1 also indicates that the proportion of AIDS cases among females is higher in Harlem than in New York City (20% vs. 12%). Tables 32.2 and 32.3 provide a breakdown of AIDS cases by risk category for males and females, respectively. For New York City as a whole, the risk factor of intravenous drug use (IVDU) accounted for about 36% of the cases. In Harlem, IVDU was a risk category for more than half (57%) of the male AIDS cases. For females, intravenous drug use was the major risk category both in Harlem and citywide, although it accounted for a higher percent of the female cases in Harlem (75% vs. 60%). As indicated by the ethnic distribution of cases, Harlem is primarily a minority community, with the vast majority of cases occurring among the black and Hispanic populations.

PROJECT COMPONENTS

Table 32.4 provides a schematic diagram of the project structure from recruitment through follow-up. The following presents a brief description of each of these components:

Recruitment

Outreach will be conducted in two locations, on the streets and in the waiting rooms of the OBS/GYN clinics of Harlem Hospital. Street outreach will be conducted by staff of the AIDS Outreach and Prevention Project (AOP), an NDRI project funded through the New York State Division of Substance Abuse Services to provide outreach to IVDUs and

TABLE 32.1

Adult AIDS Cases: Harlem and New York City (as of 12/14/88)*

	Central Harlem (Morningside Heights)	East Harlem	Total Harlem	NYC
Male	570	448	1,018(80%)	15,556(88%)
Female	145	112	257(20%)	2,198(12%)
Total	715	560	1,275(100%)	17,754(100%)

*Source: NYC Department of Health, AIDS Surveillance Unit

sex partners in the highest risk areas in the four largest boroughs of New York City.

Outreach to women in the waiting rooms of the OBS/GYN clinics of Harlem Hospital will be conducted by two outreach workers. They will distribute flyers that describe the project and will talk to clients in the OBS/GYN clinics.

Clients who are recruited for the project must meet the following criteria:

1. Intravenous Drug Users
   —must have shot IV drugs within the last 6 months prior to the date of the interview
   —have not been in treatment within the last 30 days
2. Sexual partners of IVDUs
   —have not shot IV drugs within the last 6 months (even if the person is in treatment)
   —have had sex with an IVDU within the last 6 months

Clients who meet these criteria will be escorted to the research site by the outreach worker.

Interview

After arriving at the research site, the client will be introduced to an interviewer and the informed consent form will be reviewed and signed by the client. The initial client interview will then be conducted.

The initial client interview consists of two components. The AIA (AIDS Initial Assessment) is required of all the NIDA-funded AIDS

TABLE 32.2

Adult Male AIDS Cases by Risk Factors and Ethnicity: Harlem and NYC (as of 12/14/88)

	White	Black	Hispanic	Other	Harlem Total	NYC
Sex Partner of Man at Risk	61	255	55	6	377(37%)	9,131(59%)
IVDU	15	334	150	2	501(49%)	4,767(31%)
Sex Partner and IVDU	5	55	18	0	78(8%)	753(5%)
Other	0	45	17	0	62(6%)	905(6%)
Total	81	689	240	8	1,018(100%)	15,556(101%)

Source: NYC Department of Health, AIDS Surveillance Unit

TABLE 32.3

Adult Female AIDS Cases by Risk Factors and Ethnicity: Harlem and NYC (as of 12/14/88)

	White	Black	Hispanic	Other	Harlem Total	NYC
Sex Partner of Man at Risk	2	23	14	0	39(15%)	510(23%)
IVDU	5	151	37	1	194(75%)	1,318(60%)
Other	2	15	7	0	24(9%)	370(17%)
Total	9	189	58	1	257(99%)	2,198(100%)

*Source: NYC Department of Health, AIDS Surveillance Unit

TABLE 32.4

Harlem AIDS Project

RECRUITMENT—— FOLLOW-UP PROCESS

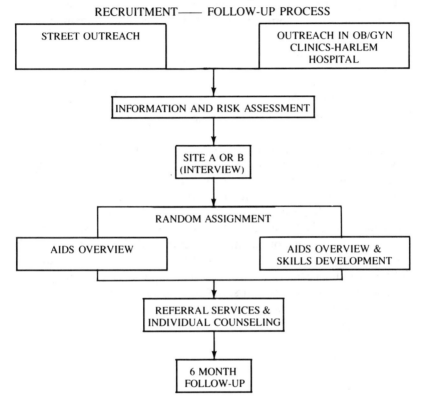

outreach research and demonstration projects and obtains information about the following:

1. Demographics
2. Drug use and needle use behaviors
3. Drug treatment and mobility
4. Sexual behaviors
5. Health indicators

6. Beliefs regarding AIDS and HIV testing

A supplement to this interview was developed for use within the project. Supplementary information collected includes the following:

1. Psychological scales. Includes measures of self-efficacy and assertiveness.
2. Self and others risk reduction. Includes information on any risk reduction efforts clients or their partners have made.
3. Measure of Spanish language usage (for Hispanic clients only).

As part of the interview, clients will be asked if they have been tested for the AIDS virus. If they have, they will be asked for their Department of Health card, which has their code number. These numbers will be submitted by the central research office to the Department of Health and test results are obtained. Clients who have not been tested will be told that if they are tested afterward, they should return to the site with their test number. At the end of the interview clients will receive a $15 money order and will be introduced to the health educator. The health educator will tell the client about the group session and encourage him or her to come to the next scheduled first session. Insofar as possible, attempts will be made to have the clients return for the group session the same day or the next day. Clients will receive a $10 money order as an incentive for attendance in each group session.

Intervention

At the end of the first group session, the entire group will be randomly assigned to the AIDS Education Group (standard intervention, one session only) or to the AIDS Education and Skills Development Group (enhanced intervention, three sessions). Table 32.5 summarizes the contents of the three group sessions. Session number 1, which both groups participate in, involves basic AIDS information and provides information on AIDS transmission and risk reduction. Sessions 2 and 3 are based on a cognitive-behavioral social learning model, and involve demonstrating skills necessary for risk reduction and giving clients the opportunity to practice these skills in the group. A set of guidelines for conducting the three group sessions has been developed. This type of social learning model, as formulated by Botvin (e.g., Botvin, Baker, Renick, Filazzola, and Botvin 1984) has met with considerable success in substance abuse

TABLE 32.5

Harlem AIDS Project: Goals and Content of Group Sessions

Session 1: AIDS Overview

Basic Information about AIDS
    · Modes of Transmission
    · Methods of Prevention
Self-Assessment of Risk
AIDS is Preventable
Introduction of Referral Coordinator

Sessions 2 and 3: Skill Development

Session 2:

    · Learn Behaviors which Can Reduce Risk
    · Discuss Alternative Behaviors
    · Demonstration and Practice for Needle Cleaning and Condom Use

Session 3:

    · Learn to Use Risk-Reduction Behaviors
    · Discuss Methods of Using These Behaviors
    · Practice Negotiation Techniques

prevention efforts. As indicated by Des Jarlais and Friedman (1988), a social learning prevention effort to prevent AIDS among intravenous drug users must include three components: basic AIDS information, means for behavior change, and methods for reinforcing the new behaviors. These three aspects are all part of the enhanced intervention.

Individualized services

At the end of the first group session, clients will be told about the availability of a referral coordinator and of individual counseling with the health educator. Clients who request referral services can meet individually with the referral coordinator. An extensive referral directory of services available to clients in the Harlem community has been developed for use in this project. Clients can also meet individually, on a short-term basis, with the health educator. Those who may require more extensive counseling will be referred to other services.

Follow-up

Six months after the initial interview, clients will be contacted for a second interview (the follow-up phase will begin in November 1989). This will consist of the AFA (AIDS Follow-up Assessment), an instrument in use by all AIDS outreach, NIDA-funded projects, and a supplement developed for the specific project. After the follow-up interview is conducted, clients will be recruited to participate in a "booster" session, to review the material provided in the initial group sessions. A twelve-month follow-up is planned.

PROCESS AND QUALITATIVE DATA COLLECTION

Intervention implementation measures

In addition to the interview information described previously, measures related to intervention implementation will also be collected, as follows:
   1. *Group sessions*
   At the end of each group session, the health educator will complete a form that contains information on client attendance and ratings of clients' participation. An evaluation form will also be completed by clients after their last session. Thus, clients in the standard intervention will complete the form after Session 1 and clients in the enhanced intervention complete the form after Session 3. This will provide a brief measure of the information they learned, their confidence in using risk-reduction efforts, and their intention to incorporate risk-reduction behaviors.
   2. *Individualized services*
   The referral coordinator will complete a form for each client requesting referral services that includes the date of referral and the type of referral made. A similar form, to be completed by the health educator, provides information on clients who have had individual counseling, and the nature of that counseling.

Ethnographic component

The project ethnographer collects information about the surrounding community and its responses to the AIDS epidemic. In addition, through conducting life history interviews with individual HAP clients, patterns in the way in which individuals make decisions regarding risk behaviors are being studied. These patterns are examined with regard to four major

TABLE 32.6

Harlem AIDS Project Data Collection

I. Baseline and Change Measures

  A. Initial and Follow-up Assessments
    1. Demographics
    2. Drug Use and Needle Behavior
    3. Treatment and Mobility
    4. Sex
    5. Health
    6. AIDS and HIV Testing

  B. HIV Test Results

  C. Supplementary Information
    1. Psychological Scales
    2. Self and Others Risk Reduction
    3. Measure of Spanish-Language Use

II. Measures Related to Intervention Implementation

  A. Group Sessions
    1. Health Educator's Ratings of Client's Participation
    2. Client's Rating of Information Obtained and Confidence in Implementation

  B. Individual Services
    1. Summary of Counseling Contacts
    2. Summary of Referral Contacts

demographic characteristics: gender, age, ethnicity and socioeconomic variables.

Table 32.6 contains a summary of the data collection instruments and domains of information which will be collected. Multivariate analyses will be used to assess the impact of a wide range of predictor variables on behavior change regarding risk reduction. Outcome variables will be based on Time 1–Time 2 behavior changes, and predictor variables will include baseline data, psychological measures, and measures related to clients' participation in the group and individual components of the intervention.

REFERENCES

Botvin, G. J., Baker, E., Renick, N. L., Filazzola, A.D., and Botvin, E. M. (1984). A cognitive-behavioral approach to substance abuse prevention. *Addictive Behaviors* 9: 137–47.

Des Jarlais, D. C., and Friedman, S. R. (1988). The psychology of prevention AIDS among intravenous drug users: A social learning conceptualization. *American Psychologist* 43: 865–70.

New York City (1989). *Community District Needs. Fiscal Year 1989 Manhattan.* N.Y.C. Office of Planning Management and Support, Department of City Planning.

CHAPTER 33

Drug Abuse and AIDS: NIDA's Clinical Medicine Branch and Opportunities for German-American Research Cooperation*

Peter I. Hartsock

INTRODUCTION

The U.S. Scene

The President's Commission on the Human Immunodeficiency Virus Epidemic (1988), the Centers for Disease Control (Curran 1987), and the National Research Council of the National Academy of Sciences (1989) have recognized that drug abuse is a prime factor in the spread of AIDS throughout the United States.

The International Scene

According to Dr. Jonathan Mann (1986), WHO (World Health Organization) AIDS Coordinator, the primary barrier inhibiting the fight against

*The opinions expressed herein are the views of the presenter and do not necessarily reflect the official position of the National Institute on Drug Abuse or any other part of the U.S. Department of Health and Human Services.

AIDS is not a technological one; it is a human problem: the inability of people or institutions to share information and work together. This problem is exacerbated by the interdisciplinary and international nature of AIDS. It is complicated enough for people in various disciplines, let alone different countries, to cooperate.

The U.S. and the International Scene

In January 1989, Surgeon General C. Everett Koop recognized three major challenges for the U.S. Public Health Service, two of which complement the challenges recognized above by Jonathan Mann. The third challenge dealt with federal-state relations, but the first two have special implications for this study:

1. Greatly improved international cooperation in public health.
2. Greatly improved sharing and coordination of health-related data and information (Koop 1989).

These challenges regarding AIDS and drug abuse have special implications for United States and international cooperation and provide a context for recognizing opportunities for German-American cooperation in drug abuse and AIDS research.

I will begin by discussing the work of the National Institute on Drug Abuse (NIDA) Clinical Medicine Branch (CMB). NIDA has the lead responsibility in the United States for supporting research on drug abuse and CMB has had the initial responsibility in NIDA for AIDS research. I will then discuss where opportunities lie for cooperation between Germany and the United States; in areas directly related to the CMB program and also outside of it.

THE CLINICAL MEDICINE BRANCH (CMB)

Introduction

The Clinical Medicine Branch (CMB) was created within NIDA early in 1986 to focus directly on drug abuse and AIDS research. This responsibility is now shared with other programs in NIDA, such as the Community Research Branch, which handles AIDS outreach demonstration projects. Representatives from the other programs in NIDA will discuss their work and the possibilities for German-American cooperation. I will confine my direct comments to CMB's mandate and where German-American research cooperation is most possible within this mandate.

To begin, it should be pointed out that, while CMB was created with AIDS as its most important mandate, we are also interested in the relationship of other diseases and medical conditions to drug abuse. Furthermore, while most of our work has dealt with intravenous (IV) drug use, we are also interested in drugs taken in ways other than IV (e.g., "Sex for Crack").

We encourage cooperation in all of these areas.

Areas of Concentration

Natural History Studies

CMB is currently funding AIDS natural history studies, focusing on adults and on children. In general, the studies of adults intend to determine seroprevalence at base line in cohorts of intravenous drug users and to follow the seronegatives over varying periods of time, determining serostatus at different intervals. In the studies of children, progression of the disease over time is being monitored.

Prevention-Intervention Studies

The emphasis in these studies is to lessen the spread of AIDS among drug addicts, their sexual contacts, and their offspring. While our prevention research program has two components—behavioral strategies and technological strategies—the two areas are not mutually exclusive and there is interaction between the two.

1. *Prevention: Behavioral Strategies*

CMB is funding prevention/intervention studies that include on-the-street outreach contact interventions. Some of our more innovative projects analyze methods for training IV drug abusers in syringe cleaning and recruiting addicts into drug abuse treatment. Other studies include multiple didactic/discussions/skills training sessions; additional projects use social learning theory, including the health belief model, self-efficacy training, and fear-arousal-reduction approaches to impact behavior.

Other work we fund combines outreach, syringe cleaning, bringing addicts into treatment, and developing means to keep addicts in treatment longer. This last issue is important because the duration of treatment appears to be a critical component of AIDS prevention.

Treatment may lead to behavior modification in the long run, but the actual treatment process may be valuable in controlling addicts' AIDS-related risk behavior while they are in treatment. If this is true, then the possibility arises that retaining patients might be encouraged not simply to control or end drug abuse but also to prevent AIDS. Research is being conducted and is encouraged in this area.

2. Prevention: Technological Strategies

Research related to prevention technology is presently underway. CMB now has a Small Business Innovation Research (SBIR) grant program which deals with the research and development of non-reusable syringes in order to reduce needle/syringe sharing and HIV transmission among intravenous drug abusers. This is the only such program in the federal government. The surgeon general of the United States has been very interested in this work and has requested that the U.S. Patent Office expedite patent applications for such technology.

In the area of prevention technology, CMB is also interested and encourage research in:

- Evaluation of the dynamics of HIV transmission via needle sharing, including laboratory and human studies of the conditions under which HIV gains entry, survives, and is subsequently released from needles, syringes, cookers, and strainers ("works"). The amount of contaminated blood particles or plasma and the time of viral residence in the "works" under various conditions should be among the variables studied. Studies that evaluate HIV viability in injection equipment by focusing on the effects of commonly injected illicit drugs, substances often used to dilute the concentration of those drugs (e.g., quinine, lactose), or viricidal agents that could be added to illicit drugs are also encouraged. This research would help to provide a basis for developing new techniques to prevent HIV transmission among needle users.
- Research on objective methods for assessing needle sharing by addicts. These studies may include the development and application of micromethods for analysis of residual sera for mixed blood types in syringes or needles, and research to determine the validity of self-reports of needle sharing by addicts.

Biomedical Studies

CMB funds biomedical studies dealing with a variety of areas, including the effects of drugs of abuse on the immune system and the interaction of these effects with HIV in determining vulnerability to initial infection and the disease manifestations of HIV. Research is also encouraged on the development of indices that predict susceptibility of the immune system to separate and joint disruption from stress, drugs of abuse, pharmacotherapeutics used in treatment programs (e.g., methadone, naltrexone, levo-alpha-acetylmethadol [LAAM], and buprenorphine), and HIV.

Immunohematological parameters are sought that predict the effects on HIV or other disease progression from further exposure to drugs of abuse, treatment drugs, and other co-factors beyond the point of initial infection.

Modeling

The rapid spread of AIDS has made special demands on researchers, planners, and policymakers who seek to understand this disease. A major demand has been for rapid development of efficient and useful models for understanding AIDS. In order to meet this challenge, CMB's AIDS modeling grants have placed maximum emphasis on pragmatism and efficiency. The key to this emphasis has been the exploration of extant data sets to determine what their strengths and weaknesses are for answering basic questions about the spread of AIDS (particularly as related to drug abuse). From this research, models are being developed which often access large data sets, many of which are already available and updated on a regular basis. Where gaps are seen in these data sets, recommendations are made for upgrading them, but the robustness of the sets finally selected often enables their use even while upgrading takes place.

Through this process, exploratory theories are being developed that begin to answer in a timely fashion the questions that interest us concerning AIDS and drug abuse. This work seeks a balance between theorizing on the one hand and the search for good data on the other. Most of the theorizing that originates with the CMB modeling grants is empirically based on data presently available, which assists in the work's timeliness and efficiency. The theory development based upon these data thus enable easy correction and upgrading. These qualities are important for producing valid AIDS models that can be developed and improved quickly and inexpensively.

As can be seen, the Clinical Medicine Branch's research program spans a wide range, from epidemiology, through prevention/education/intervention, through clinical studies and mathematical modeling. Because these efforts are administered under one program, we are in position to actively encourage and facilitate cooperation among the various projects and the disclipines they represent. This is important for better science and it also has strong implications for international and, in the present case, German-American, cooperation.

ENABLING COOPERATION: TOWARD A COMMON TONGUE

Introduction

I would now like to refer again to the concerns of Drs. Koop and Mann dealing with the need to share information and data in the battle against AIDS. A major barrier to sharing has been the absence of a common language in data collection, both within and among countries. Data are collected in different ways in different places and projects, and thus cannot effectively be compared.

I would like to present several examples of the kind of efforts in the CMB program that have enabled cooperation in drug abuse and AIDS research. These examples are presented as food for thought and are not meant to limit consideration of topics for cooperative work. The CMB's scope of work, which I have already described, can serve as an outline, albeit a preliminary one, of areas for such consideration.

Examples of Cooperation in Drug Abuse/AIDS Data Gathering and Research/Analysis

Coordinated international data-gathering and analysis

Our largest modeling project presently involves three universities: one on the West Coast, one on the East Cost and one in Canada. It emphasizes systematic data collection and analysis among the universities, using computer links and group meetings. Data span the range from epidemiologic to biomedical. Oxford and Cambridge universities are now applying to become a part of this project.

10-State Prison AIDS/Drug Abuse Modeling Project

Another project deals with the systematic collection, analysis, and modeling of AIDS and drug abuse data in prison populations across 10 states. This not only involves a CMB grantee (Johns Hopkins University), which began the project in Maryland, but also the Centers for Disease Control (CDC), which liked the initial project and has contributed sizable funding to expand it to 10 states.

CMB Questionnaire

In order to encourage uniformity in data collection and thus some comparability among data sets, CMB has developed a short AIDS/drug abuse questionnaire. This questionnaire is being used by some of our grantees and even by people we do not fund to develop a base-line core of data common to various projects. This questionnaire is designed to supplement the CDC AIDS questionnaire by expanding on the CDC's single drug abuse item of "IV drug abuser." As such, the CMB questionnaire's format is compatible with that of the CDC's and the CDC has recently incorporated much of it into its AIDS and drug abuse questionnaire.

Importance of Such Projects

The importance of such projects is that they strive for *compatibility* among data sets through the use of at least a core of variables that are shared throughout these sets and which are always in the same format. This enables greater *comparability* not only between data sets but also among the different types of research projects that supply the data (e.g., between epidemiological and intervention studies). Such comparability contributes to greater economies of scale—efficiency and power—in data access and analysis.

Computer technology enables us to capitalize on economies of scale, which are especially important both because we are in an era of limited resources and because the threat of AIDS demands rapid and extensive sharing and analysis of data and information.

These factors not only are interrelated, but are critical in the sharing of research information and the development of a common tongue for AIDS and drug abuse research.

EXAMPLES FOR GERMAN-AMERICAN COOPERATION IN DRUG ABUSE AND AIDS RESEARCH

CMB's recognition of the international challenges posed by Drs. Mann and Koop and the emphases we have placed on common language development and the sharing of data present important implications for our research cooperation with Germany. As evidenced by this book, Germany and the United States already have a strong interest in cooperation and both countries have strong research establishments that can serve as the basis for such cooperation. Some possibilities for cooperation are presented below. These are only examples and it is hoped that they and the previous discussion will serve to stimulate thinking about additional possibilities.

1. Incorporation into research projects in both countries of:
   −*common format(s)* for data collection
   −*common variables* (e.g., demographics, types of drugs)
   It is important to emphasize that we encourage input into the process of determining common formats and variables. We encourage any dialogue that contributes to the development of a common language in data collection and analysis.
2. Joint U.S.-German projects that investigate the same questions and share formats, data, and resources. Interested parties should consider applying to NIDA for funding. We will be happy to assist in the application process.
3. Holding conferences on a regular basis is important particularly in helping to develop a common tongue and to assist in the development of joint German-American research projects. There is no substitute for face-to-face meetings that focus on specific problems.
4. The contributors to this book could serve as facilitators and coordinators for determinating common formats and variables. In this context, special consideration should be made of the Center for Excellence in Addiction Treatment Research, under whose auspices the German-American conference that provided the basis of this book was made possible. The center has already done exceptional work in bridge-building, not only through its ongoing work but also through an earlier Dutch-American conference and its involvement in a second Dutch-American Conference at The Hague in June 1989.
5. Other groups, like NIDA's Community Epidemiology Working Group (CEWG), may have important input into this process. The CEWG has done excellent work in coordinating information and data sharing.
6. Again, it is important to emphasize that working for at least some common core or format of variables offers the opportunity for comparison of research findings not only between Germany and the United States but also among different kinds of drug abuse research areas, such as treatment, prevention, and epidemiology, which impact upon our understanding of AIDS.
7. Although I have been using terms of learning to communicate in a common tongue (within as well as among nations) specifically in the AIDS/drug abuse context, this dialogue has implications that apply to drug abuse, whether AIDS is the question or not, and then to many other areas of health and social investigation. A common language

that begins in an area of research as beneficial to all humanity as that which is now being presented has a good potential for enhancing communication and trust in many other areas.

8. I have been employing fairly focused terms of German-American cooperation in the area which is the purview of my program. I want to emphasize, however, that I do not think the possibilities for cooperation fall only within this jurisdiction. We should think of all of the topics covered in this book as a beginning list of areas where we can work together.

9. Above all, we must do more than just pay lip service to the term "cooperation." In its fullest sense, cooperation is a partnership and it is essential to building anything that lasts. It demands the active involvement of all parties and is not a one-way process. Cooperative international efforts are required in drug abuse and AIDS research and I firmly believe that material presented here will help to lay a foundation for the partnerships necessary to implement these efforts. Furthermore, because this effort plays a role in building a foundation for German-American cooperation, it helps in turn to meet the international challenges recognized by the surgeon general of the United States (Koop 1989) and the AIDS coordinator of the World Health Organization (Mann 1986).

REFERENCES

Curran, J. (1987). *Comments at International Conference on AIDS in Children and Heterosexuals.* Atlanta, Ga., Feb. 17.

Koop, C. (1989). *Speech on the Occasion of the Centennial Celebration of the Commissioned Corps of the U.S. Public Health Service.* Bethesda, Md.: National Institutes of Health, January 5.

Mann, J. (1986). Seminar on International Implications of AIDS. Rockville, Md.: U.S. Department of Health and Human Services, Dec. 15.

National Academy of Sciences, National Research Council (1989). *AIDS: Sexual Behavior and Intravenous Drug Abuse.* Washington, D.C.: National Academy Press.

Presidential Commission on the Human Immunodeficiency Virus Epidemic (1988). *Final Report of the Presidential Commission on the Human Immunodeficiency Virus Epidemic.* Washington, D.C.: U.S. Government Printing Office.

CHAPTER 34

A Report on the National AIDS Demonstration Research Program

Barry S. Brown

INTRODUCTION

Currently, intravenous drug users are the most rapidly growing portion of the AIDS population. As of 1989, 30% of new AIDS cases could be attributed to intravenous drug use, either by virtue of the drug use of persons afflicted with the disease or the number of persons who contracted the disease consequent to sexual activity with intravenous drug users. Findings by gender and ethnicity are even more dramatic. Fifty percent of all AIDS cases in both the black and Hispanic communities can be attributed to intravenous drug use; 71% of AIDS cases among women can be attributed to contacts with intravenous drug users or use of intravenous drugs by the women themselves (CDC 1990).

With the threat posed by intravenous drug users both to themselves and to the communities in which they live, two clear courses of action have appeared. On the one hand, there is an immediate and continuing need to develop and maintain drug abuse treatment slots to allow intravenous drug users access to drug abuse treatment. Treatment remains our surest strategy for effecting long-term behavior change. Second, outreach strategies need to be developed to provide education and behavior change programs in communities where treatment slots either remain unavailable or are seen by intravenous drug users as inappropriate to their needs. Consequently, the U.S. federal government appropriated funds to increase the availability of treatment slots, and—through its National Institute on Drug Abuse (NIDA)—initiated a program of outreach/intervention designed to encourage entry into treatment where possible and to work with intravenous drug users in the community to reduce risk-taking behaviors where treatment entry was not possible.

POPULATIONS OF CONCERN

In all, four populations were identified for NIDA's outreach/intervention program. These were: intravenous drug users who were not currently in drug abuse treatment, sexual partners of intravenous drug users, prostitutes, and runaway youths. A particular emphasis was placed on both the out-of-treatment intravenous drug using population and the sexual partners of intravenous drug users. Prostitutes were specifically targeted in some programs, but more frequently were accessed as part of program efforts to work with intravenous drug users and/or sexual partners, populations with which they obviously overlapped. Young people who were runaways were targeted in a few projects and were soon found to be a particularly difficult population to reach and to influence with behavior change strategies. These youngsters came to be seen as a population requiring programs specific to their needs, which the institute is now in the process of developing for implementation and study. At the same time, we cannot underestimate the risk for contracting and spreading the AIDS virus that runaway youngsters pose to themselves and to their communities. These youngsters, living on the streets, often have no commodity to exchange for survival beyond their own boles and frequently engage in sexual activity with little or no thought to the use of protective devices. Moreover, while not engaged in the use of intravenous drugs, the vast majority are involved in the use of disinhibiting drugs ranging from alcohol to crack cocaine.

PROGRAM STRUCTURE

During 1987 and 1988, through a grants and contracts program, NIDA developed 41 outreach/intervention projects in nearly 50 cities and at more than 60 sites. The programs are concentrated in the northeastern part of the United States, due to that region's higher rates of intravenous drug use and seroprevalence, but they also have been established nationwide, from San Juan, Puerto Rico, in the East to Honolulu, Hawaii, in the West. The 41 programs are of two types. Twenty-nine of the 41 are comprehensive community projects that target both out-of-treatment intravenous drug users and sexual partners of intravenous drug users located in a variety of community settings. Twelve of the 41 programs are targeted *either* to intravenous drug users or to sexual partners and focus on a particular community setting where that population can be found: for example, in the criminal justice system for intravenous drug users and housing authority programs for sexual partners.

All of the projects offer a mix of services and research. The services are designed to provide impetus to behavior change either by encouraging entry into drug abuse treatment programs, as described earlier, or through using innovative behavior change strategies developed by project staff and designed to meet the particular needs and concerns of the target population.

The studies conducted in this demonstration research program have two objectives. First, there is a concern with clarifying the characteristics and functioning of out-of-treatment intravenous drug users and their sexual partners. Virtually no studies are available that examine the characteristics and functioning of these populations. A second study objective is to assess the efficacy of behavior change strategies mounted to modify and reduce risk-taking behaviors. Findings from both types of studies will be employed to guide the initiation of outreach/intervention programs in additional communities. Thus, NIDA will share effective strategies as well as findings important to the delivery of outreach/intervention services.

OUTREACH STRATEGIES

As could be expected, outreach initiatives differ according to the population for which services are planned. Where the target population is out-of-treatment intravenous drug users, outreach programs have emphasized finding such individuals in three community settings. First, and most commonly, emphasis has been placed on providing outreach to "copping areas," that is, to open-air markets within the community where illicit drugs are bought and sold. Intravenous drug users will need to gather at copping areas at regular and reasonably predictable times, and so represent locations appropriate to outreach efforts. In order for such efforts to access drug users, the program and its personnel must be viewed with trust by both the drug users and the public officials responsible for law enforcement. Negotiation with the latter group is the task of the project leadership. As will be described below, negotiation in the street falls to recovering addict outreach workers who are known and respected by their addict peers.

In addition, many programs conduct outreach into the criminal justice system. Significant percentages of intravenous drug users become known to the criminal justice system. Surveys of state and federal penitentiaries have indicated that 15% to 25% of the prisoners have histories of heroin use (Eckerman et al. 1971); and more recent data gathered from arrestees sampled through the Drug Use Forecasting (DUF) system of the National Institute of Justice reveals still higher rates of cocaine and other drug use among those charged with felonies (NIJ 1989). At any time, from lock-up to probation or parole, programs can be structured to reach and to educate criminal justice clients regarding risk reduction strategies.

Hospital emergency rooms represent another institutional source of intravenous drug users. Overdose, or other toxic reaction, frequently accompanies intravenous heroin or cocaine use. It can be reasoned that individuals found in hospital emergency rooms may have been made more accessible to behavior change interventions by virtue of their heightened sense of vulnerability. Prior studies suggest that intravenous drug users located in hospital emergency rooms can indeed be induced to enter drug abuse treatment directly from that setting, or—where individuals do not enter formal treatment—they can be accessed for a continuing program of supportive counseling designed to reduce drug-taking behavior through contacts in the client's home or in other community settings. Moreover, in the hospital emergency room, as in the criminal justice system, the intravenous drug user will be available, on a more reliable basis, to efforts to provide support and to induce behavior change to an extent impossible in other settings.

Sexual partners of intravenous drug users are typically recruited in a variety of community settings. Sexual partners are recruited in street settings by means of mobile health screening vans, through on-site outreach in public authority housing programs, and by contacting sexual partners in launderettes and beauty parlors located in high drug use neighborhoods, and so forth. Institutional settings include obstetrical/gynecological clinics, well-baby clinics, and other health care facilities, such as sexually transmitted disease (STD) clinics and public health facilities. In addition to health care service delivery systems, social service programs are an important institutional source for sexual-partner clients. Because poverty and long-term drug use are often closely tied, sexual partners may be recruited through financial support programs for low income women. Sexual partners may also be located in homeless and/or battered women's shelters since, again, women at risk for AIDS are likely to suffer a variety of social and physical hardships, frequently associated with dependence on unreliable male support for themselves and for their dependent children.

Prostitutes, as a specific client population, are recruited through outreach into "stroll" areas (i.e., areas of a community in which women are engaged in sex trade). Prostitutes may also be recruited through the criminal justice system because the need for these women to make themselves readily available to customers also makes them readily identifiable by the police and subject to frequent arrest.

Runaways may also be recruited directly from the streets, often near or within stroll areas. Institutional sources of runaway youth are chiefly youth shelters or outreach initiatives already existing in the community and specifically tied to youthful runaways.

The individuals hired to conduct outreach are typically ones who share both a background and a set of experiences with the populations they are attempting to recruit. In particular, this has meant using a recovering drug addict population to recruit intravenous drug users. In the parlance of drug abuse treatment, "to talk the talk you first have to walk the walk." The individual who has lived the life of addiction, weathered its vicissitudes and made the lifestyle changes she or he is suggesting is thereby a credible agent for change. Similarly, women who have shared the lifestyles of the female clients they will be recruiting are typically employed to conduct outreach. Persons conducting outreach with runaway juveniles, on the other hand, are not typically themselves juveniles, although they commonly constitute a younger population than might otherwise be used to conduct outreach and are, of course, expected to be conversant with the lifestyles and functioning of the population with which they will be working.

INTERVENTIONS

As noted above, a key goal of these projects is to achieve an understanding of the efficacy of interventions to reduce individuals' risk of contracting AIDS. To this end, studies typically involve a comparison of a standard intervention (i.e., an intervention involving a single session combining instruction, educational materials and supportive counseling), to an enhanced intervention (i.e., a behavior change strategy that differs from the standard in both type of effort and quantity of effort).

In general, the interventions employed by programs comprise three major types, although interventions often exist in combination. First, and perhaps most frequently, counseling initiatives are used. These may be directed to an individual, a group, or to couples, where the intravenous drug user and his or her sexual partner are seen in the same counseling sessions. Counseling sessions for AIDS prevention are not unlike counseling sessions designed to achieve other types of behavior change. An effort is made to understand resistance to behavior change, to provide support and encouragement to induce behavior change, and to explore strategies for maintaining change over time. Group counseling offers its additional capacity to use the group as an element of support. From initial reports by the investigators, it appears that the use of groups to provide support and encouragement for behavior change is particularly significant for female intravenous drug users and for female sexual partners of intravenous drug users. Presumably, this is because female intravenous drug users are more subject to criticism and disparagement as a minority group within the larger body of intravenous drug users. Similarly, as sexual partners, women often must depend for financial and emotional support on those who at the same time threaten them with contracting AIDS.

Behavioral skills training strategies may employ any of several initiatives, again either alone or in combination. Thus, a cognitive skills training strategy will emphasize the exploration of alternative courses of behavior in situations that threaten the risk of HIV infection. Specifically, individuals can be asked to script responses with which they will be comfortable when faced with risky situations, for example, being offered used needles by a running partner. The client can then practice his or her response to that situation under simulated conditions and with comments and suggestion offered by the counselor and/or other group members where skills training is delivered in a group setting. In this way, the client can develop a body of behaviors to employ in relation to both external and internal cues for risk-taking behaviors.

Individuals can also develop skills for negotiating behaviors that pertain to sexual activity. This is of obvious significance for the sexual partners of intravenous drug users. The development of skills for negotiating with a partner to use protective devices without offending the partner may be crucial to both maintaining the relationship and reducing the threat of infection.

More fundamental skills training, including the proper administration of condoms and the cleaning and sterilization of needles, in cases where individuals are committed to continuing their needle use, are made available to all clients as appropriate. Strategies involving individual or group counseling and strategies involving behavioral skills training may also be combined. Thus, the skills acquired in the development of negotiating skills may be combined with supportive group counseling in an effort to better establish risk-reducing behaviors.

Clients are typically referred by outreach workers to individuals whose background and training allow them to employ both behavioral skills training and counseling strategies. The outreach worker functions as a specialist in locating individuals at risk, gaining their confidence, and securing their involvement in the interventions designed to reduce the threat of AIDS.

In addition, the use of behavioral skills training and counseling may also employ efforts to heighten the individual's sense of personal vulnerability. It is reasonable to posit that individuals who daily risk disease, and indeed death, through injecting substances of unknown purity and origin have developed an abnormally high tolerance for danger. Various strategies, but most particularly the use of specially designed media products (e.g., videos), may be used to heighten a client's sense of his or her own risk for contracting AIDS. Afterward, counseling and/or behavioral skills training is used to reduce the anxiety created and to provide strategies for dealing with the dangers to which they have become newly sensitive or to which their sensitivity has been increased.

A third intervention strategy relies on the outreach worker both to locate individuals at risk for AIDS and to guide the initiative to reduce that risk. In what has been described as a clinical application of ethnography, outreach workers insert themselves in the drug-using network with the avowed intention of inducing change on behalf of individuals within that network. Typically, the outreach worker will be nonjudgmental about behaviors which the larger society deems inappropriate (e.g., drug use), but will act with and for the client to encourage the adoption of behaviors that limit the risk of HIV infection. Thus, the outreach worker, working with a street corner group, will support individuals' efforts to reduce drug use and/or to enter drug abuse treatment; however, if the individual is intent on continuing intravenous use of drugs, the outreach worker will encourage the use of sterilization techniques to limit the risk of infection to the individual and to others in the community. Ultimately, it is the goal of outreach workers to change the group ethos regarding risky behaviors so that the group will act as a brake on the behaviors of its individual members, promoting a greater degree of caution about behaviors associated with contracting and spreading AIDS.

All interventions, whether they are of the three innovative types described or the standard intervention, will also involve the dissemination of educational pamphlets and brochures designed for the individual and for sharing with partners and others. In addition, interventions will typically involve the distribution of condoms and bleach kits, unless forbidden by state law or local policy.

RESEARCH DESIGN

The evaluative research design for the demonstration program involves four key elements. (1) As a part of intake, all clients (subjects) are given a structured, primarily closed-ended, interview schedule that requests demographic and background information, drug-use history, needle-using behaviors, sexual activity and behaviors, medical history (including HIV testing), and AIDS knowledge and information sources. All interviewers have received training in the AIDS Initial Assessment (AIA), the intake interview schedule. The AIA takes about 45 to 60 minutes and is delivered face to face, in a private setting and under a federally assured certificate of confidentiality.

At intake, the interviewers also collect locator data to be used for follow-up. Locator data include names, addresses, and telephone numbers of all persons likely to maintain knowledge about the subject's whereabouts. Information obtained from the AIA both provides base-line data regarding risk-taking behaviors prior to receiving a preventive intervention and offers descriptive information regarding the characteristics of out-of-treatment intravenous drug users and sexual partners of intravenous drug users. Immediately after the AIA is administered, all subjects are offered HIV testing and pretest counseling. Although subjects are not required to receive testing in order to receive the preventive intervention, they are encouraged to learn their serostatus.

(2) After the interview and (for most) after HIV testing, subjects are randomly assigned to either the standard intervention (typically one session of didactics and supportive counseling) or the enhanced intervention of a type described above. Control over assignment is the responsibility of the research staff.

(3) Six months after initial contact, researchers, using information from the locator form, recontacted subjects exposed to both standard and enhanced interventions and administered the AIDS Followup Assessment (AFA) interview schedule. That interview schedule is designed to obtain information about risk-taking behaviors involving drug use and sexual activity that will reflect change from base line (i.e., from the AIA). Change in knowledge is also obtained. As with the AIA, all interviewers receive identical training, and the interview consumes about 45 to 60

minutes. At the end of the interview, subjects are offered the option of HIV testing.

(4) All AIA and AFA data is forwarded to a central data-base management program that has the capacity to report data nationally and to make reports to individual sites. In this way, one can explore characteristics of subjects in various sites by total sample, by region, or by selected variables (e.g., treatment history).

PRELIMINARY FINDINGS

Preliminary reports from National AIDS Demonstration Research projects suggest two findings of particular consequence for outreach efforts with intravenous drug users. On the one hand, intravenous drug users show dramatic change in risk-taking behaviors. In response to behavior change initiatives, intravenous drug users lessen their frequency of needle injection, decrease the number of individuals with whom they share needles, and increase their sterilization of needles. Behavior change strategies with intravenous drug users have been less effective in encouraging the use of protective devices as a part of their sexual activity. (Iguchi et al. 1990).

In addition, we are discovering that an extraordinarily large number of intravenous drug users contacted in the community report *never* having been in drug abuse treatment. Thus, more than 40% of intravenous drug users report no history of drug abuse treatment, although they also report using intravenous drugs for an average of more than 11 years of their lifetime.

Clearly, there is an established need for outreach efforts to locate intravenous drug users who will not otherwise come to the attention of treatment authorities. Equally clearly, we have good reason to believe that the consequence of developing and maintaining these outreach/intervention efforts will be to limit the risk of AIDS infection to both the individuals served and to the communities where they reside.

REFERENCES

Centers for Disease Control. (1990). *HIV/AIDS Surveillance Report* (March 1990): 1–18. Atlanta, Georgia: Department of Health and Human Services.

Eckerman, W. C., Bates, J. D., Rachal, J. V., and Poole, W. I. (1971). *Drug Usage and Arrest Charges*. Washington, D.C.: Drug Enforcement Administration.

528 Drug Addiction Treatment Research

National Institute of Justice. (1989). *Drug Use Forecasting: April to June 1989.* Washington, D.C.: National Institute of Justice.

Iguchi, M. Y., Wiebel, W., McCoy, C. B., Chitwood, D. D., Watters, J., Biernacki, P., Kotranski, L., Liebman, J., Williams, M., and Brown, B. S. (1990). Early indices of efficacy in the NIDA AIDS outreach demonstration projects: A preliminary report from Chicago, Houston, Miami, Philadelphia, and San Francisco. *Morbidity and Mortality Weekly Report* 39, 535–38.